Richard Wagner

The Lighter Side

Richard Wagner
The Lighter Side

An illustrated collection of interesting facts, quips, quotes, anecdotes, and inspirational tales from the life and works of the German composer

TERRY QUINN

AMADEUS PRESS

An Imprint of Hal Leonard Corporation

Published in 2013 by Amadeus Press
An Imprint of Hal Leonard Corporation
7777 West Bluemound Road
Milwaukee, WI 53213

Trade Book Division Editorial Offices
33 Plymouth St., Montclair, NJ 07042

Acknowledgments of permission to quote from previously published materials and illustration credits can be found on pages 301 to 303, which should be considered an extension of this copyright page.

Printed in the United States of America

Book design by Patrick Crowley

Library of Congress Cataloging-in-Publication Data

Quinn, Terry, 1937-
Richard Wagner : the lighter side : an illustrated collection of interesting facts, quips, quotes, anecdotes, and inspirational tales from the life and works of the German composer / by Terry Quinn.
pages ; cm
Includes bibliographical references.
ISBN 978-1-57467-441-5
1. Wagner, Richard, 1813-1883--Miscellanea. 2. Wagner, Richard, 1813-1883. Operas. I. Title.
ML410.W13Q85 2013
782.1092--dc23

2013019298

www.amadeuspress.com

For Miriam, Sara, and Lisa,
who never complained about having another man in their home

There is no great genius without a touch of madness.
—Lucius Annaeus Seneca, Roman philosopher

Contents

3 Act Three 113

0 Intermission 161

4 Act Four 171

Preface

Why the lighter side? Simply because, to the likely surprise of many, there is one. Despite the many negatives about the personality of Wagner and his abhorrent views, there is plenty to make fun of. Giants, dragons, winged helmets and a man who created "the music of the future" are all priceless gifts to critics, comedians, and cartoonists. As early as 1891 books containing collections of hundreds of caricatures from the media were published in France and, a few years later, in Germany. Today Wagner enthusiasts enjoy the magnificent dramas and beautiful music but also exchange anecdotes, quotations, and information on the trivia of Wagner's life and works. They enjoy the stories of things that went wrong on the stage, and they know many of the famous criticisms and put-downs by other composers.

The British author Neville Cardus wrote in 1957, "One of the several shortcomings of contemporary musical criticism . . . is a plentiful lack of humor and an excess of solemnity. Beckmesser is winning with ease." I agree. Although virtually every aspect of Wagner's life and works has been examined, much of it is necessarily serious, occasionally heavy going, and sometimes dark. It is time for some light relief.

In addition to humorous material, I have included many little-known facts and inspirational stories that I have collected over more than twenty years about the life of Wagner and the people close to him.

I have not entirely neglected weightier issues such as Wagner's anti-Semitism and arguments over controversial modern productions of his works. I do not pretend that the latter is a balanced argument; rather, it is a statement of my own views with some support from prominent Wagnerians.

Richard Wagner: The Lighter Side is a collection of interesting or humorous quotations, little-known facts, and trivia to be delved into during a quiet moment or when your brain won't slow down after listening to some of the great works.

I am indebted to many people who have contributed valuable encouragement, advice, or items for inclusion. Inevitably I will have omitted to thank people who helped me many years ago; I apologize to any not included in the acknowledgments list at the end of the book.

I must immediately mention several people who have provided direct assistance or helped motivate me when I wondered whether it was all worthwhile.

Without Trish Benedict of the Wagner Society of Northern California, this book would never have been finished. She provided encouragement and a great deal of editing help that eliminated many silly errors.

Peter West of Hampshire, England, read an early draft, and his positive reactions and contribution of interesting anecdotes from his own Wagnerian experiences were invaluable.

Lee Acaster produced some excellent sample page layouts that not only indicated how the book might look but helped define how a diverse collection of information should be organized.

Mike Shaw commented positively on an early draft and granted permission to use extracts from the writings of the brilliant Bernard Levin.

My wife, Miriam, not only allowed my share of household chores to go undone but also contributed quotations and proofread the text several times.

Finally, my thanks go to Jenny Labbett, who helped get the manuscript into the correct format; Linda Randall, who helped with requests for permissions; and John Cerullo, Jessica Burr, Barbara Norton, and the rest of the team at Amadeus Press, who were enormously helpful and patient at every stage of a long process.

Terry Quinn
Wortham, Suffolk, England
May 2013

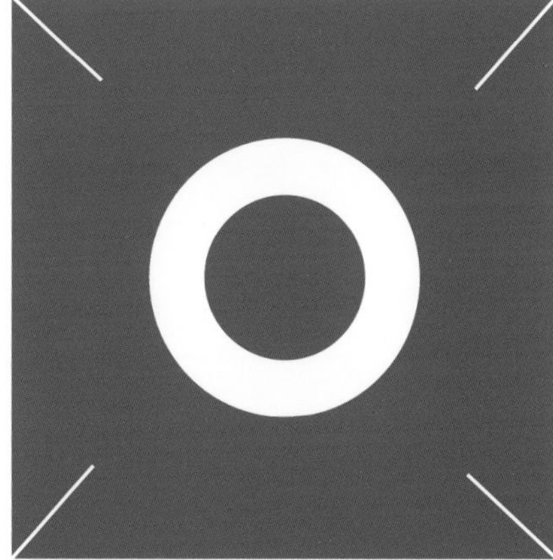

Vorspiel

In a small, little-known town in Bavaria, almost two hundred years ago, the German poet and writer Jean Paul had been thinking about music and poetry. He was concerned about the lack of a single unifying force that would bring the two together. It seemed to be a disadvantage that poets set words to someone else's music and musicians composed music to marry with words created elsewhere. He picked up his pen and wrote:

> Hitherto Apollo has always distributed the poetic gift with his right hand, the musical with his left, to two persons so widely apart that up to this hour, we are still waiting for the man who will create a genuine opera by writing both its text and its music.
>
> Quoted in Henry T. Finck, *Wagner and His Works*, 1893

• **Jean Paul, the German writer who prayed for a poet-musician. Painting by Lorenz Kreul, 1823.**

His words were the beginning of an extraordinary series of coincidences. The first was that Jean Paul wrote them in 1813, the year Wilhelm Richard Wagner was born, far away in Leipzig. Wagner was to become the poet-musician who would realize Jean Paul's wish for a unified work.

The second coincidence was that the small town in which Jean Paul wrote his plea was Bayreuth, which was to become the home of Wagner's music festival. Years later, both the poet and the poet-musician he had dreamed about were to be buried in the same cemetery in the same small Bavarian town.

The final coincidence was that the full name of the poet known to most Germans as simply Jean Paul was Johann Paul Friedrich Richter. His namesake, Hans Richter, who was not related, would become a close associate of Wagner and conductor of the first performance of *The Ring of the Nibelung* in August 1876. It seems likely that *The Ring* would have satisfied Jean Paul's dream of unity between text and music.

Jean Paul did not live long enough to see the realization of his dream. He died in 1825, when Wagner was only twelve. Just over fifty years later, the opera house that Wagner built in Bayreuth saw the launch of what has since become the world's oldest music festival. It is unique in that it is devoted exclusively to the work of one man.

Jean Paul's plea was for one person who was gifted in two disciplines: drama and music. Ernest Newman (1888–1949), a Wagner scholar and biographer, believed that Wagner went much further. He wrote that Wagner simultaneously exercised the abilities of composer, dramatist, conductor, scenic designer, singer, and mime: "Such a combination had never existed in a single individual before; it has never happened since, and in all probability it will never happen again."

Yet despite all of these talents and music that has been described as some of the most beautiful ever written, there is a sizable group of music lovers who disagree.

> No man's works have been so extolled and so censured, so popular and so detested, so worshipped and so despised, so much upheld and so much condemned, as those of Richard Wagner, the greatest composer of the century—and for some, one of the most noteworthy of all time.

So wrote the British composer-conductor Landon Ronald in an 1889 issue of *The Lady's Realm*, and in many respects nothing much has changed since. No composer in the entire history of music has created such a curious mixture of animosity and adulation—a phenomenon that goes back to the first appearance on the musical scene of the little man from Saxony.

Wagner fought for recognition of his art for most of his life. The critics ferociously rejected his works; but the public, after some early bewilderment, came to appreciate the "music of the future," and Wagner rapidly became a cult figure. In London, all-Wagner concerts were given every week in the music season, and conductors of the caliber of Hans Richter and Arthur Nikisch drew full houses. Wagner's operas were among the most frequently performed in the late nineteenth and early twentieth centuries; yet the opposition continued, and Wagner was at the same time worshipped and vilified, loved and despised, hailed as a genius and dismissed as insane.

• Richard Wagner, who was to be the answer to Jean Paul's appeal. Etching in *Illustrated London News*, February 24, 1883, artist unknown.

Wagner was never troubled by an inferiority complex or even the slightest hint of self-doubt. His ambition was as great as his considerable ego, and he firmly believed that he was the logical successor to the greats of both literature and music. As John Deathridge, of King's College, London, put it: "He has the idea of combining an opera libretto that's as complex psychologically and dramatically as Shakespeare, with a musical score that's as complex in terms of structure and form as Beethoven. So Shakespeare + Beethoven = Wagner."

One early critic compared Wagner to two other German masters, but the comparison was not favorable: he claimed that Wagner could write better poetry than Beethoven and better music than Schiller.

Perhaps it was predictable that Wagner's music would be rejected by some for the simple reason that it was new and different. This, plus his anti-Semitism and self-centered personality, resulted in his being a controversial figure during the whole of his life and beyond.

Many of the early criticisms are still heard today. Some twenty-first-century operagoers consider that Wagner's music is too heavy or too loud and that his operas are too long or too complex or too puerile, with their mixture of giants, dragons, magic fire, flying horses, and magic potions. For all of these reasons, few can honestly say that they are ambivalent about Wagner and his works: most people either love him or hate him. The top of the fence between the two groups would be a lonely place indeed. Opera enthusiasts either very deliberately avoid Wagner performances or grab every opportunity to see, again and again, the ten operas that are part of the repertoire of most international companies.

Some dismiss his music because of his unsavory character. Others, the fortunate ones, are able to

Wagner opens doors that human beings strive to keep closed."

—Bernard Levin

• An 1876 caricature from the German magazine *Ulk* had Aeschylus and Shakespeare "bow in the appropriate manner to their master."

• Plaque on a building close to the site of the Leipzig home where Wagner was born in 1883. The house was demolished just three years later.

separate the musical genius from the odious, self-centered anti-Semite. The critic Ernest Newman said, "It is only as a musician that Wagner will live. There is no need, no reason, to discuss the 'philosophy' of [his] life. He is not a philosopher: he is simply a perplexed and tortured human soul and magnificent musical instrument. All that concerns us today is the quality of the music which was wrung from the instrument under the torture." And Anatole France wrote in 1893: "It is to be observed, my son, that the greatest saints were the penitents and, as repentance is proportionate to the error, in the greatest sinners is found the stuff of the greatest saints."

One of the most astonishing aspects of Wagner's character was his total, unhesitating, unwavering belief in his own ability. His confidence was steadfast even during the worst periods of poverty and worries about the impact this was having on his long-suffering first wife, Minna. He had to live with the rejection of his life's works and the possibility that some of them would never be performed. A lesser personality would have thrown in the towel. Maybe there were other composers with the ability of Wagner but who gave up the struggle against an ungrateful world. What stunning works might have been created but were not, because the would-be composer quit too soon! Wagner persevered against all the odds, and music lovers around the world today enjoy the results. As I once said in a California lecture, Wagner was an odious jerk; but if he had been a more compassionate man with something closer to a normal conscience, it seems unlikely that he could have completed many of his great works. He was not referring to Wagner, but Albert Einstein once said that great spirits have always encountered opposition from mediocre minds.

Bernard Levin, the British journalist, writer, and enthusiastic Wagnerian, was perplexed about the diametrically opposed views on Wagner.

> I reflect . . . on the extraordinary, the unique hostility this composer, and this composer alone, provokes not only in people who have never listened to his music, but even in many who have.
>
> It is a phenomenon the great oddness of which does not seem to me to have been sufficiently remarked. There is no composer whose music pleases everybody; but those who find themselves disliking Mozart, Puccini, Bach, or Ravel are content simply

to stay away from performances of their work. In the case of Wagner, and of him alone, the dislike becomes positive; I have often encountered an antipathy so strong that it seems to take the form of a desire to prohibit Wagner's music altogether.

Of all the ways in which he is unique as a composer—his stupendous originality, his use of the orchestra as the protagonist of the drama, his weaving of a single musical fabric without joins or breaks—the strongest and most significant is surely the way in which he inspires such detestation along with the devotion. I can see no possible reason for this attitude other than the most obvious one; we hate what we fear, and what Wagner-haters hate is their own fear of what his explorations of the deepest parts of the psyche may reveal. He deals in forbidden subjects; he speaks in his music of blood and passion and will, incest, murder and revenge, love that consumes like a fire and self-sacrifice even unto death. Wagner opens doors that human beings strive to keep closed; no wonder he arouses fury when he points out what lies on the other side of those doors and that is what I mean when I say that even we who love this music feel a strange reluctance to enter his darkness and that the exception to this feeling is *Die Meistersinger*, to which we hurry on eager feet because it is the one Wagner opera that is bathed in sunshine throughout, and never goes down into the darkness below.

Bernard Levin, *Conducted Tour*, 1982

Again, little has changed in the years since Levin wrote that. There is no middle ground between the fans and the antifans. Thousands of enthusiasts join one of the 135-plus Wagner Societies around the world and attend lectures and seminars on the music, the operas, and almost every aspect of the life of the man. Fans are happy to get on a ten-year waiting list to buy tickets for performances at Bayreuth, and Wagner operas at many other houses are sold out well in advance of opening night. Yet Wagner still attracts animosity that is sometimes hard to fathom.

There is one bright side to all of this. I sometimes think that if every opera lover shared my enthusiasm for the profound beauty of much of Wagner's music, it would be even more difficult to get tickets for performances of his works. Perhaps writing a book that might create new interest in the man and his music was not such a good idea after all. ■

Act One

Wagner the Man

A Late Bloomer

Richard became a student in Leipzig and set himself some homework that included sonatas, overtures and a string quartet. Wagner was a dedicated student and composed his first works when he was sixteen. None of the early manuscripts survived. When he was eighteen, Wagner began the serious study of musical theory with Theodor Weinlig, the cantor of St. Thomas, a Leipzig church. (The musical director and organist at the same church in the previous century was Johann Sebastian Bach, who held the position up to his death in 1750.) This was to be another unique aspect of Wagner's life: none of the other great classical composers started their musical studies so late in life.

> "I hope the pink drawers are ready too???"
>
> —Richard Wagner

• **Vegetarian, snappy dresser, clown, genius. Litho by Bruno Bürger & Ottillie in the composer's birthplace, Leipzig.**

Wagner was not credited as the composer when an early overture was performed in 1830. He was probably glad of this, because the audience was unimpressed with the juvenile work and enjoyed a good laugh over it. Recognition came for the first time in 1832, when his overture for a play called *King Enzio* was given several performances. Later the same year, a performance of his Symphony in C Major was well received. In his first four years of music study Wagner had composed some twenty works, and although his first public performance was a disaster, four other performances and the publication of two of his pieces were enough to encourage him. Wagner was on his way. Perhaps his earliest major accomplishment was his appointment as conductor at Magdeburg in 1834 when he was only twenty-one.

The Snappy Dresser

It is said that Wagner's preference for nothing other than silk next to his skin was a consequence of the skin disease that made other clothing painful. But he also had extravagant tastes in clothes and always knew precisely what he wanted. Henry Finck quoted the following extraordinarily detailed specification for a dressing gown that the composer sent to his tailor:

> Pink Satin, stuffed with eiderdown and quilted in squares, like the grey and red coverlet I had of you; exactly that

• "Frou-Frou Wagner" read the caption on this 1877 caricature by F. Graetz in *Der Floh*, Vienna.

• **Flowers are regularly placed on the grave of Russ, one of several of Wagner's dogs buried at Wahnfried.**

> substance, light not heavy; of course with the upper and under material quilted together. Lined with light satin, six widths at the bottom, therefore very wide. Then put on extra—not sewn on to the quilted material—a padded ruching all round of the same material; from the waist the ruching must extend downwards into a raised facing (or garniture) cutting off the front part. Study the drawing carefully [which Wagner had enclosed]: at the bottom the facing, or Schopp, which must be worked in a particularly beautiful manner, is to spread out on both sides to have an ell in width and then, rising to the waist, lose itself in the ordinary width of the padded ruching which runs all round.
>
> Henry T. Finck, *Wagner and His Works*, 1893

On another occasion Wagner wrote to Lisbeth Völkl, who served Wagner in his Penzing home for a short time. In his December 1863 letter he wrote: "Heavens, how I am looking forward to relaxing with you again at last. (I hope the pink drawers are ready too???)"

In *The Wagner Compendium*, the Wagner scholar Barry Millington wrote, "To whom the pink drawers belonged and to what purpose they were to be put are problems that Wagner scholarship has hitherto failed to solve. More research needs to be done in this area."

> Richard Wagner wore pink underwear, climbed trees, and liked to stand on his head, but right side up he wrote some nice music.
>
> Victor Borge with Robert Sherman, *My Favorite Intervals*, 1971

Animal Lover and Occasional Vegetarian

Animals were always an important part of Wagner's life. When he was a boy the family kept several dogs. The young Richard once found a young puppy in a ditch; he smuggled it into his bedroom, where he fed it and kept it warm until its presence was betrayed by its whining. On another occasion an unpleasant smell in his bedroom was traced to a family of young rabbits.

> Only once in his life did he kill an animal for amusement. He joined a party of young hunters and shot a rabbit. Its dying look met his eyes and so moved him to pity that nothing could have induced him ever to go hunting again. The impression then made on him is echoed in the libretto of his early opera, *The Fairies* [*Die Feen*], where the doe is hit by the arrow: "Oh see! The animal weeps, a tear is in its eye. Oh, how its broken glances rest on me!"
>
> Henry T. Finck, *Wagner and His Works*, 1893

Wagner's love of animals shows in many of his operatic works. There are one or more horses in *Rienzi*, *Tannhäuser*, *Die Walküre*, and *Götterdämmerung*; a swan in *Lohengrin* and *Parsifal*; hunting dogs in *Tannhäuser*; a toad and a snake/serpent in *Rheingold*; a bear; a dragon and a bird in *Siegfried*; two rarely seen ravens in *Götterdämmerung*; and rams, even more rarely seen, in *Die Walküre*.

He owned many dogs during his life, and many of them were part of the family. One of his favorites was named Peps, and Wagner did not forget the dog when he brought home gifts after a trip abroad. On one occasion he bought the dog a new collar with his name on it. Wagner claimed that Peps "helped" with the composition of *Tannhäuser*: the dog howled whenever the music was not to his liking. When Franz Liszt visited Wagner in Zurich, he was flattered to be given the nickname Double Peps and subsequently signed letters to Wagner as "Your Double Peps," or "Double extrait de Peps," or "Double Stout Peps con doppio movimento sempre crescendo al ff ff."

Wagner recalled his dreadful sense of desolation and utter hopelessness when Peps died:

> Up to the last moment Peps showed me a love so touching as to be almost heart-rending; kept his eyes fixed on me, and, though I chanced to move but a few steps from him, continued to follow me with his eyes. He died in my arms on the night of the 9th–10th of the month, passing away without a sound, quietly and peacefully. On the morrow, midday, we buried him in the garden beside the house. I cried incessantly, and since then have felt bitter pain and sorrow for the dear friend of the past thirteen years, who ever worked and walked with me . . . And yet there are those who would scoff at our feeling in such a matter!
>
> Quoted in Henry T. Finck,
> *Wagner and His Works*, 1893

In Lucerne Wagner rescued a dog that had been run over. He attempted to wash and bandage its paw, but the frightened dog bit Wagner's hand so badly that work on *Meistersinger* was delayed for several weeks. Despite this, the dog was well cared for.

At Tribschen the family kept two dogs, two cats, mice, golden pheasants and other rare birds in an aviary, and two peacocks named Wotan and Fricka. There was also a little horse, Siegfried's birthday gift from King Ludwig. It was named Grane, after Brünnhilde's horse in *Götterdämmerung*.

The other dogs in Wagner's life were given such names as Marke, Brange, Wana, Fips, Molly, Papo, Rüpel, Russ, Runa, Pip, and Robber. The latter, a huge, much-loved Newfoundland, originally belonged to an English merchant in Riga but followed Wagner around until he was adopted by the family. He traveled with Richard and Minna to Switzerland, France, and even England. Sadly, Robber went missing in Paris, possibly in search of someone who could afford to feed him (the Wagners could barely afford to feed themselves at that time).

When Wagner bought a little dog in Meudon for three francs, he could not think of a name for the animal. "It raised no associations in his mind," Cosima said later. "Why not call it Three Francs," suggested his landlord.

Earlier, Wagner had become very fond of his pet parrot Papo, and in the Wahnfried years the family had kept chickens and more peacocks and pheasants. The children claimed that one of the cockerels sang something from the *Siegfried Idyll*. Russ, another Newfoundland, was poisoned at Wahnfried, and he and another dog, Marke, are buried close to Wagner's own tomb. A small marble slab is inscribed: "Here lies in peace Wahnfried's faithful watcher and friend—the good and beautiful Marke" (*der gute, schöne Marke*).

It was perhaps inevitable that Wagner's second wife, Cosima, would have her own dog. At her first meeting with Judith Gautier, Cosima introduced her gray pug. "My name is Cosima," she told the Frenchwoman. "And my friends at home have formed the very bad habit, which actually gives me chills, of calling me 'Cos,' so I have given that name to my dog, and since then no one dares call me anything but Cosima!"

Wagner's love of animals might also have rubbed off on his musical secretary. Anton Seidl owned several dogs during his life and named most of them after Wagnerian characters. One of them, a dachshund called Mime, had a party trick that amused visitors to the Seidl household in the United States. When Seidl sat in his armchair enjoying a cigar, Mime walked across the room on his hind legs toward his master and whined imploringly. Seidl ignored the dog for a while, but when he eventually lowered the hand holding his cigar, the dog reached out his paw to brush off the built-up ash.

Family pets included more dachshunds—Froh, Freia, and Valla—and other dogs named Hunding and Fricka. Seidl's favorite was a huge white-and-golden St. Bernard called Wotan. But tragedy struck the Seidls when Wotan grabbed the unfortunate Mime by the throat and killed the dachshund. The Seidls were heartbroken. Perhaps that particular Wotan should have been named Hagen.

When Wagner was fifty-six he wrote to the Society for the Prevention of Cruelty to Animals offering his support. At the suggestion of the SPCA, Wagner wrote a letter opposing vivisection that was published as a supplement to the *Bayreuther Blätter* and then as a pamphlet printed at Wagner's expense.

Fifty years after his death, Wagner's strong views were used by another organization. In 1933 the Millennium Guild produced two books as part of a program of propaganda in support of vegetarianism and antivivisectionism. The books were distributed free of charge to authors, editors, clergy, and other opinion leaders around the world. The volumes included quotations attributed to everyone from Voltaire to Mark Twain, Queen Victoria to Mahatma Gandhi, and Lewis Carroll to Charles Dickens, as well as hundreds of other writers, thinkers, political figures, and artists. The Millennium Guild organizers selected Wagner as their headline witness.

The Millennium Guild included one line from Mark Twain: "Man is the only animal that blushes, or needs to." Wagner's extract from *Religion and Art* ran to more than eight pages of his rambling, tortuous prose. A more transparent extract is included in the main body of the book:

> The thought of their sufferings penetrates with horror and dismay into my soul, and in the sympathy evoked I recognize the strongest impulse of my moral being, and also the probable source of all my art. The total abolition of the horror we fight against must be our real aim. In order to attain this our opponents, the vivisectors, must be frightened, thoroughly frightened, into seeing the people rise up against them with stocks and cudgels. Difficulties and costs must not discourage us.

In addition to the lengthy texts, Wagner also provided the music: the covers of the books carry the musical notation of the Holy Grail motif.

In his essay *Religion and Art*, Wagner argues that eating flesh was the root of the "degeneration" of the human race. Some of his sycophantic followers started a vegetarian club in Bayreuth, but there is scant evidence that Wagner followed their proscriptions.

Clowning Around

> I remember full well one day [in 1891], when we were sitting together in the draw-

ing-room at Triebschen [*sic*], on a sort of ottoman, talking over the events of the years gone by, when he [Wagner] suddenly rose and stood on his head on the ottoman. At the very moment he was in that inverted position the door opened, and Madame Wagner entered. Her surprise and alarm were great, and she hastened forward, exclaiming, "Ach! Lieber Richard! Richard!" Quickly recovering himself, he reassured her of his sanity, explaining that he was only showing Ferdinand he could stand on his head at sixty, which was more than the said Ferdinand could do.

Ferdinand Praeger,
Wagner as I Knew Him, 1892

Women on His Mind

At the peak of Wagner's popularity in the early twentieth century, music lovers were swamped with offers of memorabilia that included literally dozens of different biographies and everything from full-sized plaster busts of the composer to packs of Wagner-themed playing cards. Hundreds of postcards were produced featuring various portraits of the composer and characters from his operas, as well as the Festspielhaus and other Bayreuth landmarks. A popular postcard series featured metamorphic portraits of Wagner with female figures cleverly superimposed on a profile of his head.

METAMORPHOSIS 1

• **The simple superimposition of at least six figures was used in the portrait, with a seventh representing his nose and right eyebrow. Other figures include Lohengrin in his swan-drawn boat, a Valkyrie warrior maiden, and Alberich with a Rhinemaiden.**

METAMORPHOSIS 2

• **Three female figures are incorporated into this portrait, with parts of their bodies forming features of Wagner's face. The back of one maiden forms his brow, and another kneeling figure forms his nose and chin.**

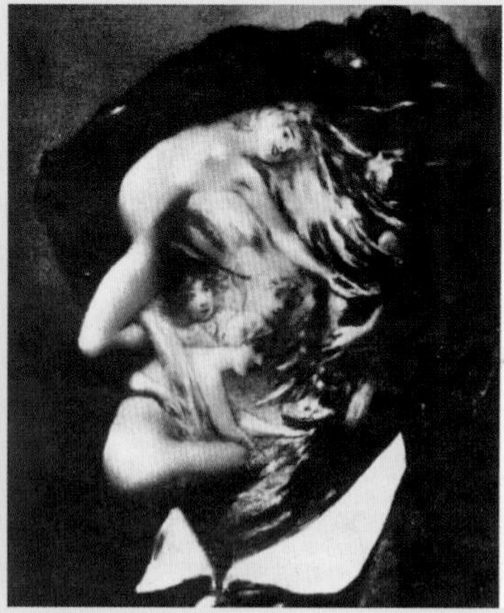

METAMORPHOSIS 3

• **Four figures are visible in this portrait. One backward-leaning figure provides his brow and nose; the buttocks of a second provide Wagner with a chin, and a third his eye, with one arm clasping the second figure to represent his mouth.**

Although William Ashton Ellis exposed some major parts of Praeger's book as fiction, it is reasonable to believe that some of the observations of Wagner's idiosyncrasies might be true. This would seem to be justified by other, more reliable observers.

> Behind the house, in that courtyard which formed part of the garden, and from which the carriage-drive started, there was a high swing, which the children were allowed to use very carefully, and with which the older people sometimes amused themselves. One day, Madame Cosima was sitting on the narrow board. Wagner offered to start the swing and give her a good flight through the air.
>
> All went well for a time, but, little by little, the motion became more rapid; higher and still higher went the swing! In vain Madame Cosima begged for mercy. Carried away by a kind of frenzy, the Master paid no attention, and the incident began to have a terrifying aspect.
>
> Cosima grew white; her hold relaxed, and she was about to fall.
>
> "Do you not see that she is fainting?" I cried, throwing myself toward Wagner. He grew pale, in his turn, and the danger was quickly averted. But as the poor woman continued to be dizzy and trembling, the Master concluded it would be wise to create a diversion. He ran rapidly toward the house, and by the side of the shutters, the mouldings and projections of the stones, he climbed nimbly up the side, and reaching the balcony of the floor above, leaped over it.
>
> He had obtained the desired effect, but in replacing one evil by another. Trembling with anxiety, Cosima turned to me, saying under her breath: "Above all things, do not notice him; do not look surprised, or you can never tell where it will end."
>
> Judith Gautier, *Wagner at Home*, translated by Effie Dunreith Massie, 1910

When I re-read my theoretical works, I can no longer understand them."

—Richard Wagner

The incident Gautier witnessed was not an isolated event. Wagner frequently alarmed family and friends by his demonstrating his climbing skills. In Zurich, he climbed a large plaster lion "to get an appetite for breakfast." He sometimes surprised visitors with his clowning. When Liszt played for the family and their friends at Wahnfried one evening, Wagner dropped to his knees and crawled up to the pianist: "Franz, to you people should come only on all fours."

In Switzerland in 1859, Wagner visited Tells Chapel with the young composer Felix Draeseke. As their boat neared the chapel, Wagner told the young man to shout as loudly as he could to hear an echo from the building. Draeseke was reluctant to shout near the chapel, whereupon Wagner started hollering all kinds of curses and was amused by the lingering responses.

In the company of the same young composer, Wagner climbed Mount Pilatus near Lucerne and demonstrated great skill and absolutely no fear of heights. Draeseke said later that Wagner had risked sections of the mountain that even experienced mountain climbers considered to be too dangerous.

Speaking and Writing for Germany

If talking had been a competitive sport, Wagner

would have been captain of the German team. He spoke rapidly and incessantly in a distinctive Saxon accent. In September 1877 members of the Wagner Societies were assembled on the stage of the Festspielhaus to discuss future plans. Wagner asked for notes to be taken, and Bayreuth's mayor, Franz Muncker, agreed to do so. He later explained in his report that taking notes on Wagner's introductory remarks was not easy. He said that Wagner had spoken very rapidly for half an hour in a conversational manner but that he constantly interrupted himself whenever a new thought occurred to him so that "sentences were abbreviated, parts of them 'swallowed,' and connecting links omitted, or crowded aside by a new thought that suddenly presented itself." He added that while Wagner's style made the speech difficult to record, it did make his words vivid and forceful.

The following year, while working on *Parsifal*, Wagner complained to Cosima about problems with the German language, saying that it did not allow one to express oneself in short sentences. "The art lies in being clear and definite within the encapsulated structure of German," he told her. It was an art that Wagner never mastered.

Wagner wrote as he spoke. He suffered from verbal diarrhea all his life. Although his personal charisma compensated for the torrential spoken outpourings, his written books and letters make for hard going—so much so that in Saint-Saëns' 1903 book *Portrait and Souvenirs*, Wagner is quoted as having said, "When I re-read my theoretical works, I can no longer understand them."

Wagner wrote letters almost every day. In a letter to his friend Theodor Uhlig, Wagner once apologized for his "confused scrawl," which he blamed on the fact that it was the sixth letter he had written that day. It has been estimated that surviving letters total between ten thousand and twelve thousand. In 1896 his letters made up three volumes, and numerous others have been discovered since. It is impossible to tell how many he wrote in his lifetime, but the Wagner scholar Stewart Spencer suggested in 1992: "Individual letters and smaller collections have continued to appear in often out-of-the-way periodicals and auction-house catalogues, so that a complete bibliography of Wagner's letters would run to one hundred separate publications."

Carl Friedrich Glasenapp (1847–1915) compiled an encyclopedia of subjects covered in Wagner's written works. The topics listed under the letter A alone begin with "Aachen music festival" and continue: Abel, Abt, Achilleus, Adam and Eve, Adolphe, Adam, Ægypten, Africa, Agamemnon, Agesilaos, Ahasver, Aischylos, Albericus, Alemannen, Alexander, Alexandrinism, Alkibiades, Alps, America, Amphion, Amsterdam, Anacker, Andalusia, Auschüstz, Antäos, Antigone, Antique tragedy, Antillen, Antoninen, Apel, Apelles, Aphrodite. And so on.

The Wit and Wisdom of Richard

Wagner described the British as a curious people, and said of the French, "It is in their inability to see anything besides themselves that they fall down." He once sent a telegram to Heinrich Vogl, who was singing Siegfried: "If in the last act you should find that your wife has gone to sleep, wake her up and give her my kind regards."

Although most of Wagner's writing was ponderous and sometimes impenetrable, he frequently showed his lighter side in his letters. Henry T. Finck wrote:

> He is constantly varying the monotony of My Dear Friend and that sort of thing by such [salutations] as:
>
> Theatre-music-fiddling-fellow;
>
> Dearest friend, brother, and register;

Kind old sinner;
Oh you most excellent fellow, man, brother, friend, chorus-director, and music-copyist;
O you wicked fellow;
Much-tortured chamber-musician.

It really is an impossible situation: No manager wants to present my things, no conductor can direct them, no singer can sing them, the entire press despises them, yet the public clamors for them.

Wagner, quoted by Cosima
in her diary, May 3, 1873

A New Approach to Opera

Innovation in the Opera House

Not content with composing thirteen operas and writing his own librettos, Wagner was an innovator in the theatre and the orchestra pit. He was instrumental in changing the role of the conductor to be an interpreter of the composer's intentions rather than a simple timekeeper. Wagner himself was chastised in one of his early appointments for departing from the tempi preferred by his predecessor.

Until Wagner rearranged the layout of the orchestra pit, not every musician had a direct line of sight to the conductor. It is hard to imagine how they could play together without that, and the truth is they probably didn't. He tried to change the physical layout of the orchestra when he was thirty, but his recommendations were rejected. Years later, another Wagner innovation brought back visibility problems: the stepped arrangement of the Bayreuth Festspielhaus orchestra pit made it difficult for some musicians to see the conductor.

Wagner is perfect proof that when God gives out talent, he doesn't care much whom he gives it to. Duplicitous, cruel, backstabbing, a vicious anti-Semite and an unconscionable sexual predator, Wagner was a nasty piece of work. Be that as it may, he is one of the five greatest composers who ever lived and probably the greatest opera composer ever.
—Joe Queenan, in the *Guardian*, © Guardian News & Media Ltd., January 29, 2007

Such was Wagner's ego it is not stretching a point to suggest that he secretly regarded himself as a god. He was sent to earth by mysterious forces. He gathered disciples unto himself. He wrote holy scriptures in word and music (the Sacred writings eventually to be gathered in ten large volumes of prose and twenty more of letters). He caused a temple at Bayreuth to be created, in which his works could be celebrated and He Himself worshipped. He cast out all those who did not agree with his divinity. But his egomania was supported by genius; and after him, music was not the same.
—Harold C. Schonberg, *The Lives of the Great Composers*, 1970

Wagner was a man untrammeled by worldly circumstance, spiritually endowed above most human levels yet often possessed by a devil. Hard, capricious, scheming, inordinately vain, contemptuous of ordinary beings, amoral, yet absolutely devoted to his art and sincere in his inner life as a musician.
—Paul Henry Lang, *The Experience of Opera*, 1972

I just admire the daring. I just admire the boldness of the whole project [of *The Ring*]. That he risked so much in his life and that he achieved so much. It takes my breath away.
—John Deathridge, Wagner scholar, in the BBC TV documentary *Great Composers: Wagner*, directed by Kriss Rusmanis, 2006

I find it very difficult to see this man sitting down and writing music. I can see him running a country or at least an airline—or probably owning a few. But I can't see him writing music.
—Roger Norrington, conductor,
in *Great Composers: Wagner*

Because the audience cannot see the orchestra, they do not know when the music will start. When it does, it seems to sound out of nowhere and everywhere.

If the Orchestra Cannot Make the Right Sound, Invent a New Instrument

When the instruments of the orchestra could not produce the precise sounds Wagner heard in his mind, he specified his own. One of them carries his name to this day: the Wagner tuba. He commissioned the manufacture of tenor and bass versions. The Wagner tuba's rich, sonorous tone quality makes a major contribution when first heard in *The Ring*. Four of the them are used in four-part harmony proclaiming the noble and majestic Valhalla motif. The Wagner tuba has since been used by other composers including Béla Bartók, Igor Stravinsky, Richard Strauss, and Arnold Schoenberg.

Anton Bruckner, a lifelong Wagner devotee, used two pairs of Wagner tubas in his Symphony no. 7 in E Major. The tubas give the opening of the first movement a regal sound that has been compared to that of the Prelude to *Das Rheingold*.

The Wagner tuba is not a tuba at all but a modified French horn, though its sound is much deeper than the horn's. Wagner wanted a tone quality somewhere between those of the horn and the trombone. In *Musical Instruments through the Ages* (1961), Anthony Baines said, "Tuba here is really a misnomer . . . It is possible that the mistake had its origin through a German conductor—presumably Richter—pronouncing the word 'tube' in the German manner (which would sound like 'tuba') when *The Ring* was first produced in London. This may not be the correct explanation, but it is a plausible one."

Wagner was also dissatisfied with the contributions from the strings. The lowest note of the granddaddy of the string instruments was not low enough for the opening bars of *The Ring*. The mystical E-flat that opens *Das Rheingold* is played on double basses that have been tuned down.

Other instruments created for Wagner include a straight wooden trumpet with a single valve, used for the shepherd's pipe in *Tristan and Isolde*, and a bassoon with a low A used in the same opera. A contrabass trombone is used in *The Ring* for the spear motif, which drops down and down for more than two octaves. Another contributor to Wagner's big sound is a bass trumpet.

When the extensive percussion sections of an orchestra were unable to create the sound Wagner wanted for the gold-mining dwarves in *Das Rheingold*, he specified that eighteen anvils be used, all tuned to F. Three sizes of anvil are used to cover three octaves, and they are divided into three rhythmic groups.

Wagner's innovations even extended to audience behavior. He disapproved of applause that interrupted the dramatic flow of his works, so he insisted that applause be withheld until the end of each act. Newcomers who showed their enthusiasm at an inappropriate time soon won cold looks or shushing sounds from their neighbors. It took some time for Wagner to impose his wishes. At an early performance of *The Ring* in Bologna, the Rhinemaidens were persuaded by an enthusiastic audience to sing their alluring song a second time, and Mime was cheered on to sing one of his contributions three times before the audience allowed the action to continue. It also took time for Wagner to control his own urges. At an early performance of *Parsifal*, someone liked the song of the Flower Maidens so much that he started shouting, "Bravo." The audience, who were aware of the

The Wagner Tuba: Rich and Noble Sound

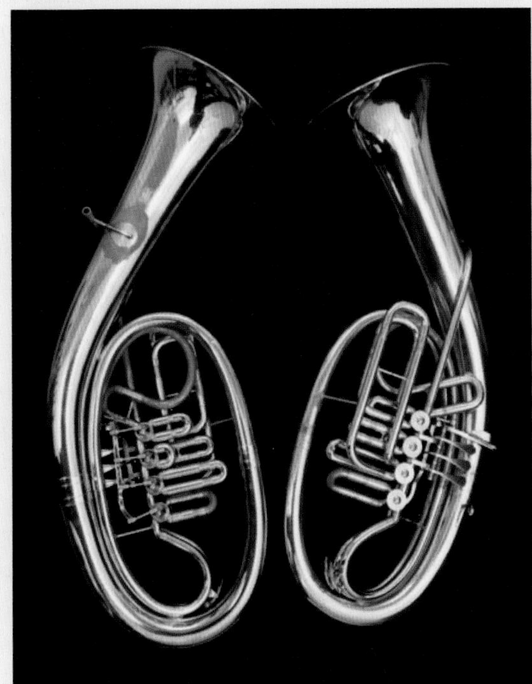

• **A pair of Wagner tubas. Photo courtesy of Woodhead Horn Repair, Bedfordshire, UK.**

The Wagner tuba is a difficult instrument to play, and its use in the scores of only a small number of composers means that horn players get limited opportunities to practice their skills. This is made worse by the fact that they are sometimes required to play both the horn and the Wagner tuba in the same piece.

Luke Woodhead, a director of his own horn repair company, explains:

> The Wagner tuba takes a very different style of playing to the horn. To start with the Wagner tuba does not allow the use of the right hand in the bell, and since horn players use this to subtly alter the tuning of most notes, the sudden inability to use the hand means that the tuning must be perfect from the embouchure [lips] alone. This can feel a little exposed! Also, they point up and out—we are used to pointing our bells backwards. Again, it leaves one feeling that there is nowhere to hide when a note is inevitably knocked over. They are clumsy-shaped instruments to hold and usually have to be picked up in a hurry—not infrequently the quick change from horn to tuba on the concert platform leads to damage to horn, tuba, or both! Added to this, they are usually picked up after a whole movement during which the player has been on horn. At this point they are invariably cold, therefore flat in pitch, and four of them are expected to play loudly and musically in tune. A big ask!

Woodhead's horn repair business in Bedfordshire, UK, services almost all of the British orchestras, including the Hallé, the City of Birmingham Symphony, the Royal Opera House, and the main London orchestras. Regular maintenance is important, says Luke: "Because the horn repertoire only calls for the use of Wagner tubas infrequently, the sets are often left unplayed for months at a time. This inactivity necessitates a service to ensure dependable valve action."

How does it sound? "If played well, the Wagner tuba can sound thrilling and provides the link between the horns and the trombones in terms of timbre. They are not subtle but provide a great racket if needed."

composer's wishes, responded with a mighty shush. Then those near him realized who the shouter was: Wagner himself.

Plácido Domingo does not agree with Wagner. He once said, "The one thing I hate at the Met is the note in the program that the public is requested not to interrupt the music with applause. That should be destroyed. What we need is to be encouraged to applaud."

Wagner did not neglect staging and presentation details. In conventional opera houses, the main curtain was lifted up or drawn open. At the Festspielhaus, both happen simultaneously. Wagner specified that the main curtain should be raised by a draw rope attached to the vertical center of the leading edge of the curtain. This curtain raising-technique still carries Wagner's name today.

Before Wagner, the house lights in the auditorium of an opera house remained on during the performance, another change that seems to us now an obvious improvement. Some of the first visitors in 1876 were surprised at the lack of a chandelier in the Festspielhaus. Several years after the darkened auditorium became standard, the eighty-year-old Princess Pauline Metternich requested a switch back to the pre-Wagner system "so that one could see the dresses of the ladies in the audience."

Arturo Toscanini was a strong supporter of several Wagner innovations in the opera house, including the darkened auditorium. But he met resistance from audiences when he conducted *Tristan* in Turin in 1897. As Harvey Sachs explained in his biography of Toscanini, "It was Toscanini's belief that a total theatrical illusion could only be created in a darkened house, and this was his first attempt at imposing this idea on a public accustomed to walking, talking, eating, looking at each other, flirting, playing cards and following libretti while 'listening' to opera."

Most of the audience members were strongly opposed to this revolutionary innovation and protested loudly. Toscanini insisted on darkness, but the noisy audience wanted to see the other half of the show—the goings-on in the auditorium. The management conceded and turned on the house lights, but Toscanini was furious and stopped conducting. The battle of wills ended in a tie. *Tristan* resumed with the house lights turned down to 50 percent.

The Italian maestro continued to impose Wagner's disciplines, introducing the Bayreuth curtain-raising method and ruling that women sitting in ground-floor seats not wear hats.

Finally, when Wagner designed his own theatre in Bayreuth, the invisible orchestra was born. The conductor and musicians in the Bayreuth Festspielhaus are concealed behind a wall that reflects the sounds of the orchestra to the back of the stage and then out to the audience. The hidden orchestra pit has been called "the mystic abyss." Because the audience cannot see the orchestra, they do not know when the music will start. When it does, it seems to sound out of nowhere and everywhere. This, combined with the superb acoustics of the Festspielhaus, makes for a spine-tingling effect.

Autographs and Manuscripts

Most of the original manuscripts of Wagner's works are held in the archives of Wahnfried, Tribschen, and other museums and libraries. Some are in private collections, and many relating to his earliest works have been lost or destroyed. Over the sixteen years of their relationship Wagner presented many of his manuscripts to his patron, King Ludwig II of Bavaria. After Ludwig's death they were held in the Wittelsbacher Ausgleichsfond, the family archives. They were subsequently purchased by the German Chamber of Industry and presented to Adolf Hitler in 1939 as a fiftieth-birthday gift. The collection included the original scores of *Die Feen*, *Das Liebesverbot*, and *Rienzi*; an orchestral sketch for *The Flying Dutchman*; the original fair-copy scores of *Rheingold*, *Walküre*, and Act III of *Siegfried*; and a copy of the orchestral sketch for *Götterdämmerung* made by Hans Richter and others. Hitler also owned a collection of Wagner's letters.

During the war Siegfried Wagner's widow, and later her son Wieland, both pleaded with Hitler to transfer the priceless manuscripts to Wahnfried's archive for safekeeping. He refused, and at the end of the war the valuable documents could not be found. Brigitte Hamann said in her book on the life of Winifred Wagner that Wieland was assured by a Hitler aide that the manuscripts were in "the safest possible place." She speculated that this might have meant Hitler's Chancellery bunker, or that the manuscripts might had been taken by air to Salzburg for storage deep under the Berghof. Bombing destroyed both the bunker and the Berghof, and no trace of any of the manuscripts has ever been found.

The Total Artwork

Before composing his later works, Wagner set about reorganizing the entire structure of opera. He believed with absolute conviction that he could bring together music, poetry, acting, singing, and scenic art in what he called the *Gesamtkunstwerk*—the total artwork. The result was works that changed opera forever. They included the groundbreaking *Tristan and Isolde*, the delightful *Meistersinger von Nürnberg*, and the colossal *Ring of the Nibelung*, which took him twenty-six years to finish. Along the way he introduced innovations that we take for granted today. The layout of the orchestra, performance in a darkened theatre, even the way the curtain is raised were all introduced by this amazing man.

But many of his changes were even more radical:

> He swept away the old idea that the libretto was one thing, the score another, and that both had to be fitted together as well as a collaboration would permit. There had to be a complete fusion of the music, text, action, and décor into a single work of art. He abolished once and for all the singer who stood immediately before the footlights beaming at his audience and giving a jolly little recital of his own, complete with any embellishments that took his fancy and as many encores as he could get. Opera, Wagner believed, had to be as convincing as ordinary spoken drama, in which the actor was expected to perform almost unconscious of the presence of an audience. But above all, he replaced the conventional recitative and aria, and acting upon his principles of unity, replaced them with what was virtually organic and continuous melody.
>
> Donald Brook, *Companion to Opera*, 1947

Wagner had the unconscious but inflexible hardihood to take up each art in turn, weigh it, and find it wanting. Each fell short of the whole reality in some respect. Painting leaves out motion and solidarity, sculpture possesses solidarity without motion, and usually without color. Poetry without drama appeals to the senses chiefly through the imagination; in itself it has neither sound, color, nor solidarity. The spoken drama lacks the intensity which it is the unique function of musical sound to give; while mere pantomime, whether of dance or drama, lacks the indefinite power of sound as well as the definite suggestion of words; and, lastly, musical sound alone provokes the eternal "why?" which can only be answered by associating the emotion raised with thought, for music is without solidarity, color, or thought, while possessing motion and sound in the highest perfection . . .

I think his critical results may be briefly summed up thus: In the musical drama, poetry, music, scenery, and acting are to be blended as that each shall have its own appropriate share, and no more, as a medium of expression. The acting must not be cramped by the music, as in common opera, where a man has to stand on one toe till he has done his roulade, or pauses in the dead of night to shout out a song about "Hush! We shall be discovered!" when there is not a moment to spare. The music must not be spoiled for the acting, as in ballet and pantomime, where acting is overstrained to express what the sister arts of poetry and music are better fitted to convey. And Poetry—which after all supplies the definite basis and answers the inevitable "why?"—must not be sacrificed, as in our opera libretti, to the demands of singers for aria and scena; while the scenery must only attempt effects and situations which can be made to look real. The object of the grand musical drama is, in fact, to present a true picture of human feeling with the utmost fullness and intensity, freed from every conventional expression by the happy union of all the arts, giving to each only what it is able to deal with—but thus dealing with everything, leaving nothing to the imagination. The Wagnerian drama completely exhausts the situation.

Hugh Haweis, *My Musical Memories*, 1884

The Thirteen Operas

Wagner wrote thirteen operas, listed below, ten of which are regularly performed by leading companies on every continent. Wagner conducted two of the premieres, *The Flying Dutchman* and *Tannhäuser*. He also conducted the closing bars at one of the

• OPERA TITLE	• CONDUCTOR	• DATE OF PREMIERE	• CITY
Die Feen	Franz Fischer	June 29, 1888	Munich
Das Liebesverbot	Richard Wagner	March 29, 1836	Magdeburg
Rienzi	Carl Gottlieb Reissiger	October 20, 1842	Dresden
The Flying Dutchman	Richard Wagner	January 2, 1843	Dresden
Tannhäuser	Richard Wagner	October 19, 1845	Dresden
Lohengrin	Franz Liszt	August 8, 1850	Weimar
Tristan and Isolde	Hans von Bülow	June 10, 1865	Munich
Die Meistersinger von Nürnberg	Hans von Bülow	June 21, 1868	Munich
Das Rheingold	Franz Wüllner	September 22, 1869	Munich
Die Walküre	Franz Wüllner	June 26, 1870	Munich
Siegfried, Götterdämmerung, and the full *Ring*	Hans Richter	August 16–17, 1876	Bayreuth
Parsifal	Hermann Levi	July 26, 1882	Bayreuth

What the Helden?

The German word *Heldentenor* means heroic tenor, a rare breed that includes very few singers. Mention *Heldentenor* to most Wagnerians and the roles that first spring to mind are Siegfried and Tristan. In addition to the specific voice qualities, these roles require strength and stamina. According to the singer and voice coach Neil Howlett, "Heldentenor implies a voice of great weight and sonority, particularly strong in the middle and bottom of the voice, in fact a tenor voice with some of the characteristics of a baritone." The German voice classification system includes *Heldentenor* for roles like Tristan, Siegmund and Siegfried. Another, *Jugendlicher Heldentenor* or "youthful heroic tenor," is more suited for Erik, Lohengrin, and Walther von Stolzing.

I have chosen to extend the use of "Helden" to include some of my heroes from the nonsinger ranks of great Wagnerians. Ten of my personal heroes are included in the following pages.

first performances of *Parsifal*. One of his early operas, *Die Feen*, was not performed until 1888, five years after the composer's death.

Helden Wagnerians 1
HANS RICHTER
The First Great Wagner Conductor

Hans Richter (1843–1916), an Austro-Hungarian, was an imposing figure. With his bushy red beard, wire-rimmed spectacles, and flowing frock coat, he cut an imposing figure striding around Bayreuth and later in Manchester and London. The music writer and critic Herman Klein wrote after meeting Richter in London, when the conductor was thirty-four:

> His hearty handshake and the open, fearless expression of his eyes prepossessed me in his favor. Thick-set and broad-shouldered, slightly below medium height, his beard square-cut and of a golden-brown tinge, he wore spectacles and spoke with boisterous vivaciousness in a broad Viennese dialect.

Richter, one of Wagner's closest associates, was entrusted with the big prize: conducting the first performance of *The Ring* in 1876. The following year he shared conducting duties with Wagner when the composer was hired by the Philharmonic Society to give a series of concerts at London's Albert Hall.

Richter also conducted the first performances of *Die Meistersinger* and *Tristan and Isolde* in England in 1882 and the first English-language *Ring* in 1908. When Charles Hallé died in 1895, the conductorship of the orchestra he had founded in Manchester was offered to Richter. He did not accept until 1899, but he then stayed until he retired twelve years later. Richter conducted regularly at Covent Garden and in many cities around the United Kingdom.

The young Richter had the best possible introduction to the works of Wagner. In 1866 the composer hired him as a copyist to produce a clean copy of the score of *Die Meistersinger von Nürnberg* for presentation to King Ludwig. For thirteen months he lived with the Wagners at Tribschen, their home in Lucerne, where he became one of the family. His work on the score and his ability to discuss nuances with the composer made him uniquely qualified for the key role of chorus master for the premiere perfor-

> "He is utterly indifferent to applause."
>
> —*Saturday Review*, on Hans Richter, 1909

mance of *Die Meistersinger* in Munich in 1868, conducted by Hans von Bülow. His detailed knowledge of the work also helped in an emergency during one of the early performances. Wilhelm Fischer, who had sung the role of Mastersinger Kothner, was too sick to perform, and there was no cover. Richter knew the role and volunteered to fill the gap. He had a passable singing voice, and his action that day saved a cancellation of the performance. It was the only appearance of his career on what was, for him, the wrong side of the footlights.

Richter was to be closely associated with *Meistersinger* for the rest of his life; he conducted the full opera 141 times and the overture many hundreds of times. Appropriately, Richter ended his career with *Meistersinger*, and after conducting five performances of the work at the Bayreuth Festival in August 1912 he never conducted again. Perhaps his only regret was that he never conducted Wagner's final work, *Parsifal*. He might have been able to do so but for his respect for Wagner's wish that *Parsifal* never be produced outside Bayreuth. Tentative plans for Richter to conduct in the Festspielhaus were thwarted due, among other things, to his failing health.

During the whole of his long career Richter recorded the minutiae of every public performance of operas and concerts. He entered the details of venues, dates, works performed, and solo performers in six notebooks that he called his *Dirigierbücher* (Conducting Books). The books include information on no fewer than 4,351 public performances over his forty-one-year conducting career. The total included 899 Wagner operas, most of them conducted without using a score. He occasionally conducted from memory an entire concert featuring works by several different composers.

• Hans Richter, first conductor of *The Ring* and close associate of Wagner, circa 1896. Artist unknown.

Georg Solti acquired Richter's notebooks while he was resident conductor of the Chicago Symphony Orchestra and made them available to Christopher Fifield for his splendid 1993 book *True Artist and True Friend: A Biography of Hans Richter*. The books made it possible for Fifield to track Richter's movements around Europe over the course of his career. In an appendix Fifield lists the thirty-three British towns and cities where Richter conducted and an astonishing forty-six others in the rest of Europe.

Richterisms

Richter was a strict disciplinarian and, unfortunately for his players, had a prodigious memory for misplayed notes or missed cues. Charles Reid, Charles Beecham's biographer, told of one mishap. In Manchester a cymbal player disastrously mistimed an entry in the finale of Antonín Dvořák's *New World* Symphony. Richter glared at him until the end of the movement and went on glaring for a full second after the music stopped. The offending cymbalist was eventually dismissed. Several seasons later he was rehearsing the *New World* again. On reaching the fateful page, Richter pulled up the orchestra two bars before the cymbal stroke and inquired in a stage whisper, "Iss he still alife?"

British colleagues and friends were often amused by Richter's problems with the English language. His wife suffered from occasional dizziness that sometimes led to a faint, the German word for which is *schwindeln*. The recommended first action then, as now, was to lie down. One day someone asked the conductor about her health. Richter replied, "My vife, she is very bad; venn she does not lie she schwindelns."

• So busy he seemed to have four arms. Caricature by Th. Zasche in *Wiener Luft*, 1891.

On one occasion he was taking a stroll around the Festspielhaus before a performance. As he passed the front of the building, he noted that it was time to sound the fanfare and shouted up to a man standing on the balcony, "You there, it's time. Blow the signal!" "I can't," said the man. "I'm the Grand Duke of Weimar, but I'm happy to have met you."

One day in England he was trying to buy rail tickets, a round trip for himself and a single for his wife. He asked the ticket clerk, "Please give me a ticket for me to come back and one for my vife not to come back."

When he became angry with a member of an English orchestra, he told the musician: "Your damn nonsense can I stand vonce or tvice, but sometimes always, by God, NEVER."

In another appendix he records the tally of works performed; not surprisingly, Wagner's music features high on the list. The numbers of performances of full operas conducted by Richter include: *Lohengrin*, 198; *Die Meistersinger*, 141; *Die Walküre*, 123; *Tannhäuser*, 85; *Siegfried*, 84; *Götterdämmerung*, 78; *Das Rheingold*, 63; *Tristan and Isolde*, 57; *The Flying Dutchman*, 55; and *Rienzi*, 15.

Hans Richter was a giant of a man, and in his younger years he had bushy red hair and a matching beard. Yet he was modest: he never once appeared on the stage at Bayreuth to take an individual bow. A 1909 article in the *Saturday Review* said: "He is utterly indifferent to applause; at the end of a great performance of *The Ring* he will step down from his desk and look up at a house shouting with enthusiasm for him alone, with a countenance no more expressive of emotion than that of a cow looking over a fence."

Even after his final appearance in the Bayreuth

PUNCH, OR THE LONDON CHARIVARI.—February 5, 1908.

RICHTER THE RING-MASTER.

Mr. Punch begs to congratulate Dr. Richter on the brilliant success with which he has conducted the first complete performance of Wagner's "Ring" in English.

• **The 1908 tribute in the British magazine *Punch* to Richter on conducting his first complete performance of *The Ring* in English.**

> "Wagner is acknowledged to be a brilliant conductor."
> —Eduard Hanslick

pit, he refused to take a curtain call. His last performance there was his beloved *Meistersinger*, but even a twenty-minute ovation failed to get him onto the stage. He believed that the composer should get all of the credit and once explained, "It is not for me to stand where the Master has stood." In an earlier demonstration of his lifelong devotion to the Master, Richter and his wife, Marie, named their daughter, the first of six children, Richardis Cosima Eva.

In his post-Bayreuth days Richter enjoyed a distinguished career in England as conductor of the Hallé Orchestra from 1899 to 1911. He became a friend of Edward Elgar and conducted the premiere performances of the *Enigma Variations*, *The Dream of Gerontius*, and the First Symphony. In 1904 a row over unauthorized stand-in players among Philharmonic musicians led a breakaway group to establish their own orchestra. Hans Richter was the first to conduct the new band, the London Symphony Orchestra.

One of the main questions is how to handle men, how to influence his musicians by his gesture or by his looks. His human qualities have very much to say on this question. If he is a man of warm heart and sincerity the musicians, even those who are far superior . . . will listen to him. If he is not a man who . . . has the passion, if he is not capable of ecstasy, he could never conduct *Tristan and Isolde*.

— Bruno Walter in 1958 on the qualities needed in a conductor

Conducting with Esprit and Fire

Many contemporaries observed that Wagner was an accomplished conductor; Hector Berlioz said that the German composer conducted with "rare precision and energy." He frequently conducted his own works and benefited from exposure to a wide repertoire at an early age. From 1833 to 1836, when he was in Würzburg, Magdeburg, and Bad Lauchstädt, Wagner conducted operas by Ludwig van Beethoven, Carl Maria von Weber, Vincenzo Bellini, W. A. Mozart, and Gioachino Rossini, and other works by François-Adrien Boieldieu, Ferdinando Paer, Giovanni Paisiello, Johann Baptist Schenk, and Ludwig Spohr.

One critic wrote of Wagner in 1861: "An excellent conductor is this man, a conductor with esprit and fire, who at the rehearsals, with voice, hands, and feet, carries along his company like a valiant officer is sure to take his fort . . . It was a real gratification to hear this *Freischütz* overture, which is usually played off at a monotonous, slovenly pace, for once with a new swing and exceedingly delicate nuances."

That critic was none other than Eduard Hanslick, who was so brutally negative about most of Wagner's compositions. He wrote again in 1872: "Wagner is acknowledged to be a brilliant conductor; he has poetic intentions, and his great authority over the players enables him to carry them into execution. His energetic reproduction of the *Eroica* Symphony, with its fine and peculiar nuances, also gave us on the whole a genuine pleasure."

In his book on conducting, Wagner told of the occasion when he conducted Weber's *Freischütz* for

• **A well-known cartoon by Spy, from the May 19, 1877, issue of *Vanity Fair*, used here on a playing card.**

the first time in Dresden: a veteran cellist from Weber's time turned to Wagner and said, "Yes, that is the way Weber took it; now I hear it correctly again, for the first time." Finck tells of the time when Wagner "taught the Viennese orchestra how to play the *Freischütz* overture in his (that is, Weber's) way; the effect was startling; many declared they had now for the first time heard this piece which constant repetition had long ago rendered threadbare."

Francis Hueffer, of the London *Times*, was in Bayreuth in 1872 and wrote:

> Wagner, in common life, is of a rather reserved and extremely gentlemanly deportment; but as soon as he faces his band, a kind of demon seems to take possession of him. He storms, hisses, stamps his foot on the ground, and performs the most wonderful gyratory movements with his arms; and woe to the wretch who wounds his keen ear with a false note! At other times, when the musical waves run smoothly, Wagner ceases almost entirely to beat the time, and a most winning smile is the doubly appreciated reward of his musicians for a particularly well executed passage.

Wagner was popular with the orchestras he conducted regularly, but sometimes a period of education was necessary. Each year in Dresden, the proceeds of one subscription concert were set aside for the benefit of the widows and orphans of former members of the orchestra. In 1846, Wagner decided that they would perform Beethoven's Ninth. The orchestra reacted vehemently against the idea: the Ninth had been performed some years earlier under the baton of the other Dresden conductor, Reissiger, and had not been a success. The orchestra members feared that another performance of the difficult Beethoven symphony would not raise much for their widows and orphans, and they appealed to their general director to overrule their conductor. Wagner refused to concede and set to work drilling his orchestra at numerous rehearsals—the schedule involved no fewer than twelve special meetings of the double basses and cellos alone. As a result of his rigorous coaching and animated conducting, the performance was a triumph, and the directors asked Wagner to make Beethoven's Ninth an annual event.

Contemporary reports tell us that Wagner preferred a brisk tempo, at least for the *Tannhäuser* overture. Under his baton, the overture took twelve minutes in Dresden. A random selection of recordings reveals that Herbert von Karajan (Berlin Philharmonic) was the slowest at 14:49, and Albert Coates (London Symphony Orchestra) was the only conductor faster than Wagner—his *Tannhäuser* overture won by twelve seconds. Adrian Boult, Lorin Maazel, Claudio Abbado, and Wilhelm Furtwängler all took longer than fourteen minutes.

> As a conductor Wagner was a man of iron energy. Almost small of stature, he seemed to grow to gigantic size when before his orchestra. His powerful head, with its sharply defined features, his wonderfully penetrating eyes, his mobile face, which gave expression to every emotion, every thought, can never be forgotten. His body stood motionless, but his eyes glittered, glowed, pierced; his fingers worked nervously, and electric currents seemed to pass through the air to each individual musician; an invisible force entered the hearts of all; every man thrilled with him, for he could not escape the glance of this great man. Wagner held everybody bound to him as by a magical chain; the musicians had to perform wonders, for they could not do otherwise. At first things went topsy-turvy at rehearsals, because of the impatience of the master, who wanted everything to be good at once; the strange, illustrative movements of his long baton startled and puzzled the musicians until they learned that the musical bars were not dominant, but the phrase, the melody, or the expression; but soon the glance caught the attention of the men, they became infused with the magical fluid, and the master had them all in his hands. Then the meanest orchestra grew and played gloriously, the tones became imbued with life and expression, the most rigorous rhythm and the loftiest face of Wagner. All hung on his glance, and he seemed to see them all at once.
>
> Once I sat beside a great actor who for the first time saw Wagner exercise this potency of look and facial expression. He stared at Wagner as if he had been an apparition from beyond the grave, and could not take his eyes off him. Afterward he told me that Wagner's face was more eloquent than all the actors in the world with all their powers of expression combined. Whoever saw Wagner, and came into contact with him in Vienna, Berlin, Hamburg, Budapest, Russia, or Switzerland, will certainly never forget this influence. He seldom conducted, but one must have seen him conduct a symphony by Beethoven in order to learn how much there is hidden away among the notes of that classic giant, and how much can be conjured out of them. To my thinking, Wagner is not only the mightiest of all musical geniuses, but also the greatest conductor that ever lived.
>
> Anton Seidl, conductor, who served as Wagner's musical assistant for six years, in his 1895 essay *On Conducting*

Wagner Conducts Wagner—or Does He?

It is unlikely that there are any authentic audio recordings of Richard Wagner conducting, but there is at least one possible contender. It has been suggested that a four-minute fragment of the *Tristan and Isolde* love theme may have been recorded by the composer. The recording was supposedly made on a cylinder around 1880 by the Bayreuth Festspiel Orchestra with Amalie Materna as Isolde and Albert Niemann as Tristan. Two versions were released on CD by Gramophone 2000 in 1997, the first from the original cylinder and the second a restored version of the same fragment.

The producers of the CD offered the recordings to musicologists "as material for consideration and examination so that they may decide upon its authenticity." The same CD includes recordings made by Siegfried Wagner conducting several orchestras in 1926 and 1927.

All of the Siegfried Wagner recordings were copied from the original discs, so the quality is rather poor. One reviewer described Siegfried Wagner's conducting as "ponderously slow and without life," but it is interesting to speculate on how much Siegfried was influenced by childhood memories of productions in the Festspielhaus. Siegfried was only twelve when his father died in Venice.

In addition to the *Tristan* fragment, the CD includes the *Huldigungsmarsch*, composed for King Ludwig's birthday in 1864. The original composition was scored for a brass band; it was adapted for orchestra several years later with help from Joachim Raff. This orchestral version was first performed in 1871.

On the final track of the two-CD set, Siegfried Wagner conducts the overture to one of his thirteen operas, *Der Bärenhäuter*, composed in 1899. Siegfried was born at Tribschen in 1869 and died in Bayreuth in 1930, just months after the death of his mother, Cosima.

Yesterday's Conductors Directing Today's Orchestras

How about the famous first conductor of *The Ring*, Hans Richter, conducting at Covent Garden, next week? Unlikely, it would seem, since Richter died in December 1916. However, if Richter had agreed to a proposal made to him a few years earlier, it might have been possible. Kind of.

The idea was to film Richter in action in front of a live orchestra; the resulting film could then be screened for another orchestra to follow. The musicians would not have the advantage of Richter's careful rehearsal, but at least his tempi and empha-

Ever since Monteverdi's day, opera performances had been directed either by the leader of the orchestra (normally from the harpsichord or pianoforte) or by a "conductor" who beat time on the floor with a long staff . . . By the early nineteenth century, a baton had replaced the staff, and conductors stood on a podium in front of the orchestra. Beethoven used a baton, as did Weber; Berlioz was one of the first to conduct from a full score. But it was Wagner who made conducting into a virtuoso art. He imposed on orchestras not only the strictest discipline but also his personal interpretation of whatever work was played. Conductors who were not famous composers—men like Hans Richter, and Anton Seidl—followed Wagner's example. Their presence sold tickets (Seidl was a cult figure in New York in the 1890s). Arturo Toscanini, however, was different. In the first half of the century, he was a superstar in his own right—not so much because of his public persona (though that was formidable) but because he was a fanatical musician, a martinet, a man totally dedicated to giving performances that were technically proficient and emotionally powerful.

—Richard Somerset-Ward, *The Story of Opera*, 1998

The ability to conduct is a gift of God with which few have been endowed in full measure. Those who possess only a little of the gift cannot write about it; and those who have it in abundance do not wish to write, for to them the talent seems so natural a thing that they cannot see the need of discussing it. This is the kernel of the whole matter. If you have the divine gift within you, you can conduct; and if you have it not, you will never be able to acquire it. Those who have been endowed with the gift are conductors, the others are time beaters.

—Anton Seidl, *On Conducting*, 1895

ses would have been preserved for future study.

Unfortunately for those of us who would pay generously to see the great man conduct, Richter declined the offer, so the film was never made. If he had agreed, we might have been able to hear *Die Meistersinger* conducted by one of its leading interpreters. And if the technology had been invented a few years earlier, we could have heard the *Siegfried Idyll* "conducted" by Wagner himself.

Most of the world's leading conductors have directed the famous Festspielhaus orchestra. They include Daniel Barenboim, Karl Böhm, Pierre Boulez, Andre Cluytens, Wilhelm Furtwängler, Herbert von Karajan, Joseph Keilberth, Hans Knappertsbusch, Clemens Krauss, Hermann Levi, James Levine, Felix Mottl, Karl Muck, Hans Richter, Wolfgang

By mid-century, the interpretive role of the composer-conductor became even more crucial with the emergence of what we today think of as the modern orchestra, whose power and expressive possibilities were exciting the imaginations of those writing for it and in turn extending its horizons. While Berlioz, Weber and Spontini were talented and often inspired as conductors, not all composers were equal to the challenge. Beethoven and later Schumann were ineffective in bringing life to their music from the podium. As Berlioz commented, conducting was a gift all its own and "as specific as the violinist's. It is acquired only by long practice, and only if one has a very marked, natural aptitude for it."

Yet, however excellent were Berlioz and others, they were but harbingers of the two men—Mendelssohn and Wagner—who would establish the precedents, precepts, and poles of conducting that still exist in one way or another. Though born only four years apart and into the same cultural environment, no two individuals or musicians could have been more disparate. Mendelssohn was an establishment figure, reserved and Apollonian. Wagner was a revolutionary, flamboyant and Dionysian. At the age of twenty-six, Mendelssohn was appointed music director of the concerts of the Leipzig Gewandhaus Orchestra, while Wagner's career as a conductor was a migrant one, largely restricted to both important and provincial opera houses.

The cool, clean, classically molded scores of Mendelssohn were also the antithesis of the heated excesses and rampant emotion found in Wagner's music. A similar gulf separated them as music-makers. Mendelssohn's conducting was characterized by quick, even tempos and imbued with what many regarded as model logic and precision. One singer in the historic revival of Bach's St. Matthew Passion conducted by Mendelssohn in 1829 has left us with a graphic prose picture of Mendelssohn's conducting and the "quiet and simple way in which he, by a look, a movement of the head or hand, reminded us of the inflections agreed upon, and thus ruled every phrase."

In contrast, Wagner's way was broad, hyper-romantic, and embraced the idea of tempo modulation—from a heightening or lessening of pace and emotions that followed the contours of a score. In rehearsal and performance he was known to hiss, storm, and stamp at his players. To him, conducting was an act of baring one's soul in public. Wagner is credited as being the first person to conduct without a score and with his back to the audience. With Mendelssohn as a model, conductors had positioned themselves diagonally to the orchestra. They had also followed his lead in wearing white gloves to conduct; a nicety Wagner would have no part of, with a single exception that created a furor. At a concert in London he conducted Mendelssohn's Fourth Symphony, the "Italian," with gloves on, and then, with obvious relish, removed them for the balance of the program.

—John Ardoin, *The Furtwängler Record*, 1994

"Those who have been endowed with the gift are conductors, the others are time beaters."
— Anton Seidl

Sawallisch, Georg Solti, Richard Strauss, and Arturo Toscanini. One notable British absentee from the list was Malcolm Sargent, possibly because his summers were spent in London: he was the chief conductor of the Proms from 1948 to 1967. And despite Wagner's anti-Semitism, he relied heavily on Jewish singers and conductors during his life. Most prominent, perhaps, was Hermann Levi, who conducted the first performance of *Parsifal* in 1882.

In the summer of 1933 John Barbirolli traveled to Germany with his friend Charles Parker. After visiting the Hans Sachs house in Nuremberg, the pair moved on to Bayreuth, where they attended performances of *Parsifal*, conducted by Richard Strauss, and *Die Meistersinger*, conducted by Karl Elmendorff.

> Bayreuth itself was commemorating the fiftieth anniversary of Wagner's death with an exhibition of relics. Barbirolli was deeply moved to be able to examine manuscripts and to enter Wagner's study. Twenty years afterwards his eyes filled with tears and he gripped my arm in his unforgettable way as he described seeing sketches from which Tristan had grown. He was especially interested to discover the original number of players in the Siegfried Idyll and usually conducted it with this small orchestra because he thought the music's peculiar intimacy was lost with a large orchestra.
>
> Michael Kennedy, *Barbirolli: Conductor Laureate*, 1971

After returning to England, Barbirolli wrote to Parker:

> It is I who has to thank you, for I should never have gone alone, and undoubtedly I profited much from the experience . . . I shudder to think what it would have been like to see some of the things we did, with anybody incapable of feeling the sense of wonder and grandeur they undoubtedly call forth.

When Jeremy Isaacs, then general director of Covent Garden, made a comment to Solti in 1983 about conducting Peter Hall's *Ring* at Bayreuth, Solti quickly corrected him: "Peter Hall will direct *my Ring*."

In 1899, when Thomas Beecham was only twenty, he made his first visit to Bayreuth. Though awed by the music, with which he was already familiar, he was disappointed by the productions and the family feuds and backbiting, which are still all too evident today. The number of foreign visitors also amazed him:

> With the splendid snobbery of youth I declined to believe that this familiar crowd of knickerbockered sportsmen, gaitered bishops, and equine-visaged ladies could have any real affinity with the spirit, the mighty genius who completed on the stage the task which Walter Scott a century earlier had begun in the novel, the reconstruction of the age of chivalry and romance. I coveted the happiness and applauded the prejudice of the royal Ludwig and had I been a millionaire would have waited until the close of the Festival and engaged the company to play its program all over again for the

audience of one, myself.

Thomas Beecham, *A Mingled Chime*, 1943

The Biographies: Fact, Fiction, and Lies

Most of the Early Efforts Are Suspect

It is likely that more has been written about Wagner than any other composer. Even in his lifetime, a torrent of articles, pamphlets, and books attempted to satisfy the thirst for knowledge about the remarkable creator of the music of the future. The biographers included some who had been close to Wagner or who had access to family records and recollections and who, therefore, were judged to have an inside track in telling the true story.

But many of the contemporary accounts—including Wagner's own biography, his own notebook, and biographies by people close to the composer—were either disingenuous or plain dishonest. Some were produced to flatter or glorify, and others were created by writers anxious to get aboard the Wagner bandwagon. None of the early biographies painted the warts-and-all pictures necessary for full understanding.

Many of the so-called biographies contributed little or no new information, and many were rehashes of earlier works. While the following are regarded by many as the main contributors to knowledge and understanding of Wagner's life, some of the facts in them have been challenged, and at least two have been exposed as more fiction than biography.

Houston Stewart Chamberlain

The Hampshire-born son of a British admiral, Houston Stewart Chamberlain was a cousin of Neville Chamberlain, the British prime minister.

> "The autobiography is simply the last and longest of a thousand speeches for the defense."
>
> —Ernest Newman

Chamberlain was educated in France, Switzerland, and Austria. He settled in Bayreuth, where he met and married Wagner's youngest daughter, Eva, in 1908. He became a German citizen in 1916, and during World War I he wrote in support of the kaiser. He was the author of *The Foundation of the Nineteenth Century*, which claimed that Aryans were uniquely responsible for creative endeavor and that Jews had been a negative influence.

Although he never met his father-in-law, he wrote a biography that has variously been dismissed as muddled or sycophantic. The renowned Wagnerian scholar Stewart Spencer, in his book *Wagner Remembered*, describes the Chamberlain book as "one of the most egregious attempts in the history of musicology to misrepresent an artist by systematically censoring his correspondence."

A great opportunity was wasted, because Chamberlain had access to valuable material through the family. His biography, *Richard Wagner*, was translated into English by G. Ainslie Hight and published in London in 1900. Chamberlain died in Bayreuth in 1927.

The Praeger Affair

Ferdinand Praeger was born in 1815 in Leipzig, Wagner's birthplace, but settled in London when he was only nineteen. He became a composer, and his works were performed in London and Paris. He was more successful as a music teacher and played both the piano and the cello.

Wagner stayed with him when he visited London in 1855 to conduct the Philharmonic. Praeger later claimed that he and Wagner were bosom buddies and that "it was through my sole exertions" that the Philharmonic Society invited Wagner to London to conduct a series of six concerts in 1877. However, apart from his letters to Minna and others from London, and the brief references in *My Life*, Wagner did not mention Praeger as a close friend. In fact, he was not impressed by his Leipzig compatriot. In a letter from London, he dismissed Praeger as "a poor German lesson-giver."

Praeger claimed that during Wagner's London stay the two men discussed many aspects of the composer's life and works, including his involvement in the Dresden uprising of 1849. Two years after Wagner's death Praeger published his book *Wagner as I Knew Him*, which supposedly relied on information obtained directly from the composer.

Bernard Shaw welcomed the book in his column in *The World*: "It is an account of Wagner by a man who was not ashamed of him as he really was and who was not afraid of being denounced for exposing the failings of a 'gentleman recently dead,' as Augustus Harris would call Wagner. A more vivid and convincing portrait than Praeger's was never painted in words: even the bluntest strokes in it are interesting."

But others began to suspect that the book included much that was fiction. Several of the statements in Praeger's book aroused the suspicion of Houston Stewart Chamberlain and William Ashton Ellis (1853–1919), an English doctor and the prominent Wagnerian who translated most of Wagner's prose works. Ellis was particularly critical of Praeger's account of Wagner's role in the events in Dresden in 1849. He conducted an intensive research study that included contemporary reports in the *Deutsche Allgemeine Zeitung* (the principal Saxon newspaper of the period), numerous letters, and three books on various aspects of the uprising. These included a publication by August Roeckel, who had been with Wagner in Dresden and who was arrested, charged, found guilty, and given a life sentence for his role in the uprising. Ellis also communicated with one of the participants, delved into records held by the British Museum, and reexamined some of Wagner's own letters and prose works, including *A Communication to My Friends*.

Ellis spelled out his findings in a slim, seventy-two-page volume titled *Wagner Sketches, 1849: A Vindication* (London: Kegan Paul, Trench Trübner, 1892). By careful crosschecking of statements, letters, dates, and even times, Ellis was able to show that Praeger's work includes numerous blatant errors and untruths that could have been picked up with minimal checking.

William Ashton Ellis did not argue that Wagner was completely blameless, only that Praeger's account suggested he was much more actively involved than the evidence shows. Ellis argued that Wagner was an activist against what he saw as a social injustice. "No doubt there were agitators," said Ellis, "and probably some of them self-seeking ones; but were there no agitators when our Barons wrenched from John the Magna Carta or none when America declared its Independence?"

Six months after his initial welcome for Praeger's book, Bernard Shaw suggested that a copy of the slim Ellis booklet should be bound up with every library copy of *Wagner as I Knew Him*. "Yes, but you didn't know him," was the message Shaw relayed regarding the result of the English doctor's detective work.

When word of Ellis' detective work reached the publishers of the German edition of Praeger's book, they immediately withdrew it from the market. Others began to question some of Praeger's statements, and it is now generally agreed that Praeger

At one point, when Cosima was giving birth, Wagner himself made entries in her diaries.

played little or no part in the decision to invite Wagner to England. Because of this and other blatant inaccuracies, some scholars have dismissed the whole of Praeger's book as a fabrication.

It is a great pity that Praeger devalued his own book, because he did have some contact with Wagner that should have provided additional insights into the mind of his countryman.

A Communication to My Friends

In 1851, while exiled in Zurich, Wagner wrote *A Communication to My Friends*, a quasi-biographical work intended to help propagate his message. In this small publication he included the first public reference to his plan for a "Nibelung Festival." Although intended to document his artistic development, the 131-page book also included some useful autobiographical information.

My Life: Wagner's Autobiography

Wagner's longer biography, *Mein Leben* (*My Life*), provides valuable information on the life of the composer, but much of it is suspect. The book was written at the direct request of King Ludwig II, who wanted to know about the life of his obsession up to the point when they met in 1864.

Ernest Newman wrote: "The autobiography is simply the last and longest of a thousand speeches for the defense . . ." Wagner "deliberately tries to mislead the reader with regard to his relationship with Frau Wesendonck; everyone who has read Wagner's ardent letters to her must have gaped with astonishment to find him glossing over that long and passionate love-dream . . ." Newman goes on to say that Wagner was plainly guilty of serious sins both of omission and commission in his account of his dealings with several people, including Eduard Hanslick.

There are three possible explanations for what one observer called "a masterpiece of mendacity." First, Wagner, a man never troubled by an inferiority complex, was a creator, and he could not resist any opportunity to enhance the portrayal of his own genius. For similar reasons, he covered up the less savory aspects of his life. One generous interpretation might be that Wagner found it difficult to switch from creator to reporter. Perhaps the creativity for which Wagner is renowned and appreciated got in the way of an honest account. Also, because *Mein Leben* was written for King Ludwig, Wagner was careful to omit anything that would displease his patron. Wagner was not going to risk jeopardizing his relationship with his personal golden goose. Finally, *Mein Leben* was dictated by Wagner to his second wife, Cosima, and it was inevitable that Wagner would be selective in his handling of the facts, especially those relating to the other women in his life. For all these reasons, *Mein Leben* is a heavily sanitized account of a tempestuous life.

Wagner rubbed salt in the wound when he wrote in the preface:

> As the value of this autobiography consists in its unadorned veracity, which, under the circumstances, is its only justification, therefore my statements had to be accompanied by precise names and dates; hence there could be no question of their publication until sometime after my death, should interest in them still survive in our descendants, and on that point I intend leaving directions in my will.

Wagner knew that some of the content of his autobiography would prove to be incendiary if published in his lifetime, but he wanted some of his closest friends to read what he had written. (He was notorious for subjecting his friends to long readings of his prose works.) So he added to the preface:

> If, on the other hand, we do not refuse certain intimate friends a sight of these papers now, it is that, relying on their genuine interest in the contents, we are confident that they will not pass on their knowledge to any who do not share their feelings in this matter.

Wagner paid for only eighteen copies to be printed, all of which were distributed only to his closest friends and trustees. He probably hoped that the book would help them spread the word and defend him against criticism. Later, almost certainly influenced by Cosima, Wagner asked to have all of the copies returned. When *Mein Leben* was eventually published for general distribution in 1911, there were suggestions that the original work might have been expurgated by family members, particularly Cosima. It was feared that because all eighteen copies had been returned and, presumably, destroyed, history would never know what had been changed. Then a nineteenth copy turned up. More on this later.

Hans von Wolzogen

Hans von Wolzogen (1848–1938) was appointed to be, in Wagner's words, "the representative of the aesthetic and social side of my artistic activity." Von Wolzogen edited the *Bayreuther Blätter* for sixty years from its first appearance in January 1878. His access to Wagner and the composer's immediate lieutenants gave him a considerable advantage, and his contemporary accounts are an important part of the database of facts on Wagner's life.

The Brown Book

For seventeen years between 1865 and 1882, Wagner also kept notes and ideas in what he called *Das braunes Buch* (*The Brown Book*), given to him by Cosima during an enforced separation. It was a beautiful leather-bound tome with metal decoration and a lock. The book is now in the Wagner Museum at Wahnfreid in Bayreuth.

In 1980, *The Diary of Richard Wagner, 1865–1882: The Brown Book*, presented and annotated by Joachim Bergfeld and translated by George Bird, was published in English translation by Cambridge University Press. In the publicity material, the publisher said:

> *The Brown Book*, so-called by Wagner for its calf binding, was a gift from Cosima, and used by him, when apart from her, to record his thoughts and feelings about her, for her later perusal. So, in the early pages, he pours out passionate declarations and reproaches. But after they had taken up residence together at Triebschen [*sic*], its contents became more general—a prose sketch of *Parsifal*, many poems, drafts of two comedies, a moving memoir of the tenor Ludwig Schnorr, the first Tristan, whose death was a great blow to Wagner, and much else. At all times, however, his pre-occupation is his own aesthetic, and the book is often fascinatingly revelatory.
>
> This is the first complete publication of the original manuscript, and while something over half of it has been previously published here and there and at different times, these previously published parts are now difficult to access or out of print. Furthermore, the present version contains new revelations, for Eva Wagner, to whom Cosima handed on the book, censored it by

sticking together those pages of which she disapproved: revelations of Cosima's jealousy of Mathilde Maier, or Wagner's irritation over Ludwig's plan for a Munich Festival Theatre. All these pages have now been opened up.

Cosima Wagner's Diaries

From January 1, 1869, until February 12, 1883, Wagner's wife, Cosima, kept a detailed daily diary in twenty-one small notebooks where she noted the daily activities in the house, what the children said and did, and conversations with the constant flow of visitors. She gave details of their correspondence, leisure activities, and Richard's declining health. Potentially most valuable however, were the comments on what Richard said and thought, about everything—his own works and those of other composers, local and national events, and communications with King Ludwig. Cosima noted every step of the way to the completion of *Parsifal*, Wagner's final work. She recorded his comments on the satisfactions of composing on days when things went well and the frustrations when things did not go according to plan.

Richard intended that the diaries would, together with his own autobiography *Mein Leben*, form the complete record of his life. At one point, when Cosima was giving birth to their son, Siegfried, Wagner himself made entries in her diaries.

Cosima's diaries have provided invaluable insights into the daily life and thought of Wagner during the later years of his life. Unfortunately, Cosima had her children in mind when she made her daily entries. The first diary is dedicated:

> This book belongs to my children.
> Tribschen, near Lucerne, 1869
> Dedicated quite especially to Siegfried by Mama.

It was therefore inevitable that some of the story would be sanitized, adjusted, or completely suppressed. So once again at least some of her thoughts, Wagner's comments, and events chronicled in the diary were filtered by Cosima's need to protect her children from less pleasant truths. Despite these reservations, the two-volume English translation by Geoffrey Skelton is essential reading for Wagner enthusiasts. Some of the details of Wagner's life will not be found in any other publication.

Glasenapp's Early Biography

Carl-Friedrich Glasenapp (1847–1915) was born and died in Riga. He wrote the first comprehensive biography of Wagner, and it became the basis for many subsequent works. The first volume was published in time for the 1876 opening of the Bayreuth Festspielhaus; the second volume appeared in 1882. Later, after Glasenapp was given access to records at Wahnfried, he expanded the biography to six volumes, which were translated into English by William Ashton Ellis.

Glasenapp's biography was written while Wagner was still alive, and the heavy hand of the Bayreuth protectors resulted in a lack of objectivity and critical evaluation in this otherwise valuable work. Glasenapp's *Life of Richard Wagner* was an homage to the composer and has been dismissed by Philip Hodson, author of *Who's Who in Wagner*, as "an obsequious piece of hagiography." It is undeniable, however, that Glasenapp's work was the basis for several future biographers because of the wealth of detail that he included.

Ernest Newman

Ernest Newman (1868–1959), one of the earliest commentators and interpreters of Wagner's works, was born in Lancashire and educated at Liverpool University. His real name was William

Roberts, but he adopted Ernest Newman when he started writing musical criticism, explaining, "I am a new man in earnest." He wrote for several British newspapers, ending with the *Sunday Times*, where he was music critic from 1920 until 1958. He wrote several books on Wagner but is best-known for his four-volume *Life of Richard Wagner*. More than fifty years after he died in July 1959, Newman is still extensively quoted in new studies of Wagner and his works.

Dogs, Horses, Ravens, Frogs, and Dragons

One of the many challenges for stage designers and directors of Wagner's operas is the many animals in the dramas. In *The Ring* there are several horses, two rams, a songbird, two ravens, a bear, a serpent, and a dragon. Live horses, rams, and even bears have been used, but so far no director has cast a live dragon.

Wotan's Ravens

There are several references in *The Ring* to Wotan's messengers, a pair of ravens who carried the news of important events. In the source material for *The Ring*, Wotan's ravens were named Munin (Memory or Thought) and Hugin (Reason).

There is no known instance of live ravens being used, and in most productions the ravens do not appear at all. However, they did make appearances in the last two productions of *The Ring* in Seattle. François Rochaix's staging in 1986–1995 featured a stuffed raven sitting on the set overlooking the proceedings. In Stephen Wadsworth's 2005 production two ravens are seen flying from the scene to report Siegfried's killing of the dragon Fafner.

The concept of messenger ravens has been picked up in Australia by the Wagner Society of Melbourne. A Web site listing Wagner opera productions around the world is identified as Ravens Reporting.

A couple of live ravens with Wagnerian names were among the birds living at a famous address in London several years ago: Thor and Odin, in the Tower of London. (Odin was the original name for Wotan in the Norse legends.) The two birds were rescued from the New Forest in Hampshire and lived at the Tower with five other resident ravens: Branwen, Hugine, Munin, Gwyllum, and Baldrick.

In a 1939 Bayreuth production of *Götterdämmerung*, one unfortunate horse could not stand the excitement and died after the first act.

The *Tannhäuser* Dogs

In 1875 Wagner put live dogs into a production of *Tannhäuser* in Vienna. This provided further ammunition for the anti-Wagner forces of that period, and a cartoon in a local paper showed Wagner surrounded by several dogs. The caption read: "Wow! Wow! Sire! Through you, dogs have come to the Opera and through you, the Opera will soon go to the dogs. We thank you for the appreciation of our race. Wow! Wow!"

Brünnhilde's Horse

In *Götterdämmerung*, the final opera of *The Ring*, Brünnhilde's horse is named Grane. At the climax of Act III Wagner's stage direction calls for Brünnhilde to mount Grane and ride into the flames of Siegfried's funeral pyre and the burning Valhalla. Most directors consider that discretion is the better part of valor, and Brünnhilde addresses her comments to an offstage Grane. In some pro-

• **Wotan's ravens rarely appear onstage.**

ductions a mock horse has been used, but this has often had an unwanted comical effect just as the production approaches its emotional climax.

At Bayreuth in 1926 the horse playing the part of Grane kicked out and injured both Siegfried and a stagehand, who suffered a broken ankle. No singers or stagehands were injured by the Grane in the 1939 production, but the unfortunate horse could not stand the excitement and died after the first act. A replacement horse was found and performed admirably.

In the 2001 and 2005 productions of the Seattle Opera *Ring*, the director, Stephen Wadsworth, used a real horse, although not for Brünnhilde's Immolation Scene. The horse, a handsome animal with a gleaming black coat, made a surprise appearance in *Götterdämmerung*. When Brünnhilde and Siegfried trade gifts before he leaves her mountain cave, he gives Brünnhilde the ring and she tells him that she will give him her horse, Grane. Brünnhilde, played by Jane Eaglen, walked offstage and seconds later reappeared leading the magnificent animal, at which point the normally silent Seattle audience collectively gasped. Siegfried, played by Alan Woodrow, held the horse on a short bridle to reduce the chances of an unplanned movement. But he need not have worried. Grane performed beautifully during the short walk along the mountain path high on Brünnhilde's rock. The horse took a good long look at the sea of faces to its left before rounding the rock to make his exit.

Speight Jenkins, general director of the Seattle Opera, revealed later that contrary to Wagner's specification, the role of Grane was played by a filly called Blackie, but it is safe to assume that few in the audience noticed or cared. When the Wadsworth *Ring* returned years later, the role of Grane was played by Star.

The prize for bravery must go to the director of the Vienna Opera's first production of *The Ring* in 1877. It featured eight Valkyries hurtling around the stage on live horses. The director had enlisted the help of the riding teacher of Empress Elizabeth to help train the eight army horses borrowed for the occasion. He also hired accomplished Polish horsemen who were outfitted with wigs and helmets and doubled as Valkyries for the scene.

Live horses had been used the year before, in the first Bayreuth *Ring*, but there Wagner decided to take no risks, and the singers walked the horses onto the stage. In Vienna no punches were pulled, and even the critic Eduard Hanslick found the sight appealing. It all went according to plan. The only problem was complaints from the Polish riders that the music was too loud.

However, it was not such smooth going for Amalie Materna, the Vienna Brünnhilde. During rehearsals she had problems with the horse playing the part of Grane and could not persuade it to stand still. The director, Franz Ritter von Jauner, came up with a cunning plan. He hid a soldier from the Army Service Corps behind a stage rock and instructed him to feed the horse a handful of oats whenever it became restless. But there were some negative audience reactions, according to Marcel Prawy in his book *The Vienna Opera*: "Malicious tongues maintained that every now and then a great red orb came bobbing out from behind the rock; it was generally assumed to be

• **This 2011 Luxembourg stamp celebrated the two hundredth anniversary of Liszt's birth.**

the rising sun—in fact it was only the seat of the soldier's trousers."

One of the many risks of using live animals is their complete lack of consideration when taking a toilet break. When a horse on the stage at Covent Garden decided to spread a little manure on the stage, Thomas Beecham was heard to exclaim, "Egad! A critic."

Siegfried's Bear

Siegfried came on stage with a live bear in the Seattle *Ring*, but this caused a minor problem. Animal-rights activists carried placards outside the opera house protesting the use of the animal. In a later Seattle production, when the bear should have made his entrance, Siegfried entered trailing a long leash that extended back into the wings. The bear did not appear, and after a few minutes of exchanges with the hapless Mime, Siegfried threw his end of the leash back into the wings. Those in the audience who thought this was a cop-out were confounded a few seconds later when a real live bear cub scampered across the stage.

Helden Wagnerians 2
FRANZ LISZT

Friend, Banker, Supporter, Father of the Second Wife

The Hungarian-born keyboard maestro Franz Liszt was one of the earliest Wagnerians, and over the course of their long friendship he provided Wagner with a constant source of money and encouragement during some of the darkest periods. His daughter Cosima became Wagner's second wife, though it took some time for Liszt to accept their relationship.

In the difficult early years when nobody believed in Wagner except Wagner himself, Liszt was a constant source of encouragement and support. In January 1854 Wagner wrote to Liszt:

> None of the past years has gone by without having at least once driven me to the very verge of suicide . . . I cannot live like a dog, cannot sleep on straw and drink fusel (cheap alcohol): I must have some kind of sympathy, if my mind is to succeed in the toilsome work of creating a new world.

The good friend provided the sympathy and encouragement that Wagner needed. In one of his letters, Liszt wrote:

> Your letters are sad—and your life sadder still. You want to go out into the wide world,

• **Bust of the Hungarian pianist and composer outside the Liszt Museum in Bayreuth.**

live, enjoy revel! Ah! How cordially I wish you could! But do you not feel, after all, that the thorn and the wound which you have in your heart will leave you nowhere, and can never be healed?—Your greatness constitutes also your misery—the two are inseparably united, and must ever annoy and torture you.

Liszt first met Wagner in 1847, and when Wagner fled from Dresden after becoming involved in the 1849 uprising, Liszt sheltered the refugee at the virtuoso's home in Weimar. The close friendship was interrupted for several years after Cosima left her husband, Hans von Bülow, to live with Wagner.

In addition to providing Wagner with a wife,

• Liszt's mausoleum in Bayreuth cemetery was designed by his grandson, Siegfried Wagner.

albeit against his wishes, Liszt was also responsible for identifying Anton Seidl as the man who would become one of the composer's closest musical associates.

Wagner's selfish egomania was visible even in relationships with his closest friends:

> Whereas Wagner accorded to Liszt no more than a grudging homage in so far as he identified himself with the Wagnerian cause, Liszt reverenced Wagner with something approaching idolatry; he was prepared to abandon his own creative work if only he could raise adequate funds to finance a production of *The Ring*. Yet though Wagner's genius is self-justificatory, he himself admitted that "since my acquaintance with Liszt's compositions my treatment of harmony has become very different from what it was formerly." He added, characteristically, that, "It is, however, indiscreet to babble this secret to the whole world."
>
> Wilfrid Mellers, *Man and His Music*, 1962

While Wagner was exiled in Switzerland, Liszt worked hard on the premiere of *Lohengrin* in Weimar, conducting an astonishing forty-six rehearsals. This was probably a record, exceeded only by the seventy-two rehearsals conducted by Wagner himself before *Tristan and Isolde* was abandoned as "unsingable" in Vienna. Among the many prominent musicians in the audience for the premiere on August 28 was Giacomo Meyerbeer.

Some music scholars believe that Liszt gave Wagner more than funding and psychological support. The conductor and composer Howard Goodall suggested in his television series *The Story of Music* that musical innovations credited to Wagner should be attributed to Liszt. Goodall suggested that the emotion-charged diminished and augmented triads in Wagner's music had been prominently used by Liszt years before they appeared in *Tristan* and other works.

When Wagner's new opera was criticized, Liszt came to his defense with a paraphrase of Luther's defense to the Diet in Worms: "Here I stand. I cannot do otherwise than stand or fall with Wagner's operas."

When Trish Benedict of the Wagner Society of Northern California heard this in a September 2012 lecture in San Francisco, she wrote:

> What a guy! For one of the most famous musicians of the time to champion this obnoxious upstart and his difficult-to-comprehend operas was a magnanimousness that Wagner rarely demonstrated, it was simply the soul of graciousness.

"
Tristan."
—Franz Liszt's last word

Liszt joined a Franciscan order in 1857 and after the death of two of his children, Daniel and Blandine, he retired to a monastery in 1863. He died in Bayreuth not long after leaving the Bayreuth Festspielhaus. His last word was simply, "Tristan." He is buried in Bayreuth cemetery in a mausoleum designed by his grandson, Siegfried Wagner.

Wagner in London

The First Visit in 1839

The first time Wagner visited London, in August 1839, he was unheralded, unrecognized, and unknown. Wagner, Minna, and their dog Robber were on their way to Paris from Pillau, near Königsburg. Originally estimated at eight days, the trip took three and a half weeks because of a series of storms. Wagner said later that it was a grueling journey across rough seas and claimed that one of the storms was the inspiration for the overture to *The Flying Dutchman*. In London they stayed at a boarding house in Great Compton Street, in Soho. On a later visit to London Wagner tried to find the house but failed.

Keen to meet with the Norfolk-born writer Baron Edward Bulwer-Lytton (1803–1873) to discuss an opera based on his novel *Rienzi, Last of the Roman Tribunes*, Wagner visited the Houses of Parliament. Upon being told that the author was out of town, he bullied an official to permit him to witness a House of Lords debate on the Anti-Slavery Bill and listened to exchanges between the premier, Lord Melbourne, and the Duke of Wellington. The duke "looked so comfortable in his gray beaver hat, with his hands diving deep into his trousers pockets, and . . . made his speech in so conversational a tone that I lost my feeling of excessive awe," said Wagner in his autobiography.

The Second Coming

In 1855 Wagner received an invitation from the London Philharmonic Society to visit London for four months to conduct eight concerts. The fee was to be £200, the highest ever paid by the Society to that date. Some thirty years earlier they had commissioned Beethoven to write his Ninth Symphony and paid him the princely sum of £50. Wagner arrived in London in early March and stayed in Portland Terrace, near Regent's Park. "It seemed to me that spring never came, the foggy climate so overclouded all the impressions I received," he said later.

Wagner expressed concerns about being limited to one rehearsal for each concert and was not impressed by the quality of the orchestra. "You are the famous Philharmonic Orchestra," he shouted at the musicians (presumably with the help of an interpreter, as his English was almost nonexistent). "Raise yourselves, gentlemen, be artists!" he is reported to have told them. During the series of concerts he conducted performances of Beethoven's *Eroica* and the Ninth Symphony in addition to some of his own works.

Defying the normal custom, Wagner declined to pay obeisance to the all-powerful media critics, including James Davison, who was both the music critic of the *Times* and editor of the influential *Musical World*. The critic had become used to visiting musical figures calling on him to acknowledge his importance and curry favor with him. Wagner's failure to do so got him off to a bad start with Davison, who "adopted a most hostile attitude, and it was from this that I first realized, clearly and definitely, the effect of my essay entitled *Judaism in Music*," Wagner wrote later.

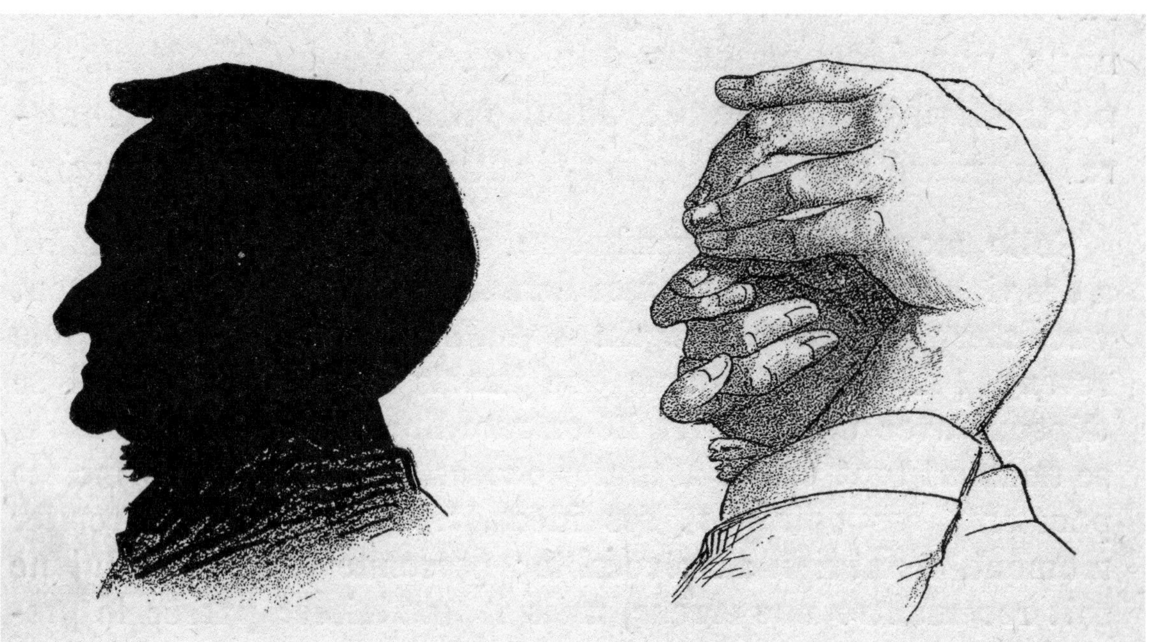

• **An 1877 caricature on how to cast a silhouette shadow of Wagner. But it is not as easy as it looks. Caricature by Kreutzberger after an original composition by F. Trewey.**

To Wagner's dismay the *Times* critic covered the first performance with "furious contempt and disparagement." Despite appeals from the Society, Wagner dug in his heels and refused to doff his hat to Davison. At the beginning of his visit, late in the eighteenth century, Joseph Haydn spent three whole days visiting all of the main newspapers; but Wagner considered his own refusal to genuflect to the great and good of Fleet Street a matter of pride. "The hostility of the media," he told an unidentified friend, "only showed the whole world that I did not bribe them; on the contrary, it gave me pleasure to observe how they always kept the door still open for me, so that the least advance on my part would have changed their minds; which of course I would not think of doing." He wrote in his autobiography: "As I saw later, the [Philharmonic] Society began from that time forward to regret my appointment, realizing that they had an entirely intractable and pig-headed person to deal with." He seriously considered packing his bags and departing to Zurich but was persuaded to stay to avoid creating problems for his friends.

The gentlemen of the Philharmonic Society for the seven-concert series chose works by twenty composers. Beethoven headed the list with ten works, followed by Mozart (nine), Weber (eight), Spohr (seven), Felix Mendelssohn (five), and Luigi Cherubini (four). Also on the program were Charles Lucas, Meyerbeer, Heinrich Marschner, George Onslow, Fernando Paer, Frédéric Chopin, Luigi Ricci, Cipriani Potter, Giovanni Battista Pergolesi, George Frederick Handel, George Alexander Macfarren, and Johann Nepomuk Hummel.

Wagner said in his autobiography that his own compositions were restricted to selections from *Lohengrin* and the overture to *Tannhäuser*. When the latter was performed at the fifth concert, the

• **Selling the "music of the future" in London. Caricature from *Entr'acte*, London, 1877.**

audience rose, waved their handkerchiefs, and cheered enthusiastically. Wagner had originally planned to include music from *Parsifal*. He wrote later, "I had drawn up an explanatory . . . but the words 'Holy Grail' and 'God' were struck out with great solemnity as that sort of thing was not allowed at secular concerts."

The seventh concert, on June 11, 1855, was part command performance, because the Queen let it be known that she would like to hear the *Tannhäuser* overture, which had already appeared on one of the earlier programs. It was duly added to the program for a second playing together with Macfarren's overture *Chevy Chase*, a Spohr aria from *Jessonda*, a scene from Weber's *Oberon*, and Mozart's *Jupiter* Symphony.

The Queen's brother-in-law, Ernest II of Saxe-Coburg-Gotha, was both a Wagnerian and a composer of opera himself. Perhaps he told Victoria something like, "This you must hear," or maybe the Queen herself had read about the audience reaction at the earlier concert. The Duchess of Wellington was among the other dignitaries in the royal party. It is not known whether Wagner was able to mention that years earlier he had heard her husband participate in a House of Lords debate.

Wagner wrote to his friend Wilhelm Fischer on June 15 and quoted the Queen as telling him: "I am delighted to make your acquaintance, your composition has enraptured me." In a letter to Liszt on July 5, Wagner commented, "In truth they were the first in England to venture to speak up for me without disguise. If one reflects that they were dealing with a political outcast, under warrant of arrest for high treason, one will surely think me right to thank the pair of them right heartily."

London held few charms for Wagner. On April 5, 1855, he wrote to Minna at their home in Zurich.

> First of all, I never escape the cold: the abominable London air paralyses mind and body. Besides, there is the unbearable coal vapor, which cannot be avoided either in the house or in the street. Every moment one has hands like a chimney sweep, and I have to wash once every hour; the laundry also gets dirty very quickly; I cannot, for decency's sake, let people see a shirt which I've worn once—except the laundress, for she sees her profit in it. Most harmful of all, the air and the vapor settle in my chest, which is never clear, so that I've already completely lost my nice little voice. I find it most bearable when

> I'm at home. Don't think for one moment that my apartment is luxurious: the living room—salon—was far too small to accommodate the grand piano so I have had to devote the so-called *salle à manger* next to it solely to the piano and the desk; the rooms are together—the doors have been taken out, thus forming a single, moderately spacious room—and are heated by only one fireplace. My bedroom is on the floor above; it is in pretty good shape, and in the large bed you'd have had ample room too.
>
> The location of my house is by no means elegant: it is at the upper end of Regent's Park and attracted me only because of its seclusion and cheerfulness. But even here I'm now and then entertained by hurdy-gurdies and brass instruments. In the house I'm otherwise pretty well off, and when I'm not invited out I always eat at home; then I order in the morning what I want to have, beef or veal; sometimes some fish beforehand, *Kartoffeln*—which they very proudly call potados—[*sic*], or cauliflower, etc. Wine, at three shillings, I have in the house lately—Moselle wine as Rahn advised me through you. My bills are generally considered very reasonable: for meat, butter, bread, coffee, milk, etc., for all that they charge me the cost price, and then a few pence for wood, and eggs and butter for cooking; salt, mustard, etc., I get for nothing.

But at other times, Wagner was less than content with the local food. In a letter to his friend E. B. Krietz, he wrote: "I'm taking pills to counteract the English diet."

His letter to his wife continued:

> I've already had Klindworth for dinner several times, and both of us had enough.

"I'm taking pills to counteract the English diet."
—Richard Wagner

> The bill for everything together amounts on the average to between £3½ and £4 a week (including the rent). Small, indispensable purchases are mostly very expensive, and for less than one shilling one gets absolutely nothing. The other day I wanted to do myself a favor, and ate with Klindworth at a French restaurant, which was very expensive and confirmed me in my decision to eat at home . . . Usually we stay together until midnight. At last we had a fine day; I promptly went to the Zoo; it is absolutely magnificent, very gorgeous, beautiful animals, very neatly kept, pretty garden, etc. During the fair season the visit to this garden will certainly be my main pleasure. I don't like to go to town at all: their Parliament building, etc., can go to blazes. The parks are always the best. I have not yet gone to any other amusements: no theatre has so far attracted me. There are as many concerts here as sand on the seashore but no English concert will soon find me in the audience again! How these people make music defies description. But more on that some other time.

The British: They Love Me, They Love Me Not

Wagner was supported by some fervent enthusiasts in Britain but opposed by many who were equally vociferous in their rejection of his "new" music. His works must have shocked the ear just as much in 1855 as the music of composers like

Stravinsky decades later.

Wagner complained about the inadequacies of the critics and the hostility of the media. A later exception, Ernest Newman, said: "Wagner was convinced that most of the critics were in the pay of Meyerbeer. There was no need to assume that: the trouble was simply that they were men of ordinary intelligence brought face to face, for the first time in their professional lives, with a contemporary phenomenon that was extraordinary and failing to see how much bigger it was than themselves."

The hostility of the media was due, at least in part, to the leadership position enjoyed by Davison. He was an influential figure, and once he took a position, few of his colleagues had the courage to present opposing views.

Despite all of this, Wagner was well received by many in London audiences, and his interpretation of the works of other composers received an enthusiastic response. Even some of Mendelssohn's supporters made complimentary comments about Wagner's interpretation of the *Hebrides Overture*.

Although disappointed with the reception he had received, Wagner left at least one new supporter behind when he left London: Queen Victoria.

The Third and Final Visit

William Quirke, a violinist who played under Wagner's direction in 1877, wrote in his memoirs in 1914:

> The immortal Wagner is coming to London when at the zenith of his glory. A large orchestra is engaged for a series of ten concerts [later cut to seven].
>
> On a particular day, the first rehearsal is held in the lower room of St. James Hall beginning at 10 o'clock, and expected to last till about 3 in the afternoon, the work selected being *Das Rheingold*, and Herr Wagner to take the baton, although Hans Richter is looked upon as the probable conductor of the festival. The orchestra numbers nearly two hundred members, containing something like fifty first and fifty second violins. The descriptive music of the Rhine, which opens the work, gives a deal for the second violins to do, and is exceedingly difficult to perform.
>
> The members of the orchestra are all in their places, when Herr Wagner appears, descending some steps, followed by Herren Richter and Franke. By some strange accident, in descending Herr Wagner has his hat crushed through coming in contact with some projection, and this gives a most undignified, if not comical appearance, as, strutting into the room, he approaches the orchestra, assuming a very haughty air. Those in his immediate presence seem to look at him with too much awe to propose taking off his hat and restoring it to a proper shape. Among the English members of the orchestra the incident provokes unmistakable signs of merriment, as the individual players call each other's attention to the condition of the hat. But this is not shared by the German members of the orchestra, who view the English conduct in the matter as almost sacrilegious and most reprehensible. Herr Wagner, noticing this hilarity, and not divining the cause, glares at the perpetrators with surprise and disgust. However, a tap with the baton, and the rehearsal begins. The second violins with their long, rolling *arpeggi*, like waves, make the atmosphere quite damp with the water of the Rhine, and this is more strongly emphasized, as, after rehearsal, I see two or three members of the orchestra causing a small

crowd to collect as they pretend to wring water from the tails of their frock coats.

The work has not proceeded far before the conductor taps his desk violently, and shouts, "Zürück!" (Back!). A fresh start is made but ere long another misunderstanding, this time through the conductor, who, carried away by the music, relinquished his baton, expecting this huge machine to follow a beat, given only with one of his fingers on his shirt-stud. This time, white with ill-conceived rage, the composer turns to Richter, and walking to and fro, repeats the word "schlecht" (bad) two or three times. This little performance is not lost on the English portion of the orchestra, who, seemingly unable any further to control their mirth, burst into an unmistakable chuckle, to the consternation of the German and other foreign elements.

Here Herr Deichman, leader of the second violins, springs to his feet, and passionately tapping the music stand with his bow, says in bad English, "It is no tink to laugh." So violently does he strike his desk that the little piece of ivory at the top of his bow flies across the room and strikes Herr Wilhelm in the face. This last occurrence draws perfect howls of laughter, in which a good number of the foreign section freely join. Herr Wagner is by this time in a frenzy of passion. But this is the opportunity for the perfect tactician, Herr Richter, who, taking the great composer by the arm, leads him away, speaking in a soothing, conciliatory tone. The orchestra in the meantime indulge in unrestrained jubilation.

In a few moments the conductor returns, without Herr Wagner, and with the baton in his hand, says only two words, "Now boys!" Every man in that orchestra looks back to the eye which seems to read into their very souls, as, electrified by the wonderful personality of the great conductor, each one pushes his chair nearer to his music-stand, and a volume of sound, as if from one instrument, conveys to the ear of the glorious effects in that wonderful conception of one of the greatest musical and dramatic geniuses of the century.

Now we know we are playing *Das Rheingold*, for we feel it illuminated by the soul of Richard Wagner.

William Quirke,
Recollections of a Violinist, 1914

Do not look at the trombonists, as it only encourages them."

—Announcement before a San Francisco Symphony performance of the *Tannhäuser* overture

---

The Reluctant Portrait Sitter

Hubert Herkomer (1849–1914) was a talented artist and such an enthusiastic admirer of Wagner's music that he named his first two children Elsa and Siegfried. The twenty-eight-year-old artist kick-started his career by painting portraits without charging any commission. Alfred Lord Tennyson, Robert Baden-Powell, and John Ruskin were among his subjects, and his original plan was to hang the paintings in his own home. Perhaps his best-known work was *The Last Muster*, an emotion-charged picture of Chelsea pensioners in a church hall. This and many other sketches and paintings by Herkomer are reproduced in Lee MacCormick Edwards' splendid biography *Herkomer: A Victorian Artist*.

When the young Herkomer learned that Wagner would be spending several weeks in London in the summer of 1877, he spotted a double opportunity—to meet the great composer and to paint his portrait. He persuaded the German Athenaeum, an art gallery in Mortimer Street, to commission a watercolor portrait of Wagner. The only problem was that Wagner was not enthusiastic. The Bavarian-born Herkomer, who was to become Sir Hubert Herkomer, R.A., later told the story:

> The whole business of the portrait was disagreeable to him, but I was at least allowed free admission to his abode (12 Orme Street), so this "seeing" instead of "sitting" went on for nearly a month; my patience was sorely tried, and my independence got chafed.
>
> But I was wrought up to a curious pitch of excitement during this training, for I was affected by the personal power of the man over those around him, by the magic of his music, and by the face of this poet-musician, which, when stirred by emotion, was a grand reflection of his work.
>
> Now I doubt whether any man since Napoleon has ever been known to exercise such powers of fascination over his admirers as Richard Wagner does daily, and will do to the termination of his life. You lose your identity when in his presence, and are inclined to forget that there is something else in the world besides Wagner and his music.
>
> You are under the influence that sets every nerve at its highest key. He has been able to make people frantic with enthusiasm.
>
> Wagner was in my mind day and night—a constant vision which barred out every other thought, willing or unwilling—and it was in a moment of anger arising from this constant putting off of the sittings that I determined to try what my memory could furnish, and with his face only inwardly visible to me, I set to work. I worked all day, and it grew I knew not how. The next day I worked still harder and more excitedly and finished the portrait. On the third day I took it to Wagner.
>
> Up to that time he had but suffered me to be near him paying little more attention to me than to an animal, but from the moment that he saw his portrait his demeanor changed, and never did a man show admiration more truly and heartily than did Richard Wagner on this occasion, and ever since to me.
>
> How I had done it puzzled him. "You use 'witchcraft,'" he said to me.
>
> So then he was ready to sit for me, and I was intensely eager, not to say nervous,

Herkomer's watercolor of Wagner was destroyed, but this later etching by the artist survived.

> to compare my impressional portrait with the original subject.
>
> Quoted in Henry T. Finck, *Wagner and His Works*, 1893

The *Art Annual* of 1892 said of the watercolor portrait of Wagner: "There was the most curious contrast between the expression of the man as Herkomer designed him and that which he saw before his eyes. The artist had made his face full of emotion; the composer, as he sat before him, only looked pleased and contented. As a likeness, however, it was highly valued by Wagner's family, and now it hangs in Mrs. Wagner's house at Bayreuth."

In 1878 Herkomer painted a portrait of Cosima. Both pictures were displayed in Wahnfried for almost seventy years but were destroyed when the house was partially demolished by an Allied bomb in 1945. Fortunately, Herkomer created an etching based on the original painting, and copies of this survive.

A photograph of the two originals is reproduced in Lee MacCormick Edwards' book. Coincidentally, another Wagnerian subject appears opposite *The Last Muster*: the great Hans Richter, with his bushy red beard.

The Music

As Different as Gaslight to Electric Light

> No other composer has had such an unerring instinct for beauty of sound, such imaginativeness in originating novel tone-colors, such a keen sense of the fitness of the various combinations for intensifying the expression of definite dramatic emotions, as Richard Wagner. The general quality of his orchestral sound is as different from that of his predecessors as electric light is from gaslight. And the secret of this superiority lies largely in this, that Wagner may be said to have revived a medieval practice . . . Early makers built their instruments in four sizes, corresponding to soprano, alto, tenor and bass. Now, while the modern composers up to and including Beethoven were contented with two oboes and two bassoons, two clarinets, two trumpets, and so on, Wagner added a third to each pair, besides a bass trumpet, contrafagotto (bassoon), bass clarinet, etc., thus making a perfect quartet in each family, and immensely enlarging the orchestral palette for either mixed tints or for pure tints of single instrumental groups.
>
> The *Götterdämmerung* orchestra calls for eighty-nine players. Of the brass instruments included in the list, six—two tenor tubas, three bass tubas, and the bass trumpet—were undoubtedly new in orchestral scores. The current notion that Wagner thus enlarged his orchestra for the purpose of securing a greater degree of loudness is supremely absurd. He does indeed know how to combine instruments at a climax into an overwhelming torrent of sound; but more frequently he uses his brasses softly, to secure rich and warm new colors. Thus, in the Valhalla music of *Rheingold* he produces the most stately, majestic harmonies with thirteen brasses playing softly.
>
> Wagner thought out his tone-pictures in colors, and when his palette did not contain the tint his imagination called for he invented it. Thus the dragon in *Siegfried* is musically heralded by the unearthly, slug-

gish sounds of the new contrabass tuba. For the shepherd scene in *Tristan* he had specially made to his order a wooden trumpet, which enabled him to make the change from the shepherd's lament to his joyous strains. In *Die Meistersinger* he uses a lute, an ox-horn in G flat, and other devices for special realistic effects. The rainbow sound in *Rheingold* is irised in the tones of six harps, and so on. But, in spite of all this multiplying of particulars, Wagner did not change the balance of forces. With him, as with Beethoven, the strings, greatly enriched by subdivisions, continue to be the nucleus of the orchestra. As Saint-Saëns wrote in regard to a scene in the *Walküre*, "By the manner in which a composer makes the string quartet speak, the master is revealed."

The Standard Musical Encyclopedia, 1910

The Brass: Powerful but Dangerous

The brass instruments feature prominently in much of Wagner's music, and some people believe that the trombones, horns, and trumpets are responsible for criticisms that the music is too loud. To enthusiasts, however, Wagner's brilliant use of these instruments adds depth, richness, and majesty.

But even Wagner himself recognized that the power of the brass should be used with caution. On one occasion while rehearsing *Rienzi*, he gently chastised the trombones for playing too loud: "Gentlemen, if I mistake not, we are in Dresden, and not marching round Jericho, where your ancestors, strong of lung, blew down the city walls."

Richard Strauss suffered from the same overenthusiasm. He wrote in his *Ten Golden Rules for the Young Conductor*, "Never look encouragingly at the brass, except with a short glance to give an important cue."

• Wagner made masterly use of the brass to create a new sound. Caricature from *Moonshine*, April 1, 1882.

Now even audiences are warned not to encourage the strong-of-lung men and women of the brass section. Andrew Rombakis, a San Francisco doctor, told me that a San Francisco Symphony performance in September 2012 began with the *Tannhäuser* overture. Before it began came an announcement over the loudspeaker: "Please turn off your cell phones, and do not look at the trombonists, as it only encourages them."

Leitmotifs—Weaving *The Ring*

Leitmotifs are musical themes or leading motifs. Although they were used before Wagner, he perfected the concept and used it to extraordinary effect, particularly in the four operas of *The Ring*. Yet scholars have found only one instance of Wagner using the word. In a letter to Hans von Wolzogen, Wagner rebuked him for not adequately explaining the composer's use of the "so-called leitmotifs." Wagner preferred to describe the musical phrases as "melodic moments."

In *The Ring* there is a leitmotif for each of the main characters; inanimate objects such as Wotan's spear, Siegfried's sword, and the magic Tarnhelm helmet; and emotions like love, anger, fear, or frustration. Fate, a three-note motif, appears throughout *The Ring*. The great musical parodist Anna Russell called leitmotifs "signature tunes," and Debussy likened them to the calling cards of every character in *The Ring*.

> The value of Wagner's themes lay not so much in their repetition and development as in the fact that they were singularly arresting and musically significant in themselves . . . Whether they "represent" or "depict" the ideas associated with them is a matter of opinion, but they serve their purpose; the entry of an important theme at a critical moment always impresses us by its musical value, even if we have forgotten its particular name in the directory.
>
> Edward Dent, musicologist, in 1934

Wagner's leitmotifs range from two or three notes up to several bars of music, and they include many beautiful phrases. Each leitmotif is marvelously appropriate to the person, thing, or emotion it represents; but the composer's real genius was the way the musical themes evolved to fit changing circumstances or emotions. An example is the Spear motif, which signifies Wotan's authority as the leader of the gods. When it is first heard it is powerful, confident, and impressive. Later, when Wotan goes through a period of great anguish, the Spear motif is twisted to reflect his frustration. His agony is perfectly matched by the music.

Some leitmotifs take on a different meaning when slowed down or speeded up. A fragment of one leitmotif can form the root of another, and some leitmotifs are even played backward and thereby take on a different meaning. For example, when inverted, the eerie Erda motif becomes the Twilight of the Gods theme.

Wagner is also unique in the way that he com-

I know of no instance amongst the voluminous writings of Wagner where he discusses his own [composition] technique, and takes us into his musical workshop. On most other subjects, how to do this or that, physical, metaphysical, animal, vegetable, mineral; from *The World as Will and Representation* to Vegetarianism; from Greek tragedy to alliteration in verse; from anti-Semitism to Vivisection—on all things under the sun does he seek to enlighten us, except on his own method of composing. He left us mountains of self-explanation of Wagner the philosopher; Wagner the poet; Wagner the political theorist; Wagner the critic; Wagner the complete 'ologist, in fact. He expounded on other composers; his essay on Beethoven is a masterpiece of interpretation. Upon the important question of the how of his own music he gives us scarcely a word of illumination; he tells us endlessly what it means but seldom does he give us a peep into his technical workshop.

—Neville Cardus, *Composers Eleven*, 1958

bines themes and weaves them together with such consummate skill. Leitmotifs overlap, alternate, and interweave. "From the jumble of leitmotifs emerges a symphonic fabric of endless imagination and of a thousand hues," writes Paul Henry Lang in *The Experience of Opera*.

Once familiar with the plot and the major leitmotifs, it is possible to follow the action just by identifying the motif playing at a given instant. My favorite party trick was to have a guest randomly select one of the fourteen CDs that usually make up *The Ring* and then play any part of a sixty- to seventy-minute disc. Within a few seconds I could usually identify the opera, the act, and scene and describe who was on stage at that point in the drama. I achieved this by identifying which mix of leitmotifs were playing, from which I was able to identify the point that had been reached in the fifteen-hour drama.

Even Wagner's detractors were impressed by his leitmotifs. James Davison, the music writer with the London *Times* who was such a vociferous critic of the composer, nonetheless wrote after attending the inaugural performance of *The Ring* in Bayreuth in August 1876: "Wagner's symphony may be likened to an omni-colored kaleidoscope, where the same bits of painted glass incessantly appear and disappear, yielding prominence to others that have been seen before, and puzzling the eye of the examiner, as the Wagner orchestra puzzles, while it frequently enhances the ear."

Monday Night Is Wagner Night

Concerts devoted exclusively to Wagner's music are a rarity these days, but at the end of the nineteenth century they were popular weekly events in England. The weekly "Monday Night Is Wagner Night" tradition started in 1873 in the Hanover Square Rooms. The Wagner Society sponsored the concerts with Edward Dannreuther, its founder, as conductor. The Monday-night tradition switched to the new Queen's Hall when it opened in 1893. The Queen's Hall Orchestra was founded in 1893 under the direction of Henry Wood; and their first public concert started with the *Rienzi* overture. Three years later the promenade concerts adopted the theme-night idea. Monday was Wagner Night, Tuesday was devoted to Arthur Sullivan, Wednesday was classical night, Thursday was Franz Schubert only, and Friday night was classical night. Saturday was promoted as popular night.

In addition to Henry Wood, prominent conductors who led the Wagner Monday-night concerts included Hermann Levi (the first conductor of *Parsifal*), Hans Richter (the first conductor of *The Ring*), George Henschel, Felix Mottl, and the then-twenty-five-year-old Siegfried Wagner.

Queen's Hall, on Langham Place, was destroyed by an incendiary bomb in December 1940.

Top of the Proms

The BBC Promenade Concert series, popularly known simply as the Proms, is still the largest classical music festival in the world and a regular summer feature of classical music performance in Britain. Most of the concerts are given in London's Royal Albert Hall, where the younger, fitter participants stand or sit in the "promenade." What has now become a British institution started in the old Queen's Hall and was conducted by the series' cofounder, Henry Wood, for the first fifty years. Wood was knighted for his services to music.

The first concert, on August 10, 1895, included the overture to *Rienzi*, and over the next 115 years works by Wagner were to be performed more than those of any other composer. This has been revealed in a new Web-based archive that lists every piece of music performed at the Proms. The archive was produced by the BBC, sponsor and organizer of the concert series since 1927, and took a team of four some two years to research and compile. In addition to the name of each composition, the database includes information on the orchestras, conductors, and soloists at every performance up to the end of the 2013 season. The BBC plans to update the archive the morning after every new performance during future Festivals.

The high scores achieved by Wagner are surprising, perhaps even to Wagnerians. Wagner appeared in the program 4,694 times up to the end of the 2010 Proms. Wagner's total was more than twice that of the second-place composer, Beethoven. The archive reveals that thirty-six different Wagner compositions have been included over the years. In addition to the expected concert-hall favorites, the Proms list includes performances of lesser-known Wagner works such as *Kaisermarsch*, *Huldigungsmarsch*, *Traüme*, *Two Grenadiers*, *Albumblatt*, and music from the early operas *Die Feen* (*The Fairies*) and *Das Liebesverbot* (*The Ban on Love*). The overture to *Tannhäuser* has been the most frequently performed single composition by any composer.

It may be that because of the enormous popularity of Wagner's music in the early years, other composers will have to do some catching up. Compared to Wagner's 4,694, performances of works by other primarily operatic composers include Weber with 510, Verdi 444, Bizet 430, Rossini 426, Britten 309, Meyerbeer 142, Puccini 109, Monteverdi 79, Donizetti 60, and Bellini 13. There are usually only a few Wagner compositions annually, but 2010 was an exception, with fourteen items in the two-month-long program. The 2012 season included the *Siegfried Idyll*, *Tristan and Isolde* (Prelude to Act I), *Parsifal* (Prelude to Act III with the Good Friday Music), the *Meistersinger* overture, and *Lohengrin* (Prelude to Act I).

He may sometimes use his system (which is much older than he) of leading motives too abundantly, or inconsistently, but how much more often does he use it with incomparable and unforgettable art; and what creative power these themes show, especially the shorter and more plastic ones in the post-Lohengrin period. How superb is his orchestral scene-painting, the way in which he bathes each scene, darkness and dawn, sunlight and shadow, calm and storm, in its appropriate light. How evocative are the themes allotted to material things, Wotan's spear, Siegmund's sword; how unforgettable are his nature pictures, the Rhine and the sea, forest, garden and spring meadows. But all these felicities pale before the music that portrays human nature in all its phases and complexities, love and hate, trust and treachery, heroism and cowardice, joy and sorrow, expressed, as never before, in the great symphonic canvases of his music dramas.

To the true Wagnerian, his characters, except one or two in the earlier operas, are real persons—be they gods or mortals—with whom we love and hate, suffer or rejoice.

—Alec Robertson, *Decca Book of Opera*, 1956

The BBC announced in April 2013 that the two hundredth anniversary of Wagner's birth would be celebrated at the Proms with no fewer than seven full-length operas. For the first time in its history, the Proms program would include the complete *Ring*, with Daniel Barenboim conducting the Berlin Staatskapelle. Three other orchestras were scheduled to participate as well: the BBC Symphony Orchestra was booked to perform *Tristan and Isolde*, conducted by Semyon Bychkov; the BBC Scottish Symphony,

Up to the end of 2010, Wagner appeared in the Proms 4,694 times—more than twice that of the second-place composer, Beethoven.

conducted by Donald Runnicles, was listed for *Tannhäuser*; and Hans Richter's old band, the Hallé, was to perform *Parsifal* under the baton of Mark Elder.

All of the Wagner works in the top twenty were overtures or orchestral highlights from the thirteen operas. Below is the top-twenty list, with the number of times performed:

1. *Tannhäuser*, 739
2. *Die Meistersinger*, 591
3. *Lohengrin*, 567
4. *Götterdämmerung*, 419
5. *Tristan and Isolde*, 378
6. *Parsifal*, 334
7. *Die Walküre*, 322
8. *The Flying Dutchman*, 290
9. British National Anthem, 252
10. *The Marriage of Figaro* (Mozart), 243
11. *The Damnation of Faust* (Berlioz), 220
12. *Rienzi*, 215
13. *Siegfried*, 205
14. *Faust* (Gounod), 204
15. *Don Giovanni* (Mozart), 181
16. *William Tell* (Rossini), 179
17. *Mignon* (Thomas), 175
18. *Hungarian Rhapsodies* (Liszt), 174
19. *Peer Gynt Suite* (Grieg), 173
20. *1812 Overture* (Tchaikovsky), 153

Wagner appeared twice more on the top-forty list, with the *Siegfried Idyll* coming in at number thirty with 132 performances and music from *Rheingold* at thirty-two with 130.

The BBC Proms Archive can be found at www.bbc.co.uk/proms/archive.

Bleeding Chunks in the Concert Hall

The works of Giuseppe Verdi are performed more frequently in world opera houses than those of Wagner. Maybe this has something to do with the fact that Verdi wrote twenty-six operas against Wagner's thirteen. Or perhaps it is because of the cost of staging Wagner's works, or the shortage of high-caliber singers with the necessary range and stamina. Or could it be a shortage of audiences with the stamina to cope with frequent long operas?

But it is a different story in the concert hall. Overtures to the operas of other composers occasionally make it on to concert programs, but Wagner is alone in providing enough material for a complete concert. The overtures or preludes to *Rienzi*, *The Flying Dutchman*, *Tannhäuser*, *Lohengrin*, *Tristan*, *Die Meistersinger*, and *Parsifal* are all perennial favorites.

What makes Wagner unique is the popularity of orchestral pieces taken from the body of his operatic works, the musical tapestries woven from leitmotifs. Favorites from *The Ring* include the Entry of the Gods into Valhalla, the Magic Fire Music, Siegfried's Rhine Journey, and Siegfried's Funeral March. Others include the overture to *Die Meistersinger*, the Prelude and Liebestod from *Tristan*, and the Prelude and Good Friday Music from *Parsifal*.

Wagner was not keen on orchestral performances of his music ripped out from the dramatic context. He called them "bleeding chunks." But he has only himself to blame for the popularity of his orchestral extracts today. In response to popular demand, he made changes to his orchestrations to make stand-alone performance possible. ■

Act Two

The Early Operas

In his autobiography Wagner mentioned his earliest work, *Leubald*, and regretted that the manuscript had long since disappeared. One of his recollections of the libretto was that he had killed off so many of the characters that he had to bring them back as ghosts in the second act.

Years later it was discovered that his youthful work had in fact survived. His handwritten outline for *Leubald* was acquired by the Honorable Mary Burrell, an English Wagner enthusiast, and was featured in her biography of the composer, *Richard Wagner, 1813–1834.*

After recapping Wagner's own recollection of *Leubald*'s plot, Burrell wrote: "Pardon me, readers, for repeating these words of his which have made the round of myriads of little pamphlets and booklets, the weary student meets them at every turn doing duty as padding. This time they are at last the prelude to something new and historical about the celebrated tragedy." She then suggested that Wagner's biographical note about the death of forty-two people was a figure of speech: "One might as well say four hundred and two, or four thousand and two, whole Clans are slain; only one ghost appears and enough characters remain alive to fall down dead at the end."

Die Hochzeit (*The Wedding*)

Written in Prague in the summer of 1832 when Wagner was nineteen, *Die Hochzeit*, claimed Wagner in his autobiography, *My Life*, was written in secret. He could not write in his cold hotel room, he said; he spent his mornings in the home of his friend Moritz but hid the manuscript behind the sofa whenever his host approached. The introduction, chorus, and septet were completed in Würzburg in March 1833.

The rest of the opera was never completed. Wagner's sister Rosalie did not care for the subject matter or libretto and persuaded her brother to abandon the work. Wagner destroyed most of the libretto but stored the score and some completed sections of the text. The only music composed was an orchestral introduction, a chorus and a septet. The fragments were published in Germany in 1912 and broadcast by the BBC some years later.

Synopsis: In his autobiography Wagner wrote of *Die Hochzeit*, "I do not remember where I found the medieval subject. An insane lover climbs through the window into the bedroom of his friend's betrothed, who is awaiting her bridegroom; the bride struggles with the madman and throws him down into the courtyard, where he gives up the ghost. At the funeral rites the bride utters a cry and falls dead on the corpse."

Wagner recycled four of the characters from the abandoned *Hochzeit*—Lora, Harald, Ada, and Arindal appear in his next work, his first full opera, *Die Feen*. Many years later, in *Tristan and Isolde*, he would also revive the idea of the distraught lover falling dead on the body of her beloved.

Die Feen (*The Fairies*)

• *Die Feen* was never staged in Wagner's lifetime, but he did conduct the overture at Magdeburg in 1834. The libretto was inspired by *The Serpent Woman*, by Carlo Gozzi (1720–1808), the Italian poet and dramatist. Richard's uncle Adolf Wagner was an admirer of Gozzi and had translated one of his works into German.

Completed: 1833, when Wagner was twenty.

Premiere performance: June 29, 1888, Hoftheater, Munich, more than five years after Wagner's death.

UK premiere: May 17, 1969, Great Hall of the University of Aston, Birmingham, by an amateur group. The first London production was in Fulham Town Hall on May 4, 1973.

US premiere: February 24, 1982, New York City Opera, as a concert performance.

Wagner included this brief synopsis in *A Communication to My Friends* in 1851. The translation is by William Ashton Ellis.

> A Fairy, who renounces her immortality for the sake of a human lover, can only become mortal through the fulfillment of certain hard conditions, the non-compliance wherewith on the part of her earthly swain threatens her with the direct penalties; her lover fails in the test, which consists in this, that however evil and repulsive she may appear to him (in an obligatory metamorphosis) he shall not reject her in his unbelief. In Gozzi's tale the Fairy is now changed into a snake; the remorseful lover frees her from the spell by kissing the snake: thus he wins her for his wife.

Wagner missed out a few interesting details. The first problem encountered by the fairy Ada and the crown prince, Arindal, is the condition that he must not ask who she is for eight years. This was an idea Wagner recycled later in *Lohengrin*. The test set for the couple by the king of the fairies is that Arindal must not denounce Ada whatever she does. Ada throws the couple's two children into a fiery trench. Arindal, not knowing it is a test, understandably fails.

Following the first performance of *Die Feen* in Munich in 1888 conducted by Hermann Levi, Wagner's first complete work became something of a hit. Over the next seven years, it was performed more than fifty times.

***Das Liebesverbot* (*The Ban on Love* or *The Novice of Palermo*)**

Completed: 1836, when Wagner was twenty-three.
Premiere performance: 1836, Stadtheater, Magdeburg.
UK premiere: An abridged version was presented by students at the Collegiate Theatre, University College, London, on February 16, 1965; Edward Dent translated the libretto.
US premiere: The first American performance was at the Glimmerglass Festival in New York in the summer of 2008.

Wagner was an admirer of Shakespeare and an avid reader of his works all his life. *Das Liebesverbot* was based on Shakespeare's *Measure for Measure*. Wagner changed the nationality of Shakespeare's viceroy from Italian to German. He also changed his name from Angelo to Friedrich. The plot is thin.

Wagner started composing the score in 1834 and completed it in 1836 when he was just short of his twenty-third birthday. It has been said that the overture to *Das Liebesverbot* has a very Italianate sound.

When *Das Liebesverbot* was first staged in 1836 it caused quite a stir. Authorities in Magdeburg were concerned about an opera with the provocative title of *Forbidden Love*, and Wagner was informed that his opera could not be produced. Somehow Wagner and his supporters succeeded in convincing the police that an opera based on Shakespeare's *Measure for Measure* must surely be perfectly respectable. He was, however, persuaded to change the title to *The Novice of Palermo*, and two performances were given.

But Wagner's problems were only beginning. On opening night the tenor forgot his part, panicked, and started singing something he could remember from Daniel Auber's *Fra Diavolo*. It was even worse on the second night, when a fight broke out between a married couple who were singing leading roles in the production. It seems that each had just learned of the other's infidelity, and they quickly came to blows, after which their respective friends and supporters joined in creating a mini-riot backstage. The performance was canceled, and *Das Liebesverbot* was never performed again in Wagner's lifetime.

The junior lead in the company was a popular twenty-seven-year-old actress named Wilhelmina Planer. Her friends knew her as Minna, and a few years later she became Frau Richard Wagner.

Rienzi, der Letzte der Tribunen (Rienzi, the Last of the Tribunes)

Completed: 1840, when Wagner was twenty-seven, although there were several later revisions.

Premiere performance: 1842, Dresden.

UK premiere: 1879, Her Majesty's Theatre, London, performed by the Carl Rosa Opera Company.

US premiere: 1878, New York Academy of Music, the Pappenheim Opera Company.

The Bare-Bones Plot

An attempt to abduct Irene, the most beautiful girl in Rome and the sister of Rienzi, creates enmity between the followers of Orsini and those of Colonna. Irene is saved by Adriano, with whom she is in love. Rienzi appears and rebukes them for their conduct. The nobles continue to fight outside the gates of the city. Rienzi closes the gates and rouses the people to free themselves from their oppressors.

The nobles send messages of peace and are admitted into the city on agreeing to take the oath of fealty. They plot Rienzi's assassination, Adriano reveals the conspiracy to Rienzi, and the plotters are condemned to death. However, Adriano intercedes for them, and they are pardoned on their oath of submission.

I always was a bungler in lying."
—Richard Wagner

The nobles again conspire against the tribune, and Rienzi decides to exterminate them despite Adriano's pleading.

After the nobles have been killed in battle, Rienzi returns to celebrate his victory with a Te Deum but is excommunicated by the Pope on account of his jealousy of Rienzi's power. The people desert Rienzi.

Besieged by the populace, alone with his sister Irene in the Capitol, the Tribune dies with her while the building burns. Adriano, who tried to save Irene, also dies.

Rienzi was first performed in Dresden in 1842, with Wilhelmine Schröder-Devrient and Joseph Tichatschek leading a strong cast. According to Wagner, the premiere was a triumph, with the audience calling all the way through the performance for the author or composer. This held up the performance so many times that it lasted five and quarter hours. Wagner's production set two precedents that were to become familiar in his works: it was a long, long evening, and the three main characters died at the end.

Rienzi has never been performed at the Bayreuth Festival. It was, however, put on the map in Bayreuth—literally: there is a street behind the Festspielhaus named Rienzistrasse.

When Wagner sent a copy of the libretto of *Rienzi* to his friend Anton Pusinelli around 1870, he included a picture of himself in a Napoleonic stance with the words "Tribune of the People." Inevitably, this was to provide support for those

***Rienzi* was Meyerbeer's greatest opera.**
—Hans von Bülow

***Rienzi* was Meyerbeer's worst opera.**
—Charles Rosen

***Rienzi . . .* is music of decadence rather than of the future.**
—Georges Bizet

***Rienzi* was an attack of musical measles.**
—Ernest Newman

***Rienzi* is much better than its reputation.**
—John Deathridge

who believe that Wagner identified himself with most of the heroes of his dramas.

> I always was a bungler in lying. For example, nothing injured me more than the fact that, conscious of being able to do better things than Rienzi, I made a speech to the artists at the dress rehearsal in which I declared the exaggerated demands made on the artists by that opera as an "artistic sin of my youth." The reporters immediately dished up this expression before the public and made it feel in regard to this work that, inasmuch as its composer himself had declared it to be a "thorough failure" its production before the art-cultivated Berlin public was an impertinence deserving of castigation. Thus my ill success in Berlin was in truth [due] more to my badly played role as a diplomatist than to the opera itself, which, if I had approached it with full faith in its value and in my eagerness to make it appreciated, might have been as successful as operas of much less attractiveness that were produced in that city.
>
> Richard Wagner, quoted in Henry T. Finck, *Wagner and His Works*, 1896

In 1928, when the Soviet Republic celebrated the tenth anniversary of its formation, the overture to *Rienzi* was played at the opening ceremony.

The Italian composer Gaspare Spontini told Wagner, "When I first heard your *Rienzi*, I said, 'This is a man of genius, but he has already done more than he can do.'" When Wagner pressed for an explanation, Spontini said, "With *Rienzi* Wagner had exhausted all operatic possibilities, so that it was useless and foolish to try to write any more operas." Fortunately, Wagner ignored the advice.

Like *Die Feen* and *Das Liebesverbot*, *Rienzi* is not considered to be part of the regular Wagner canon of major works and has never been performed in the Bayreuth Festspielhaus. The Intermezzo Web site gives as one of the reasons "that they're (shhhh!) not that good." Nevertheless, as part of the celebration of the two-hundredth anniversary of Wagner's birth, all three of the early operas were to be performed in Bayreuth in 2013, but not in the Festspielhaus.

It is said that a copy of a book about Rienzi was found in Napoleon Bonaparte's baggage after the Battle of Waterloo.

> If operatic rank were to be determined by the number of works each composer has

written, Wagner, with his 11 [*sic*] operas and music-dramas, would come near the end of the list; while Donizetti, with his 63 operas, would rank first. In reality, there is more musical material in a single act of *Lohengrin* or *Tristan* than in a dozen or a score of the old-fashioned Italian operas, many of which were composed in a few weeks; while Wagner in most cases devoted several years to a new work—the Nibelungen having, in fact, occupied him at intervals during a quarter of a century, being comparable in this respect to Goethe's Faust.

Henry T. Finck, *Programme for a Four-Day Wagner Festival*, 1884

Wagner: You've Got to Laugh

Birgit Nilsson was loved for her mischievous sense of humor. After a disagreement with Joan Sutherland, she was asked if she thought the Australian diva's famous "big hair" was real. "I don't know," she replied, "I haven't pulled it yet!" She once had an argument with Franco Corelli and accused the tenor of biting her neck; subsequently she canceled some of her performances, claiming that she was suffering from rabies.

Rudolf Bing claimed that each year when Birgit Nilsson returned to the Met, he was so thankful that he went down on his knees. After he became Sir Rudolf Bing, he went through the annual ritual when the singer arrived. Nilsson told him, "You do that much better since you practiced it for the Queen."

A 1967 Herbert von Karajan production of *Die Walküre* involved a very dark and gloomy set. During a rehearsal Karajan and others were astonished when Birgit Nilsson made her entry onstage wearing a miner's helmet complete with lamp.

In 1981 Nilsson was awarded the highest decoration of the Swedish government. She expressed her thanks for the honor by singing Brünnhilde's "Ho-jo-to-ho" battle cry. She repeated the famous call in 1996 when she made a surprise appearance on the stage of the New York Metropolitan Opera in a gala tribute to celebrate Maestro James Levine's twenty-fifth anniversary as artistic director. By then she was seventy-seven and had been retired for fourteen years. Yet she hit every note of the very difficult war cry. Predictably, the audience went wild.

She could take as well as she gave. Knowing of her sense of humor, Decca engineers working on the groundbreaking 1965 recording of *Götterdämmerung* sprang a surprise for her. Just before recording started of Brünnhilde's Immolation Scene in Act III, Birgit was amazed when TV stagehands led a live horse onto the stage. Grane had arrived for Brünnhilde's last journey. Nilsson enjoyed the joke enormously and let out a tremendous peal of laughter.

Singer Snippets

At the beginning of her career, Dame Joan Sutherland, later dubbed La Stupenda by Italian enthusiasts, was encouraged by her mother to become a Wagnerian soprano. She said in a TV documentary on her life that she wanted to emulate her particular idol, Kirsten Flagstad, the Norwegian soprano: "I think I admired the quality and warmth and roundness of the sound, the musical sound. I wanted to have a voice with that richness and quality. I didn't want to be a pipsqueak coloratura." In the late 1950s the management of Covent Garden wanted Sutherland to study the role of Sieglinde, but her husband, Richard Bonynge, was strongly opposed and insisted that she focus on the great bel canto roles.

The American soprano Lillian Nordica once had a major confrontation with Nellie Melba when the Australian claimed that she had exclusive rights to the part of Brünnhilde one season. Melba insisted on singing the role, even though her voice was simply not up to it and it showed. Her performance was a disaster, and Nordica was acknowledged as one of the top Wagnerian sopranos of the age.

Ludwig Schnorr von Carolsfeld was the first tenor to sing Tristan. In 1865, as he was dying, he was told that preparations had begun for the performance of *The Ring* at Bayreuth. He sighed and responded, "Then after all, I shall never sing Siegfried."

Maria Callas, one of the greatest of all sopranos, sang in only three Wagner operas: *Tristan and Isolde*, *Parsifal*, and *Die Walküre*. She sang Isolde in Venice and Genoa, Brünnhilde in Venice and Palermo, and Kundry in Rome. The only published recordings are the Rome Kundry, with Boris Christoff and the Rome Radio Orchestra, conducted by Vittorio Gui. Callas never sang a Wagner role outside Italy.

There has always been fierce competition among the recording studios to sign up the operatic megastars. For most of Kirsten Flagstad's illustrious career, she was under contract to EMI. In the early 1950s she recorded all three acts of *Tristan and Isolde* with Furtwängler conducting. Then in an unbelievable blunder, someone at EMI revealed something that should have remained confidential to protect their star: the company let slip that Isolde's two top Cs had been sung by Elisabeth Schwarzkopf, and that EMI had dubbed the notes into the Flagstad recording. Understandably, Flagstad felt betrayed by her recording studio and was so upset that she vowed never to make another recording. Fortunately for opera enthusiasts, Decca officials persuaded her to change her mind.

Das Barbecü—A Spoof Western Ring

The Ring is a serious drama, but that does not mean that Wagnerians need to take themselves too seriously. In 1991 Speight Jenkins, general director of the Seattle Opera, had an idea that would give visitors to Seattle something to do on the rest nights between performances of the four *Ring* operas. The Dallas-born Jenkins commissioned two Texans to create a spoof on *The Ring*. The resulting musical, *Das Barbecü*, played in a small hall in Seattle during *The Ring*'s run in the summer of 1997.

The show is not a parody—it includes none of Wagner's music, and the plot is only loosely related to *Götterdämmerung*. With lyrics by Jim Luigs and music by Scott Warrender, the musical is based on the romance of Siegfried and Brünnhilde. The result is a hilarious mixture of bawdy songs, guacamole, and a wedding barbecue that gives the show its name, with the Brünnhilde-Gunther and Gutrune-Siegfried ceremonies billed as "a double shotgun wedding." The original production had only five actors playing thirty-five roles, and the audiences appreciated the extra-quick costume changes and country music. Luigs claimed that the show was intended for general audiences, but it seems likely that knowledgeable Wagner audiences would get more out of it. The cast includes Alberich, a "good-for-nuthin' dwarf," and Hagen, who is portrayed as a narcoleptic. When Alberich visits his son, Hagen, in *Götterdämmerung*, he asks, "Are you sleeping, Hagen, my son?" In *Das Barbecü* the action is interrupted every few minutes when Hagen drops his chin to his chest and goes to sleep in mid-sentence. The Wagnerians also got more out of hearing Brünnhilde speak with a Texas drawl and seeing the Rhinemaidens performing as a synchronized swim team.

Several of the singers from the Seattle *Ring* saw the show in 1991, and Nancy Maultsby, who sang Erda, caused some concern among the *Das*

Barbecü audience. "She was laughing so loudly, I thought she might do some harm to her voice," said one observer.

Since its premiere in Seattle the show has been seen in several parts of the United States, and an updated, expanded version was staged in Seattle to coincide with the 2009 *Ring*.

In the *Ring* parody *Das Barbecü*, Brünnhilde spoke with a Texas drawl and the Rhinemaidens performed as a synchronized swim team.

Fun in the Mystical Abyss

Every year around two hundred musicians in Germany give up their summer to perform at the Bayreuth Festival. They are the crème de la crème of the country's leading opera and symphony orchestras and over the years have included several prominent soloists and professors of music. The selected musicians commit to no fewer than ten weeks of rehearsal and performance and spend most of the time in the Festspielhaus orchestra pit, dubbed the "mystical abyss" because of the glorious sound that comes from musicians hidden from sight.

Summer in Bayreuth is a long period of intense, exhausting work, so some light relief is necessary. Each year the musicians present a satirical concert for their colleagues who make up the massive staff assembled to stage the annual Festival. Directors, conductors, family, and friends gather for the popular concert, one of which was recorded and issued on a CD, *Bayreuther Schmunzel-Wagner*.

The Festspiel Chorus has fun with everything from Marlene Dietrich to "Hello Dolly" and "Alexander's Ragtime Band" on a track called "Wir sind von Kopf bis Fuss auf Wagner eingestellt" ("We are totally obsessed with Wagner"). Other tracks feature polkas, waltzes, and marches and there are no prizes for guessing which operas are parodied on the track named "Tanny und Lissy." Elsewhere Mozart, Beethoven, and others get a look in, but then, without warning, up pops the Valhalla theme, the Nibelung anvils strike up, or the *Flying Dutchman* sails in.

There are no fears about accusations of sacrilege; it is said that Wolfgang Wagner welcomed the annual event. His grandfather enjoyed lampoons of his own works and was particularly amused by Johann Nestoy's parodies of *Tannhäuser* and *Tristan*.

Irreverence Welcome Here

Making fun of the German composer started during Wagner's lifetime, at a time when cartoons and caricatures were regular features of both general newspapers and music magazines. Most of them laughed at Wagner, not with him, and many were quite cruel. A collection of 130 drawings and caricatures, *Wagner en Caricatures*, by John Grand-Carteret, was published in France in 1891; another, *Richard Wagner in der Karikatur*, by Ernst Kreowski and Eduard Fuchs, was published in Germany in 1907. This latter included 223 caricatures, several of which are included in this book.

She's Not Making This Up, You Know

There are not many laughs in *The Ring*—unless it is Anna Russell's version. She tells the story of the four operas in twenty-one minutes and forty seconds, complete with much irreverence and hammed-up leitmotifs, or "signature tunes," as she called them.

Anna Russell was born in Paddington, London, in December 1911. She was educated at the prestigious Royal College of Music in London, where she studied voice in addition to piano, cello, and composition, the latter under, among others, Ralph

> "
> A sort of Eurovision contest, sadly restricted to German competitors."
> —Robert Thicknesse, describing the song contest in *Tannhäuser*

Vaughan Williams. When World War II started, Russell and her Canadian-born mother moved to Toronto, and over the following years she entertained the troops, made regular provincial tours, and appeared on local radio stations. She composed much of her own material. After a mediocre career as a contralto, Russell became a star attraction thanks to her merciless lampooning of classical music, singers, and musicians. Her main targets were pomposity and overinflated egos. She had a go at Russian folk songs, Women's Club officials and her own people, the British. When she was asked about the qualities necessary to become a prima donna, Russell replied that she should be "a glorious voice, sexy, independently wealthy, politically motivated, backstabbing bitch."

But it was her hilarious take-off on *The Ring* that made Russell so popular among Wagnerians. She dismisses Wotan as a "crashing bore" and calls Erda the "green-faced torso, because that's all we ever see of her." Russell's influence is such that many people believe that Wotan and Erda produced the other eight Valkyries in addition to Brünnhilde. They believe it because Russell said so, but Speight Jenkins has pointed out that there is no mention of this in Wagner's text.

When Russell explained that Gutrune was the first woman that Siegfried had ever met who was not his aunt, she brought the house down. And then she delivered her best-loved line: "I'm not making this up, you know."

Anna Russell died in Australia in October 2006. Her merciless spoof of *The Ring* deserves a place in every Wagnerian's collection.

The Plot Summed Up with a One-Liner

One of the best of the current generation of gentle satirists is Robert Thicknesse, previously opera critic of the London *Times*. His reference work *The Times Opera Book* (2001) is a slim volume covering some ninety operas, with comments on the music, libretto, and plot, along with numerous quips and quotes. It is a valuable addition to the library of any operagoer. Thicknesse is clearly an opera enthusiast himself, and his references to Wagner's works are serious and mostly positive. It is in the one-liners that Thicknesse excels. The act-by-act plots for each opera are beautifully written, with jabs of hilarious irreverence. The involvement of the Woodbird in *Siegfried* is covered by "a talking bird, operating as a dating agency, arranges a meeting with Brünnhilde." And then, in Act III: "Guided by the bird, Siegfried arrives at Brünnhilde's mountain. He shouts at her until she wakes up, whereupon they fall in love."

The plot for *Parsifal* opens with "Amfortas, head of a brotherhood of misogynous knights." He refers to the song contest in *Tannhäuser* as "a sort of Eurovision contest, sadly restricted to German competitors."

He provides a synopsis of each opera in the form of still more one-liners. *Rheingold*, for example, is summarized as: "A hot item of jewellery changes hands several times." *Siegfried*: "A bold, but academically challenged German undresses an unconscious Valkyrie, and finds it a whole lot scarier than killing a singing dragon."

Private Joke for Wagnerians

While attending *Ring* performances in many cities, I have enjoyed wearing the T-shirt I bought in Seattle. The Giants who build Valhalla demanded that they should take Wotan's sister-in-law Freia as payment. They later agreed that instead of Freia, they would to take the Nibelung gold and the ring. The T-shirt carries the words:

FASOLT & FAFNER
GENERAL CONTRACTORS
fees negotiable

I enjoy it because it is a private joke for Wagnerians, and I wondered how long it would be before someone stopped me in the street to talk about it. It eventually happened in Phoenix, Arizona, when I was in town for the Arizona Opera production of *Die Walküre*. A woman passed me in the street and I saw her glance at the shirt. She walked past me and I heard running steps as she returned to ask, "Excuse me, but where did you get your T-shirt? I must have one." She was disappointed to learn that they were not locally available.

• Senta dreams of the Dutchman in this scene on a French edition of the meat-extract company Liebig's souvenir cards.

Der fliegende Holländer (The Flying Dutchman)

• *The Flying Dutchman* is the earliest of the ten Wagner operas that are regularly performed today. Wagner's inspiration was a version of the legend of the wandering seafarer written by Heinrich Heine.

Completed: 1841, but updated several times for almost twenty years. Started in Meudon near Paris during a period when Wagner and his first wife, Minna, were suffering great hardship and close to starvation.

UK premiere: July 1870, Theatre Royal, Drury Lane, London. It was sung in Italian.

US premiere: November 1876, Academy of Music, Philadelphia. Again sung in Italian.

The Bare-Bones Plot

Two ships arrive at a fishing village on the Norwegian coast. One is captained by Daland, a Norwegian sea captain, and the other is the ghost ship of the Dutchman. He has been cursed to wander the oceans but is permitted to come ashore once every seven years; he will be freed from the curse if he can find a woman who will remain true to him to the end of her life. Daland makes a deal to provide his daughter, Senta, in exchange for treasure. The Dutchman and Senta fall in love. The Dutchman overhears a conversation between Senta and Erik, her longtime admirer, and concludes that Senta will be unfaithful to him. He sets sail to resume his lonely wanderings. Claiming that she has now proved that she would remain true unto death, Senta throws herself into the sea, and the Dutchman is freed from the curse.

Wagner was not happy with the first performance in Dresden, and the critics were not very impressed either. It is understandable that after the years of poverty and rejection, the prospect of a second success so soon after *Rienzi* excited Wagner greatly. Largely as a result of his impatience, the production was carelessly prepared with an inadequate cast saved only by the inclusion of Wilhelmine Schröder-Devrient, creating the first Senta. Years later Wagner described the staging as "incredibly awkward and wooden." The media coverage was highly negative. "I hear everywhere complaints about the lack of agreeable melodies that can be retained in the memory, and about over-heavy orchestration," wrote the *Neue Zeitschrift für Music*.

Another leading musical paper included only a two-line report on the opera: "Wagner's latest opera, *The Flying Dutchman*, has been given at Cassel. Two imposing ships, which sailed across the stage with marvelous ease, created great enthusiasm." There was no mention of the story, the music, or the singers. The negative coverage went on for several years. A Milan paper described the first performance in that city as "an infernal racket." Not to be outdone, a French critic claimed that he was made seasick by the production.

But the worst was to come from London, where a critic for the *Musical World* wrote:

> This man, this Wagner, this author of *Tannhäuser*, of *Lohengrin*, and so many other hideous things,—and, above all, the overture to *Der fliegende Holländer*, the most hideous and detestable of the whole,—this preacher of the "Future," was born to feed spiders with flies, not to make happy the heart of man with beautiful melody and harmony. What is music to him or he to music? His rude attacks on absolute melody may be symbolized as matricide . . . Who are the men that go about as his apostles? Men like Liszt, madmen, enemies of music . . . not born for music, and conscious of their importance, revenge themselves by endeavoring to annihilate it.

Franz Liszt responded with a 107-page essay. Of the opera that the British writer found so hideous, Liszt said: "One feels tempted to exclaim, as in looking at Preller's marine pictures, 'It is wet!' One scents the salt breeze in the air . . . One cannot escape the impressiveness of this ocean-music. In rich, picturesque details it must be placed on a level with the best canvases of the greatest marine painters. No one has ever created a more masterly orchestral picture."

The combined effects of the inferior early performances and the negative media reports sank *The Flying Dutchman* for more than a decade. Following the performances in Dresden and Cassel, the opera was performed in Berlin in 1844; this was followed by a long period when the opera was not performed anywhere. It was not heard in Vienna until 1860, Munich and Stuttgart had to wait until 1864 and 1865 and the Dutchman's ship did not pull into Hamburg until 1870. Dresden got over the initial failure: 1883, the year of Wagner's death, saw the one hundredth staging of the *Dutchman*.

In his autobiography Wagner claimed that the inspiration for *The Flying Dutchman* was a perilous sea voyage in 1839, when the composer was twenty-six. Wagner, Minna, and a shaggy Newfoundland dog named Robber were on a voyage from Pillau on the Baltic coast heading for Paris. The couple's passports had been confiscated, and they were fleeing to escape their creditors.

The small cargo ship, the *Thetis*, provided no luxuries and few comforts, but it had the tremendous advantage of being inexpensive. They boarded for a supposed eight-day journey that ended up taking more than three weeks. Several times they were hit by rough seas, and during one severe storm the captain of the tiny *Thetis* headed for refuge in a Norwegian fjord. According to Wagner's account, they stayed for three days in a small hamlet called Sandwike, where they were accommodated by the wife of an absent sea captain.

After resuming their journey, Wagner, Minna, and the dog sailed up the Thames and spent eight days in London. The couple stayed at the Hoop and Horseshoe, near Tower Hill, and then at the King's Arms in Old Compton Street, Soho.

In an effort to verify Wagner's account of his one and only visit to their country, Norwegian Wagnerians embarked on a detective mission to verify the information in the composer's autobiography. Milton Brener details the search in his 1996 book *Opera Offstage*. In his autobiography, written some thirty years after the voyage, Wagner said that they stayed in a small hamlet called Sandwike, which name he subsequently used in *The Flying Dutchman*. "Sandwike here, how well I know the bay," sings Daland in the opera. Then, in 1935, an Austrian opera singer pinned it down when he unearthed a list of vessels that called at the island. Further confirmation came in 1947 with the discovery of a pilot's log that mentioned the arrival of the *Thetis* and several other ships sheltering from the storm. Scholars were even able to identify the house in which Richard and Minna stayed by consulting shipping invoices that recorded which captains were absent at the time of the couple's visit. Wagner may have used more than one local name in *The Flying Dutchman*: just a few miles from Sandwike is an estate named Daland.

There Is No Sandwike in Norway

In his autobiography Wagner identified the town where the Thetis took refuge as Sandwike. Linda Randall, who helped proofread the manuscript of this book, wrote: "I believe this should be spelled Sandvika. I know this because I lived there for two years." She checked the atlas and confirmed that it was indeed Sandvika. Kristian Evensen, a Norwegian Wagnerian, includes the correct spelling in his retelling of the *Thetis* story on his excellent Web site Wagneropera.net. Linda Randall speculates that the misspelling in Wagner's autobiography may be the result of the frequent confusions caused by the German pronunciation of *w as v*.

Ten years later, around the time that Wagner was involved in the Dresden uprising, the *Thetis* was lost at sea. Wagner never knew what a close escape he had during the mighty North Sea storms. In April 1998 the composer's grandson, Wolfgang Wagner, traveled by the same route as his grandfather and visited Sandwike. Had the *Thetis* gone down in 1839, Wolfgang would never have been born, and his grandfather would barely rate a footnote in the history of music and opera.

In 1914 Siegfried Wagner worked on a new production of the *Dutchman*. Rehearsals were successfully completed, but the performance was canceled. After a *Parsifal* performance opened the

Festival, World War I began, and all performances were scrapped. The lights of the Festspielhaus were to remain out for ten years.

Helden Wagnerians 3

FATHER OWEN LEE

It's OK to Like Wagner

It might seem strange that a man like Wagner should be so appealing to a Catholic priest. Yet Father M. Owen Lee is not only a keen Wagnerian, he is a prolific writer, lecturer, and scholar who has done much to popularize the works of the flawed genius. Now in his early eighties, Father Lee is a professor emeritus of classics at St. Michael's College at the University of Toronto.

• Father Owen Lee, author of several books on Wagner and his works. Photo by Iain Scott.

When Father Lee was only eleven he heard a Saturday afternoon Met broadcast of *Tannhäuser* on Valentine's Day of 1942. He became an instant victim of the Wagner bug. "I had never heard such beautiful melody and harmony. The music simply swept over me like a tidal wave," he said. Wagner was to become a lifelong passion, and Father Lee went on to become a prominent writer and broadcaster on the composer and the wider world of opera. Many of his books, including *Wagner's Ring: Turning the Sky Round* and *Wagner: The Terrible Man and His Truthful Art* are now among the books considered essential for the libraries of committed Wagnerians. However, it was Father Lee's live intermission talks during the Met broadcasts that made him such a well-loved commentator in North America on the works of Wagner and other composers.

Father Lee has been an outspoken critic of modern productions and likes to quote Bernard Shaw, who once said, "When I get on this subject I really cannot contain myself." Shaw was talking about "the execrable impostors in tights and tunics who did so much damage to the reputation of Verdi a hundred years ago." Father Lee focuses his ire on producers and directors who "love themselves more than they love Wagner." He spent several years living in Germany in the 1970s and for a while reveled in the numerous productions available to Wagner enthusiasts. But he soon became disenchanted by the work of deconstructionist directors; he cites tilted stages, tipped-over chairs, and the title character crawling on his stomach as the three most boring clichés of modern productions. His frustration shows when he quotes an unnamed Englishman who said, "Directing opera is what Germans do nowadays instead of invading Poland."

In an article titled "Ancient and Modern," published in *Opera Canada* in 1998, Father Lee wrote:

> On both sides of the Atlantic, deconstructionist producers cite Wagner himself to justify their staging to duped managements and docile audiences. "Next year we'll do it differently" (Wagner's remark when the first Ring cycle did not live up to his expectations) is made to mean, "Next year we'll get rid of the forests, rivers and rainbows and substitute rubbish cans, traffic signs and oil derricks." "Children! Create something new!" is made to mean, "Let those who follow me mount scandalous productions." But when Wagner said. "Kinder! Macht neues!" . . . he was talking about writing new operas, not tinkering with old ones.

When asked for his opinion on the new regime in Bayreuth, Father Lee says that he is not pessimistic. Then, after a brief pause, he adds, "But I am not optimistic either. Time will tell. I am pleased that Christian Thielemann will continue to be involved."

Father Lee cites *Die Meistersinger* as his favorite Wagner opera, and his reasons say much about the priest and Wagnerian. In an interview with Iain Scott of *Opera Canada* in 2001, he said:

He is an educator who teaches how to think and feel."
—Father Owen Lee on Hans Sachs

> What moves me most about *Die Meistersinger* is the humanity of Hans Sachs. He is, in fact, a model for me. He is an educator who teaches not just rules and techniques, but how to think and feel. He loves music as much as he loves his chosen profession, and he sees the connection between the two. He is a celibate whose true children are the lives he touches and enriches. He is the good man I would like to be. He comes to see deeply into life, to accept its inevitable limitations, and to embrace it fully.

Father Lee's most recent book is *Wagner and the Wonder of Art: An Introduction to "Die Meistersinger."* It includes an articulate response to those who claim that there is a "dark underside, a fascist brutality, an ugly anti-Semitic level" in this magnificent work.

Is it strange that a man of the cloth should become a leading advocate for Wagner, who featured murder, theft, and even incest in his operas? Father Lee has a response: "I have spent my life with the literature of Greece and Rome and many of the classics involve unsavory things that are a part of life. Beyond that, I can only quote the catchphrase of the politician played by Ian Richardson in the wonderful British television series *House of Cards*. Whenever he was faced with a difficult truth, the politician Francis Urquhart replied, 'You may think so; I cannot possibly comment.'"

The first time Father Lee addressed the Wagner Society of Toronto, he spoke about *Die Meistersinger*. When he sat down he was surprised by the rapturous applause. He said later, "I just could not believe that my lecture deserved such a prolonged ovation from a knowledgeable audience. I asked one of the Society officials what it was that the audience liked so much. He replied. 'You are a Catholic priest and you are a Wagner enthusiast. It is OK to like Wagner.'"

Tannhäuser und der Sängerkrieg auf dem Wartburg (Tannhäuser and the Song Contest on the Wartburg)

• The full name is rarely used; the work is known simply as *Tannhäuser*.

Completed: April 1845. Revised several times up to 1875.

Premiere performance: October 19, 1845, Dresden.

UK premiere: May 1876, Covent Garden, London. Sung in Italian.

US premiere: April 1859, Stadt Theatre, New York. This was the first performance of any Wagner opera in the United States.

The Bare-Bones Plot

Tannhäuser returns from his sensual adventure with Venus and joins his friends, who are competing in a song contest. The minstrels are singing of love. When it comes to Tannhäuser's turn, he sings of his passionate time in the Venusberg. He escapes punishment because Elisabeth, the niece of the Landgrave, intervenes on his behalf. As penance, he heads for Rome with a group of pilgrims, all hoping to be granted forgiveness by the Pope for their sins. But Tannhäuser's offense is such that his plea is rejected, and he returns without hope when told that he will only be forgiven when the Pope's staff grows buds and flowers. On his return home he learns that Elisabeth has died, and he joins her in death. As the pilgrims sing, fresh green leaves sprout from a papal staff they carry, signifying that Tannhäuser has found redemption.

The first performance of *Tannhäuser* was given in Dresden in October 1845. Audience reactions were positive, and Wagner was called in front of the curtain at the end of each of the twenty performances. However, not everyone was enthusiastic. The famous Wilhelmine Schröder-Devrient, who sang Venus, told Wagner: "You are a man of genius, but you write such eccentric stuff, it is hardly possible to sing it."

• **The Wartburg castle in Eisenach that Wagner used as the setting for *Tannhäuser*.**

The director of the Dresden Opera told Wagner that Weber at least knew how to create a happy ending for his operas. Henry T. Finck has pointed out that there was a popular craving for "happy endings" in that period. The audience for a production of Shakespeare's *Othello* in Hamburg were so affected by the first performance that the city fathers ordered the manager to alter the end of the play. Othello and Desdemona were made to kiss and make up, and from the second performance, everyone left the theatre happy.

Twenty-first-century Wagner followers might wonder what would have happened if the premieres of some of his operas had been staged in Hamburg. Hans Sachs might have married Eva, Tristan and Isolde would have raised several children in a Cornish castle next door to Brünnhilde and Siegfried, the burning of Valhalla would have turned out to be an optical illusion, and Wotan would have lived there happily with Fricka. And maybe Erda would have lived next door.

Mayhem in Paris

The first performance of *Tannhäuser* in France on March 13, 1861, was one of the most astonishing debacles in the history of opera. The performance was ordered by no less than the emperor, Napoleon, and Wagner did everything possible to ensure a successful production, including 160 hours of rehearsal. But those who were opposed to Wagner resented the support of the emperor and Pauline von Metternich, wife of the Austrian ambassador, and they were intent on wrecking the evening.

A group of members of the Jockey Club had another reason to object. Wagner had refused to go along with the local tradition of a ballet sequence in the second act of an opera. The dandy members of the Jockey Club dined before the opera and usually turned up late, most of them well lubricated. Wagner had made a minor concession by including a ballet sequence in the first act of *Tannhäuser*, and when the Jockey Club members discovered that they had missed the whole thing, they started a noisy, extended protest.

The performance was a disaster. The Jockey Club came with hunting whistles and a determination that the opera would not be heard. They blew hunting horns, shouted, hissed and whistled despite protests from the great majority of those present.

One of the supporters of Wagner was the French poet Charles Baudelaire. He said afterward, "Ten obstinate people armed with shrill whistles can . . . cut through the voice of an orchestra as powerful as that of the Opera."

The Jockey Club turned up again on the second evening, and after a repetition on the third evening, Wagner had no option but to agree that the production should be withdrawn. Baudelaire added, "What will Europe think of us? A handful of boors maligned us all."

The French composer Charles Gounod saw it differently. Following the negative comment on the performance, he wrote, "I wish God would grant it to me to write a flop like that."

In an 1845 letter to Mendelssohn, Schumann wrote:

> Wagner has just finished a new opera; no doubt a clever fellow, full of eccentric notions, and bold beyond measure. The aristocracy is still in raptures over him on account of his *Rienzi*, but in reality he cannot conceive or write four consecutive bars of good or even correct music. What all of these composers lack is the art of writing pure harmonies and four-part choruses. The music is not a straw better than that of *Rienzi*;—rather weaker, more artificial! But if I wrote this I would be accused of envy; hence I say it only to you, as I am aware that you have known all this a long time.

Three weeks later, Schumann wrote again to Mendelssohn:

> I must take back much of what I wrote

> regarding *Tannhäuser*, after reading the score; on the stage the effect is quite different. I was deeply moved by many parts.

Shortly after that, he wrote to another friend:

> I wish you could see Wagner's *Tannhäuser*. It contains profound and original ideas, and is a hundred times better than his previous operas, though some of the music is trivial. In a word, he may become of great importance to the stage, and, so far as I know him, he has the requisite courage. The technical parts, the instrumentation, I find excellent, incomparably more masterly than formerly.
>
> Robert Schumann, quoted in Henry T. Finck, *Wagner and His Works*, 1893

In 1864 Wagner remarked about the composition of *Tannhäuser*: "Before I undertake to write a verse or sketch a scene, I am already filled with the musical spirit of my creation. All the characteristic motifs are in my brain so that when the text is done and the scenes arranged, the opera itself is completed, and the detailed musical treatment becomes rather a thoughtful and quiet after-work which the moment of actual composition has already preceded."

Wagner made many changes to *Tannhäuser* after the first performance in Dresden in 1845. An explanatory note is often added to programs to denote which version is being staged, Dresden or Paris. Despite all the changes, Wagner was never happy with his early opera; just days before he died in 1883, Cosima wrote in her diary, "He says he still owes the world a *Tannhäuser*."

> The first production of the [*Tannhäuser*] opera was miserable . . . Luckily, some important critics were in the house, and they wrote long articles complaining that the love scenes with Venus were disgraceful and immoral and ought to be banned. Business picked up at once.
>
> Victor Borge with Robert Sherman, *My Favorite Intervals*, 1974

The Norwegian composer Edvard Grieg went to a performance of *Tannhäuser* in Leipzig in 1858 and was so enthusiastic that he returned for another thirteen consecutive performances.

George Szell was engaged by Met's general director, Rudolf Bing, to conduct a series of performances of *Tannhäuser*. The two men did not get on, and the fiery Szell clashed with the equally difficult Bing. The rock crashed straight into the hard place. Szell upset everyone and eventually quit after only four performances. Someone suggested to Bing that "George Szell is his own worst enemy." "Not while I'm alive," replied Bing.

In 1872, after the cornerstone-laying ceremony and concert in Bayreuth, Gustav Engel, a leading Berlin critic, wrote in *Vossische Zeitung*, "However much *Tannhäuser* and *Lohengrin* may dominate the German theatres, there is as yet no evidence of his being celebrated by his countrymen as were Mozart and Beethoven, as even Mendelssohn was in his day; only the fanatic zeal of his special admirers could deceive foreigners on this point."

Engel wrote this several years before Wagner's death. History does not relate whether he was aware of an earlier contribution by a predecessor of his at the same newspaper. Writing about *Don Giovanni* three years before Mozart's death, a critic wrote: "It is the product of a freak, a caprice, and not inspired by the heart . . .

Stamps He Might Not Have Liked

Dozens of postage stamps have been issued around the world to honor Wagner and his works. He would have been pleased by most of them, but perhaps not the one issued in Paraguay. First, they got his name wrong. Was it a confusion with his uncle Adolf? Probably not, because the spelling is also wrong, and so are the years of his birth and death. Richard's uncle Adolf was born in 1774 and died in 1835. The dates on the caption show that the Paraguayan postal authority confused Richard with Adolph Wagner, an eminent economist who was born in 1835 and died in 1917.

Another possible reason Richard might have disapproved was the inclusion of a ballet scene. With one notable exception, he resisted the idea of the traditional ballet scene in his operas.

Another stamp issued in Ras al-Khaima, one of the United Arab Emirates, repeated the use of a ballet scene. If Wagner had ever been tempted to include such a scene in his later operas, he would have been deterred by the fiasco in Paris at the premiere of *Tannhäuser*. Pressure from the Jockey Club for such a scene led to pandemonium and the abandonment of the performance.

> "What I felt in composing this music he felt in performing it."
> —Richard Wagner, on seeing Liszt conduct a rehearsal for *Tannhäuser*

Besides, we have never heard that Mozart was a composer of note."

At several points in his life Wagner expressed concern that he might die before completing his current project. As early as 1844, while composing *Tannhäuser* in Dresden, he said: "Into this work I had precipitated myself with my whole soul and with such consuming ardor that, the nearer I approached its end, the more I was haunted by an idea that a sudden death would prevent me from completing it."

The strong mutual affection between Wagner and Liszt was cemented when the Hungarian composer conducted *Tannhäuser* in Weimar. Wagner said later, "I saw Liszt conduct a rehearsal of my *Tannhäuser*, and was astonished to recognize my second self in this achievement. What I felt in composing this music he felt in performing it; what I intended to say in writing it down he said in making it sound. Wonderful!"

After visiting King Ludwig's castle, Neuschwanstein, the Wagnerian and journalist Bernard Levin bought a walking stick in a nearby village. He described it as a "noble staff, tapering from a solid boss to a thumb's thickness." He swore that he inspected it occasionally "for signs of sprouting, in accordance with the miracle in *Tannhäuser*."

Charles Baudelaire for the Defense

Many of those present at the aborted Paris performances of *Tannhäuser* were horrified by the behavior of the Jockey Club. Several tried to silence the noisy critics, but to no avail. One defender, who had become an enthusiastic supporter of Wagner more than a year earlier, was Charles Baudelaire (1821–1867), one of France's greatest literary figures. After attending concert performances of some of Wagner's music, he wrote to Wagner in February 1860 thanking him for "the greatest musical pleasure I've ever experienced." His effusive letter must have warmed Wagner's heart. He went on:

> I've reached an age where one hardly enjoys writing to famous men anymore and I would have hesitated much longer to express my admiration to you through a letter had I not day after day set eyes on unworthy, ridiculous articles where all possible efforts are made to defame your glory. Yours is not the first case where my country has caused me suffering and shame. In short, it's indignation that has led me to express my gratitude. I said to myself: "I want to be distinguished from all those jackasses."
>
> The first time I went to the theatre to hear your works I was pretty ill-disposed toward them. I admit I even had a lot of bad prejudices. But I had an excuse, for I've so often been a dupe. I've heard so much music by charlatans making great claims. I was instantly won over. What I felt is beyond description.
>
> From *Selected Letters of Charles Baudelaire*, translated and edited by Rosemary Lloyd, 1986

Baudelaire's enthusiasm for Wagner's music wavered later in his life. He was quoted as saying, after attending a performance of *Tristan and Isolde* in Paris, "I love Wagner, but the music I prefer is that of a cat hung up by its tail outside a window and trying to stick to the panes of glass with its claws."

Misery in the French Capital

Wagner's time in the French capital was probably the most miserable of his life. Not only had his early opera been rejected, but he was so poor that he and Minna were close to starvation and sometimes stayed in his cold apartment because his only pair of shoes was worn through. Then, to cap it all, Wagner's Newfoundland Robber left home and never returned. Maybe he was hungry too? (Wagner claimed later that the dog had been stolen.)

Wagner wrote of his experiences and feelings.

> In these dark days I am beginning to feel more and more deeply the necessity of keeping a regular diary. I hope that the writing down of my prevailing moods, and the reflections springing from them, will afford me relief, as tears do to a heart oppressed. Tears have come into my eyes unbidden this moment; is it a proof of cowardice or of unhappiness to yield willingly to tears? A young German journeyman was here; he was in poor health, and I bade him come again for his breakfast. Minna took the occasion to remind me that she was about to send away our last pennies for bread. You poor woman! Right you are; our situation is a sad one, and if I reflect on it, I can foresee with certainty that the greatest conceivable misery is in store for us; an accident only can bring improvement; for an accident, I must almost consider the contingency of being helped by others voluntarily and without any personal interest; this last hope would be humiliating if I were convinced that I could expect nothing but alms; fortunately, I am compelled to assume that men like Meyerbeer and [Heinrich] Laube would not help me unless they believed that I deserved help. Weakness, caprice, and accident may, however, still intervene and estrange these persons from me. That is a terrible thought; and this doubt and the uncertainty regarding their goodwill is painful and sickens my heart.

Four days later, he wrote:

> How this is to come out next month I do not know; my fears are turning to despair. I have now indeed an opportunity to earn a trifle by writing articles for the Gazette Musicale; I shall also send articles to [August] Lewald in Stuttgart for Europa, to see if I can make some money that way. Yet in the most favorable case I cannot avoid being crushed by what is impending at this moment. Twenty-five francs is all I have left. With this I am expected to pay on the first a bill of exchange for 150 francs, and on the fifteenth my quarterly rent is due. All fountains are dry. From my poor wife I am still concealing the pass at which we have arrived. I constantly hoped Laube would send something; I would then have told her how, without him, we could have had nothing to count upon, and how I had kept it secret from her, so as not to add to the cares which have already shaken her constitution. But now I fear this will be impossible. On the first I shall have to reveal the secret. The Lord help us! That will be a terrible day, unless assistance arrives.

Quoted in Henry T. Finck,
Wagner and His Works, 1893

Around that time Wagner was forced to suggest to Minna that she raise some temporary loans by pawning her trinkets; Minna confessed that she had already done so some time earlier. The man who was to compose *Tristan and Isolde*, *Die Meistersinger von Nürnberg*, and *The Ring of the Nibelung* was saved from starvation by some work arranging music and by writing for musical papers.

After the *Tannhäuser* fiasco, it was thirty years before a Wagner opera was produced in France. The breakthrough came when *Lohengrin* was mounted at the Grand Opera—but only with police protection. It was an immediate success, and in its first year there were sixty-one performances.

Despite this triumph, Wagner never forgot his treatment in France. Years later, when discussing his own involvement in the revolution in Dresden, Wagner wrote to his friend Theodor Uhlig: "I assure you that I no longer believe in any other revolution save that which begins with the burning down of Paris."

After the 1855 premiere, the *Times* wrote of the *Tannhäuser* overture: "A more inflated display of extravagance and noise has rarely been submitted to an audience, and it was a pity to hear so magnificent an orchestra engaged in almost fruitless attempts at accomplishing things which, even if practicable, would lead to nothing."

In 1933 Arturo Toscanini pulled out of a commitment to conduct at Bayreuth as a protest against the Nazi persecution of Jewish musicians. The job was then offered to Fritz Busch, who, although not a Jew, had quit Nazi Germany for good earlier that year. He contemptuously rejected the Bayreuth offer. Hermann Goering was furious. He told the conductor that he could be compelled to conduct. Busch responded, "Just try it! A compulsory performance of *Tannhäuser* conducted by me would be no pleasure to you. You haven't heard anything in your life so stinkingly boring." Goering gave up.

Seattle Opera: America's Premier Wagner Company

It started, appropriately, in Bayreuth, where Glynn Ross (1914–2005) worked during the summers of 1953 and 1954. Ross was bitten by the Wagner bug, but, having lived through Wieland Wagner's minimalist productions, he wanted to get back to something closer to Wagner's original ideas. He yearned for stagings that incorporated the rocks and trees specified by Wagner in his original stage directions.

He observed that productions of *The Ring* were rare in the United States in the early 1970s, even among the major houses, and he was keen to implement his own ideas. In 1963 he became the founding general director of Seattle Opera, but it was to be another ten years before he was to begin work on his first *Ring*. It was staged in 1975, and the first step had been taken toward the creation of a company with a strong commitment to Wagner's works. The four operas were presented in a single week, and Ross kept his promise to move closer to Wagner's original ideas by producing a naturalistic *Ring* brought up to date by modern stage technology.

The Seattle *Ring* became an annual summer event, and Ross also broke new ground by presenting one of the annual cycles in English. The British baritone Malcolm Rivers, who had already sung the role in the Goodall *Ring* of the early 1970s, was chosen to sing the Alberich in both the German and English cycles. Rivers was until recently chair-

• **The final scene from Seattle's *Ring*. Unlike many productions, Wadsworth's *Ring* ends on a positive note, with new saplings growing from fallen dead trees, signifying renewal and growth. Photo by Chris Bennion, courtesy of Seattle Opera.**

man of the London Wagner Society.

In 1980 Glynn Ross presented a new production of *Tristan and Isolde*. By now Seattle was well on the way to creating an audience that is probably more knowledgeable and enthusiastic about Wagner and his works than may be found in any other city in the world outside Germany.

However, there were rumbles of discontent among the non-Wagnerians on the board, who feared that the high cost of producing Wagner was starving other operas of necessary investments. In 1983 Ross and Seattle Opera parted company, and, after the already-contracted 1984 production, the annual *Ring*s were canceled. However, the commitment to Wagner remained.

The board did well in appointing Speight Jenkins as Ross's successor. He is a lawyer and one-time journalist, music critic, and radio and TV commentator with a passion for Wagner. Shortly after he was appointed, Jenkins said he would like to lead Seattle in staging all ten of the Wagner's frequently performed operas. This was a bold ambition for one of the smaller US companies, but he achieved his goal twenty years later, in 2003, when Seattle Opera staged a new production of *Parsifal*.

Jenkins' first *Ring*, produced in 1986 and directed by François Rochaix, was a departure from the natural look favored by his predecessor, and he received hundreds of letters of complaint. Then Seattle experienced the Chéreau effect. When the production was repeated in 1987 and again in 1991 and 1995, the Rochaix *Ring* was applauded by both the critics and the knowledgeable Seattle audience. One memorable staging feature of that production was the flying horses of the Valkyries appearing out of the clouds. All three of the first cycles were sold out, and that was to become the norm for Seattle *Ring* productions. Seattle's reputation was established.

In 2001 Seattle introduced a new staging of the cycle, dubbed the "Green *Ring*" because of its focus on a natural look inspired by the beautiful landscapes of the northwestern United States. This new production was directed by Stephen Wadsworth

• The Valkyries on their flying horses. Their appearance brought gasps and applause from the normally disciplined Seattle audiences. Photo by Ron Scherl, courtesy of Seattle Opera.

and designed by Thomas Lynch, with costumes by Martin Pakledinaz and lighting by Peter Kaczorowski. It was a critical and public success. Three cycles were staged, and the Green *Ring* returned to Seattle in 2005, 2009, and 2013, after which it is scheduled to be retired. It was sold out each time, and in 2009 the audience came from forty-nine states and twenty-three foreign countries.

The huge success of this Seattle *Ring* is due to a combination of Wadsworth's clarity of vision and ability to get the most out of his cast and Jenkins' absolute commitment to getting it right, keeping it clear, and maintaining respect for the composer's intentions. After seeing the August 2005 production, I wrote to friends, "This was my twenty-fourth *Ring*. I have seen productions in Bayreuth, London, New York, San Francisco, Chicago and several other cities. Seattle's production was remarkable because the production was so clear, everything on the stage supported and clarified the story line and there were none of the irrelevant staging nonsense and self-indulgent claptrap that ruins so many European productions. The Seattle *Ring* avoided the problem seen too often in Europe where what the audience sees is out of kilter with what they hear. Most pleasing however, was the way I was uplifted by the optimism seen and felt at the end of *Götterdämmerung*."

The quadrennial Seattle *Ring* has become a major cultural event in Washington state. In addition to the acclaimed production, Seattle Opera mounts a series of related events, including all-day seminars in which internationally renowned Wagnerian scholars participate and pre-curtain talks for *Ring* beginners. For several years now, the city parks authority has joined in the summer celebration by reprogramming the musical fountains in Seattle Center to include Wagner's music.

In 2009 the company introduced another innovation, *Confessions of a First-Time Operagoer*, a series of behind-the-scenes videos chronicling the discovery process of the nineteen-year-old Cassidy Quinn Brettler. The videos featured interviews with key members of the team responsible for both the artistic and the technical aspects of a *Ring* production.

In fewer than fifty years, Seattle Opera has gone from a modest beginning to become America's leading Wagner company. Some believe that if Wagner were to come back for his two hundredth anniversary, the Seattle production would be his *Ring* of choice. After all, Seattle Opera is probably the only company, apart from Bayreuth, that includes his name in its mission statement.

Curtains for *The Ring*

Or, more accurately, just one curtain. The Seattle Opera production of *The Ring* in August 2005 saw the first appearance of a new house curtain, which is only used every four years. The magnificent curtain, with a beautiful abstract design, was made by the Seattle Opera craftsmen and -women. It was donated by Linda Nordstrom (whose family runs the namesake American retail chain) in honor of her late husband, Christian Seifert. Following its use during the 2013 *Ring*, it is now back in storage. Next appearance: August 2017.

A Secret Fan

Young Bruno Schlesinger was born into a musical family and showed signs of talent when his mother gave him piano lessons. Even as a young student, he grabbed every opportunity to attend local opera houses and concert halls. But he was discouraged from attending performances of Wagner's works: his middle-class Jewish parents disapproved of Wagner because of his anti-Semitism, and Bruno's teachers disapproved of the composer's radical musical ideas.

But young Schlesinger wanted to judge for himself, and one day he secretly attended a performance of *Tristan and Isolde*. The experience was to change his life. He wrote later:

> There I sat in the topmost gallery of the Berlin Opera House, and from the first sound of the cellos my heart contracted spasmodically . . . Never before had my soul been so deluged with floods of sound and passion, never had my heart been consumed by such yearning and sublime bliss, never had I been transported from reality by such heavenly glory. I was no longer in this world. After the performance, I roamed the streets aimlessly. When I got home I didn't say anything and begged not to be questioned. My ecstasy kept singing within me through half the night, and when I awoke on the following morning I knew that my life was changed. A new epoch had begun: Wagner was my god, and I wanted to become his prophet.

The young man made rapid progress, and when he was only twenty he was offered a position with the Breslau Stadttheater. There was a condition: he had to change his surname. He resisted, but when it became clear that it was an essential requirement if he wanted the job, he agreed. Still an enthusiastic Wagnerian, he chose the name of one of Wagner's heroes.

That young man went on to become one of the world's great conductors. The musical world re-

> "It's as stupid to underestimate Wagner as it is to overestimate him. He doesn't need either."
> **—Otto Klemperer**

members him today as Bruno Walter. He died in Beverly Hills, California, in 1962.

Arturo Toscanini had a phenomenal memory and usually knew every last note in a score. He once corrected a note that the Met cellists had been playing incorrectly for years. It is said that he even surprised the Festspielhaus orchestra when he asked about a cymbal crash at the end of *Tristan*'s first act. The percussionists thought they'd caught the maestro out because their scores did not show a cymbal crash. But Toscanini knew his Wagner: he insisted that the original manuscript be brought out from the vaults. Sure enough, Wagner had specified a cymbal crash.

In a 1991 book titled *Furtwängler on Music: Essays and Addresses*, the conductor offered his thoughts on Wagner the man: "If he were to fulfill his mission Wagner, too, had to be hard. However unpleasant it may have been for those immediately affected by it, we must concede that his egoism was thoroughly justified, even necessary. He was compelled to act thus—his works are his vindication."

Richard Strauss had a relaxed podium style that was sometimes interpreted as lack of interest. He was a one-handed conductor and explained: "The left hand has nothing to do with conducting. Its proper place is the waistcoat pocket . . . It is better to conduct with the ear instead of with the arm: the rest follows automatically."

> I must confess that when I recently conducted the first act of *Die Walküre* it was as though I were encountering a woman I had loved forty years ago. And the strange thing was that she hadn't changed or grown older. I find the music thrilling. Thrilling! One can say this or that about Wagner but no one else could have written that music. No one! It's as stupid to underestimate Wagner as it is to overestimate him. He doesn't need either.
>
> Otto Klemperer in a radio interview by Peter Heyworth, retold in *Conversations with Klemperer*, 1969

Helden Wagnerians 4
ANTON SEIDL
The Essential Right-Hand Man

Anton Seidl (1850–1898) was an Austro-Hungarian conductor who studied with Hans Richter and later became Wagner's musical secretary. He worked on arrangements for Wagner's Albert Hall concerts and conducted the first performances of *The Ring* in Leipzig and all 133 performances of Angelo Neumann's traveling Nibelung Circus in 1882–83.

Seidl moved to the United States in 1885 and conducted the first American performances of *Die Meistersinger* in 1886; *Tristan* in 1886; *Siegfried* in 1887; *Götterdämmerung* in 1888; and *Rheingold* in 1889. When he died in 1898, New Yorkers gave him a funeral rivaled only by that of Wagner himself.

Earlier, in a letter to Liszt, Wagner wrote: "I am working with all my energies. Could you not send

• Anton Seidl, Wagner's musical assistant, who was to become a favorite conductor in New York.

me a man who would be able to take my wild lead-pencil sketches and make a cleanly copied score of them? I am working this time on a plan quite different from my former one. But the copying is killing me! It makes me lose time of which I might make more precious use; and, besides, the constant writing fatigues me so much that it makes me ill, and causes me to lose the mood of the real work of creating. Without such a clever assistant I am lost; with him I could have the whole [tetralogy] completed in two years."

The man who took on this assignment was Anton Seidl. He became an indispensable aide and lived with the Wagner family for six years during the completion of *Götterdämmerung* and the composition of *Parsifal*. Throughout that period, Seidl had a unique opportunity to become familiar with every detail of Wagner's works and, of particular value, the composer's interpretation of his own works.

In 1875, the twenty-five-year-old Seidl accompanied Wagner on a trip to Berlin, where he was to give two concerts. Franz Fridberg reported in the *Berliner Tagblatt* on how Seidl had come to be appointed to assist Wagner and went on:

> In time he became Wagner's right hand; he was, in fact, the real conductor of our rehearsals. It was impossible to conceive all that this young man from Budapest heard and knew by heart. Before Wagner himself had noted errors in his own music, Seidl could be seen flying over chairs and desks to correct the blunder. The master viewed the actions of his young famulus with paternal love, and repeatedly I heard him murmur, "Ho, he! What would I do without my Seidl?"
>
> Five years later I heard *Götterdämmerung* under Seidl's direction in Leipsic. Not long before I had heard the first and second performances of the tremendous work in Munich under Levy. Without wishing in the least to depreciate the merits of this great artist, I must say that, for me, Seidl's conception was the greater. There was in it more life, more movement, more poetry. In fact I received the impression that night that all of the conductors I had got acquainted with, Seidl was the chosen interpreter of Wagner.
>
> In 1879 Seidl assisted at rehearsals for the Wagner concert in London and later won acclaim for a performance of *Tristan and Isolde* in Leipsic. Wagner wrote to the manager, Angelo Neumann: "You are aware that I had made up my mind to allow this problematic work to be given hereafter only under my personal supervision: now it has succeeded without me—and that astonishes me! Well, good luck! I certainly discover in Seidl hidden faculties which only require a fostering warmth to surprise even myself; therefore, I beg you now, for the sake of the ensemble, to allow him even in the scenic department more authority that is usually granted to conductors, for in that direction lies what he especially learned from me."

In 1882 the Travelling Wagner Theatre visited London for a performance of *The Ring*. Seidl took some time out from rehearsals to have his hair cut; because he spoke little English at the time, he communicated his wishes to the barber with a series of hand signals. Shortly afterward the artists began to arrive for the rehearsal. There was some mild panic: the man at the podium with his back to them was clearly not their beloved Seidl! What had happened, and who was this replacement? Then the man turned around. It *was* Seidl—but his trademark long hair had gone. He stood there wearing what we might today describe as a crew cut. Seidl had not done as good a job of communicating with the barber as he'd believed. As soon as he'd succeeded (or so he thought) in telling the barber to take an inch off his long hair, he buried himself in a newspaper. When he next looked up at the mirror, he discovered to his horror that the barber had taken his hair down to an inch long. There was much leg pulling for the next hour, but the company was relieved that they had not lost their popular conductor.

Seidl traveled with a chest in which he kept some of his most prized possessions. These included important papers and his letters from Wagner. In the book *Anton Seidl: A Memorial*, Henry T. Finck wrote: "One day a friend said to him, 'Mr. Seidl, your trunk is burst open at the railway station, and the wind has scattered your papers. The people are picking up your valuables; if you hurry you may be able to save some of them.'"

It is not known how much he was able to recover, but Finck reported that he never retrieved many of his letters from Wagner and that "the loss was a deep anguish to him."

According to Finck, the last letter that Wagner wrote was addressed to Angelo Neumann and included the words, "Seidl delights me greatly." The combined results of Seidl's leadership of the Neumann touring musicians and other conducting engagements around Europe resulted in Wagner's protégé being the first to conduct his master's greatest works in many German cities as well as in England, Italy, and then America.

Seidl made his debut at the Metropolitan Opera House on November 23, 1885, with a performance of *Lohengrin*. In the following years he introduced New York audiences to *Die Meistersinger* (January 1886), *Tristan and Isolde* (December 1886), *Siegfried* (November 1887), *Götterdämmerung* (January 1888), and *Das Rheingold* (January 1889). He became a US citizen, and in addition to his work for the Met, he was appointed conductor of the Philharmonic Society in 1891. Seidl became one of the most popular conductors New York had ever known and also enjoyed considerable international success.

Seidl's sudden death on March 28, 1898, at the age of only forty-eight, shocked his adopted city. He had appeared to be healthy just days before, when he rehearsed the Met orchestra playing Siegfried's Funeral March for a performance of *Götterdämmerung*.

A service was held at the Met, where a cathedral-like setting on the stage was lit by many candles. The catafalque was positioned over the place where Seidl had conducted and enjoyed so many enthusiastic ovations from grateful New York audiences. It was surrounded by masses of flowers from friends, musicians, singers, and supporters all over the world. One took the form of a conductor's desk with the flowers forming an open score. Embedded in the flowers were photographs of Wagner and Seidl with the inscription "Vereint auf Ewig" (Eternally united).

Five different conductors led the music components of the memorial service, concluding with Siegfried's Funeral March, played by the New York Philharmonic Orchestra. This was introduced by a tremulously voiced Henry Krehbiel, who read a message from Seidl's friend Colonel Robert G. Ingersoll that was guaranteed to increase the flow of tears:

> Anton Seidl is dead. Play the great funeral march. Envelop him in music. Let its wailing waves cover him. Let its wild and mournful winds sigh and moan above him. Give his face to its kisses and its tears.
>
> Play the great funeral march, music as

> "
> Seidl delights me greatly."
> **—Richard Wagner, in his last letter**

> profound as death. That will express our sorrow—that will voice our love, our hope, and that will tell of the life, the triumph, the genius, the death of Anton Seidl.

At these last words, the Philharmonic Orchestra started the Funeral March as they had been rehearsed by Seidl only days earlier. A procession escorted the coffin out of the opera house, and tears and sobs spread out to the streets when they appeared. It was overwhelmingly poignant and more heartrending than any opera ever presented on the Met stage.

The eulogies continued long after the funeral. The year after Seidl's death, a group of friends asked the Wagnerian writer Henry T. Finck to write a biography and tribute to the much-loved conductor. The resulting book included tributes from the Philharmonic Society, several music critics, and singers, including Lilli Lehmann, Lillian Nordica, and Jean and Edouard de Reszke. Only a thousand copies of the 290-page book were published; these are prized by Wagnerian collectors.

Die Fledermaus in *The Ring*...

Die Fledermaus appeared in the Bayreuth Festspielhaus in 1995. It was not the Strauss opera but a real live *Fledermaus*, or bat, that appeared during a performance of *Die Walküre*. The creature presumably entered through the huge stage doors when they were opened to aid ventilation during the intermission.

Act III began with the fearless Valkyrie warrior maidens onstage, and all was going well until the bat appeared. It swooped and dived over the singers, several of whom took an instant dislike to the tiny mammal. Some of the ladies were visibly terrified, but like true pros they kept singing while ducking and diving with one eye on the conductor and the other on the bat. It is not known how the problem was solved, but the bat did not make an appearance for the rest of Act III.

... And *The Ring* in *Die Fledermaus* ...

Four of the cast of Seattle Opera's highly successful 2005 *Ring* appeared in a production of *Die Fledermaus* a few months later. But it went a bit further than using some top-class Wagnerian singers, because the spoof production included some creative tampering with Strauss' libretto. Most audiences would not have noticed, but Seattle operagoers know their Wagner. Lisa Burkett, of the Wagner Society of Northern California, tells the story.

> When the action began, we heard a tenor serenading his former lover, Rosalinde, outside her salon window. In Seattle Opera's production, he was a German heldentenor, Alfred. He climbed through the window and launched into a phrase from the Awakening Scene, prompting Rosalinde to plead with him to sing anything but *Siegfried*. He complied with her request by singing the opening line of Walther's Preislied. Rosalinde swooned, employing the fainting couch for its intended purpose. As Alfred exited through the window, he quoted Tristan's hallucination about a ship approaching the shore.
>
> I had the pleasure of seeing the production with the audience known to be Seattle

> Opera's most sophisticated, which erupted with laughter at each of these jokes.

The jesting didn't end with libretto liberties: the singer playing Alfred turned up at the party wearing Siegfried's splendid purple lamé coat, and he brought a friend—Siegfried's bear.

The Wagnerian singers who found their way into *Die Fledermaus* were Jane Eaglen (Brünnhilde) as Rosalinde, Richard Berkeley-Steele (Siegmund) as Gabriel von Eisenstein, Alan Woodrow (Siegfried) as Alfred, and Nancy Maultsby (Waltraute) as Prince Orlofsky.

The audience laughed at the clever Wagner-Strauss mélange, but there were tears too after Speight Jenkins, the general director, appeared in front of the curtain to pay tribute to Birgit Nilsson, who had died only a few days earlier. Eaglen completed the tribute by singing Isolde's Liebestod.

. . . And *Die Fledermaus* in the Festspielhaus

The Glenn Miller Band and the Radio City Music Hall Rockettes performed at the Festspielhaus in 1945 after the American forces took over the building. Religious services and a variety of entertainments were staged before the end of 1945. The following year the Festspielhaus was handed over in trust to the town of Bayreuth. It was used for concerts and operas including *Fidelio*, *Madama Butterfly*, *La traviata*, and yes, *Die Fledermaus*.

The Most Difficult Roles in Opera

Despite the difficulty of the roles and the requirement that they commit themselves to a long period of summer rehearsal and performance, most singers jump at the chance to sing at Bayreuth. Even the megastars grab the opportunity. The great Birgit Nilsson said of her first visit:

> I thought my heart must burst. I simply could not believe that I might be allowed to sing in this temple, in this hall, where Wagner lived and worked. It just seemed a dream. With a pounding heart, I entered the Festspielhaus and had the feeling that Wagner's spirit hovered over everything.

In an 1872 letter, Wagner instructed the banker Friedrich Feustel that singers performing at the first Festival would receive expenses but no salary. "He who does not come to me from glory and enthusiasm can stay where he is. A lot of use to me a singer would be who came to me only for a silly salary! Such a person could never satisfy my artistic demands."

Nothing much has changed in the 130-plus years since then. Bayreuth still attracts the best singers in the world, but they do not come for the money. Singers, no matter how big a name they may be, are paid a flat fee for the role. The leading soprano Astrid Varnay once said, "One goes to Bayreuth to work; to earn money, one goes elsewhere."

Birgit Nilsson's first Isolde in Bayreuth was a tremendous success, and at her curtain call she was greeted by thunderous applause. The adrenalin was also pumping for the conductor, Karl Böhm. At the post-performance reception in the Neue Schloss, Nilsson was seated between Böhm and the mayor of Bayreuth, Hans Wild. The conductor was still euphoric and still in the thrall of Nilsson's stunning performance. He turned to her and said, "Miss Nilsson, when you stop singing, I will stop conducting." It was a generous comment, and the mayor desperately searched for words that would express his own enthusiasm for the Swedish soprano. After a long pause, he turned to

"
Have I ever done you any harm?"
—Adelina Patti, soprano, when asked why she had not sung any Wagner roles

her and said, "Miss Nilsson, we would be honored to have you buried in Bayreuth."

Why was Wagner so important to her? Waltraud Meier was asked. "There isn't a short answer to that," she said and went on:

> There are so many areas you could begin to tackle in Wagner. You can work endlessly just on the details. Let's say you decide to look just at the psychological aspects, and then just at the philosophical aspects, and then just at the text as text, purely technical. And then you look at the orchestration, the handling of melody, the handling of the voices, and then you look at everything together as a whole again—it's endless. I feel I could go on doing it forever without anywhere near reaching the end. I hope I have another life, so I can go on doing it. That's what I find so fascinating.
>
> Much as I appreciate other opera composers, compared to Wagner they all seem a bit one-dimensional. Lovely music, of course, incredible melodies, great for the voice, all very touching and moving. But for the universal perspective, no one rivals Wagner.
>
> Waltraud Meier, mezzo-soprano, in Annette Schreier's documentary film *I Follow a Voice Within Me*, 2001

Adelina Patti (1843–1919) sang at Covent Garden for twenty-five years and was reputed to be the highest-paid soprano of her time. Felix Semon, the laryngologist, once asked her why she had never sung any of Wagner's roles. "She looked at me with her beautiful eyes," he said in his memoirs, "and simply asked me, 'Have I ever done you any harm?'"

But later the great Patti did sing Wagner on at least two occasions. Bernard Shaw wrote in May 1894 that she had sung the "Dream" from the *Wesendonck Lieder*. Shaw said that she sang it extremely well, and, when the inevitable encore came, repeated it instead of singing "Home, Sweet Home" or "Within a Mile."

A few weeks later, Shaw reported that Patti had sung another Wagner work, Elisabeth's Prayer from *Tannhäuser*. But Shaw clearly had mixed feelings about the possibility of seeing the formidable singer in a full Wagnerian role.

> If Patti were to return to the stage and play Isolde, though she might very possibly stop the drama half a dozen times in each act to acknowledge applause and work in an encore—though she might introduce Home Sweet Home, in the ship scene, and The Last Rose in the garden scene—though nobody would be in the least surprised to see her jump up out of her trance in the last act to run to the footlights for a basket of flowers, yet the public might learn a good deal about Isolde from her which they will never learn from any of the illustrious band of German Wagner heroines who are queens at Bayreuth, but who cannot sing a gruppetto for all that.

Wieland Wagner invited Birgit Nilsson to sing at the reopening of Bayreuth after the war, but she had to decline because she had already committed to sing at Glyndebourne. She was later invited to visit Bayreuth to audition but again had to decline because of a prior commitment. She confessed later to being pleased about that clash of dates because she was not keen on auditions. "It reminds me of a country horse market—the only difference is they can't examine your teeth to see if you've lied about your age," she wrote in *La Nilsson: My Life in Opera*.

The following year she did perform at Bayreuth, but not in a Wagner role: she sang the soprano part in Beethoven's Ninth Symphony. She agreed to sing some Wagner for Wieland, and after delivering extracts from *Die Walküre*, *Lohengrin*, and *Tannhäuser*, Wieland fell to his knees in his office and told her that she could select her own role. "Express your wish and the role is yours," he said. Despite Wieland's enthusiasm, it was to be ten years before Wieland invited Nilsson to sing Isolde in Bayreuth. It was the younger brother, Wolfgang, who brought Nilsson to Bayreuth in 1954 to sing Elsa in his production of *Lohengrin*.

Tenors are usually short, stout men (except when they are Wagnerian tenors, in which case they are large, stout men) made up predominantly of lungs, rope-sized vocal chords, large frontal sinuses, thick necks, thick heads, tantrums and amour propre . . . It is certain that they are a race apart, a race that tends to operate reflexively rather than with due process of thought.
—Harold Schonberg, 1961

Of course, we've all dreamed of reviving the castrati; but it's needed Hilda to take the first practical steps towards making them a reality . . . She's drawn up a list of well-known singers who she thinks would benefit . . . It's only a question of getting them to agree.
—A character in Henry Reed, *The Private Life of Hilda Tablet*, 1954; quoted in Ned Sherrin, *Oxford Dictionary of Humorous Quotations*, 2000

Helden Wagnerians 5
BRYAN MAGEE
Author of the Best Small Book on Wagner

I am often asked by people who have just found Wagner (lucky people—they have it all to discover and savor), "Which book do you recommend for me to learn more about this composer and his works?" Without hesitation I recommend *Aspects of Wagner* by the Oxford philosopher Bryan Magee. It is one of the slimmest of the five hundred or more books in my library of Wagner and opera. At not even a hundred pages, it covers the basics and responds to most of the common fallacies and unjustified criticisms.

Magee writes with all the clarity and economy absent from Wagner's own prose works. *Aspects of Wagner* includes six essays on Wagner's theories, the Jewish issue, what he calls Wagnerolatry, the composer's influence on other artists, performance of his works, and his works as music. He covers as much ground in a page as others could only achieve with several pages (and for which Wagner himself might have required a chapter).

Aspects of Wagner was first published in 1968. Since then it has been reprinted many times, and a wholly new, revised edition appeared in 1988. Foreign translations are still being published.

Magee was born in London in April 1930 and educated at Keble College, Oxford, on a history scholarship, although he tried unsuccessfully to switch to music. During his studies he developed an interest in philosophy and took a second Oxford degree. It was to be a preoccupation for the rest of his life. He still found time to become a poet and novelist, a television broadcaster, and a member of Parliament for the Labour Party and later the Social Democrats. He is still remembered by many for his television dialogues with philoso-

Magee writes with all the clarity and economy absent from Wagner's own prose works.

phers in the 1970s, and his talent for expressing complex thoughts in a clear and digestible form became apparent at that time.

He inherited his interest in Wagner from his father, whom Magee describes as a "Wagner junkie." He soon learned that not everyone recognizes the genius of the little man from Saxony. He recalls with puzzled horror the comment made by a friend on seeing his record collection: "I had no idea Bryan was a bit of a Nazi." "My position is that I don't think the anti-Semitism gets into the works in any significant way," explained Magee in an interview with *The Guardian* in 2003. "The fact is that anti-Semitism was very widespread in European culture, with the result that an enormous number of very famous writers and artists were anti-Semites. But in most cases it doesn't significantly affect their work and with Wagner I think it is demonstrably the case."

Magee has written a total of twenty-one books, of which *Aspects* is by far the shortest. There has been only one other on Wagner, *Wagner and Philosophy*, published in 2001. In 1983 he published a major work titled *The Philosophy of Schopenhauer*, the greatest of all nonmusical influences on Wagner.

Wagner and Philosophy was published in the United States as *The Tristan Chord*—a much better title, admits Magee. It's better because it does not frighten off anyone worried that a book on philosophy might be hard going. Only occasionally does Magee the philosopher show through, and he succeeds in delivering his complex message without resorting to the sometimes unfathomable language used by others in his field. This gifted Wagnerian gets into Wagner's head and succeeds in

• **Bryan Magee, Oxford philosopher and Wagnerian.**

simplifying the philosophy of Schopenhauer and Wagner's thinking when he wrestled with alternative approaches to *The Ring*.

The book was widely acclaimed when it was published in 2000. Speight Jenkins of Seattle Opera said it was the most important books on Wagner in at least ten years. "Those of us who love Wagner are more than fortunate to have Bryan Magee among our number."

Now in his eighties, Bryan Magee is a member of Wolfson College, Oxford. He says that he still has several other books in his head, which is why he writes every day of the week. "Anything more in your head about Wagner?" I asked him. "I have an idea for something but I am not sure if I will write it," he replied. The world of Wagner hopes that he will.

Wagnerians and Anti-Wagnerians

Prominent Enthusiasts, Past and Present

Wagnerian or Wagnerite? In the early years Wagnerite was more common, but it was mostly used by critics in derogatory connotations. It became part of the language when Bernard Shaw published his book *The Perfect Wagnerite* in 1895. In his musical criticisms published in various British newspapers and magazines, Shaw later referred to supporters and enthusiasts as Wagnerians. The list of Wagner enthusiasts is long and distinguished, and at the top is King Ludwig II of Bavaria: it is almost certain that without his support, Wagner would never have completed *The Ring of the Nibelung* or built his Bayreuth opera house.

Other Wagner enthusiasts have included:

- **Franz Liszt,** both a moral and a financial supporter from Wagner's early days.
- **Richard Strauss,** who conducted many of Wagner's works.
- **Gioachino Rossini,** despite some oft-quoted negative quips.
- **Gustav Mahler,** who was not only a public supporter of Wagner but also a renowned conductor of the composer's works.
- **Queen Victoria,** who asked for a repeat of the *Tannhäuser* overture at the Albert Hall concerts in 1877.
- **Oscar Wilde,** who attended Wagner operas in New York and Bayreuth but is also known for his critical comments.
- Journalist **Bernard Levin,** who admitted to being more profoundly and helplessly addicted to Wagner's music than he was to writing for a living.
- **T. S. Eliot,** who composed his little-known poem *Opera* after attending a performance of *Tristan and Isolde*.
- **Nicolai Rimsky-Korsakov,** who kept a portrait of Wagner over his desk.
- **Virginia Woolf,** who went to Bayreuth in 1909 and wrote an essay on her experiences for the *Times*.
- **Hugo Wolf,** who, as a fifteen-year-old in Vienna, hung around Wagner's hotel hoping to meet his hero and succeeded in a brief encounter with the composer.
- **Albert Schweitzer,** whose high school organ teacher gave him his enthusiasm for Wagner's music and who in 1896 visited Bayreuth for performances of *The Ring* and *Parsifal*.
- **Friedrich Nietzsche,** who went from being a passionate supporter to a rancorous critic.

Fictional fans have included Arthur Conan Doyle's Sherlock Holmes and Colin Dexter's Inspector Morse (played by John Thaw), who tried to educate the hapless Sergeant Lewis on the wonders of Wagner.

Current prominent Wagnerians include:

- **José Manuel Barroso,** president of the European Commission.
- **Stephen Hawking,** who was seen at the Royal Opera House in 2005 for a performance of *Die Walküre*. Some members of the audience wondered why a physicist of such eminence was seated in the upper balcony. Then they realized that the sight line to the stage was perfect for him because it is difficult for him to look up. He tells on his Web site that he started listening to Wagner as a young man shortly after his ALS was diagnosed.
- **Norman Foster,** the prominent architect, who was in Bayreuth when he conceived the idea of what has now become the iconic arch

Wagner, the composer who was first heralded as the writer of marvelously complex and intricate works which could only be understood by the advanced musician, is now demanded by popular audiences. I rarely play a program without a Wagner number, and my band has in its repertoire practically everything which Wagner has written.
—John Philip Sousa, "Music the American People Demand," *Etude*, 1910

When I came out of the Festspielhaus, unable to speak a word, I knew that I had experienced supreme greatness and supreme suffering, and that this experience, hallowed and unsullified, would stay with me for the rest of my life.
—Gustav Mahler, describing his reaction at age twenty-two to the first performance of *Parsifal* in July 1882

So overwhelming is the power of Wagner that after hearing one of his works one vows never to compose another thing. Afterward, one forgets a little and begins again.
—Jules Massenet

Unforgettable beauty that silences all criticism.
—Claude Debussy

Wagner is Verdi with the addition of style!
—Georges Bizet, in 1862

that lights London's Wembley Stadium.

- **George Osborne,** British Chancellor of the Exchequer in the coalition government, who took a day off to see *Götterdämmerung* at the Royal Opera House in September 2012. He was accompanied by the education secretary, Michael Gove, and the arts minister, Ed Vaizey.
- **Ignacy Jan Paderewski.** In his day the man who became prime minister of Poland was probably the most famous pianist in the world. In *Wagner Moments*, J. K. Holman wrote: "When asked what single score he would save from a universal conflagration, [Paderewski] replied, without a moment's hesitation, that it would be Wagner's *Die Meistersinger*, which he thought 'the most prestigious effort of the human brain in the domain of art.'"
- German chancellor **Angela Merkel**, who is a regular visitor to the Bayreuth Festival. The annual pilgrimage to Bayreuth is one of the few times in the year that the chancellor is seen in public with her husband, the eminent scientist Joachim Sauer. Because of this rare appearance, German journalists have dubbed Herr Sauer "the Phantom of the Opera."

And Some Notable Opponents

After attending the first performance of *Götterdämmerung* in 1876, Pyotr Ilyich Tchaikovsky said he felt as if he had been released from a prison. He added, "How many thousand times finer is the ballet of Sylvia." Reporting for the Russian paper *Russky Viedomosty*, Tchaikovsky wrote, "Throughout the whole duration of the festival, food forms the chief interest of the public; the artistic representations take a secondary place. Cutlets, baked potatoes, omelets—all are discussed more eagerly than Wagner's music."

He began to relent when he wrote, "If *The Ring* bores one in places, if much is incomprehensible . . . if the harmonies are open to objection . . . even if the immense work should fall into oblivion . . . yet the *Nibelungen Ring* is an event of the greatest importance to the world, an epoch-making work of art." He concluded, "The *Nibelungen* may be a great work of art—it is possible—but it is certainly a crashing bore; it goes on far too long."

Leo Tolstoy said that *Siegfried* was "the supreme example of 'counterfeit art'—mere hypnosis and maniacal ravings." He added, "To sit in the dark for four days in the company of people who are not quite normal, and through the auditory nerve subject your brain to the strongest action of sounds best adapted to excite it, is a guaranteed method of reducing yourself to a peculiar condition in which you will be enchanted by absurdities."

The Belgian-born composer César Franck wrote "Poison" across his copy of the score of *Tristan and Isolde*, which resided permanently on his desk. But as one observer pointed out, it is interesting that he owned a copy in the first place and kept it conveniently to hand.

The Irish writer James Joyce said that *Die Meistersinger* was "pretentious" and *Tannhäuser* "ridiculous." In his groundbreaking book *Ulysses* he made fun of the scene in *Die Walküre* where Siegmund removes the sword from the tree. Joyce's hero raises his ash plant to shatter a lampshade in a Dublin brothel.

One of the most vociferous opponents of Wagner was the critic Eduard Hanslick, a professor of music at the University in Vienna and a regularly published critic. In 1858 he damned the composer of *Lohengrin* as "an antimelodious fanatic," and in 1868 he said, "The prelude to *Tristan and Isolde* reminds me of the Italian painting of the martyr whose intestines are slowly being unwound from his body on a reel." On another occasion he criticized Wagner's music as "tyrannized by leitmotifs" and "a chromatic-enharmonic confusion."

Of *Siegfried*, Hanslick said, "This tuneless, plodding narrative recalls the mediaeval torture of waking a sleep-crazed prisoner by stabbing him with a needle at every nod."

That old poisoner.
—Claude Debussy, referring to Wagner in a letter to a friend

There is absolutely nothing there! They are the work of a man who, lacking all harmonic inventiveness has created eccentricity . . . I like Verdi 100 times more!
—Georges Bizet, in a letter to his mother after first hearing Wagner's music

---

For me, Wagner is impossible . . . he talks without ever stopping. One just can't talk all the time.
—Robert Schumann

It is impossible to communicate with Schumann. The man is hopeless; he does not talk at all.
—Richard Wagner

Stravinksy's piano teacher Leokadia Kashperova tried to discourage her pupil from an interest in Wagner, but that did not stop the young Igor from learning all of Wagner's works from the piano scores by the time he was sixteen. The future composer of *Firebird* and *The Rite of Spring* called his teacher a blockhead, but whether this was in any way related to her antipathy to Wagner is not known.

Mark Twain: A Confused Wagnerian

Wagner has many gifts for comic writers and humorists, and one of the best remarks has been attributed, incorrectly, to Mark Twain: "Wagner's music is better than it sounds." In his 1924 autobiography Twain put the record straight. What he said was, "I have been told that Wagner's music is better than it sounds." He was quoting Edgar Wilson "Bill" Nye.

The gifted American writer was not an anti-Wagnerian, although it may seem as though he could not make up his mind. Twain saw Wagner operas in both New York and Bayreuth, where he visited in August 1891. He wrote of his experiences in *At the Shrine of Wagner*. But in a letter to his friend William Dean Howells, he once wrote:

> I wish I could give those sharp satires on European life which you mention, but of course a man can't write successful satire except he be in a calm, judicial good-humor—whereas I hate travel, & hate hotels, & hate the opera, & I hate the Old Masters—in truth I don't ever seem to be in a good enough humor with ANYthing to satirize it; no, I want to stand up before it & curse it, & foam at the mouth—or take a club & pound it to rags and pulp.

He must have been in a good mood when he saw *Tannhäuser*, his favorite Wagner opera, since he saw it in his youth. He describes it as "an opera which has always driven me mad with ignorant delight whenever I have heard it." He wrote about sitting in the dark waiting for the third act to start. Finally, the hidden orchestra began to play. And in time, the curtain was drawn aside disclosing a forest in the twilight, a white-robed girl praying, and a man standing nearby. Soon a chorus of men was heard approaching and singing. "It was music, just music—music to make one take scrip and staff and beg his way around the world to hear it."

The Wagnerian scholar William O. Cord wrote:

> On another day Twain said *Tristan and Isolde* broke the hearts of all in the audience, all who were of the faith. He [Twain] went on to say that he felt out of place among these dedicated Wagnerians. "I feel like the one blind man whereas all the others see, the one groping savage in the college of the learned, and always during service I feel like a heretic in heaven."

Twain wrote of the "absolute attention and petrified retention, of the audience. You know that they are being stirred to the profoundest depth that there are times when they want to rise and wave handkerchiefs and shout their approbation and times when tears are running down their face. One does not even hear any sound until the last note of the music has faded." He suggests that anyone seeking to become instantly famous should stand up and leave the house in the middle of an act. "Instant celebrity!" he says.

In *A Tramp Abroad*, Twain talks about an operatic evening in Germany.

> Another time we went to Mannheim and attended a shivaree—otherwise an opera—the one called Lohengrin. The banging and slamming and booming and crashing were something beyond belief. The racking and pitiless pain of it remains stored up in my memory alongside the memory of the time I had my teeth fixed . . . The recollection of that long, dragging, relentless season of suffering is indestructible. To have to endure it in silence, and sitting still, made it all the harder.

Mark Twain saw *Tannhäuser* several times, and *Walküre*, *Götterdämmerung*, *Meistersinger*, *Tristan and Isolde*, and *Lohengrin* at least once. He spent at least twenty-four hours in opera houses listening to Wagner's works. Curious for a man who claimed that he hated opera.

Helden Wagnerians 6

SPEIGHT JENKINS

Insisting on Clarity and Respect

Speight Jenkins is unique among general directors of opera companies. In addition to his general management responsibilities, he is a key member of the production team, participates in all concept meetings, and gets involved in staging decisions for every major production. He does this because of a dual priority. He is strongly committed to ensuring that a production does not depart too far from the wishes of the composer. It could be said that he demonstrates more respect for the creator of a work than most directors, let alone general directors. Stephen Wadsworth, director of the highly acclaimed Seattle *Ring* in 2001–13, says that what distinguishes Jenkins from many of the European producers is that "he cares about the audience."

Jenkins also feels a strong sense of duty to achieve the highest possible level of clarity. Insiders say that when he attends production meetings, he applies constant pressure to make certain that everything is clear and that everything that happens on the stage helps to tell the story.

Jenkins has been a Wagner enthusiast since he saw his first *Ring* at the New York Met at the age of eleven. But he heard it even earlier: "My earliest memories are of Pearl Harbor, having my tonsils removed, and *Walküre*. It touched me at the extremely young and impressionable age of seven." He has been building his knowledge of the composer ever since, and Seattle audiences are benefiting. When the curtain falls at the end of a *Ring* opera in most cities, the audience heads wearily back to their homes or hotels. Five or more hours in the opera house can be both physically and emotionally draining and audiences need to recuperate.

But not in Seattle. After the performance, a sizable part of the audience files into the adjoining four-hundred-seat Nesholm Family Lecture Hall to participate in a question-and-answer session on the production. All of the sessions are led by Jenkins, who has an encyclopedic knowledge both of Wagner's operas and of his life. After performances of *Die Walküre*, *Siegfried*, and *Götterdämmerung*, Jenkins answers dozens of questions on the stories, production minutiae, general interpretation, symbols, and technical staging details, including, "How did you make those rocks?"

It is hard to think of another general director anywhere in the world who would have the knowledge, courage, or stamina to handle questions on any and every aspect of a production just after it

• **Speight Jenkins, a unique general director. Photo by C. Yuen Lui, courtesy of Seattle Opera.**

has concluded. And how many would be prepared to do so into the early hours of the morning? It is a testimony to the popularity of this prominent Wagnerian and the feel-good reaction to the Seattle production that there was standing room only for late arrivals at these sessions. Even more amazing, he runs these post-performance question-and-answer sessions after every performance of every opera by every composer.

Jenkins' respect for Wagner's works has protected Seattle audiences from the distortions and pretentious nonsense that has blighted other productions around the world. Jenkins achieved this by choosing his directors and the other members of his production team with great care. "In 1994 I wrote to four directors and said that for the first seventy-five years we did *The Ring* the way Richard Wagner did it," he explained. "Then for the next twenty-five years we did it the Grecian way that Wieland Wagner pioneered. And since then we've modernized it and done it the Chéreau way, but what's next? I've seen all sorts of *Rings* . . . a Japanese *Ring*, an outer-space *Ring* . . . but what I hadn't seen is a *Ring* that emphasizes nature. And this is something very appropriate to the American northwest, so I asked these four how they would respond to the idea of nature, and Stephen Wadsworth gave the most interesting answer."

Wadsworth was appointed, and the Green *Ring* was first staged in 2001 and revived in 2005, 2009, and 2013. It has extraordinary realism, and its trees, rocks, running water, and cliffs look stunningly beautiful. "No one who has seen them has failed to come away amazed," says Jenkins.

The popularity of Seattle's Wagner productions has not been achieved by using big names to draw in the audience. With only a few exceptions—and onetime local resident Jane Eaglen was certainly one—Seattle has avoided the international megastars. This helps in tight budget situations but has not hurt the overall standards achieved: Seattle's productions have been enthusiastically acclaimed by critics from around the world. As early as 1982, the sometimes hard-to-please *New York Times* said that Seattle had become a serious rival to Bayreuth. I agree, and today Seattle Opera is the best Wagner opera company in the United States—probably the world. I have seen three different *Ring* productions in Seattle and have never winced, never become angry, and never accused any of the production team of desecration. I cannot say that of any other company.

> "My earliest memories are of Pearl Harbor, having my tonsils removed, and *Walküre*."
> **—Speight Jenkins**

In 2009 Speight Jenkins completed twenty-five years with Seattle Opera, and in his honor the mayor of Seattle declared April 25 Speight Jenkins Day in the city. The Wadsworth *Ring* returned to Seattle in August 2013, and Speight Jenkins will retire in September 2014. He will be replaced by Aidan Lang, who has held senior positions with New Zealand Opera, Glyndebourne, the Buxton Festival, and Opera Zuid.

If Speight Jenkins were British, he would be a racing certainty for a knighthood or better.

A Secret in the Attic

Captain Lew Besymenski, of the Russian army, knew something that most historians of music and World War II did not. Were it not for his daughter, his knowledge might have been lost forever following his death in July 2007.

More than fifty years earlier, the Russian officer was one of a party assigned to prepare an inventory of items that survived the destruction of Hitler's bunker and the Reich Chancellery above it. Once the party had completed their task, some of the Red Army soldiers took the opportunity to collect some souvenirs, and many of Besymenski's comrades smuggled out monogrammed silver and porcelain decorated with the Nazi swastika. The young captain, however, was more interested in some boxes that had been packed ready for shipment to the "Führer headquarters," Hitler's mountain retreat at Berchtesgaden. Most of the contents were electrical appliances and other domestic equipment that was of little interest, but Besymenski was intrigued to find that the boxes contained Adolf Hitler's collection of some one hundred gramophone records. Surprisingly, in addition to the inevitable Wagner, Beethoven, Brahms, and Mozart recordings, the collection included works by composers who had been derided as worthless by the loathsome Hitler. The captain realized that he had found something very special when he noticed that the collection included recordings featuring prominent Jewish artists such as the Russian baritone Fyodor Shalyapin, the Austrian pianist Artur Schnabel, and the Polish violinist Bronisław Huberman.

The Russian officer, himself a Jew, had exposed Hitler's secret: while he had prohibited his followers from listening to works by non-German composers, he had accumulated for his own pleasure a collection that included many of the forbidden works composed, played, or sung by Jewish artists. And judging by the scratches on the discs, he had played them frequently.

Captain Besymenski knew that this revelation would astonish World War II historians and music scholars, but he did not dare inform anyone of his discovery. After the war he became a respected historian and lecturer at the Moscow Military Academy, and he was afraid of the consequences of admitting his pilfering, even though many, even more senior, officers had accumulated truckloads of valuable paintings, jewelry, and other souvenirs. Marshal Georgy Zhukov, leader of the Russian troops at the battles of Stalingrad and Berlin, was believed to have taken more than fifty oil paintings and many other valuable items.

Besymenski took his more modest souvenirs home and hid them in his dacha outside Moscow. He played the records occasionally for his own pleasure and the entertainment of a small circle of trusted friends.

For many years he did not even tell his family; his daughter Alexandra was first shown the collection in 1991. Her father died in 2007, and she discovered the collection in the loft while she was looking for something else. She decided that the world needed to know that as well as being a detestable despot, Hitler was a cowardly hypocrite. "I think my father found it astonishing that millions of Jews and Russians had died because of the ideology of Hitler, and here he was all the time enjoying their art," she told *Der Spiegel*. While Hitler was listening to the recording of the Jewish violinist, Huberman was living in exile, having fled from Vienna a year before the Anschluss spread German Jews' misery to the Austrians.

Now Wagner scholars are hoping that Hitler's priceless collection of original Wagner manuscripts might also have been pilfered from the chancellery and that, like the records, they will show up some day. The collection included the original scores of *Die Feen*, *Das Liebesverbot*, and *Rienzi*, as well as other orchestral sketches.

The Russian officer who took the records has one other claim to a place in the history books. He claimed that he was present at the autopsy on the charred remains of Hitler's body and was able to confirm what every British schoolboy had sung about for years: Adolf Hitler had only one testicle.

> “Here he was all the time enjoying their art.”
> **—Alexandra Besymenski, on Hitler’s owning well-worn records by Jewish and Russian artists he had banned**

The Lesser Orchestral Works

Wagner is best known for his operatic works, particularly the ten works starting with *The Flying Dutchman* and ending with *Parsifal*. “What a pity that Wagner did not compose more purely orchestral music,” is a frequent comment from newcomers to Wagner. In fact, Wagner did compose a great deal of other music. The problem is that, with only one major exception, it was not of the same quality as the operas, and most of these works are rarely played today. In his indispensable book *The Wagner Compendium*, the renowned Wagner scholar Barry Millington provides details of all of Wagner’s known compositions, including many that have been lost or destroyed. The Millington list comprises:

- 23 orchestral works, plus information on fragments and uncompleted works
- 13 choral works
- 3 chamber works
- 6 works for solo voice and orchestra
- 17 works for solo voice and piano
- 15 piano works

The Symphony in C

Wagner started work on his Symphony in C Major when he was only eighteen. It took him only six weeks in the early summer of 1832, or so he claimed in a letter to a friend. It was first performed in Prague in November 1832, and after a performance in Leipzig the following year Wagner gave the manuscript to Mendelssohn and asked him to “take it under his care.” Mendelssohn did not respond, and the manuscript disappeared.

Years later Wagner conceived the idea of establishing a Wagner museum for his son, Siegfried, and he wanted the manuscript of his symphony to be included in the collection. He remembered that he had not sent the separate orchestral parts to Mendelssohn and, wondering whether they still existed, asked his friend Wilhelm Tappert to use his detective skills to locate the missing parts. Tappert started by asking Mendelssohn’s heirs if they had any knowledge of the manuscript and contacted possible leads in Magdeburg, Riga, and Dresden. Then, in November 1877, the royal librarian at Dresden located something that Wagner had left behind when he fled the city. A box left with the singer Josef Tichatschek contained manuscripts of several early overtures and the violin part of the symphony. After further searches, all of the parts except those for the two trombones were located. Tappert sent the material to Bayreuth, where, according to Henry T. Finck, in *Wagner and His Works*, “Cosima surprised and delighted her husband by playing to him the motif of one of the movements; he jumped up excitedly, and exclaimed, ‘My old symphony—that is it!’”

Wagner instructed his assistant Anton Seidl to combine the separate parts into a score and to add the two missing trombone parts. The resurrected symphony was then lodged in the Siegfried archives. Years later in Venice, just weeks before his death, Wagner organized a private performance of the symphony as a surprise for Cosima's birthday. The symphony lasts approximately forty-five minutes and was written for a large orchestra. Shortly after Wagner's death, an agent paid the family $12,000 for the performance rights for just one year.

It is believed that a May 1833 report on the Leipzig performance was the first reference to Wagner in a British publication. According to American writer Anne Dzamba Sessa, the *Harmonicum*, an obscure, long-defunct publication, said that the performance had been applauded. It seems likely that the Leipzig audience were being polite in approving the work of the twenty-year-old. The unexceptional symphony has not been applauded much since then, for the simple reason that it has been rarely performed.

Although Wagner talked about composing further symphonic works, he never did so. Toward the end of his life he said: "Perhaps when *Parsifal* is finished, I shall write nine symphonies. The Ninth with choruses."

At various times, both Neville Cardus and Ernest Newman speculated wistfully on what might have been. If only he had lived later—would he not have dispensed with the scaffolding of words and plot? Perhaps the *Siegfried Idyll* was a portent of what might have been.

Rule Britannia

Writing of Wagner's first visit to London in 1840, the Reverend Hugh Haweis said:

> While here he playfully seized the musical motif of the English people. It lay, he said, in the five consecutive ascending notes (after the first three) of Rule Britannia; there was expressed the whole breadth and downright bluff "go" of the British nation. He threw Rule Britannia into an overture, and sent it by post to Sir George Smart, then omnipotent musical professor in London; but the postage being insufficient, the MS was not taken in, and at this moment is probably lying in some dim archive of the Post Office, left till called for.
>
> Hugh Haweis, *My Musical Memories*, 1884

The Honorable Mary Burrell was an admirer of Wagner who planned to publish the definitive story of his life and works and traveled Europe buying up Wagnerian papers and memorabilia. After she died in 1898 her extensive collection was found to include a bundle of orchestral parts, and the music critic of the *Times*, J. A. Fuller-Maitland, was invited to examine them. When the sheets of music were laid out on a table it was immediately clear that they were parts of the lost *Rule Britannia* overture. A full score was prepared, and the work was performed.

Rule Britannia was not one of Wagner's finest works. Another critic said many years later that it might have been better if the unremarkable overture had remained lost.

The Love Feast of the Apostles

Shortly after taking up his appointment as Royal Conductor of the Dresden Opera in January 1843, Wagner accepted the leadership of the Dresden Liedertafel, a local choral society. The society was scheduled to participate in a festival with several other choirs in the summer, and Wagner agreed to compose something for combined male voice choirs and orchestra. The result was *Das Liebesmahl der Apostel* (*The Love Feast of the Apostles*).

The work lasts about thirty-three minutes, with the choirs singing unaccompanied for the first thirty minutes or so. When the orchestra appears, there are some hints of *Tannhäuser* and *Lohengrin*. It must have been rather crowded in the Dresden Frauenkirche: there were twelve hundred singers and an orchestra of one hundred.

Wagner, who was never slow to blow his own trumpet, did not even sound the tin whistle for this choral work. "I do not mind including it in the list of my uninspired compositions," he said.

Write a Centennial March for Us, Please?

In 1875, after Wagner had declined several offers to conduct in the United States, he accepted an invitation to write a march for the centennial celebrations the following year. Theodore Thomas had selected several American composers for the choral works and suggested that Wagner be commissioned to write an instrumental piece. The Women's Centennial Organization agreed to raise the funds, and Wagner requested $5,000 for the US rights only. In justifying his fee, Wagner mentioned that "Mr. Verdi has received from his publisher about half a million francs for the unconditional rights to the publication and performance of his *Requiem*." The full title of Wagner's contribution to the festivities was inscribed "Grand Festival March for the Opening of the Centennial, Commemorative of the Declaration of Independence of the United States of America. Composed and dedicated to the Women's Centennial Committees by Richard Wagner."

At the head of the score he wrote a couple of lines from Goethe:

> Nur der verdient sich Freiheit wie das Leben,
> der täglich sie erobern muss.
> [He only earns the right to freedom and to life
> Who daily is compelled to conquer them.]

Unfortunately, the first group to examine the score mistranslated the German word *erobern*—to conquer. Wagner was greatly amused when he heard that the second part of Goethe's line had been translated as "Who daily is compelled to rob them."

The march was first played in Philadelphia on May 10 by an orchestra of 150 and was enthusiastically applauded. However, it seems Wagner himself was not so keen on it. When it was played in London the following year, he remarked: "Unless the subject absorbs me completely, I cannot produce twenty bars worth listening to." While he was working on the composition, Cosima noted in her diary, "R still working . . . but he can think of nothing but the 5000 dollars he has demanded and perhaps will not get."

She was wrong. Henry T. Finck wrote in the notes for a Wagner festival in 1884: "The stipulated price was five thousand dollars; but through the efforts of his American friends he received twice that sum at a time when he was very much in need of money for his first Bayreuth festival." Finck also reported that when Wagner heard about the success of the march in America, he said, "Do you know what is the best thing about the march? The money I got for it."

The *Centennial March* was one of the weakest compositions of Wagner's adult life. Bernard Shaw wrote in May 1893: "When he replenished his exchequer by the *Centennial March*, he came rather nearer disgracing himself than Beethoven did in the *Battle of Vittoria*; and that is saying a good deal. Wagner must have known that his march was undistinguished and needed something to spice it up. His instructions with the score suggested that the 'long solemn pauses' could be augmented by a salute of guns and rifles at some distance."

Helden Wagnerians 7

BERNARD LEVIN

Finding Excuses to Mention Wagner

Bernard Levin was a British writer and critic of huge talent. He wrote at various times for the *Daily Mail*, the *Daily Express*, the *Spectator*, and the *Observer*. Perhaps he will be remembered mainly for his columns and criticisms published in the *Times* from 1971 until 1997. His unflinching style made him unpopular with politicians, but this contrasted with his popularity among operagoers, particularly Wagnerians. He was a true eccentric and frequently turned up at the opera wearing a silk-lined cloak.

His criticisms were usually incisive and always entertaining. When he was displeased with a performance or a production, he made his point with a gentle but acerbic wit that was frequently more devastating than the broadsides delivered by some of his less subtle colleagues. His lack of reverence made him an ideal candidate to join the team of the groundbreaking satirical revue *That Was the Week That Was* in the early 1960s, along with David Frost and others.

Levin's passion for Wagner's music was equaled only by his dislike of the man. Yet he recognized the benefits of Wagner's selfish perseverance. In the introduction to his 1988 book *All Things Considered*, he wrote, "I was repelled at the lengths, and depths, to which he would go, and the rebuffs, setbacks and failures he was willing to endure, in order to give an ungrateful world the fruits of his genius."

Levin's frequent mention of Wagner in his columns became something of a standing joke. Even in his travel books, he missed no opportunity to include some Wagnerian information. His 1987 book *To the End of the Rhine* presented several opportunities: "The Nibelungenlied takes place on its waters and its banks, and Wagner set to music not only the legend but the river itself; the *Rheingold* prelude is one of the most lifelike musical depictions of a tangible scene ever written and a blind man who had never heard of the composer, or for that matter the Rhine, could be in no doubt that he was listening to the flowing of a mighty river."

• **Bernard Levin. Sketch by David Mitchell.**

Bernard Levin was made a Commander of the British Empire in 1990 for his services to journalism. He was equally appreciated by his fellow writers. The novelist Philip Toynbee said, "There must surely be very few of his readers who would deny that he is the most remarkable journalist of our time."

Fortunately, the anthologies of his best columns from the *Times* are available so that Wagnerians can enjoy Bernard Levin's considerable wit and wisdom. I only met him once. We had engaged him to address an executive conference in Florida on the UK political scene in the 1970s. Between discussions on his role I suggested that we must find a few minutes to talk about Wagner. His face lit up and he said, "Yes, yes. What a good idea." Sadly, business got in the way, and the discussion never happened before he had to fly back to the United Kingdom.

The suspicion of some non-Wagnerian *Times* readers that Levin was just a little bit crazy might have been confirmed if they knew that he once won a bet by standing on a table in a small restaurant in London's Little Venice and singing the whole of the *Tannhäuser* overture as a duet with a friend. The lengthy interruption to the peacefulness of the small restaurant was made worse by the fact that, by his own admission, Levin's singing voice was abominable. Yet he claimed that this could sometimes be useful. "I once scared off a huge Alsatian [German shepherd] . . . by bawling Siegfried's Forging Song in its horrible face." It worked, and German shepherd owners might want to pass on the news to their postman.

Bernard Levin died on August 7, 2004, aged seventy-five, after a long struggle with Alzheimer's. His writings on Wagner will continue to delight fellow enthusiasts for years to come. One of my personal favorites covered the difficulty of finding Wagnerian singers.

Several other extracts from Bernard Levin's writing are included elsewhere in this book by kind permission of Mike Shaw, the copyright owner.

Levin once won a bet by standing on a table in a small restaurant and singing the whole of the *Tannhäuser* overture as a duet with a friend.

For and Against

Speaking about *Tristan and Isolde*: the giant structure fills me time and time again with astonishment and awe, and I still cannot quite comprehend that it was conceived and written by a human being. I consider the second act, in its wealth of musical invention, in tenderness and sensuality of musical expression and its inspired orchestration, to be one of the finest creations that ever issued from a human mind. This second act is wonderful . . . wonderful . . . quite wonderful.

Giuseppe Verdi

I once told Wagner that I was the best Wagnerian of our time.

Johannes Brahms

It has been said of Liszt that Wagner was indebted to him for much besides money—including sympathy and a wife. The two men were friends, if somewhat tempestuously on Wagner's part, and Wagner came to rely on Liszt as mentor and guide. Musically they influenced each other considerably. Wagner, by far the most popular composer, once wrote to Liszt to say that he had unconsciously used a theme of his. Liszt replied, "Now at least it will be heard."

Clifton Fadiman, *Little Brown Book of Anecdotes*, 1985

I knew *Parsifal* . . . from the score and was influenced by it as late as 1908—the slow section of my *Scherzo fantastique* . . . derives from the Good Friday music.

Igor Stravinsky, *Expositions and Developments*, 1981

The last act of *Götterdämmerung* . . . appears, in its almost supernatural grandeur, like the chain of the Alps seen from the summit of Mont Blanc.
—Camille Saint-Saëns

Of the wonderwork, *The Nibelung's Ring*, I have lately heard more than twenty rehearsals at Bayreuth. It overtops and commands our whole art-epoch as Mont Blanc does our other mountains.
—Franz Liszt, in a letter to a friend

> This is the most extraordinary work of the whole of our history of culture—doubly extraordinary because it is miles ahead of our time
>
> Edvard Grieg, after seeing *The Ring* at Bayreuth in 1886

> Wagner has some lovely moments but some terrible quarters of an hour.
>
> Gioachino Rossini

Speaking of Wagner's orchestrations:

> The glowing colors of *Parsifal* seem to be illuminated from behind.
>
> Claude Debussy

And on Wagner's use of leitmotifs:

> A play in which every character presents his visiting card every time he enters the room.
>
> Claude Debussy

Rossini was no more an admirer of Wagner than were other Parisians of his day. A friend who entered his study found him studying the score of *Tristan and Isolde* and asked him what he thought of it.

> "Ah," said the master, "It is a beautiful work! I never expected to find such grace of expression, such power of invention in the music of the reformer of our old dramatic operas, the scores of Mozart, Gluck, Cimarosa, Weber, Mercadante, Meyerbeer—and my own."
>
> His visitor, coming closer, was dumbfounded when he observed that Rossini was reading Wagner's score wrong side up.
>
> Whereupon, inverting the score, Rossini said after a glance, "Alas, now I cannot make head nor tail of it!"
>
> Leopold Auer in his autobiography, *My Long Life in Music*, 1924

And the following is also attributed to Rossini.

> "Do you know what Wagner's music sounds like?" he asked me one day. Opening the piano and seating himself heavily on the keys, he exclaimed, "There! That's the music of the future."
>
> Louise Héritte-Viardot, *Memories and Adventures*, 1913

Wagner on Other Composers

Wagner rarely had a kind word for composers other than Bach, Beethoven, Mozart, and occasionally Bruckner, Haydn, and Weber. Wagner hung engravings of four composers in his study in Tribschen. The engravings, in their original frames, still hang in the house that is now the Richard Wagner Museum. The four composers are Beethoven, Mozart, Christoph Willibald Gluck, and Haydn. They all died before Wagner was born (except for Beethoven, who died in 1827, when Wagner was only fourteen). Wagner's compliments to dead composers and scurrilous castigation of living ones contradicted something he wrote in *Opera and Drama* in 1851: "In the survey of our operatic history, there is something most painful about being only able to speak good of the dead, and being forced to pursue the living with remorseless bitterness!"

- **Beethoven.** Wagner's greatest idol. When he was still a young man, he knew Beethoven's quartets and sonatas by heart and conducted a remarkable performance of the Ninth Symphony in Dresden at a time when the work was out of favor.
- **Haydn**. Speaking to Anton Seidl about the Andante in Haydn's Symphony no. 94 in G Major, he remarked, "One of the loveliest things ever written and how wonderful it sounds."
- **Mozart.** Of *The Magic Flute*, Wagner said, "What celestial magic prevails in this work from the most popular melody to the most sublime hymn!" A review of a concert that included Mozart's Symphony no. 40 in G Minor included the statement, "There is not much of it." The dismissive remark made Wagner indignant. He said of the themes of the first and second movement that "they should be set in diamonds." But Wagner then put down his other idol by adding that Beethoven had lived on those themes in his early works. He could hurt with faint praise too. He once said of Beethoven's Eighth Symphony, "One has to be in the right mood."

  "Mozart died when he approached the secret [of music]," said Wagner. "Beethoven was the first to enter it." Earlier, while living in Paris, he wrote about an imaginary German musician who dies a lonely death with this confession of faith on his lips: "I believe in God, Mozart, and Beethoven!"
- **Chopin.** "A composer for the right hand."
- **Saint-Saëns.** Wagner became acquainted with Camille Saint-Saëns during his stay in Paris in 1860. Wagner writes in his autobiography *Mein Leben* about the then twenty-five-year-old Saint-Saëns: "With an unparalleled sureness and rapidity of glance with regard to even the most complicated orchestral score, this young man combined a not less marvelous memory. He was not only able to play my scores, including *Tristan*, by heart, but could also reproduce their several parts, whether they were leading or minor themes. And this he did with such precision that one might easily have thought that he had the actual music before his eyes."
- **Mendelssohn.** Although Wagner had little positive to say about Mendelssohn's works, he was enthusiastic about the *Hebrides Overture*, calling it "one of the most beautiful pieces we possess. Wonderful imagination and delicate feeling are here presented with consummate art. Note the extraordinary beauty of the passage where the oboes rise above the other instruments with a plaintive wail, like sea winds over the sea."
- **Schumann.** Wagner said that he could not discern a single melody in the works of Schumann and added, "When he does produce a theme, it is a Beethoven one. How there can be Schumann devotees, I cannot imagine." He once dismissed the unfortunate German composer as "a very fragile talent." On another occasion he observed, "Since all present-day composers are Schumannians, Beethoven lived in vain."
- **Gounod.** Wagner described Gounod's *Faust* as "music for sluts."
- **Brahms.** The love-hate relationship between

Music for sluts."
—Richard Wagner, on Gounod's opera *Faust*

> Wagner and Brahms is well-known, yet both made positive comments about the other. Later they appeared to change their minds.

But Wagner did not have a monopoly on witty or caustic comment. The following were collected by the Grinning Planet Web site:

> Beethoven always sounds to me like the upsetting of a bag of nails, with here and there an also dropped hammer.
>
> John Ruskin

> Beethoven's last quartets were written by a deaf man and should only be listened to by a deaf man.
>
> Thomas Beecham

> Too many pieces of music finish too long after the end.
>
> Igor Stravinsky

> If anyone has conducted a Beethoven performance, and then doesn't have to go to an osteopath, then there's something wrong.
>
> Simon Rattle

> Opera is when a guy gets stabbed in the back and, instead of bleeding, sings.
>
> Ed Gardner

> A good composer is slowly discovered and a bad composer is slowly found out.
>
> Ernest Newman

> Nietzsche is worse than shocking, he is simply awful: his epigrams are written with phosphorus on brimstone . . .
>
> Never was there a deafer, blinder, socially and politically inepter academician . . .
>
> And what can you say to a man who, after pitting his philosophy against Wagner's with refreshing ingenuity and force, proceeds to hold up as the masterpiece of modern dramatic music, blazing with the merits which the Wagnerian music dramas lack—guess what! *Don Giovanni*, perhaps, or *Orfeo*, or *Fidelio*? Not at all: *Carmen*, no less. Yes, as I live by bread, as I made that bread for many a year by listening to music, Georges Bizet's *Carmen*.
>
> Bernard Shaw, *Saturday Review*, January 1895–May 1898

Two Operatic Geniuses on Parallel Tracks

Wagner and Giuseppe Verdi were both born in 1813, and both had their first major successes in 1841 with their third operas, Wagner with *Rienzi* and Verdi with *Nabucco*.

In 1870 Verdi fell out with his longtime friend the conductor Angelo Mariani, and, according to some reports, Wagner was the unwitting cause of the schism. Mariani had agreed to conduct *Aida* in Cairo but withdrew after losing a battle with Verdi for the affections of the soprano Teresa Stolz. In an act of revenge, Mariani dropped his plan to conduct *Aida* and instead conducted the Italian premiere of *Lohengrin* in Bologna, with Verdi in the audience. It was a sensational success, and Wagner sent his portrait to Mariani with the inscription "Eviva Mariani!!!" (Long live Mariani!). Another version of this story suggests that Mariani withdrew his promise to conduct *Aida* because he did not feel well enough to travel to Egypt. Verdi did not believe him, and the friends fell out after an argument in the spring of 1871. It may be that the unfortunate Mariani had been telling the truth, because he died of cancer two years later.

Wagner or Verdi? Paul Henry Lang wrote in *The Experience of Opera*: "One group of partisans maintains that Wagner's works represent the summit of opera and that Verdi's, with the exception of the last operas, are little more than hurdy-gurdy music. The other party sees in Verdi the culmination of almost three centuries of operatic history, allowing Wagner musical merits but deploring his operatic ideal."

"Outside the theatre," said Neville Cardus, Verdi's music "is only half-alive; imagine a concert of Verdi's numbers given in the manner of a Wagner program."

Crazy for Wagner

"He Keeps Me Young"

In August 2006 Verna Parino traveled alone from San Francisco to Munich. At the end of the ten-hour flight, suffering from jet lag thanks to a nine-hour time difference, Verna headed for the car rental desks. She rented a large Mercedes and set off on the long drive to Bayreuth, where she had tickets for *The Ring* and three other operas in Bayreuth's Festspielhaus.

So what? Fans from all over the world make long journeys to attend the annual Festival. The difference here is that Verna Parino of San Francisco was ninety years old at the time, and she made the journey alone, including the 150-mile (240 km) drive.

Since then this amazing lady has witnessed *The Ring* several more times and by August 2012 the now ninety-five-year-old had seen Wagner's masterpiece sixty-eight times in thirty-four cities and nineteen countries. When word got out that Verna had booked a ticket to see *The Ring* in Shanghai in September 2010, one of China's oldest and largest evening newspapers splashed the story under the headline "93-Year-Old Lady Longing for 58th Cycle of *The Ring* in Shanghai." Unlike most companies, the Shanghai group staged *The Ring* on four consecutive days, so that experience was more tiring than the usual *Ring*, with two rest days.

• Verna Parino enters the Festspielhaus with the essential cushion.

Verna says that she started loving Wagner when she was at high school and since then has not counted the performances of the composer's other operas that she has attended. Her husband, Richard, who died in 1967, was born to Italian parents and therefore, quite naturally, was a Verdi enthusiast. Fortunately, the Verdi and Wagner enthusiasts managed to live together without friction.

She is not keen on ultramodern Wagner productions but enjoys "new interpretations that make me appreciate Wagner even more." She says that "*The Ring* is about the world around us and when we look inside ourselves, it is all there."

When she saw a much-criticized *Ring* in Los Angeles in June 2010, she was not only disapproving, she was angry. She has been a regular contributor of reviews for the magazine of the Finnish Wagner Society and started to write about what she had experienced in Los Angeles. "However, I set it aside because I did not want to be so negative. Then I read that the L.A. production had lost almost $6,000,000, so I decided I should explain why that was." The article she submitted to Helsinki began, "When a 'nice-little-old-lady,' aged 93, has to stop at a nearby sports bar for a double cognac and loud rock music to recover from a performance of *Das Rheingold*, you know something is wrong."

A founding member and previous president of the Wagner Society of Northern California, Verna has also been active in the San Francisco Opera Guild and Opera Guilds International (now renamed Opera Volunteers International) and has been recognized by the organizations for her services to their specific aims and opera in general.

Back at that Bayreuth visit in August 2006, it was close to eleven o'clock at night before Verna left the Festspielhaus after *Götterdämmerung*. Her wake-up call came at four o'clock the next morning, and she soon climbed into the rented Mercedes and headed back to Munich to catch her flight home. Did she have any problems on the drive back? "Not really, but I would have preferred an automatic car," she said. "The auto rental company gave me a stick-shift model, and I'm not used to that!"

Verna's future plans include the Seattle *Ring* and a trip to Australia. She has made a nonrefundable deposit on *Ring* tickets and hotel tickets for the 2013 Melbourne *Ring*, during which time she will be celebrating her ninety-seventh birthday.

Does Wagner help keep you young? I asked. Her face lit up. "Sure he does—just look at me!" It is no surprise that some of her Wagnerian friends call Verna Parino Superwoman.

The Wagnerian Cop

The fictional Inspector Morse was a Wagner enthusiast and frequently berated the hapless Sergeant Lewis for failing to appreciate the music of the Bayreuth magician. Colin Dexter set his Morse stories in Oxford, but little did he know that in the same university city was a police sergeant who did not need to be persuaded to listen to Wagner.

Sergeant Peter West was a lifelong Wagnerian and not afraid to tell anybody who would listen. Among his duties was communicating from the police station to the radios carried by officers on the beat in the town. One of the regular messages was to advise that their shift was over and that they should return to the station. Most duty sergeants simply sent a voice message, but Sergeant West recalled his men by playing a recording of Siegfried's horn call.

One night, officers on patrol had been asked to keep an eye open for a woman who had wandered away from a local mental hospital. A young policeman spotted a woman walking alone, stopped her and started asking questions. It soon became clear that she was not the missing patient, but by then she had become irritated about the questioning, so the officer started to explain.

Just then, Siegfried's horn call sounded from the radio strapped to the officer's shoulder. "What on earth was that?" the startled woman asked. The officer explained about his quirky, Wagner-loving sergeant who used Siegfried's horn call as a signal. "And you thought I was the crazy one," the young woman exclaimed before walking off.

I'm a Ringhead

Perhaps in an attempt to show that not all Wagnerians take themselves too seriously, *Ring* enthusiasts sometimes adopt irreverent labels. One enterprising enthusiast in Seattle for *The Ring* few years ago sold buttons reading "I'm a Ringhead." The idea was picked up by the *Los Angeles Times* a few years later when Louise Roug wrote that followers of the Grateful Dead are known as Deadheads, fans of Plácido Domingo are known as Domingan Nuns, and aficionados of Richard Wagner are known as Ringheads.

In Australia, according to Leona Geeves of Sydney, enthusiasts are known as Wagneroos. "Terrence, another Wagneroo," she was heard to call out during a visit to Orange County, California, for a *Ring* cycle in October 2006.

No special qualifications have been established to qualify as a bona fide Ringhead or Wagneroo, but most belong to one of the 140 Wagner Societies and have attended multiple *Ring* cycles. Many devotees have spent a significant part of their lives and a sizable chunk of their personal wealth traveling the world to see yet another *Ring*. One candidate for king of the Ringheads was Sherwin Sloan, onetime president of the Wagner Society of Southern California. The *Ring* he attended in Orange County was his first in southern California, but only because it was the first time the full cycle had been staged there. It was special for another reason: it was his eightieth *Ring*. Sloan, a retired ophthalmologist, died in June 2010. His record will be hard to beat because he ran a company called Performing Arts Tours, so attending *Ring* performances was part of his job. Tough work, but . . .

The Curious Tale of the Fireman's Tribute

Richard and Cosima were taking a walk in Lucerne one summer evening in 1869 when they came upon the scene of a serious house fire. They stood for some time watching the efforts of the local firefighters to get the blaze under control. Wagner was so impressed by their bravery and expertise that when he returned to Tribschen, he dashed off a short musical passage in their honor.

The manuscript survived, but more than a hundred years later it was a copy of the brief work that was displayed in Wagner's Lucerne home, Tribschen, now the Richard Wagner Museum. A caption explained that a copy was on display because the original had been stolen some years earlier.

When Peter West (yes, the same Wagnerian cop) read about this in the Tribschen visitors' guide, loud bells began to ring in his head. Peter takes up the story:

> I had a feeling that I had been present at a Sotheby's sale in London some twelve years earlier (one of the largest Wagner auction sales ever held) and that a manuscript of that description had been sold under my very nose. I dropped everything and made a frantic search through my papers and found the catalogue that quickly confirmed my belief. The original of the *Fireman's Tribute* had sold for £5,000—I had even marked the exact selling price in the margin!
>
> I sat down that evening and composed a long letter regarding my findings, which I sent to Tribschen, suggesting that if they contacted Sotheby's or the Metropolitan police in London, there'd be a sporting chance they could trace the stolen item, maybe even the thief.
>
> I expected a return call from the museum straight away, but nothing was forthcoming. A couple of weeks passed and there was not a word from anyone. I was annoyed about the lack of response—then surmised that they may have thought that my letter

was a hoax. I was going to write again or phone, but because of one thing another, I never actually got around to doing anything. Eventually I forgot all about it.

Three years later I was at Sotheby's "out of town" auction room in Sussex. The person I needed to see was engaged with another client so I waited around in reception and with nothing better to do idly browsed some old catalogues that were on the table in the waiting room. I picked up a Books and Musical Manuscripts catalogue—which referred to a sale at Sotheby's London the previous year, and automatically turned to the Wagner section—as one would.

My jaw hit the floor, for there, right in front of me, was the same item. The original of the *Wahrspruch für die Luzerner Feuerweh* was listed. It appeared that the manuscript had been sold twice in the same saleroom in fifteen years. I could not believe what I was reading—but yes, there it was in all its glory. That evening I wrote another letter to Tribschen, telling them of my new find and berating them for ignoring my earlier letter.

A few days later I received a telephone call from the mayor of Lucerne. "Mr. West," he said, "No wonder there was no reply to your first letter. You had inadvertently written to the thief."

Yes, the villain was the curator of the Wagner Museum, who had long since been dismissed from his post. And the outcome? Well, of course you never get to hear all the details, but the officer at Interpol who dealt with it told me they had recovered the manuscript intact.

Peter West, speaking in 2007 ■

Act Three

The Dysfunctional Wagner Family

> It is true that almost all of the family of Richard Wagner, from his birth (probably illegitimate—the argument continues) to the youngest member of the clan, are, and always have been, such as to bring a shudder through any ordinary person's body. As if that were not sufficient, they are always quarrelling—to such an extent that it is a miracle that nobody in that gang has yet been murdered. (They make up for it with regular and frequent banishments.) But if you knew nothing at all of that, and just went into an opera house with a programme, a translation and a subtitle, you would never guess either that the Wagners are awful, or that wonderful music was written by an awful man.
>
> Bernard Levin, the *Times*, 1996

The story of the dysfunctional Wagner family is more extreme than anything Wagner ever wrote. "It is tempting to read the family saga as a Wagnerian myth, with a dash of Ibsen," says the *Telegraph*'s Ian Hewett. "Throw in the jealousies, nastiness, backbiting, and skulduggery of the television series *Dynasty*," and the plot would still fall short of the saga that started with Wagner's death in 1883 and continues to this day. Most notable have been the squabbles over the leadership of the family firm. Cosima inherited the empire but for many years insisted that everything continue to be done as the Meister had done it, right down the minutiae of stage designs and direction. Some scholars believe that her rejection of change and any form of updating jeopardized the future of the institution she was so intent on preserving. She is nevertheless credited with managing Bayreuth through a series of financial and other crises.

> "She is the only Nazi left in Germany."
>
> **—Heinrich Mann, on Winifred Wagner, after World War II**

Cosima retired in 1906 and at first was very much a back-seat driver after Wagner's only son, Siegfried, took over management of the Bayreuth machine. Cosima died in April 1930, and Siegfried survived her only by a few months. After his death in August 1930, the reins were taken up by his widow, the English-born Winifred Williams. Had it not been for her adoration of Hitler, the Wagner name might have escaped close association with the Nazi regime. But Winifred not only admitted Adolf Hitler to her family, she continued to worship him until her death in 1980. She told a writer in a 1975 interview that "if Hitler were to come in the door today, I would be as happy and glad to see him and have him here as I always was." "She is the only Nazi left in Germany," said the writer Heinrich Mann after the war.

On the other hand, but for Winifred's close relationship with the Führer it is likely that Bayreuth would have gone broke during the war. And the Austrian historian Bridget Nauman uncovered a great deal of evidence that Winifred used her influence to save the lives of many Jews.

Some of this came out at her denazification trial, but she still had to pay a heavy price for her support of the monster her family befriended. After Wieland and Wolfgang took over management, once the war was over, she was banned from entering the Festspielhaus. Wolfgang looked after the administration, and Wieland revolutionized operatic production. In the forty-four years after

Wieland's premature death in 1966, the autocratic Wolfgang, who died in 2010, ruled Bayreuth. When he was born, in 1919, his grandfather had been dead for thirty-six years. His only contact with the thinking of Richard was therefore gained through his grandmother.

Bayreuth continues to be one of the most successful music festivals in the world, as well as the oldest. Paradoxically, while it becomes progressively more difficult to procure tickets for the summer music dramas, many believe that standards have slipped, and that Bayreuth is no longer setting the standard. Since the landmark 1976 production by Patrice Chéreau, new productions of *The Ring* have been greeted by negative comment by the critics and sometimes fierce hostility by audiences. Toward the end of the last decade, pressure began to build for a changing of the guard.

Wagner vs. Wagner vs. Wagner

Control of the Bayreuth Festival and ownership of the Festspielhaus was transferred from the family to the Richard Wagner Foundation in 1973. At their meeting in March 2001, its twenty-four-member board suggested that it was time for Wolfgang to retire. They named Wolfgang's daughter Eva Wagner-Pasquier as the new head, but Wolfgang had other ideas. He had already suggested that his wife, Gudrun, should succeed him and thumbed his nose at the board. He reminded them that he had a contract for life and effectively told the board that if they did not accept his nominee, he would continue indefinitely. For a while, the board threatened to get tough. The Bavarian culture minister, Hans Zehetmair, was quoted in the *New York Times* as having said, "If he doesn't do anything, we are required to appoint an emergency director." But Wolfgang dug in his heels and got on with managing the Festival.

Eva Wagner-Pasquier was associate director of the Aix-en-Provence Festival in France, and her career history included New York's Metropolitan Opera and a brief spell at Covent Garden. Jeremy Isaacs, who headed the Royal Opera House at the time, said in his memoirs that Eva "is the best qualified Wagner to succeed her father Wolfgang but . . . Gudrun will freeze her out."

A few months after the board named Eva to succeed Wolfgang, she said that she no longer wanted the job. Her lawyer admitted that they had grossly underestimated her father's hardheadedness.

Nike (then sixty-two), the musicologist daughter of Wieland Wagner and artistic director of the Kunstfest Weimar Arts Festival, then declared herself a candidate, but Wolfgang again gave a thumbs-down. He had another candidate in mind, and in 2004 Wolfgang appointed his daughter Katharina to produce the 2007 Bayreuth production of *Die Meistersinger*, making her the first woman to direct at the Festspielhaus since her great-grandmother, Cosima. Her production was greeted by howls of protest, and the critics were not impressed. A caricature of Richard Wagner was seen dancing in his underpants, there were topless dancers, and the Meistersingers themselves strutted around the stage with massive penises. This was too much for the traditionalists and even offended those who enjoyed adventurous productions. The *BBC Music Magazine* review appeared under the headline "Meister Clanger."

Nike did not miss an opportunity to score points over her cousin and dismissed Katharina's production as "old wine in a new wineskin." She also had a go at Uncle Wolfgang: "Both the institution of Bayreuth and its director are going senile." The younger half sister then mounted a PR offensive and issued glamorous pictures of her that appear to have backfired.

• **Winifred and Siegfried Wagner in the main square of Bayreuth, circa 1916.**

The tabloids immediately dubbed Katharina the "Bayreuth Barbie" and "Bayreuth Hilton."

After Wolfgang's death the two half sisters, Katharina and Eva, were appointed joint administrators of the Festival, and for a while life on the Green Hill settled down. But the two women have plenty of opponents, and it seems likely that this soap opera will run on and on.

Winifred and Friedelind

In 1940 Wagner's granddaughter Friedelind was concerned about what was happening in Germany and disapproved of her mother's support for Hitler. She left the country to live in Switzerland, and Hitler insisted that the British-born Winifred should follow to persuade her errant daughter to return. Friedelind refused, and her furious mother threatened that if she worked against the Nazi interests, she would be "destroyed and exterminated." Brigitte Hamann, author of the excellent biography of Winifred, challenges the popularly accepted version of this story. She says that it appears to be untrue that the encounter ended in conflict, because a letter exists in which Friedelind thanked her mother for "coming all that way" and added, "But it was worth it, wasn't it?"

• **Siegfried as seen by Olaf Gulbranson, date unknown.**

Despite this note of warmth, Friedelind refused to return to Germany and eventually settled in the United States, where she promoted the Allied cause. She became a US citizen in June 1947.

The Disadvantage of a Famous Father

When Felix, the youngest son of Robert and

[Winifred's] relations with Fidi, twenty-eight years her senior, gradually declined into a marriage of convenience. Once the family bloodline had been secured, the spouses went their separate ways. The husband returned to his bachelor existence and cultivated his homosexual friendships. One of his lovers was an Englishman, Clement Harris, who boasted that he had shared a bed with Oscar Wilde.
—Guido Knopp, *Hitler's Women*, 2001

The next question to ask is whether Siegfried is lucky or unlucky in having Richard . . . for his father. On the one hand, had he not been the son of his father there would have been a far greater difficulty over the production of his opera at the chief houses of Germany than there has been; on the other hand, once produced, it is likely that the work has been subjected to a censorship and a sifting far more severe and searching than would have been the case if the young composer had had to confess to any less notable a begetter.
—Vernon Blackburn, *Bayreuth and Munich: A Travelling Record of German Operatic Art*, 1899

I have seldom met such a natural and profoundly kind and noble man like him.
—Albert Schweitzer

Siegfried Wagner is a deeper and more original artist than many who are very famous today.
—Arnold Schoenberg, in 1912

There are people who want to make a tragic figure of me. They look at me with a compassionate smile and what they think may well be something like this: "Poor human being, how much must the burden of your colossal father's glory oppress you! How we do pity you. And that you possess the boldness to be an opera composer yourself, that you are so naïve to believe you can succeed in it! Poor, pitiable human being." I answer them: Do I really look that oppressed and crushed, dear reader? I would be sorry to give such an impression because I feel very well and sound. But I willingly admit that things are not made very easy for me.
—Siegfried Wagner in his 1922 memoirs

Karl Kraus, alluding to Siegfried's "unnatural likeness" to his father, foisted upon him the words: "Even if I can't write music, at least I look the part."
—Brigitte Hamann, *Winifred Wagner: A Life at the Heart of Hitler's Bayreuth*, 2005

Clara Schumann, announced that he would like to become a violinist, his mother offered him some wise advice. In an 1867 letter to her thirteen-year-old son she wrote:

> Your grandmother and Ferdinand [Schumann, Felix's older brother] write me that you are going about with the idea of becoming a violinist. That would be a grave step, more serious than you can realize. If you are not a distinguished violinist, no matter how clever you are, you will have a burdensome part to play as the son of Robert Schumann . . . I do not at all believe that you have such a gift as is required for high artistic rank.

Two years later, Siegfried Wagner was born at Tribschen in Switzerland, but it seems that the boy received no such advice as Clara gave her son. When he was only three his father encouraged his interest in music, and he later arranged for the child to study with his father's friend Engelbert Humperdinck. It may be that Siegfried himself recognized the disadvantages of being the son of a musical genius, and for a while he became interested in architecture as a career. The mausoleum of his grandfather Franz Liszt in the Bayreuth cemetery is an example of his work.

It was probably inevitable, however, that Siegfried would be drawn into the Bayreuth machine. His apprenticeship included general assistance at Bayreuth, and in 1906 he produced *The Flying Dutchman*. When he was made general director of the Bayreuth Festival he was always in the shadow of his mother, who insisted that Richard's way was the only way.

Siegfried Wagner completed sixteen operas between 1898 and 1929, the year before his death. Unlike his father, all of Siegfried's completed works were performed before his death, and some were favorably received. It is impossible to say whether his brief success was due to the appeal of his works or to the mere curiosity with which the sons and daughters of famous composers must contend.

Siegfried's operas were modeled on the style of his teacher Humperdinck, and he wrote his own librettos. The following list includes works that were never completed.

• TITLE	• DATE OF COMPOSITION
Der Bärenhäuter (The Bear-Skinned Man)	1898
Herzog Wildfang (Duke Wildfang)	**1900**
Der Kobold (The Goblin)	1903
Bruder Lustig (Brother Mirth)	**1904**
Sternengebot (The Command of the Stars)	1906
Banadietrich (Dietrich the Banned)	**1909**
Schwarzschwanenreich (Kingdom of the Black Swans)	1910
Sonnenflammen (Sun Flames)	**1912**
Der Heidenkönig (The Heathen King)	1913
Der Friedensengel (The Angel of Peace)	**1914**
An allem ist Hütchen schuld! (Everything Is Little-Hat's Fault!)	1915
Das Liebesopfer (Love's Sacrifice*)	**1917**
Der Schmied von Marienburg (The Blacksmith of Marienburg)	1920
Rainulf und Adelasia (Rainulf and Adelasia)	**1922**
Die heilige Linde (The Holy Linden)	1927
Wahnopfer (Delusion's Sacrifice)	**1928**
Walamund	1928–29
Wernhart	**1929**
Das Flüchlein das Jeder mitbekam (The Little Curse Everyone Got)	1929

***Siegfried was not happy with *Love's Sacrifice* and returned to it years later when he reworked it as *Wernhart*. Neither of these works progressed beyond the libretto stage.**

The Operas of Siegfried Wagner

After the outbreak of World War I in 1914, Siegfried conducted the Berlin Philharmonic on several occasions, and other efforts on the podium brought mixed reactions. After one concert at which he conducted some of Richard Wagner's works, Antonio Guarnieri, another conductor who was present, told him, "Your father's works are so great that not even you can ruin them."

He also conducted performances of some of his own operas, but they are rarely heard today outside Germany. He does, however, have followers. The International Siegfried Wagner Society, which supports and encourages the performance of his works, was established in 1972 and currently has around a hundred members, including several prominent musicologists, composers, directors, singers, and musicians. Members meet twice a year, and the organization is administered from Nuremberg. The Society organized an international symposium in Cologne in 2001.

Not surprisingly, the Society's members believe that Siegfried's works have been neglected. Siegfried undoubtedly suffered from unreasonable and unattainable expectations. He once said that he thought he would die before being discovered. He may have been right. Current members of the Society are optimistic that Siegfried will be recognized: "His time has come," proclaimed the Society in one of its publications. Members might be encouraged to learn that music from two of Siegfried's operas has been played at the BBC Proms. But it is unlikely that any current member was in the audience the last time Siegfried was on the bill. Music from *Der Bärenhäuter* was last included in 1899, and *Herzog Wildfang* was on the bill in 1901.

Siegfried and Winifred in the United States

Richard Wagner never visited the United States, but his son and daughter-in-law did. In January 1924 Siegfried and Winifred Wagner set sail for the United States, where they hoped to raise at least $200,000 to bail out the nearly bankrupt Festival. The series was billed as *Music of Three Generations*, and Siegfried was to conduct his own music with that of Liszt and his father on a program scheduled be given in twenty cities in four weeks.

Plans started to go awry early on when they were ambushed by waiting journalists interested in a story that Winifred had donated $100 from Festival funds to a representative of Hitler's organization. The defense was that the $100 was from private funds, and eventually the storm blew over. At least for a while.

The first stop on the tour was Detroit, and Siegfried's organizers engineered an invitation to Henry Ford's country home. The automobile pioneer was known for his anti-Semitic views and support for Germany's right wing. Siegfried was probably hoping that he would receive a generous donation, but Winifred had her mind on something else: she was hoping that Ford would offer her a two-seat convertible. Ford did not satisfy either wish.

After traveling safely across the Atlantic on the liner *America*, it was not until he attended a dinner given in New York just after he arrived that Siegfried hit an iceberg. The Jewish community was then among the most enthusiastic and generous supporters of the arts in New York City, as it possibly still is. After dinner Siegfried launched into a pro-Hitler, anti-Semitic tirade—forgetting that his host was a prominent member of the Jewish community. To make matters worse, one of the witnesses was a journalist. News of Siegfried's comments spread like wildfire.

The fund-raising tour was a flop, and only ten concerts were given. The profit made on the exhausting tour was less than $10,000, only 5 percent of the original target.

On Music and Musicians

Who is there that in logical words can express the effect music has on us?

Thomas Carlyle, in *The Hero as Poet*, 1840

Words are poor interpreters in the realms of emotion. When all words end, music begins.

Richard Wagner

Yes, the theatre should be full.

Response by Giuseppe Verdi when a journalist asked if he, like Wagner, had a theory about theatre

I think there is no work of art which represents the spirit of a nation more surely than *Die Meistersinger* of Richard Wagner. Here is no plaything with local color, but the raising to its highest power all that is best in the national consciousness of his own country. This is universal art in truth, universal because it is so intensively national.

Ralph Vaughan Williams, *National Music*, 1932

There was only Beethoven and Wagner.

Gustav Mahler

For nearly half a century there was no one to believe in Richard Wagner except Richard Wagner.

Hugh Haweis

Wagner never wrote an opera that wasn't in some way about himself.

Father Owen Lee

"Is Wagner a human being at all? Is he not rather a disease?"

—Friedrich Nietzsche, *Der Fall Wagner*, 1888

There is not one of his operas which would not benefit by the lopping of about half the text.

Anthony Burgess

Never and never will I write my memoirs. It is enough for the world of music to have to put up with my notes for so long. I will never condemn it to read my prose.

Giuseppe Verdi

Is Wagner a human being at all? Is he not rather a disease? He contaminates everything he touches—he has made music sick. I postulate this viewpoint: Wagner's art is diseased.

Friedrich Nietzsche, *Der Fall Wagner*, 1888

I am the child of a mixed marriage. My mother was a Wagnerian and my father was anti-Wagner.

Herbert Lindenberger, professor of humanities at Stanford University

His was a brain of the rarest and subtlest composition, put together cunningly by nature as no musician's brain has been put together before or since. The Muse of Poetry seems to have dipped her wings into the lucid stream of music, disturbing it with suggestions of a world it had never reflected before, deepening its beauty by closer association with the actual world of men. This was the brain of Wagner.

Ernest Newman, *A Study of Wagner*, 1899

Later, Wagner ran off with Cosima, had two more children with her, and married her. In that order. While we're on the subject, you might be interested to know that Isolde's brother was born right in the middle of Wagner's *Siegfried*. The opera, that is. Naturally, Wagner had enough to worry about without having to think up names, so he simply called the baby Siegfried. The way I look at it, the kid was pretty lucky. Another couple of years, and he would have been called Götterdämmerung.

Victor Borge with Robert Sherman, *My Favorite Intervals*, 1974

I like Wagner's music better than anybody's. It is so loud that one can talk the whole time without other people hearing what one says.

Oscar Wilde

Wagner once said to Cosima that English is not a real language. After reading Shakespeare's great scene between Henry IV and the prince, Cosima wrote: "Yesterday we compared the English text with the German. The German seemed to us much more noble."

Your husband does not like Jews; my husband is one.

George Eliot to Cosima Wagner when they met in London in 1877

Nothing proves more conclusively the power of his music than its ability to survive his librettos.

Paul Henry Lang

It is only fitting to admire Beethoven and Wagner for their pretensions as well as for their achievement. They dared more than other men. If they won greater glory, they also risked a more disastrous failure.

Deems Taylor, *Of Men and Music*, 1937

I must say that anyone who puts his faith in the civilizing power of art is bound to take away from Bayreuth a very positive impression of this marvelous artistic enterprise which—through its innate value and its effect on us—can be nothing less than a milestone in the history of art. That much is certain, that something has taken place at Bayreuth which our grandchildren and their children will still remember.

Tchaikovsky, after attending the first Bayreuth Festival in 1876

The theatre was dusty (curtains included), props shoddy, mise-en-scène prehistoric.

Adrian Boult, after a visit to Bayreuth in 1912

In 1876 Karl Marx told his daughter that people who wanted to know what he thought of Wagner constantly pestered him. His usual response was that the extended Wagner family was every bit as queer as the Nibelungs and merited its own tetralogy.

Bernard Levin wondered how far around Europe an opera-loving traveler could go using only the Italian, German, and French picked up from the operatic stage. He reported his findings in his book *Conducted Tour*: "The briefest study of *Die Walküre* will tell you what to do should you happen to fall in love with your long-lost sister, and from *Siegfried* you may learn the proper etiquette for conducting an affair with your aunt."

After a performance of a Wagner opera at the Royal Opera House in 1996–97, the general director, Jeremy Isaacs, proposed a toast to Wagner. But he inadvertently proposed a toast to the Master's health more than 110 years after his death. Noticing the accidental insertion of the extra word, the bass singer Gwynne Howell was heard to mutter, "I did not know he was ill."

> Wagner never forgave Mozart for writing Italian operas.
>
> Paul Henry Lang

> We've been rehearsing for two hours now, and we're still playing the same bloody tune!
>
> Thomas Beecham, while working on the prelude to *Das Rheingold*

Helden Wagnerians 8
BERNARD SHAW
The Original Perfect Wagnerite

He was born George Bernard Shaw but disliked his first name and never used it except as an initial; some of his musical criticisms were signed simply "GBS." He was born in Dublin and resisted formal education—he did not go to university and was virtually self-educated. He left Dublin for London in 1876 and lived with his mother, who had separated from her husband and moved to England when Shaw was only sixteen.

Shaw established himself as a music critic in London, writing for papers including the *Dramatic Review*, the *Pall Mall Gazette*, the *Star*, the *World*, and the *Saturday Review*, sometimes using the pseudonym "Corno di Bassetto." He became a supporter of Wagner's works and frequently used his newspaper and magazine reviews to promote the idea of a Wagner theatre on Richmond Hill, London.

Toward the end of the century he was operated on for necrosis in his foot and was unable to put his weight on it for a year and a half. During this period he wrote *Caesar and Cleopatra* and *The Perfect Wagnerite* (1898), a commentary on *The Ring*. He said later in a letter to a friend, "I have no reason to believe that they would have been a bit better if they had been written on two legs instead of one."

• **Bernard Shaw, portrayed on a stamp issued in Romania.**

Shaw became a prominent socialist. He was a founding member of the Fabian Society and worked with Kier Hardy. Shaw's literary career is well-known, and in 1925 he was awarded the Nobel Prize for Literature. His erudite music criticisms and devastating wit are familiar to Wagnerians. It was used to great effect to condemn second-rate performances by musicians, sing-

• **Ticket for the Wagner Festival in Berlin in 1936.**

Wagner at the Berlin Olympic Games

The 1936 Olympic Games presented an opportunity for Bayreuth to bolster its coffers by capitalizing on the inflow of foreign visitors to the country. It was apparently Hitler who came up with the idea of dividing the cultural festival into two cycles, one before the games and a second immediately afterward. He provided funds for a spectacular new production of *Lohengrin* staged by Heinz Tietjen and conducted by Wilhelm Furtwängler. Some of the lavish costumes were decorated with pearls; Lohengrin wore a suit of gleaming silver chain mail, and Elsa was followed by no fewer than seventy pages, all carrying candles.

In her well-researched book *Winifred Wagner: A Life at the Heart of Hitler's Bayreuth*, Brigitte Hamann included a story that demonstrated the depth of Hitler's knowledge of Wagner's works. The difficult second part of the Grail legend had been cut from the original Weimar production because of concerns about the tenor's voice. Tietjen was confident that Franz Völker could handle it, however, and the missing material was reintroduced for the first time in Bayreuth. When the singer reached the new territory, Hitler reacted immediately. Winifred Wagner said later that at first Hitler had been startled and clutched her hand, but then he seemed to appreciate the additional music. He clearly knew *Lohengrin* very well indeed.

Hitler was delighted with the new *Lohengrin* and at one point discussed the idea of making a gift of the whole production to Britain's newly crowned King Edward VIII for staging at Covent Garden. When the word was discreetly dropped in the royal ear, he is reported to have replied that he had nothing against it, as long as he didn't have to go to the damned opera himself. As a result of Edward's spectacular indifference, the plan was quietly shelved. Even if the new king had been more enthusiastic, the chances are that the plan would have come to naught when Edward abdicated a few months later because of his planned marriage to Wallis Warfield Simpson.

Tickets for the event showed the five Olympic rings in the background in a faint green. There was nothing subtle about the swastika and the imperial eagle, however: they were printed in solid black, front and top.

Cycle 1 was given from July 19 to July 30, and Cycle 2 from August 19 to August 31. During the period between the two Bayreuth cycles, a Richard Wagner Festspiel reception was given at the Berlin State Opera.

ers, conductors, or anyone else. His friend Henry Hamilton Fyfe once challenged Shaw on his constant use of ridicule. "If I said what I really mean without making people laugh," replied Shaw, "they would stone me."

Shaw was a frequent visitor to Bayreuth and a staunch supporter of the Wagnerian cause. He also shared Wagner's views on Brahms. He once said of his *Requiem*, "It could only have come from the establishment of a first-class undertaker."

The idea of a Wagner Theatre in London became a long-running crusade, and Shaw promoted Primrose Hill as a possible location. He wanted a Bayreuth in London mainly because he was critical of the stultifying effect of Cosima Wagner's insistence on doing everything precisely the way the Master dictated. Shaw saw other benefits in a Wagner theatre in London. He detested the sea and train journey to Bayreuth and resented paying £1 admission for each performance, which he considered "prohibitive as far as the average amateur is concerned."

The Wagnerian conductor Hans Richter shared Shaw's dislike of cross-Channel crossings and was usually violently ill. But he was more realistic about the prospects of a Wagner theatre in London. Not long after he retired to live in Bayreuth, he wrote to his longtime friend Percy Pitt: "A gentleman from the Wagner Society in London hopes to have finished building a theatre in one of the large parks there in time for 1913; in it he wants to stage *Parsifal* with Bayreuth forces. I think this bold optimist is called Parker. If the man can bring *that* off, I shall publicly convert to Islam in Trafalgar Square and marry the Pope! There are some wonderful dreamers about!"

Shaw fell off a ladder while trimming a tree at his home in Hertfordshire in 1950. He died a few days later.

Tickets, Please

A First in Berlin

The fiftieth anniversary of Wagner's death saw commemorative events in several cities. In Bayreuth the mayor and other dignitaries marched in procession past Wagner's grave, on which had been laid floral tributes from, among others, Adolf Hitler, Crown Prince Rupprecht of Bavaria, and the exiled ex-Kaiser Wilhelm II. The Festspielhaus team was determined to create something memorable for a performance of *Die Meistersinger* directed by Heinz Tietjen. If sheer numbers achieved that, they were successful. The Festival meadow scene featured some eight hundred people on the massive stage.

But it was Berlin that pulled off an amazing coup. Tietjen was again involved when Berlin State Opera staged eleven of Wagner's operas, from *Das Liebesverbot* to *Parsifal*. It was an astonishing artistic and logistical feat that has not been repeated anywhere in the world to this day. The team of Harry Kupfer and Daniel Barenboim came close in 2002, when ten of the works were performed in two weeks and then repeated in a second cycle. The only opera omitted from the original Berlin eleven was Wagner's second surviving opera *Das Liebesverbot*. It is rarely performed today and has never been staged in Bayreuth. Neither have the two other early works, *Die Feen* and *Rienzi*.

Hang On to Those Ticket Stubs . . .

Someone in Ohio cleared out their attic in 2006 and found a collection of ephemera from a trip their grandparents had made to Europe 105 years earlier. The collection included a ticket for a performance of *The Flying Dutchman* at Bayreuth in August 1901—the first year the opera was performed in the Festspielhaus. The ticket, not

• **Bayreuth ticket stub for *Tannhäuser*, 1901.**

much larger than a postage stamp, was sold on eBay for more than $30 in September 2006.

. . . But Be Careful in Case They Become Exhibit A

Tickets for a performance of *The Ring* were presented as evidence in a sensational trial in the United States in 2007. Conrad Black, the former owner of the *Daily Telegraph*, was on trial for fraud and charges that he skimmed off $60 million of company funds for his own use. Evidence in the case included the use of a corporate jet for a $500,000 personal holiday in the French Polynesian island of Bora Bora, with return via Seattle. Black offered to refund half of the cost of the trip in a corporate jet, but his defense argued that the segment between Seattle and Honolulu should be allowed as a business expense. Prosecutors then played their ace. They produced sets of tickets bought for Black and his wife for performances of all four of the operas of the Seattle *Ring* during a stopover on the way back.

The opera tickets helped to convict him of fraud and obstruction of justice. He was sentenced to six and a half years' imprisonment.

Lohengrin

Completed: April 1849.
Premiere performance: August 28, 1850, Weimar.
UK premiere: May 8, 1875, Covent Garden, London. It was sung in Italian and was the first Wagner opera performed at Covent Garden.
US premiere: April 3, 1871, Stadt Theatre, New York.

The Bare-Bones Plot

Elsa, heir to the throne of Brabant, is under threat of disqualification. If she is barred, the crown will be awarded to Telramund. Elsa has been accused by Telramund and his wife, Ortrud, of murdering her brother, Gottfried. Elsa calls for the knight in shining armor that she has seen in her dreams to come to her aid and represent her in the coming battle for the crown. Lohengrin arrives, riding across the lake on a swan, and when he imposes a condition for helping her—she must not ask his name—Elsa agrees. Telramund is defeated in the battle, but he and Ortrud continue their efforts by sowing doubts in Elsa's mind about the knight's true identity. On their wedding night, she cannot resist asking his name. He tells her that he is Lohengrin, but that as she has broken her vow, he must return to Montsalvat. Ortrud then reveals that the swan is her lost brother, who would have been freed if Elsa had kept her promise.

It has been suggested that anger at the refusal of the Saxon authorities to produce his new opera was one of the reasons Wagner became involved in the 1849 uprising in Dresden, rather than some loftier political ideal. He had completed composition in August 1847 and did not hear any of the music played by a full orchestra until almost six years later in Zurich. On that occasion a concert was given by an orchestra of seventy-two that included many specially invited musicians from several German cities. The program included parts of *Lohengrin*, with a newly completed concert ending for the Bridal Chorus. The concert was such a success that it was repeated twice, each time to a full house. The third performance coincided with Wagner's fortieth birthday, and the people of Zurich presented him with a gold cup and organized a torchlight parade through the town. Wagner wrote of this later: "It was really pretty and festive, and such a thing had never happened before. A stand for the orchestra had been erected before my house; I thought at first they were building a scaffold for me. There was playing and singing—speeches were exchanged, and hurrahs were given me by a countless multitude."

Wagner did not witness a full production of *Lohengrin* until May 1861 in Vienna. When the audience saw him enter the Kärntnertor Theatre, a storm of cheering and applause erupted that brought tears to his eyes. It was twelve years after he had completed the work and almost eleven years after Liszt had arranged the Weimar premiere.

After hearing Wagner read the text of his newly completed *Lohengrin*, one of his acquaintances, the composer and conductor Ferdinand Hiller, said: "What a pity that Wagner means to set it to music himself. His musical gifts are not equal to that."

Wagner recalled his first meeting with the very large tenor Ludwig Schnorr von Carolsfeld in Karlsruhe in 1862:

> While the sight of the swan-knight, approaching in his little boat, gave me the somewhat odd impression of the appearance of a young Hercules, yet his manner at once conveyed to me the distinct charm of the mythical hero sent by the gods, whose identity we do not study but whom we instinctively recognize. This instantaneous effect that touches the inmost heart can only be compared to magic. I remember to have been similarly impressed in early youth by the great actress Schroeder-Devrient, which shaped the course of my life, and since then not again so strongly as by Schnorr in *Lohengrin*.
>
> Ludwig Nohl, *Life of Wagner*, 1884

• Lohengrin arrives with his swan on a stamp issued by Ras Al-Khaima.

According to the *Victrola Book of the Opera* (1917), *Lohengrin* was the second most popular of all operas performed in Germany in the first decade of the twentieth century. There were 3,458 performances. Top place went to Georges Bizet's *Carmen*.

> Yesterday, at last, I received my scores! I played a few things in *Lohengrin* at the piano, and I cannot tell you what a wonderfully deep impression this, my own work, made on me.
>
> Wagner, in a letter to Theodor Uhlig in 1849

One can't judge Wagner's opera *Lohengrin* after a first hearing, and I certainly don't intend hearing it a second time.
—Gioachino Rossini

Ortrud is a woman who does not know love. This expresses everything, even the most terrible. Her sphere is politics. A political man is detestable, but a political woman is an atrocity: such an atrocity I had to portray.
—Wagner, in a letter to Liszt, 1852

The saddest of my creations.
—Richard Wagner

By an odd coincidence, while Liszt was conducting the world premiere performance of the swan knight *Lohengrin* in Weimar in August 1850, its composer was staying in the Schwann Hotel in Lucerne. He could not set foot in Germany for fear of immediate arrest and was on an extended visit to the Swiss city by the lake. But that evening Wagner's thoughts were far away from the Schwann Hotel or Lucerne. At the moment the performance started in Weimar, Wagner began pacing around his hotel room, watch in hand, following the actions of the swan knight in his mind. Many years later Stravinsky told his biographer, Robert Craft, that in 1968, after a visit to Tribschen, he sat in the same Schwann Hotel and recalled that incident while drinking tea and thinking about Wagner and *Lohengrin*.

In 1899 Henry T. Finck commented on Anton Seidl's first appearance in the United States. He conducted *Lohengrin*, which was already familiar to New York audiences, yet several people were puzzled. The Seidl interpretation, they said, sounded different. Finck thought he had the answer.

When Hans Richter conducted his first *Lohengrin* in London, it was discovered that the scores used by the orchestra contained no fewer than 186 errors. And this was not a onetime problem. The same scores, complete with all the errors, had been used in the British capital for some twenty-five years. Finck's suspicions on the cause of the "different sound" in New York were reinforced when someone asked Seidl why his version sounded different. Seidl just smiled and winked.

Seidl once sat at a dinner table with a group of musicians and singers who argued the merits and otherwise of Italian opera. Seidl said nothing until the subject seemed to have been exhausted. He then spoke up. Victor Herbert recorded his statement:

> "In the property room of the Metropolitan Opera House, gentlemen, there is a helmet." He paused for a moment, reflectively puffed at his cigar, and then resumed: "It may be tarnishing now, but a year or two ago it was brightly burnished. If you were to hunt it up you would find that this specimen is much like other helmets save for the 'Schwanritter' emblem which it bears. It was made for *Lohengrin*, and my dear friend Campanini wore it in a truly magnificent performance of the role. Yet if you were to find that helmet today you would discover that in addition to the prescribed dimensions and insignia of this piece of knightly headgear Mr. Campanini had put on a blue plume, probably three feet in length. That, my dear gentlemen is Italian opera."
>
> Victor Herbert, in *Anton Seidl: A Memorial*, 1899

King Ludwig II of Bavaria grew up with pictures of the legendary swan knight but became totally obsessed with the story after seeing *Lohengrin* for the first time. Five years after he met Wagner, he built a new castle in Bavaria. He called it Neuschwanstein (New Swan Stone), and its design is said to have been influenced by the sets of some of the operas, particularly *Lohengrin* and *Tannhäuser*. Wagner never visited this most famous of Ludwig's grand designs. The obsession with swans continued all of Ludwig's life: on Wagner's sixty-ninth birthday, Ludwig had a pair of black swans delivered to Wahnfried. They were given a home on a lake in the Hofgarten public park behind the house.

In Ludwig's Schloss Linderhof there is a Venus grotto with an indoor lake and fountain backed by a huge painting showing Venus surrounded by her cupids. But there is no Tannhäuser in the painting—because Ludwig imagined himself in that role. As Rudolf Ciri the archivist put it, "Ludwig did not live only in his dreams. He lived his dreams."

Robert Schumann considered writing an opera on the same subject as Wagner but decided that it was not suitable. He told Mendelssohn in an 1845 letter that he was therefore unpleasantly surprised when Wagner showed him his completed poem.

At a reception given by Cosima Wagner in 1894 after a performance of *Lohengrin*, the American soprano Lillian Nordica, who had sung the role of Elsa, approached the great Lilli Lehmann and asked if she might call on her some time. The great diva gave her potential American rival a frosty look and responded, "I am not taking pupils this season."

In 1953, *Lohengrin* was the first of the postwar Bayreuth productions to be a sellout. The following year 100 percent of the tickets were sold for all productions, and so it has continued to this day. This is probably worthy of a place in the *Guinness Book of Records*—unless there is another festival somewhere that has sold out every year for more than half a century?

"

All autobiographies are lies."

—Bernard Shaw, *The Rejected Statement*, 1916

Mary Burrell's Mission

After Wagner's death in 1883, Cosima stepped up her work as the self-appointed guardian of the Meister's image, and she targeted anything that detracted from Wagner's almost godlike status among the Wagner Societies. She took every opportunity to demand the return of documents and anything else that she thought might be used to besmirch her late husband's reputation.

But in her campaign to round up Wagner's letters, Cosima was about to have a competitor. Enter the Honorable Mary Burrell, daughter of Sir John Banks, the royal physician at Trinity College, Dublin, and wife of the Honorable Willoughby Burrell. She was wealthy, idolized Wagner, and both wrote and spoke excellent German. She had visited Bayreuth in Wagner's lifetime and had become both a keen supporter and a dedicated student. However, she condemned the biographical output of those she deemed to be under the influence of the family and other Wahnfried enforcers. She was particularly critical of the early biographies by Carl Friedrich Glasenapp and Houston Stewart Chamberlain. She also criticized *Wagner as I Knew Him* by Ferdinand Praeger, which had already been publicly exposed as unreliable.

In *The Rejected Statement*, Bernard Shaw wrote in 1916:

> All autobiographies are lies. I do not mean unconscious, unintentional lies: I mean deliberate lies. No man is bad enough to tell the truth about himself during his lifetime. And no man is good enough to tell

> the truth to posterity in a document which he suppresses until there is nobody left alive to contradict him.

Mary Burrell apparently agreed and decided to write her own *Life of Richard Wagner*, basing her work on original documents so that no room would be left for questions. In the years immediately following Wagner's death in 1883, she set about finding the source material she needed. She became a Wagnerian with a mission and with great tenacity followed up every clue that would lead her to letters, records, manuscripts, official documents, performance details, and anything else that could become the basis for her book. Although Cosima had already attempted to retrieve as much original material as possible, Wagner's prodigious letter writing and the sheer volume of other material written about him meant that there was still a great deal of potentially useful correspondence and ephemera out there. The problem was finding it.

Mary Burrell was helped in her quest by the resentment and distrust of the Bayreuth machine that existed at the time. This applied particularly to Cosima, who was not regarded as likely to cooperate with anyone intent on an honest biography. Burrell contacted the family members and friends of Wagner and their descendants all over Europe. Whenever possible, she bought the original letters and manuscripts; otherwise she acquired certified copies for her collection.

Then, one day in 1891, Mary Burrell hit the jackpot. She located a relative who owned material that had belonged to Minna Planer, Wagner's first wife. During her marriage to Wagner, Minna had accumulated an extensive collection of ephemera and documents, including 128 letters from Richard to her, plus numerous other theatre programs, official documents, and miscellaneous papers. When Minna died in 1866, her collection passed to Natalie Bilz, Minna's illegitimate daughter, born before she met Wagner. (For many years Natalie was passed off as Minna's younger sister.) After Minna died, Wagner demanded the return of his letters and intimidated Natalie with threats of repercussions if she refused. She eventually conceded and returned many of the letters and other documents, but she retained others that were special to her. After Wagner's death it was unthinkable that Natalie Bilz-Planer would turn over more of her hoard to Cosima, who was, after all, the "other woman" who had ousted her mother. Mary Burrell worked hard to gain Natalie's trust and eventually succeeded in convincing her that she wanted to tell the first truthful account of Wagner's life. At that point, Natalie gradually began to part with items from her collection.

When Mary Burrell found her, Natalie was living in impoverished circumstances in an almshouse in Leisnig in Saxony, so it is likely that she needed the money that this wealthy Englishwoman was willing to pay for the letters and other materials. A special prize for Mary Burrell was the draft of one of Wagner's earliest works, *Leubald*. Up to that point it was believed that Wagner's youthful literary effort had been lost or destroyed. In 1892 Mary Burrell hit the jackpot again. She located the widow of the printer who had produced the eighteen copies of Wagner's *My Life* some twenty years earlier. Wagner, almost certainly influenced by Cosima, had tried to recover all of the copies that had been distributed, and for several years it seemed that they had succeeded. But no one knew that the printer, Bonfantini, had kept an unbound copy of the pages for himself. The now-priceless document was still in his widow's possession when Mary Burrell made contact. This was to be the jewel in the crown of what became known as the Burrell Collection.

At the time scholars did not have access to *My Life*, and it proved to be a treasure trove of information. But Mary Burrell did not accept Wagner's entire story as gospel, and when she started her biography of Wagner she corrected errors that had resulted from Wagner's imperfect recollections of his early life or from deliberate distortions to enhance the picture he was creating for King Ludwig II.

After fifteen years of tireless pursuit, Mary Burrell had accumulated an astonishing collection of 840 items, including autograph letters, musical and literary sketches, pictures, photographs, notebooks, completed manuscripts, and even passports and marriage and birth certificates. Back in England she started work on the book that she was determined would be the definitive, accurate biography of Wagner. Her manuscript reached the point where Wagner was in his twenty-first year when she died in 1898. None of her family had any interest in continuing work on the biography, but her husband and daughter published the part already completed: *Richard Wagner: His Life and Works from 1813 to 1834*.

Mary Burrell wrote in a chatty, casual style, and she switched back and forth between English and German. It seems likely that no book editor was allowed to correct any of her informal language and abbreviations. She made frequent use of the ampersand and interrupted the flow of her own narrative with various interjections and questions to the reader ("Behold Readers," "Can Readers believe it").

The amateur sleuth set herself a difficult target. She vowed not to include anything in her book that "did not rest on documentary evidence I had seen myself." She was able to correct many of the details in the biographies by Glasenapp, Houston Chamberlain, and Wagner himself. (She referred constantly to these earlier biographical works as simply "the Books.") She was a stickler for detail, and nothing in the earlier material was too trivial to be corrected. On one page she berates those before her who wrongly reported the house number of Wagner's mother: "It is very troublesome to mention these trifles, the inventions of the Biographers are a constant worry."

Another example was her quest for details of Wagner's first home in the Brühl area of old Leipzig:

> The house the Wagners lived in had the sign of the Red and White Lion, their neighbors lived at the sign of the Green Fir Tree, the Black Wheel and the Crane . . . All of this may seem easy to write by reference to the Books,—not at all!—so elementary a fact as the number of the house these books have contrived to confuse. I have a romantic reminiscence to guide me to the cause of such mistakes. The first time I went to Bayreuth I lodged in a house numbered 673, my friends imagined me in a Franconian Rue de Tivoli (but the explanation for the high number was simply that) it was the six hundredth & seventy third house in Bayreuth. When I arrived there in 1889 & found the old-world village numbering changed into street numbering in consequence of overbuilding to accommodate tourists (a vision of the red brick "bicoques" spotted with white that have sprung up like Fungi round the Temple rises before me) I felt it was part of the ruinous prosperity that had spoiled my beloved Bayreuth.

She went on to describe how she had decoded "the Books" to identify the Wagner house. Her task was complicated by the fact that Friedrich Wagner had registered the birth of Wilhelmine Ottilie, giving the address as the Red and White Lion, not the White and Red Lion, as "the Books" have it. The house in which Wagner was born was demolished in

1886 as part of a redevelopment plan; Burrell even tracked down the municipal record of that event.

One of the documents that Burrell bought from her sources was the script of a children's play written by Wagner's stepfather, Ludwig Geyer, for his mother's birthday in 1816. Burrell devoted fourteen pages of her book to the script for the play, including the cast list of the Wagner children: Albert, Rosalie, Julius, Luise, Clara, Ottilie, Richard, and Caecilie. Burrell notes that this was "the first appearance in any theatrical performance of the precious Richard at 3 years & 3 months." Elsewhere she records that in September 1820, when Richard was seven, he played a minor role in Schiller's play *William Tell* in Dresden. She also reproduced a copy of an early school register in which the young Wagner had been required to enter his own name.

Mary Burrell was only forty-eight when she died. Her husband, Willoughby Burrell, and his daughter decided that the results of her fifteen-year mission should be published, and they sponsored one of the most expensive and lavish books ever issued on Richard Wagner or any other composer. Whatever other claims can be made for her book, it is almost certainly the largest and heaviest book ever published on any aspect of Wagner's life or works. It measured approximately 25.5 × 22 inches (70 cm × 56 cm) and weighs an astonishing 36.6 pounds (16.6 kg). This was a coffee-table-sized coffee-table book. The massive weight of the book has resulted in the covers of Copy Number 11 parting from the binding, but the inside pages are in good condition. Every word in the book was engraved in a beautiful copperplate script printed within a ruled rectangle with notes alongside in a separately ruled column. A frontispiece notes, "This book has been engraved and printed in London by Allan Wyon, Chief Engraver of Her Majesty's Seals." The illustrations were entrusted to a heliogravure specialist in Paris. The handmade paper carries Wagner's signature as a watermark. The binding is equally sumptuous, incorporating gilded vellum and silk endpapers. The book includes twenty-six portraits and views, sixty-four facsimile copies of original documents, and a two-page-spread plan of Leipzig, Wagner's birthplace.

An unalterable and unquestioned law of the musical world required that the German text of French operas sung by Swedish artists should be translated into Italian for the clearer understanding of English-speaking audiences.
—Edith Wharton, *The Age of Innocence*, 1920

Only a hundred copies of the lavishly produced book were printed. It is not known how many survive, but there are two numbered copies in the British Library next to St. Pancras station in London. One is identified as Number 11, and the title page notes that it was presented to the library by Mary Burrell. Willoughby Burrell or his daughter presumably presented it to the library in her name. The other copy of Mary Burrell's magnum opus is identified as Copy Number 54.

The poignant note at the end of the massive book reads:

> This much the Writer of these Pages achieved of her purpose to copy out as far as possible the Ideal Biography. Her call to higher service on June 26, 1898 prevented its completion & from her Manuscript, her Husband & Daughter have now had this first Volume brought out according to her wishes & instructions as a worthy Foundation for the Monument she had hoped to erect to the genius of Richard Wagner. Perhaps at some future date the important and interesting collection she made preparatory to this Work and to which so many nobly contributed of their best, may be given to the public.

Following the publication of the book in 1898, the collection of letters and other documents was not seen for more than thirty years.

Sale in New York

In 1930 what had come to be known as the Burrell Collection was found in the loft of Mary Burrell's daughter, Lady Henniker. The collection was sold to Mrs. Mary Louise Curtis Bok, who continued to add to the hoard; within a few years it had grown to 865 items. In 1944 the entire collection was donated to the organization Bok had founded in 1924 in Philadelphia, the Curtis Institute of Music. The Burrell Collection was renamed the Curtis Institute of Music Richard Wagner Collection.

The Curtis Institute of Music is a foundation dedicated to the promotion of music and musical education. For more than fifty years the organization provided free education to talented young musicians from many countries. The institute needed to top up its original endowment fund, so in 1978 it was decided to sell the collection of Wagner documents. Hundreds of items went under the hammer at Christie's in a New York City auction on October 27, 1978. For Wagner scholars and enthusiasts, it was the sale of the century: letters, musical manuscripts, prose texts, pictures, and not one but two copies of the lavishly produced first volume of Mary Burrell's biography of Wagner printed in 1898. The treasure trove of Wagneriana included an original letter signed by Ludwig Geyer, Wagner's stepfather, and a letter from Wagner to Mathilde Wesendonck. This was the famous letter that Minna intercepted and that ultimately led to the separation of the Wagners and their estrangement from the Wesendoncks. Otto Wesendonck, a wealthy partner in a New York silk trading firm, had provided to Wagner his home, the Asyl, and, some believe, his wife Mathilde. Some scholars believe that Mathilde was Wagner's mistress; we will probably never know for certain. One thing is sure: Mathilde inspired Wagner while he was composing *Tristan and Isolde*.

Wagner's Influence on Art and Literature

While I am deep into one of my pile of new books on Wagner and his works, my wife, Miriam, gets through several fictional works a week. She will occasionally look up to tell me, "Here's another reference to your man!" This week she was reading *Requiem*, by Clare Francis, and was amused to find that the aptly named hero, Richard, decided to impose some culture on his girlfriend, Daisy, and take her to a performance of *Götterdämmerung*. Daisy was not impressed and during one of the intermissions asked "who this Wagner geezer thought he was anyway, rambling on for longer than Ben Hur, giving people stiff bums and tired brains."

Another best-selling author, Danielle Steele, wrote a book that was guaranteed to catch the eye of Wagner enthusiasts because it was titled simply *The Ring*. However, Wotan, Brünnhilde, and Siegfried were excluded from this version. It was the story of a Berlin family in the 1930s, and the titular ring was an heirloom that was passed down through the women of the line.

The book was made into a teleplay with a more direct Wagner link. The titles were backed by the opening bars of the prelude to *Tristan and Isolde*, but that was it. Wagner enthusiasts hoping for more were disappointed.

Sepulchre, by Kate Mosse, features a lengthy description of the experiences of a young woman at a Paris performance of *Lohengrin*. Shortly after the prelude begins, catcalls are heard from the upper tiers, and it goes downhill from there. The

> "There occurs in nature something similar to what happens in Wagner's music."
> **—Vincent van Gogh**

interruption deteriorates into a riot, and panic in the audience results in the abandonment of the performance. The date selected by Mosse for the opening of her novel was September 1891—thirty years after the infamous *Tannhäuser* fiasco in the French capital.

Great music inspires great art, and Wagner's works have inspired many of the world's leading artists and illustrators. Arthur Rackham (1867–1939) was a British artist best remembered as an illustrator of children's books. His catalogue of successes includes *Grimm's Fairy Tales*, *Rip Van Winkle*, *Peter Pan*, and *Alice's Adventures in Wonderland*. Perhaps one series preferred by adults was his illustrations for Shakespeare's *A Midsummer Night's Dream*, which some believe to have been his finest work.

Rackham visited Bayreuth to see *The Ring* in 1897 and again in 1899. After his first visit he was reportedly disappointed and felt "deceived by the pedantic and over-detailed sets that destroyed the atmosphere." The problem was probably Cosima, who was insisting that everything be done precisely as specified by her husband, who had been dead for more than fourteen years.

But some of the staging details clearly stuck in Rackham's memory, because in 1910 he started work on a series of sixty-four illustrations for *The Ring* that were published in two volumes with an English text. The first volume, with illustrations for *Rheingold* and *Walküre*, was published in 1910 by Heinemann; the second, depicting *Siegfried* and *Götterdämmerung*, followed in 1911.

The Rackham illustrations are magnificently executed and are mostly true to Wagner's descriptions of characters and settings. The artist was able to achieve what has been virtually unattainable for the opera director—his Brünnhilde is slim and beautiful, and Siegfried is a handsome young curly-haired blonde.

Curiously, Rackham departed occasionally from his otherwise accurate visual representation of Wagner's instructions and illustrated "scenes" that do not appear in any of the four operas. In one instance he illustrated Grimhilde, the mother of Hagen, who does not appear on the cast of characters of *The Ring* and is never seen onstage. The illustration shows a human woman standing with Alberich.

The story of how Mime found Sieglinde in the forest where she died giving birth to Siegfried is told by Mime but does not appear in any scene. Another beautiful illustration shows Loge, the God of Fire, chatting with the Rhinemaidens. This meeting is mentioned by Loge to Wotan but the meeting is not shown on stage. In yet another departure from the staged version of the story, Rackham shows Alberich beckoning to a very young Siegfried to come eat the meal the dwarf has prepared. Siegfried in this illustration appears to be about three or four years old. Why Rackham included these scenes among the sixty-four illustrations is not clear. Perhaps he was relying on an imperfect recollection of his visits to Bayreuth eleven and thirteen years earlier.

The first editions of the two Heinemann books are sought after by collectors and change hands for hundreds of dollars. Some of Rackham's illustrations of *The Ring* can be viewed at www.artpassions.net/rackham/wagner_ring.html.

Auguste Renoir sketched the composer in his Palermo home in January 1882, a year before Wagner's death. It was reported that he completed

• **Wagner, by Renoir.**

his sketch in just thirty-five minutes. He subsequently produced an oil painting that now hangs in the Musée d'Orsay in Paris.

Wassily Kandinsky once said that hearing *Lohengrin* in Moscow was one of the two events "that stamped my life and shook me to the depths of my being." In her book *Kandinsky Compositions*, Magdalena Dabrowski said that it was a performance of Wagner's *Lohengrin* that stirred Kandinsky to devote his life to art and "convinced him of the emotional powers of music . . . The performance conjured for him visions of a certain time in Moscow that he associated with specific colors and emotions . . . His recollection of the Wagner performance attests to how it had retrieved a vivid and complex network of emotions and memories from his past. He said, 'The violins, the deep tones of the basses, and especially the wind instruments at that time embodied for me all the power of that pre-nocturnal hour.'"

Salvador Dalí's painting of *Tristan and Isolde* now hangs in the Salvador Dalí Museum in Figueres, Spain. The oil on canvas work is—well, it's Dalí. In 1939 Dalí created a set design for a ballet danced to music from *Tannhäuser*.

(When I was browsing in a New York artists' materials store in the early '80s, every assistant rushed to serve the important customer who had just entered. It was Salvador Dalí. He was wearing carpet slippers and his famous moustache was Scotch-taped to his cheeks, presumably for protection from a windy day in the city.)

Aubrey Beardsley was born in Brighton in 1872 and became a prolific painter of Wagnerian subjects, including characters from *Tannhäuser*, *Siegfried*, and *Tristan and Isolde*.

Vincent van Gogh wrote in a letter to his sister Wilhelmina in March 1888: "But by intensifying all the colors one arrives once again at quietude and harmony. There occurs in nature something similar to what happens in Wagner's music, which, though played by a big orchestra, is nonetheless intimate." The thought was still in his mind a few months later when he wrote to his brother Theo: "I made a vain attempt to learn music, so much did I already feel the relation between our color and Wagner's music."

Pablo Picasso was a Wagner enthusiast, and one of his works was inspired by *Parsifal*. He was a member of a Barcelona literary group who called themselves Valhalla. Not much is known about the activities of the group, but one British art historian, Mark Harris, has suggested that they may have seen Wagner performances at a local bar/restaurant, El Quatre Gats.

A 1934 drawing contains an important Wagnerian theme that appears to be unique in Picasso's work. It depicts what is probably the most dramatic scene in *Parsifal*—the moment when the spear hovers over *Parsifal*'s head after being hurled at him by the evil magician Klingsor.

Paul Cézanne was perhaps unique among the greats: as a member of the Wagner Society of Marseilles, he was literally a card-carrying Wagnerian. He called his 1867 painting of a girl at a piano *Overture to Tannhäuser*. It was painted in oils on canvas and is now displayed in the Hermitage Museum in St. Petersburg. In January 1868 he attended a concert in Paris whose program included the overtures to *Der fliegende Holländer* and *Tannhäuser* and the prelude to *Lohengrin*.

David Hockney was born in Bradford, England, and has lived near Los Angeles since 1978. He has designed sets for works by Puccini, Strauss, Mozart, and Stravinsky, and in 1987 he created the sets for a production of *Tristan and Isolde* in Los Angeles. In a review in the *New York Times*, John Russell was particularly enthusiastic about the artist's contribution:

Hockney rose to the notorious challenge and whisked us in a matter of seconds to a world in which all life was extinguished and all light doused, and from there to a transfigured universe in which time past, time present and time to come were somehow in equilibrium. It was as awesome a moment as we shall ever see on a stage.

The Wagnerian Experience

My thanks to various friends and Wagner Society members who have contributed anecdotes from their Wagnerian experiences. Some have remained anonymous in order to protect the guilty.

In 1989 I was in the Festspielhaus with another member. We'd just sat through *Rheingold*, and during clapping the lady next to my friend took out a libretto and was furiously looking through the cast of characters. She turned to my friend and whispered, "Which one was Siegmund?" R—— and I looked at each other and our jaws dropped. R—— turned back to the woman and hissed, "He's in the next opera!" Then she turned to me and said, "I've been trying to get tickets for ten years—how did *she* get in?!"

We decided that there should be a test to qualify for tickets and that it should be something like, "Who dwells on the earth?"

Trish Benedict, California

At the back of the Festspielhaus there are several creatively named "semi-viewing seats." The seats are behind pillars, and the unfortunate ticket holder has to lean to one side to see part of the stage. One visitor remarked later, "Last year, I saw half of *Parsifal*. To be more precise, I saw the right half."

Anonymous

I once asked a friend if he'd like to come with me to the opera to see the *Ring* cycle. "No thanks," he said. "I'd rather stay home, do my laundry, and watch the rinse cycle."

On another occasion I told a patient that I would not be able to see her again for a couple of weeks because I would be traveling. This large lady with the wonderful accent asked, "Where are you going to this time, Doctor?" I uttered one word, Bayreuth, and paused while I speculated on the possible response. I have found that many Americans have never heard of Bayreuth or confuse it with Beirut, Lebanon. But not this lady. Her immediate reply: "You IS? I just LOVE that Brünnhilde!"

Dr. Andrew Rombakis, California

I followed two ladies leaving the screening of the Met *Rheingold* at our local cinema. I overheard one saying: "We've got a long way to go in our first *Ring*, Gladys, but I have already decided that this Wotan fellow is a shit."

Anonymous

Peter West complained to his doctor about severe pains in his legs. After an examination the doctor told him that the problem could be serious and referred him immediately to the Royal Berkshire Hospital. There a consultant surgeon confirmed a major arterial blockage in both legs and told him that he had to undergo surgery as soon as possible. The details of the operation are not for the squeamish.

Because of the life-threatening nature of the

• **Siegfried splits the anvil with his sword, Nothung. Cartoon by Emil Wagner, 1921.**

problem, the surgeon consulted his operating schedule and said, "Look, I can fit you in next Tuesday. How does that suit you?"

"I don't suppose you could do me the following Tuesday?" said Peter.

"Why, are you going on holiday?" the surgeon asked.

Peter West smiled. "Holiday? No, more like a duty. I have tickets for the ENO [English National Opera] *Ring* cycle at the Coliseum."

The astonished surgeon replied, "Do you realize, my boy, that if you don't have this operation you may die?"

"If I don't see *Siegfried* at the Coliseum then I almost certainly will," Peter told him.

The surgeon laughed, shook his head in disbelief and rearranged his busy schedule.

Shortly after Peter arrived back at his home that afternoon, the telephone rang. It was the press office at the Coliseum. "We have received a call from a guy called Rothney who said he is a cardiovascular surgeon at the Royal Berks Hospital in Reading. He claims that one of his patients has put off a lifesaving operation to see the Ralph Koltai *Ring*. Was that you, and is it true?" Peter confirmed the story, and the Coliseum press office set to work. Thirty minutes later, the *Evening Standard* was the first to call. The next day the story was all over the morning papers.

Peter West saw the performance of *Siegfried*. Happily, he survived the surgery a few days later. Two days after the operation he received a message asking him to call "Siegfried" when he was discharged from the hospital. Two weeks later the Wagner enthusiast called ENO and spoke with the now legendary Alberto Remedios. The tenor had clearly been impressed by the idea that someone would risk his life to see the production and asked if he could come to visit the recovering patient in Newbury some time. He did so, and Peter was then invited to visit Alberto and the rest of the ENO team at the Coliseum.

The Best-Laid Plans...

Staging an opera, any opera, is a complex operation involving a team of several hundred singers, musicians, stagehands, musicians, special effects technicians, lighting specialists, producers, directors with numerous assistants, and front-of-house staff. There is plenty of scope for things to go wrong, and the history of Wagner productions has more than its fair share of catastrophes.

Possibly the first was at the premiere of *Das Liebesverbot*, in Magdeburg, directed by Wagner himself. On the second night a fight broke out between members of the cast and the performance was canceled. There was no third night, and *Das Liebesverbot* was never performed again in Wagner's lifetime.

The climax of the third opera of *The Ring* sees Siegfried test his newly reforged sword by cleaving the blacksmith's anvil apart. This scene has gone wrong so many times in various productions that experienced *Ring*-goers get quite nervous when the end of Act I approaches. On several occasions the anvil has failed to split apart when Siegfried strikes it. In at least one production the singer had the presence of mind to take a second swing at the anvil and was rewarded when the anvil split apart. Better late than never.

> "When does the next swan go?"
>
> **—Leo Slezak, tenor, after his swan transport in *Lohengrin* left without him**

Others were not so lucky, and sometimes the reverse of this problem occurs. In one production, Lauritz Melchior raised the sword, Nothung, above his head, but before he could begin the downward slash, the anvil split apart prematurely. The tenor froze with the sword raised above his head as he looked down at the split anvil and wondered what to do next. After a lengthy pause while he tried to remember plan B, he made another halfhearted swipe at the anvil and walked off.

In *The Bumper Book of Operatic Disasters*, Hugh Vickers quotes Lionel Salter as saying that during one period the premature anvil split happened so often that younger members of the Covent Garden audience thought it was part of the story. Presumably they thought that Nothung was so powerfully magical that it could cleave metal without even touching it.

Wagner demanded so many special effects for Siegfried's sword in *The Ring* that the props departments produce five or six versions for most modern productions. Kate Bebbington, the assistant armorer at Covent Garden, looked after no fewer than ten swords, including spares, for the Keith Warner production in 2007. Special soldering techniques were required to repair the shattered swords so that they were strong enough to withstand some vigorous waving around but weak enough to shatter on cue. That, too, does not always go to plan, and tenors have been known to throw the still-complete sword to the ground in disgust.

Fire on the stage brings a whole new set of potential problems. In the 2005 Covent Garden production of *Die Walküre*, the director, Keith

• Eva and scenes from *Die Meistersinger* on a French trade card issued by Liebig.

• Scenes from *Tristan and Isolde*.

Wagner with a Cup of Oxo

In the 1840s Stollwerck, a German chocolate maker, started printing colored pictures in the packaging of its products. The company hoped that its customers would save the cards and come back for more. It worked and other companies quickly followed. When meat extract company Liebig started issuing high-quality trading cards with its bouillon cubes around 1870, a new industry was born.

Over the next 105 years Liebig distributed cards covering more than eleven thousand wide-ranging subjects, mostly in sets of six. Many of the cards were printed in thirteen colors by a high-quality lithographic process, and versions in several languages were produced in various countries, mainly England, Belgium, France, Germany, and Italy. The sets covered popular subjects (famous people, history, buildings, ships, paintings, literature, geography), as well as more esoteric ones (types of oysters, national drinks, jungle gyms).

Opera composers and their works were represented, including Beethoven, Bizet, Meyerbeer, Mozart, Verdi, and Weber. Wagner was well represented: in addition to a set of six cards on his life, there were two series covering Wagnerian heroes and heroines and another on scenes from *Die Meistersinger*. The sets are sought after by card collectors and Wagnerians and frequently are bought and sold on eBay. No cards were printed in England after Liebig was acquired by Brooke Bond, which marketed the famous bouillon cubes in the United Kingdom as Oxo.

A selection of the original Liebig cards on Wagner and his operas appears in this book. Unfortunately, modern color printing involves only four colors, and so some of the brilliance of the thirteen-color originals has been lost. A few years ago an Italian magazine reprinted some of the Liebig cards as gifts for its readers, but it proved impossible to match the quality of the original chromolithographs.

Lambert, and stage designer, Stefanos Lazaridis, came up with a remarkable effect when Wotan calls upon Loge to create the fire around Brünnhilde's rock. A small flame of about four or five inches high appears near the front of the stage. Wotan appears to pick it up and, holding it in his cupped hand, walks across the stage. He then sets it down, where it begins to spread and encircle the rock.

To achieve this spectacular effect, Bryn Terfel was equipped with a small concealed propane gas tank with a tube leading to his left hand. In his right hand Terfel held a switch that controlled the flow of gas to the nozzle in his left hand. "It looked wonderful in all the rehearsals," said Terfel in a radio interview appropriately called "It was *not* all right on the night."

The magical effect went badly wrong at the first performance when the switch failed. The flame from the singer's left hand leapt several feet in the air, and he was unable to extinguish it. "I could not blow it out because I was in mid-phrase," he said. "I had to wait until the end of 'Leb wohl,' which is not a short piece of music." To his great credit, Terfel kept his cool in a hot situation.

Despite the beautiful effect of the hand-carried flame, Terfel was not enthusiastic about Laziridis's set designs. Commenting on the negative audience reaction, the Welsh baritone told the Sunday *Times*, "If the simplicity of those sets had matched the simplicity of the directing [by Keith Warner] I don't think there would have been any cause for complaint." Some observers wondered whether his feelings about the production had anything to do with his withdrawal from the full *Ring* at Covent Garden in 2007. He had cited family reasons for dropping out, leaving John Tomlinson to perform the role of Wotan in all three cycles.

One of the favorite stories of David Webster, general administrator of the Royal Opera House from 1944 to 1970, concerned the soprano Hilde Konetzni. She was singing Sieglinde in a touring performance of *Die Walküre* conducted by Reginald Goodall. Montague Haltrecht told the story in his 1975 book *The Quiet Showman*: "He loved describing the moment of great ecstasy in the love duet when quite suddenly she performed a beautiful sweeping movement, one he'd not seen before, and ended kneeling at her lover's feet. He was deeply moved, and tears sprang to his eyes."

But what had actually happened was that the lady had lost a tooth and had seen it caught in the light—gleaming like Rhine gold! Her swooping cry was the joy of discovery, not the ecstasy of love.

Webster went on to explain the total consternation that reigned backstage during the interval. Konetzni was not sure whether she could continue singing with a tooth missing. Fortunately Elizabeth Latham, the resourceful stage director, came up with an inspired idea to keep the tooth in place: chewing gum! It worked: the gum kept the tooth in place until Sieglinde left the stage carrying Siegmund's shattered sword.

Perhaps the best-known ad lib from a singer was delivered during a staging of *Lohengrin*. In some early productions, the hero is supposed to come onstage riding on the back of a swan, but one fateful night Leo Slezak missed his cue, and the cable-drawn swan took off without him. Slezak did not miss a beat, turned to the audience, and asked, "When does the next swan go?" Thirty years later, in 1936, the great Lauritz Melchior had the same problem at the New York Metropolitan Opera and repeated Slezak's famous line.

In an otherwise wonderful production of *Die Walküre* in San Francisco, the huge doors at the back of Hunding's hut burst open as required, letting in a stream of sunshine and setting the scene for Sieglinde to sing the beautiful "Du bist der Lenz" (You are the spring). But the carefully created atmosphere was destroyed when a stagehand was

> "It is, after all, only planned to be a provisionary structure."
> **—Richard Wagner, on the Bayreuth Festspielhaus**

seen strolling across the back of the stage, hands in his pockets. He looked left, saw 3,250 audience faces staring at him, and completed his traverse at a gallop. History does not relate whether the stagehand survived the wrath and winter storm of San Francisco's fiery leader at the time, Lotfi Mansouri.

Bayreuth Festspielhaus: Magical, Mystical Acoustics

The 140-Year-Old Temporary Building

Wagner considered several options before deciding to build his festival theatre in Bayreuth. There were approaches from Munich, Berlin, Weimar, London, and even Chicago, among others. An offer to build an opera house in Weimar and sponsor the production of *The Ring* was received from the Grand Duke of Weimar.

The leaders of Baden-Baden thought that they had a strong case because of the large number of visitors to the popular Black Forest resort. But this was the very reason Wagner was opposed to the location. He wanted people to come to his festival theatre only to see his operas, not to provide an entertainment break while taking the cure. In a letter to Emil Heckel, founder of the first Wagner Society in Mannheim, Wagner wrote:

> The place must not be a large city with a permanent theatre, nor one of the larger summer resorts, where during the season an absolutely undesirable public would offer itself; it must be centrally located in Germany, and moreover be a Bavarian city, as I also intend to take up my permanent residence in the place, and consider that I could do this only in Bavaria, if I hope to enjoy the continued patronage of the King of Bavaria.

Hans Richter, who would conduct the first performance of *The Ring*, suggested that Bayreuth would be an ideal location. But Wagner clearly hoped that once the Festival was over, others would take up the cause. In an April 12, 1872, letter to banker Friedrich Feustel, he said, "In this building we are only giving the outline of the idea, and hand it over to the nation to perpetuate it as a monumental structure." In another letter to his financial adviser he wrote that "the dimensions of the auditorium as well as of the stage must be so estimated that they may serve as the foundation of the future massive structure." But Wagner did not want to skimp on the equipment to be used in the "temporary" building: "On the other hand, the heavy and ingenious machinery must be made thoroughly *solid*; as this, together with the foundation, shall, if God wills, outlast our lightly-put-together provisionary structure."

King Ludwig had already provided generous financial support, but Wagner was counting on more. Ludwig favored Munich as the location of the theatre, and he commissioned the prominent architect Gottfried Semper, designer of the Dresden opera house, to produce some ideas. Ludwig, builder of dream castles, wanted something more elegant and more permanent in stone.

In the end Wagner prevailed, and what some were calling his Nibelung Theatre was started in Bayreuth. It was designed to his specifications by Otto Brückwald of Leipzig, and Wagner laid the foundation stone on his fifty-ninth birthday,

THE WAGNER FESTIVAL AT BAYREUTH — EXTERIOR OF THE THEATRE

• **The Festspielhaus as it appeared in 1902.**

May 22, 1872. A tin box under the stone carried a telegram from the king, the statutes of the first Mannheim Wagner Society, some coins, and a few of Wagner's verses. The translation reads:

> A secret great I here enclose;
> Many hundred years here let it rest!
> So long as the stone guards it well,
> To the world it will itself reveal.

The stone-laying ceremony was preceded by a Beethoven concert at the Margrave opera house, a beautiful building opened in 1748. Wagner had dismissed this ornate building as too small when he checked its suitability to house his Festival. Indeed, it is so small that Bernard Levin once said, tongue in cheek, that the entire building would fit onto the stage of the Festspielhaus.

Financing of the building project continued to be a problem. Despite broad promotion, only about a quarter of the patron tickets were sold to Wagner Society members, and the project teetered on the edge of collapse. In early 1874 Wagner appealed to Otto von Bismarck for financial help, but his letter went unanswered. The kaiser made a small contribution, but the public remained indifferent in the face of a massive media onslaught that included references to "the Wagner Swindle," Wagner's "coarse big-mouthedness," and "a farce and simply nauseating."

• **The kaiser attended the opening of the Festspielhaus and admitted to Wagner, "I did not believe you would be able to carry it through." Card by Liebig.**

Once more it was King Ludwig who advanced funds to rescue the project, supplemented by a small donation from the Viceroy of Egypt and further contributions from Wagner Society members.

The opening of the first Festival in 1876 was the culmination of a twenty-five-year dream. Wagner's first public mention of his plans for an opera house was in *A Communication to My Friends*, in 1851. The original capacity was 1,645, but seats were added in later years to bring the capacity up to the present 1,925.

The unique acoustics of the Festspielhaus results in a magical, mystical sound that has never been matched by any other opera house in the world. However, Bayreuth is close to the bottom of the opera-house comfort league. It has always been feared that plush seating and carpeting might jeopardize the legendary acoustics of the house that Wagner built, so there is none of either, although a token thin cover has been added to the seats and backs. Five hours or more can be an uncomfortable experience, and regulars take their own cushions as a minor concession to twenty-first-century comfort. Furthermore, anyone taller than about five and a half feet finds the space between rows inadequate.

No extraneous sound is tolerated, not even the faintest hum of air conditioning—of which, again, there is none. Temperatures close to 100 degrees Fahrenheit (37.7 degrees Celsius) have been recorded in the auditorium, and occasionally even the normally ultraformal German men have been

• **Traffic jams are not new. Slow-moving carriages on the Green Hill up to the Festspielhaus. Sketch by David Mitchell.**

known to remove their tuxedo jackets.

The hourlong intermissions provide an opportunity to cool the audience and the Festspielhaus. The audiences enjoy cold drinks in cooler air, and the roof of the building is sprayed with cold water for an hour.

When he first conceived the idea of a special opera house whereupon to stage his Nibelung music-drama, Wagner told friends that the work would be performed only once and the theatre then burned to the ground. In 1872 he was still talking about his festival theatre as if it would not be around long. He wrote to the banker Friedrich Feustel from Lucerne on April 10 and continued a discussion on the allocation of the available funds. He told Feustel the 50,000 Thalers allocated for decoration of the building was unnecessarily high: "It is, after all, only planned to be a provisionary structure." Two days later he wrote again to Feustel: "The theatre building to be considered *absolutely provisional*; it would please me if it were entirely of wood, like the gymnasiums and *Saengerfest* halls: no further solidity that what is necessary to ensure against collapse. Therefore, economize—no ornamentation."

At the beginning of the second act of *Die Walküre*, Wotan sings, "Vollendet das ewige Werk" (Completed, the eternal work). He was celebrating the completion of Valhalla by the giants Fasolt and Fafner. When Wagner entered the Festspielhaus for his first rehearsal of *The Ring*, the orchestra stood up and sang "Vollendet das ewige Werk." Both Wagner's *Ring* and the theatre in which it would be performed were finished at last.

The Bayreuth Experience Then . . .

> More than an hour before the time fixed for the play a long line of carriages forms to bring the public to the theatre. These carriages, too few for the number of rich amateurs, are taken by assault; it is well to engage them in advance if you do not wish to go on foot, which you can do in a delightful walk of about twenty minutes along the shady lanes parallel with the principal avenue. The landaus and victorias, somewhat out of date and made to be drawn by two horses, have never more than one, harnessed to the right side of the shaft (as horses are scarce), which produces the most comic effect.
>
> If you are among the first to arrive, you have ample leisure to examine the newcomers and to notice that the toilettes have singularly gained in elegance during the past years . . . The sole annoying point for them [the ladies] is the hat which they

• **Operagoers promenade outside the Festspielhaus and await the fanfare that calls them to take their seats.**

> will not consent to leave with the attendants during the acts, when it is strictly forbidden to keep it on the head. They resign themselves to holding it on their lap, which is scarcely comfortable.
>
> Albert Lavignac, *The Music Dramas of Richard Wagner*, 1898

Stravinsky was not impressed by the architecture of the Festspielhaus, calling it "a crematorium, and a very old-fashioned one at that."

When Gabriel Fauré made the pilgrimage to Bayreuth in August 1896 he wrote to his wife, Marie, giving details of his experiences and impressions. The following comes from one of his lengthy letters.

> We are absolutely overcome by all those wonderful things and all our discussions—and we have very many—come to nothing. It's rather like *The Ring* itself in fact, which is built on a philosophy and all sorts of symbolical ideas which ultimately reveal nothing but our hopeless misery and impotence . . .
>
> It's very, very tiring. Every evening after the performance I feel as if I had walked from the Madeleine to the Bastille and

back ten times over.

Gabriel Fauré, translated by Edward Lockspeiser, in *The Literary Clef*, 1958

. . . And Bayreuth Today

Opera in the Bayreuth Festspielhaus is a lengthy but leisurely event, with the work of Europe's top fashion designers much in evidence. Most of the audience is in formal attire for every opera, and unoccupied seats in the eighteen-hundred-seat auditorium are rarer than modern performances of a Meyerbeer opera. Fifteen, ten, and five minutes before the performance is to start, a group of brass players appears on the balcony facing down the hill to play a series of leitmotifs from that evening's performance.

The longer operas start at 4 P.M., and there are two intermissions. Those who have no fear of falling asleep enjoy aperitifs and a starter course before the opera starts, a main-course meal at the first intermission, and dessert and coffee during the final break.

At the appointed hour all of the entrances to the auditorium slam shut in unison, and anyone arriving late is doomed to wander around the Festspielhaus grounds or to drown their sorrows in the restaurant. There are no exceptions, even for very important persons. And there are no television monitors in the lobby area. Most of the operas end around 11 P.M., but few of the enthusiasts go back to their hotels to sleep. The final curtain is the starting gun for impassioned debates on every aspect of the production. Bayreuth bars and restaurants clock up a lot of overtime during the Festival.

• **Dozens of streets in Bayreuth are named after Wagner family members, the operas, or their characters.**

> "If someone needs to cough, he would be well advised to consider choking to death."
>
> **—Birgit Nilsson, on Bayreuth audience etiquette**

Knowledgeable Wagner audiences everywhere are usually well disciplined, but the discipline of audiences in the Festspielhaus in Bayreuth is exceptional. Even before the house lights are dimmed, chatter in the auditorium dies down and the famous "Bayreuth hush" takes over. On the instructions of Wagner himself, audiences actually listen to preludes and overtures; attempts at conversation will draw the wrath of other audience members. The great Birgit Nilsson said in her memoirs, "If someone needs to cough, he would be well advised to consider choking to death rather than die by the sharp elbow and murderous glare of his neighbor."

Bayreuth audiences never applaud individual singers, sets, or scenes, waiting instead until the last bars of music fade to silence. Then the place erupts. If the audience is pleased with a performance they stamp their feet, creating a thunderous rumble when singers, directors, costume designers, and others step through the gap in the curtains. But when displeased, Bayreuth audiences are totally uninhibited, and loud boos and roars of disapproval are quite common.

Perhaps the first time whistling and booing were heard in the Festspielhaus was in 1956, when the audience disliked Wieland Wagner's new production of *Die Meistersinger von Nürnberg*. It was the Mastersingers *without* Nuremberg. Wieland had stripped away the medieval turrets and spires, and the Festspielhaus audience did not approve. Years later, Rosalie, designer of the much-derided costumes for Alfred Kirchner's production of *The Ring*, took only one small step out from between the curtains and retreated immediately when she was hit by a torrent of very loud booing, whistling, and shouting. She did not reappear. Katharina Wagner suffered a similar fate at the conclusion of her first production in the Festspielhaus, *Die Meistersinger*, in 2007, but Wagner's great-granddaughter is made of sterner stuff. She stood her ground and smiled out at the audience, most of whom were booing.

A leading contender for the loudest, longest, most hostile reception in recent years was the disapproval of Christoph Schlingensief's production of *Parsifal* in 2005. The worst features were a decomposing rabbit and clerics with blood on their hands from a menstruating woman. Some believe that it was the most controversial production ever seen in the Festspielhaus.

The first English singer to appear in the Bayreuth Festival was the mezzo-soprano Marie Brema, who had been mentioned in one of Bernard Shaw's reviews. He said that although she sang a Brahms piece "without two penn'orth of feeling, she had a thousand pounds worth of intelligence and dramatic resolution." Hermann Levi was the talent scout who brought Brema, who sang Ortrud in *Lohengrin* and Kundry in *Parsifal*, to the attention of Cosima Wagner, who ruled the Bayreuth Empire in the 1890s. Irene Dalis, now the successful leader of Opera San José, was the first American to sing Kundry in Bayreuth in 1962.

The Austrian composer Anton Bruckner was a regular visitor to Bayreuth. It is said that he spent hours just looking at Wagner's house, Wahnfried, but that in the Festspielhaus he listened with eyes closed. He did not even try to understand the story of *The Ring* and once asked, "Why do they burn Brünnhilde at the end of *Walküre*?"

Latecomers, Be Warned

A Viennese millionaire missed the first act of the first Bayreuth performance of *Die Walküre*. He arrived after the doors had been closed and was forced to wait until the intermission before taking his seat. The man's name? Rothschild. But there were no exceptions for latecomers to the Festspielhaus then, and there are none today.

The Invisible Orchestra

In prefatory remarks to the first edition of the text of *Der Ring des Nibelungen*, published in 1862, Wagner spelled out his ideas for the "temporary" opera house that he would build for its performance. After discussing the idea of a temporary theatre in one of the smaller German cities, he had this to say about one of the many innovations, the invisible orchestra:

> To complete the impression of such a performance, I should lay great stress upon an invisible orchestra, which it would be possible to effect by the architectural illusion of an amphitheatrical arrangement of the auditorium.
>
> The importance of this will be clear to anyone who attends our present operatic performances for the purpose of gaining any genuine impression of the dramatic art work, and finds himself made the involuntary witness of the technical evolutions caused by the

unavoidable view of the mechanical movements made by the musicians and their leader. These should be as carefully concealed as the wires, roped canvas, and boards of the stage machinery, the sight of which, as everyone knows, creates a most disturbing impression and one calculated to destroy all illusions.

After having experienced what a pure, etherealized tone the orchestra gains by being heard through an acoustic soundingboard which has the effect of eliminating all the indispensable but non-musical sounds which the instrumentalist is obliged to make in producing the tone; and after having realized the advantageous position in which the singer is placed to his listeners, by being able to stand, as it were, directly before them—no one could arrive at other than a favorable conclusion as to the effectiveness of my plan for an acoustic-architectural arrangement.

The artistic success of this innovation in theatre building is without a single drawback. The singers and the players are easily and perfectly heard, the merest whisper or a drum-roll or a tremolo travelling clearly all over the house; and the fortissimo of the total vocal and instrumental force comes with admirable balance of tone, without rattle, echo, excessive localization of sound, or harsh preponderance of the shriller instruments. The concentration of attention on the stage is so complete that the afterimage of the lyric drama witnessed is deeply engraved in the memory, aural and visual. The ventilation is excellent; and the place is free from the peculiar odor inseparable from draped and upholstered theatres.

Wagner, quoted by Bernard Shaw in the *English Illustrated Magazine*, 1889–90

Wagner delivered on almost all of his promises. Certainly the acoustics are near perfection and have not been matched in newer opera houses, despite all the advantages of twenty-first-century acoustic technology. The beginning of *The Ring*, the famous E-flat played on the basses, seems to come from everywhere and nowhere. This creates a mystical effect that is also spine-tingling at the beginning of the prelude to *Parsifal*.

> If one has not heard Wagner at Bayreuth, one has heard nothing.
>
> Gabriel Fauré, in an 1884 letter

It Sounds Even Better in the Dark

The arrival of the famous E-flat is so much more spine-chillingly effective in complete darkness. But the rulings of the health and safety departments make this impossible in most opera houses.

Not, however, at Covent Garden in October 2012, when the full *Ring*, conducted by Antonio Pappano, was broadcast by BBC Radio 3. The audience in the Royal Opera House heard the beginning of *Das Rheingold* in a completely darkened auditorium. As the sound of orchestral tuning faded away, the BBC presenter announced to the radio audience in hushed tones: "And now the house lights are dimming. Absolutely every light in the house will go out including the ones in the pit and even the emergency exit signs . . . Let the magic begin."

"Did you require special permission from Health and Safety to turn all the lights off during a public performance?" I asked the Covent Garden press office. "Uh, we'll get back to you on that," I was told. They never did.

Working in the Mystic Abyss

James Levine, of New York's Metropolitan Opera, usually conducts rehearsals with a towel over his shoulder, presumably to mop up perspiration.

• **The conductor Hans Richter was tired of people asking for tickets so he inserted a sign in his hat reading, "Please do not ask me if I have main rehearsal tickets. I do not."**

In the opera house, he is obliged to don the regulation black tie and tails. But not in the mystic abyss of the Festspielhaus. The sound-reflecting cowl hides the conductor and the orchestra from the audience, and so the inhabitants of the Bayreuth pit can wear anything they like. Levine conducts in a T-shirt and has the ubiquitous towel slung over his shoulder. (I once spotted Levine wandering around the upmarket Pflaums hotel at Pegnitz, near Bayreuth. Even for a discussion with colleagues, Levine had the inevitable white towel over his shoulder.) The members of the orchestra also wear T-shirts. Following the last notes of the performance, the conductor probably has enough time to take a shower before climbing into his tuxedo to take his curtain call.

When it is 80 or 90 degrees in the auditorium, it can be unbearable in the cramped space of the orchestra pit, but the largely German musicians are stoic and dedicated. When the American Thomas Schippers appeared in the pit in 1963 to conduct *Meistersinger* wearing shorts, though, some of his German colleagues thought this was going a bit too far. At the next performance the conductor found a tennis racket on his music stand. He wore long trousers for the third performance.

The conductor in the Bayreuth orchestra pit can see the singers but not the audience. The audience can see the singers but not the conductor or orchestra. The orchestra can see the conductor but neither the audience nor the singers. Even though the conductor has an advantage over his players, working conditions are not ideal. Daniel Barenboim once said that conducting in the pit at Bayreuth is "like being 150 feet underwater without a diver's helmet."

The hidden orchestra at Bayreuth is sometimes a surprise to performers. When Birgit Nilsson sang Elsa in 1954, she looked down at the conductor, Eugen Jochum, for her cue and was astonished to see that he was wearing a short-sleeved plaid shirt. Nilsson could see both the casually dressed conductor and the serried rows of formally dressed audience members. She did not realize until later that the audience could not see the conductor or orchestra.

> It might take nine or ten years of applications to get one's first ticket to Bayreuth.

How Can I Get Tickets?

First-time applicants will receive a very brief, polite letter that says, essentially, tough luck. They try again the following year, with the same unhappy result. Try again in year three and add another rejection letter to their collection. And again, and again, and again. Each time a would-be pilgrim applies, his or her name rises up the rankings until after a long, patient wait, they might get tickets for one or more productions. The current expectation is that it might take nine or ten years before would-be Festspielgoers can pack their bags for Bavaria.

It is very important that you apply every year. If you fail to apply in any future year, your name drops to the bottom of the waiting list, and you start over again. I did not know about this essential detail and waited thirteen years before I got my first ticket. (Grateful thanks to Leise Bauer for making possible my first visit to Bayreuth.)

The difficulty in obtaining tickets for the Bayreuth Festival is not a new phenomenon. The large, red-bearded figure of Hans Richter, first conductor of *The Ring*, was so recognizable that when he walked the streets of Bayreuth he was frequently pestered by fans seeking tickets. He got so tired of this that he stuck a sign in his hat that read: "Please do not ask me if I have main rehearsal tickets. I do not."

There are only 55,000 tickets available for the operas performed during the short summer Festival, but more than half a million applications are received. The number of applications increases every year for a fixed number of tickets, so the chances of success decrease each year. And help from a friendly ticket scalper is unlikely: Bayreuth administrators have established strict rules that forbid the resale of a ticket. Every ticket carries the name of the person to whom it was issued, and spot identity checks are sometimes mounted at the doors. There will be some tough questions for anyone whose ID does not match the name on the ticket.

Choosing the Bayreuth Orchestra and Chorus

There are up to 125 musicians in the Bayreuth pit for performances of *The Ring*. However, around 180 musicians are in the pool because of the need to give players rest periods during the intensive cycle of rehearsals and performances. There is fierce competition for a place on the exclusive Bayreuth team, and musicians are drawn from most of the major German orchestras. Yearly turnover is low, usually not more than a dozen or so, and many of the musicians have been in the orchestra for twenty-five years or more. Even so, every member of the exclusive group is evaluated each year before receiving an invitation to return.

Contrary to popular belief, the musicians who play the warning fanfares before each act are not members of the orchestra. They are drawn from a separate group of ten brass players. Once the triple fanfare has been sounded for the third act, or the single act of *Das Rheingold* or *Der fliegende Holländer*, the work of the fanfare team is over. They can head for home, or possibly some local bar.

Unlike the predominantly German orchestra players, the 134 members of the chorus are drawn from a wider area. In 2008 the singers were drawn from choirs all over Germany and the rest of Europe. Again, competition is fierce and turnover low, typically no more than twenty a year. Auditions are held in London, Manchester, Frankfurt, Hamburg, Vienna, and Bayreuth. The chorus is made up of seventy-six men and fifty-eight women, and many believe that the Bayreuth chorus is the finest in the world. There have been only three chorus masters at Bayreuth since the Festival restarted after World War II. Eberhard Friedrich has been the chorus master since 1991; his two predecessors were the legendary Wilhelm Pitz and Norbert Balatsch.

It's All Rubbish

In 1988 Yuri Lyubimov, a Russian, was appointed to direct a new *Ring* at the Royal Opera House. The problems that followed should have been anticipated. First, the Russian spoke no German, a major obstacle when conducting German opera. He might have got around that problem except that he spoke very little English either and worked with the singers through an interpreter.

Then, in a conversation with Jeremy Isaacs, he confided that he thought Wagner's text was mostly rubbish. With a director who could not communicate directly with the cast, who did not know at any given point where he was in the plot of the fifteen-hour epic, and who probably didn't care because he thought it was all rubbish anyway, the recipe for total disaster was complete.

How could such a man get the best out of world-class singers? The answer is, he didn't. The production was scrapped after *Das Rheingold* and hurriedly replaced with the Götz Friedrich production, which was shipped over from Berlin.

Are You Fully Qualified to Join This Audience, Sir?

> People do not go there [Bayreuth] as they go to the Opéra in Paris or in any other city, taking with them their cares of yesterday and their worldly indifference. Or at least they should not go thus, for it would be voluntarily depriving themselves of one of the most intense artistic emotions it is possible to experience if they entered the hall of the Festival Theatre in Bayreuth without being sympathetically attuned to what they have come to hear.
>
> Unfortunately that is what often happens now that the Wagnerian pilgrimage has become as fashionable as it is to go to Spa or to Monte Carlo. I know perfectly well that it is impossible to make all the spectators pass an examination before permitting them to enter the hall, or to make sure that, either by their musical education or by the intelligent interest which they take in matters of art, they are worthy to enter into the sanctuary, but it must be confessed that it is painful to hear the absurd remarks which show how unworthy is a certain portion of the public that now frequents Bayreuth.
>
> Albert Lavignac, *The Music Dramas of Richard Wagner*, 1898

A London Icon Conceived in Bayreuth

The acclaimed architect Lord Foster, of Thames Bank, had been working on plans for the replacement for London's famous Wembley Stadium. The British architect had already won international recognition as the designer of Hong Kong's stunning new airport, the remodeling of the Reichstag building in Berlin, and numerous other iconic buildings around the world. The original 1999 design for the new Wembley Stadium called for the roof to be supported by cables descending from the tops of four masts. It was a proven technical solution but lacked excitement. Lord Foster was taking a short break in Bayreuth. One evening, while relaxing in the Festspielhaus, a vision of tiara shapes came into his mind. "I raced back to the hotel and started faxing back rough sketches to my associate partner, Alistair Lenczner," he said later. The result was another London icon. The new Wembley Stadium was opened to the public in 2007, and the massive 1,750-ton latticed steel tiara holding up the Wembley roof is now visible from many parts of the capital. Few of those who see it realize that it was conceived in Bayreuth.

Hanny Kopetz, Wagnerian Antiquarian

From a distance, the antique shop on Brandenburger Strasse in Bayreuth looks like any other. But a closer look at the window displays under the red awnings makes it clear that this is no ordinary antique dealer. The window has several busts of Wagner, ranging from a few centimeters up to a larger-than-life forty-five centimeters, as well as various pictures, glass and porcelain figurines, and posters.

The display is a warning to Wagner enthusiasts, because one step inside this mecca for Festival visitors could seriously damage your wealth. The Wagner Antiquariat is an Aladdin's cave crammed with Wagnerian memorabilia, souvenirs, and ephemera. It seems that every shelf has a portrait of Wagner or a bust of the composer in various materials and a range of sizes: at my last visit I counted thirty-seven different busts.

The diminutive owner is Hanny Kopetz, who established the business in 1980. Her encyclopedic knowledge of Wagner and his life and works

• **Hanny Kopetz outside her Bayreuth antique store. She is sitting on one of the original Festspielhaus seats that she sold in 2006.**

• **Italian opera fans will not find much of interest in this antique shop. Everything in it relates to Wagner or his works.**

is backed up by an enormous collection of documents, photographs, books, autographs, music scores, and ephemera. And like the owner of an old-fashioned hardware store, she knows where everything is. Ask a question about some esoteric aspect of productions in Bayreuth over the course of several decades and she heads for some corner of her three-room store and rummages around before triumphantly producing something that answers the question and more.

The stock of the store turns over constantly, and during an average year she acquires items from several sources around the world. She has scouts in several locations who tip her off when interesting items come on the market. Much of it is then sold during the summer Festival, when Wagner enthusiasts from around the world come to Brandenburger Strasse to buy something for their personal collection or as a gift for a Wagnerian who could not get one of the sought-after Festival tickets.

"What special items are you offering this year?" she was asked. "Well, I bought several of the original seats from the Festspielhaus," she told me. "These are the last two," she says, pointing to a pair of wooden chairs with woven wicker seats. Then her eyes light up as she points to what looks like an ornate lamp. "Did you know that the illuminated Grail for the first production of *Parsifal* was made by a Bayreuth dentist who had the necessary tools and skills for the job?" I had to confess that I did not know that and had no idea of what the original Grail looked like. "Well, here is a reproduction that I now have for sale," she said. "It was recreated based on press photographs of the original. It will probably end up in the collection of a *Parsifal* enthusiast somewhere."

One shelf in the store is filled with piles of Bayreuth Festival programs over many years, including a few of the famous Chéreau centenary *Ring* of 1976. Another corner has racks of posters, postcards, and original

• **The Festspielhaus is flanked by the house where Wagner was born in Leipzig and the Palazzo Vendramin in Venice, where he died. Engraving by Kaeseberg and Oertel.**

artworks, including many cartoons and caricatures. I bought a cartoon showing a titanic struggle between Siegmund and a stagehand trying to hold up a flimsy set. The artist is believed to have been Emil Wagner (no relation) and dates from around 1927. The cartoon is on page 224 of this book.

Wagner's Homes

Leipzig

Wagner was born in the House of the White and Red Lion, 88 the Brühl, in the old part of Leipzig. The house was declared unsafe and was demolished in 1886. A plaque commemorating Wagner's birth home is mounted on a nearby department store.

Tribschen, the Richard Wagner Museum

Tribschen was built in 1626 on a large estate overlooking Lake Lucerne. The house was restored in 1800, and Wagner arrived in April 1866. Cosima von Bülow joined him later the same year, but she and Wagner could not be married until 1870, after her divorce from Hans von Bülow. It was in this house that both Eva and Siegfried Wagner were born, that Nietzsche became one of the family, and that Cosima started writing the daily diaries that would

• Possibly the only Chinese restaurant in the world that has a picture of Richard Wagner prominently displayed in the entrance. The Lucerne restaurant was frequented by Wagner when it was the Dubeli pub.

• Order card from Wagner's pub, the Dubeli in Lucerne.

continue until the day before Richard's death. Years later Cosima wrote that the six years they lived in the house overlooking the lake were the happiest of her life.

The Tribschen estate (Wagner insisted on adding an "e," and so the spelling "Triebschen" found its way into many books and articles) had belonged to an old Lucerne family. It was sold to the municipality of Lucerne in 1931, and after restoration the ground floor of the house was turned into the Richard Wagner Museum. Among the exhibits is the original score of the *Siegfried Idyll*, played in the house as a present to Cosima on her birthday, Christmas morning, in 1870, with Wagner conducting a group of musicians arrayed on the Tribschen staircase.

The hundreds of other exhibitions in the museum include numerous letters carrying Wagner's signature, portraits, photographs, sculptures, and concert programs, as well as several original scores, librettos, and notes. There is also one of Wagner's famous velvet berets, and a velvet jacket and silk shirt that he wore at Tribschen, and the Erard piano that traveled with him on his frequent movements around Europe.

Wagner's Bierhalle

Wagner followed a regular daily routine. He rose at six, bathed, and then read until breakfast, served at ten o'clock. He worked until four, then drove or walked until six, when he worked for another two hours before supper and an evening with his family.

On some days he would find time to walk along the lakeshore into the center of Lucerne to collect his newspaper. He sometimes visited his favorite bar, the Bierhalle Dubeli on Furrengasse, near the Chapel Bridge in the heart of old Lucerne.

Today Dubeli is no more. In 1965 the Li Tai Pe Chinese restaurant was established, but the connection with Wagner is maintained. There is a brass plaque over the front door reading "Stammlokal Richard Wagner's [*sic*]." This upmarket dining establishment is possibly the only Chinese restaurant in the world that has a portrait of Richard Wagner in a place of honor inside the main entrance.

In May 1866 King Ludwig decided to pay a surprise visit to Lucerne for Wagner's birthday, despite fears that the country might be forced to go to war. He arrived, in time for lunch, dressed in a blue cape and a large hat decorated with peacock feathers. Wagner and Cosima, unaware of the visit, were told by a servant that someone called Walther von Stolzing was at the front door. Ludwig stayed for two days. Inevitably, news of the visit leaked, and he was severely criticized for leaving his country during a national emergency.

Most historians agree that the Tribschen years were probably the happiest of Wagner's life. The Wagners left only because plans were in hand for the long-desired opera house in Bayreuth, which was to be the beginning of another exciting period. Nevertheless, there was an inevitable melancholy about the family's departure in 1871.

Wagner returned only once, six years later. He and his family called in on the way back from London in July 1877. Tribschen was then occupied by a French family. Wagner's grandson Wieland described one special moment in his essay "From Tribschen to Wahnfried." Wagner was silent and pensive. Only once did his mood change and a sarcastic smile begin playing over his lips: lying open on the grand piano was a piano arrangement of Meyerbeer's *Les Huguenots*.

In 1905 Cosima returned to visit her old home and sent a greeting to Hans Richter. Eight years later she paid a final visit and commented on how the once beautiful and peaceful town had changed. She was particularly critical of the ugliness of the railway station.

The house changed hands many times after Wagner's death and was often unoccupied for long periods. Occasional Wagnerian pilgrims coming to Lucerne could do no more than stand outside the silent, empty, shuttered house.

In 1956 the Richard Wagner Tribschen Museum was established. The house continues to be managed as part of the Lucerne museum service.

Arrival in Bayreuth

In 1871 Wagner was preparing to move permanently to Bayreuth. He had already decided to call his new home Wahnfried. But the house would not be completed until late in 1873. When he wrote to the banker Friedrich Feustel with some thoughts on temporary accommodation, he was, in typical Wagner fashion, thinking big: "I have in mind one of those large earlier estates of the nobility, pointed out to me as 'castles,' with large gardens, in fact, 'parks,' one or two hours distant from the city."

On April 24, 1872, when he was almost fifty-nine, Wagner arrived to take up residence in Bayreuth. He stayed at the home of Feustel, chairman of the Bayreuth community commissioners' board, at Bahnhofstrasse 15. Feustel was instrumental, along with Mayor Theodor Muncker, in arranging for Wagner to settle on Bayreuth for his festival theatre and his future residence. Feustel's house no longer exists; a multistory building occupies the site.

Three days later Wagner moved to the Hotel Fantaisie in Donndorf, a few kilometers outside Bayreuth, where he was joined by Cosima and the children. In September 1872 Wagner rented a house at 7 Dammalee, which was convenient for the site of the Festspielhaus, the foundation stone of which had been laid on his birthday on May 22

• **The rear of Wahnfried, Wagner's home in Bayreuth. The house is now the Richard Wagner Museum.**

of that year. While living in the Dammalee house, Wagner was visited by Liszt and Bruckner. During that time he started work on his future residence in the Hofgarten. The Dammalee house has since been replaced by a multistory building.

In February 1872 Wagner had written to Muncker to explain his ideas for the house to be built for him. Again, he was thinking big, and he went into some detail with regard to his requirements. He even specified how the garden should be laid out and planted with trees and shrubs. He urged Mayor Muncker to err on the side to too much rather than too little. The avenue of chestnuts, the shrubberies, the pine trees, and the circular lawn at the rear of the house specified by Wagner are still features of Wahnfried today. Add garden designing to the talents of this extraordinary man.

When he moved into Wahnfried, Wagner insisted that the house be furnished with the finest furniture, carpets, and tapestries: "Beauty, splendor, and brightness are a must for me! The world owes me what I need . . . or is it really unreasonable to ask for a little bit of luxury that I am so fond of? After all I am giving the world and thousands of people so much joy and pleasure."

Several problems were encountered during the construction of Wahnfried, and Wagner nicknamed it Angersheim (House of Anger). In April 1874 the family moved in, and Wagner described it as "this place, where my fantasies found peace and rest . . . The name Wahnfried is chiseled in gold over the front entrance. Wahn = illusion/delusion and Fried = Peace."

The frieze was created to Cosima's specifications by the Dresden painter Robert Krausse. Wagner's October 1874 letter to King Ludwig described it:

> The center is occupied by Germanic Myth; since we wanted to have characteristic physiognomies, we resolved to use the features of the late Ludwig Schnorr; from either side Wotan's ravens fly toward it and it proclaims the legend imparted to it to two female figures, one of which, whose features resemble those of Schröder-Devrient, represents Ancient Tragedy, while the other represents Music, with the head and figure of Cosima; a small boy, clad as Siegfried and with my son's head, holds her hand, gazing up at his mother Music with an expression of mettlesome joy.

After the years of penury, Wagner and Cosima lived well at Wahnfried. The house was extravagantly furnished with plush sofas, soft armchairs, numerous little tables and desks, and the grand piano once owned by Liszt. Deep pile carpets and silk tapestries adorned the walls. The Wagners' household staff included a cook, a governess, a gardener, a caretaker, and a chambermaid.

The Wahnfried library, formerly the drawing room, houses Wagner's eclectic collection of 2,500 books. In late March 1945 Wolfgang Wagner, concerned about the safety of this valuable collection, arranged for it to be removed for storage elsewhere.

For thirty years after Wagner's death, Cosima never touched her husband's Steinway at Wahnfried. Her granddaughter Friedelind recalled in *Heritage of Fire* that the piano remained where it was and had not been moved even an inch. Then, on the day Wieland was born, Cosima sat down at the Steinway and played a few bars of the *Siegfried Idyll*. It is said that Cosima never touched the piano again during the rest of her life. However, one witness said that she did play Schubert's "Lob der Tränen" (In Praise of Tears) only hours before Wagner's death.

Wagner's tomb, which he designed himself, is a flat, unadorned stone slab. In 1930, almost fifty years after Wagner's death, Cosima was buried alongside her husband. Plain ivy and shrubs normally surround the graves but in July and August of each year, flowers and wreaths are placed on the tombs by representatives of the Festspielhaus orchestra and visiting Wagner Societies from all parts of the world.

At least two of Wagner's dogs are buried in the garden at Wahnfried. Russ is buried alongside his master's grave. The small headstone reads, "Here rests and watches Wagner's Russ." When Festival visitors place flowers on Wagner's tomb, the dogs are not forgotten. Some unknown visitors place flowers on Russ' grave. Around the corner, close to the exit to the Hofgarten, is the grave of another of Wagner's dogs, Marke.

In 1940 British planes flew over Bayreuth for the first time, and the mayor was puzzled. It had been hoped that because there were no obvious military targets in or around Bayreuth, the Allied bombers would stay away. Then the mayor discovered that Winifred Wagner had met with Hitler on his Pullman railway coach, which had been parked near the town. Allied intelligence officers may have known what the mayor had not.

The following month Bayreuth was bombed for the first time. Wahnfried was hit, and most of the rear of the house was destroyed. It could have been worse: the house was hit by only one of the twenty-five bombs that fell in the adjacent Hofgarten. Had it not been for Wolfgang's concern about the library, Wagner's precious books would have gone up in flames. The Festspielhaus was never hit, but it was looted in the final weeks of the war. Villa Wahnfried was later fully restored and in 1976 became a museum.

> Beauty, splendor, and brightness are a must for me! The world owes me what I need."
>
> **—Richard Wagner, on furnishing his new home in Bayreuth**

Last Stop: Venice

After leaving Asyl in Zurich in the late summer of 1858, Wagner lived for eight months in one of the run-down Giustiniani palaces on Venice's Grand Canal.

The summer Bayreuth Festival in 1882 exhausted Wagner. *Parsifal*, his final opera, had had its premiere in the Festspielhaus on July 26 and was followed by another fifteen performances. The following month Wagner, Cosima, their son, Siegfried, Liszt, and several other friends left Bayreuth for Venice. They occupied twenty-eight rooms at the Palazzo Vendramin, which is prominently located on the tip of Giudecca Island on the Grand Canal, not far from St. Mark's Square.

Wagner and his entourage arrived in Venice on September 18, 1882. Four months later, on February 13, 1883, the composer died in his room in the Palazzo Vendramin, now a casino. Visits to Wagner's rooms are permitted on Saturday mornings at 10 A.M., but advance reservations are essential. ■

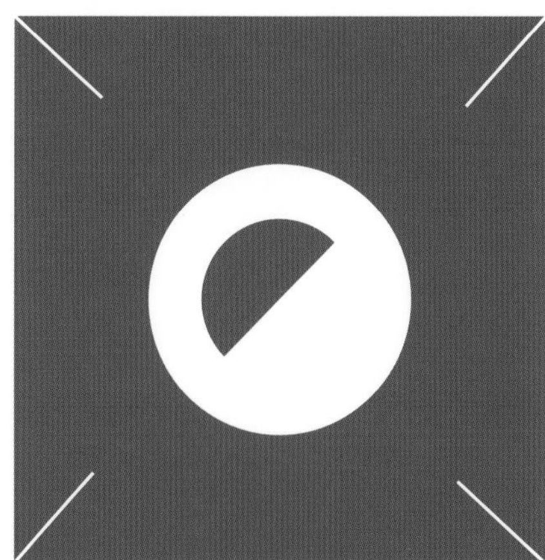

Intermission

Creativity or Desecration?

Nobody Sits on the Fence

New ideas and interpretations are both the lifeblood of opera and a source of anger and bitter argument. The question is, how far can a director go in offering his own interpretation before departing so far from the creator's intention that he becomes guilty of desecration? Few disagree that it is necessary to innovate. The staging and interpretation would very soon become boring if all productions stuck religiously to Wagner's original instructions. But how far is too far?

Some modern productions have delighted Wagner enthusiasts, but many have triggered outrage and condemnation because the constant search for new ideas and interpretations frequently leads directors into dangerous territory.

In his admirable book on the history of the Bayreuth Festival, Frederic Spotts writes:

> But the issue for Bayreuth—and for contemporary operatic production—is establishing where interpretation leaves off and violation starts, where inspiration stops and self-indulgent exhibitionism takes over, where independent critical judgment ends and trendy uncritical conformity in fear of being considered an old fogy begins. After all, the composer's motivation in establishing his own opera theatre was to prevent the disfiguration of his works.
>
> Frederic Spotts, *Bayreuth: A History of the Wagner Festival*, 1994

Roger Scruton, author of *Gentle Regrets*, hit the nail on the thumb when he said, "Wagner productions are invariably travesties—not productions, in fact, but 'interpretations,' with the ego of the producer placed squarely between the work and the audience, so turning every seat in the opera house into one with an obstructed view." Bernard Levin put it this way: "Directors should have the artistic integrity in accepting the duty to convey the spirit and meaning of the work rather than the ingenuity and perseverance of the director. Richard Wagner is not commonly regarded as a composer who didn't know his own mind, needing assistance from directors who could tell him what he was thinking." And Bernard Shaw wrote in 1894, "I hate performers who debase great works of art: I long for their annihilation: if my criticisms were flaming thunderbolts, no prudent Life or Fire Insurance Company would entertain a proposal from any singer within my range, or from the lessee of any opera-house or concert-room within my circuit." It seems likely that if writing that today, Shaw would feel the same way about pretentious directors.

> "Richard Wagner is not commonly regarded as a composer who didn't know his own mind."
> —**Bernard Levin**

In *Aspects of Wagner*, one of the best books on the composer ever written, Bryan Magee spelled out four objections to the work of modern producers.

> Producers who turn works of art into vehicles for currently topical ideas and attitudes show that they have no real understanding of what art is. But even to the least objectionable of those who treat Wagner's works as if they were primarily vehicles for social and historical comment I have many objections, of which four are salient. First, it is to treat ideas which can

> be conceptualized as if they were what is central to a great work of art, and they never are. Second, by doing that, producers ignore the work's genuinely profound aspects, thereby what I have called "superficializing" it. Third, they treat the actual setting in which Wagner placed his work as irrelevant to it, something that can be dispensed with completely without loss or injury to the rest of the work—a bizarre thing for a stage producer, of all people, to suppose. Fourth, to relate most of Wagner's works to contemporary or recent social settings is to do something that he took enormous pains to preclude: he deliberately set most of his works in a mythical or quasi-mythical world, he goes out of his way to tell us, because their content is universal and therefore not to be seen as relating to one particular society.
>
> Bryan Magee, *Aspects of Wagner*, 1968

"It is almost fifty years since I wrote that, and I still believe every word of it," Magee told me recently.

In my opinion, one recent example of a *Ring* gone wrong was the 2005–13 Royal Opera House production directed by Keith Warner, with designs by Stefanos Lazaridis. Many critics found the production confused and incoherent. They commented on bewildering visual metaphors, such as the Rubik's-cube helmet for the Tarnhelm and Wotan emerging into Mime's hut from a crashed plane. "Mostly baffling," said the *Guardian*. "Dismayingly bad . . . A disappointing *Ring* that just goes round in circles," was the verdict of the *Telegraph*. Another writer suggested, "There is something unsettling about dragons, toads and magic helmets in a high-tech modern setting with lots of stainless steel."

Most telling for some disappointed Wagner enthusiasts was the question posed by Anthony Holden, the eminent critic of the *Observer*. He asked, "Is Warner playing an elaborate joke on us or what? The boos at the end were, for once, deserved."

It was inevitable that the complexity of *The Ring* should result in endless thoughts on meanings, and the speculation, exploration, and experimentation continues to the present day. Wieland created a sensation in 1951 with his first postwar production. He stripped away everything from the original production. No rocks. No trees. No buildings, It was the first revolutionary, minimalist production. It worked because the director did not impose any of his own ideas on the work but left "interpretation" to the audience.

Regie Opera

Most Wagnerians believe that it was Patrice Chéreau who broke the mold and set the scene for superimposing a director's thinking onto Wagner's concepts. Chéreau's centenary *Ring* in 1976 (see below) was a dramatic departure from the stagings of the first hundred years. Many believe, therefore, that Chéreau was the first exponent of *Regie* opera. However, in his valuable book *Opera: The Rough Guide*, Matthew Boyden gives several examples of pre-Chéreau *Regie* opera:

> In the 1970s . . . the revolution arrived not in Bayreuth (where Wolfgang imitated his brother), but in Kassel and Leipzig. In Kassel Siegfried was a hippy, Wotan was a Texan oil millionaire (surrounded by decrepit gods in wheelchairs), the Nibelungs lived in a concrete bunker and the Gibichungs were decked out as Nazis. The Norns' broken rope at the beginning of *Götterdämmerung* was a crashed computer. The anticapitalist line was furthered in Leipzig: Wotan was now a mad industrialist, the gods lived in a decaying Grecian

temple, Fafner and Fasolt got a crowd of oppressed factory workers to build Valhalla, and the wedding in *Götterdämmerung* took place on a turbine-factory floor, surrounded by yet more Nazi thugs.

Matthew Boyden, *Opera: The Rough Guide*, 1999

For its followers, the label *Regie* is synonymous with creative, different, or adventurous. To its opponents, it is more like distortion or desecration. The word *Regietheater* is German for "director's theatre"; it implies giving almost total freedom to the director to depart from the intentions of the creator by making additions, moving the setting of a work to a different time, or introducing political or psychological interpretations. Opponents believe that in *Regie* productions the director plays too great a role compared to those of the composer, conductor, and singers.

Chéreau set his *Ring* in modern times with sets that included a hydroelectric power station. Since then the search for new approaches has gone on, and almost every new staging of *The Ring* triggers a debate on the interpretation and the relevance of the staging.

Audiences usually divide into several major camps. First there are those who welcome every new approach—the more innovative and adventurous, the better. They believe that this is the only answer to the boredom and monotony of "naturalistic" productions. They favor new solutions and approaches, and they quote Wagner, who instructed his followers, "Kinder, schafft Neues" (children, try something new).

The second sizable audience category is one that supports new approaches, provided they are executed with respect to the composer's intentions. They argue the need to avoid contradictions between what the music says and what the audience sees on the stage.

After hydroelectric power stations and glass-sided elevators, where do you go next?

John Wagner (no relation) in California suggested a fourth category to my original three:

> I would create a fourth category between the first group (welcome every new approach) and the second (new approaches OK only if they follow Wagner's intentions). I would grant more leeway for innovation not specifically tied to Wagner's statements. In general I think that once an artist puts a work "out there" into the public sphere, he or she loses control as to what future interpreters may choose to do with the work. I would not go as far as your first category and say anything goes. Of course, there are limits and I think it is totally improper to deliberately make a mockery of an artist's work.

The final group—a small and rapidly diminishing one—believes that the only way to produce Wagner's works is to follow his detailed instructions. However, not even the most conservative traditional-staging supporter would share the concerns of Vernon Blackburn, who in 1899 adopted a critical tone when he compared productions of *Die Meistersinger* in Bayreuth with the Covent Garden version.

> Whereas Covent Garden arranges the characters who sing the famous quintet in the third act in a straight line, Bayreuth arranges them in the form of a triangle. I might say that Jean de Reszke attires

> himself for the contest in pale grey velvet, where the Bayreuth man appears in claret red. I might even note that as Magdalena, an artist who in London arrayed her head in a red wig with grandmotherly side-curls, at Bayreuth appeared in the same character without so irresistibly comic an appeal to the eye.
>
> Vernon Blackburn, *Bayreuth and Munich: A Travelling Record of German Operatic Art*, 1899

The debates begin at the end of every new production, and unanimous verdicts are rare. The mixed reactions are clear immediately, especially in Bayreuth, where cheers frequently mingle with boos. And just as it took time for audiences to adjust to the new musical norms that Wagner had introduced, so later audiences have needed time to recognize the validity of new interpretations. Chéreau's production of *The Ring* was greeted by howls of protest in 1976, but just a year later he was acclaimed as a genius, and today his groundbreaking production is recognized by most as a turning point in Wagnerian interpretation.

Chéreau's production raised the bar for other directors. After hydroelectric power stations and glass-sided elevators, where do you go next? Pressures on directors to innovate have pushed many toward the ludicrous or shocking. The worst excesses of some have resulted in the use of the pejorative "Eurotrash." The label is used mainly in the United States, where views on European productions are frequently negative.

Today some enthusiasts suspect that directors purposely set out to shock the audience in order to gain attention. Examples might be the 2004–7 Bayreuth *Parsifal* directed by the enfant terrible Christoph Schlingensief, which featured clerics representing most of the world's religions waving their blood-covered hands in the air. The blood had been taken from a large model of a menstruating woman and was one of the reasons that the Schlingensief *Parsifal* was one of the most controversial productions in Bayreuth's long history of controversial productions. It was rumored in Bayreuth circles that Wolfgang Wagner tried to fire Schlingensief during rehearsals, but the idea was dropped because the likely legal costs could have been ruinous.

It gets even sillier when the pot starts calling the kettle black. Listeners to a German radio station were astonished to hear Schlingensief criticize Katharina Wagner's 2007 production of *Die Meistersinger*. He said he felt like she had set the production in a "fitness studio or a porn shop."

One of the most egregious recent examples of *Regietheater* gone wrong was the May 2013 production of *Tannhäuser* by Deutsche Oper am Rhein in Düsseldorf. The Nazi theme of this stomach-churning production brought boos from the audience within minutes of the start. No wonder. It showed people dying in a gas chamber; the rape of the heroine, Elisabeth, who was left bloodied and crying; and a scene where a mother, father, and daughter were stripped, had their heads shaved, and were then executed.

There was a near-riot on opening night, and some audience members were treated for shock after witnessing the harrowing scenes. The director, Burkhard Kosminski, refused to make changes, so the management canceled the production and substituted a concert version of the popular opera.

Now I have another name to put on my list of directors whose works I will never see.

Irrelevant Creativity

Another contender for the shock-and-horror award might be the 2004 English National Opera *Ring*, in which Brünnhilde is put to sleep on her rock by several hypodermic-wielding figures in white coats while Wotan looks on. To me, that introduced an unforgivable conflict between what is heard and what is seen. The sleep motif merging into the magic fire theme and mixed with the fate motif is one of the most achingly beautiful compositions in all of opera. To replace a gentle kiss on the eyes with a multiple attack with hypodermic needles is nothing short of desecration.

Reactions are never predictable, and the themes and production details so hated by some are enthusiastically applauded by others. However, a number of modern Wagnerians are annoyed by directors and designers who, it seems, first come up with interesting visual ideas and then try to justify them with some weak explanation. (I have labeled such efforts "irrelevant creativity.") Worst of all are directors who come up with ideas that demonstrate their lack of understanding of what a given opera is all about or who introduce ideas that conflict badly with the basic story or the music—for example, the 2006 Bayreuth *Ring*, which overlapped the mythical story of gods and giants with scenes from twenty-first-century life. There were workmen repairing telephone cables near to Fafner's cave, a courting couple sitting alongside a bicycle, a man in modern dress reading a newspaper on the stairs, and a large crowd of partygoers in tuxedos and ball gowns suddenly appearing in the Gibichung Hall. The whole thing became so confused that it seemed to me that the time controls on Doctor Who's Tardis time traveler had gone out of kilter. The idea that action in *The Ring* can be superimposed on scenes from modern life is possibly creative but, in my view, totally irrelevant.

Most singers and conductors maintain a discreet silence about what happens on the stage even when they disapprove, and few have spoken out against stagings that are inappropriate or just plain ridiculous. There have been a few brave exceptions. The Cornish-born tenor John Treleaven sang Siegfried in the controversial Royal Opera House *Ring* without any public comment. But he ran out of patience when he sang the role in the Los Angeles production in 2010. He told the *Los Angeles Times*, "The character development that I bring to the part is almost expunged by this clown-like makeup." The steep rake of the stage resulted in ankle and knee injuries, and the tenor's relationship with the director, Achim Freyer, was severely strained: "My level of trust has been severely dented. I can only open myself up to a certain extent now."

> "My advice . . . is simple: pretend you are listening to the radio. Keep your eyes closed."
>
> **—Stephen Pollard, the *Times*, on the Covent Garden *Ring* in 2007**

Linda Watson, Los Angeles' Brünnhilde, was also concerned about the steeply angled stage. "It is the most dangerous stage I've been on in my entire career . . . The entire body is tipped wrong. It's very painful to do it for hours," she told the *Los Angeles Times*. She too was concerned about the director's approach to effective character development and reportedly told Freyer, "Buy one of my CDs and put it on instead of me."

Other singers complained about uncomfortable costumes. According to the *Los Angeles Times*, one was reported to have quit the production because a mask that he was required to wear interfered with his hearing.

Werktreue, the Antidote for *Regie*?

To my knowledge, there are only two opera companies in the world that eschew the so-called *Regie* productions. The first is Seattle Opera, under the caring guidance of Speight Jenkins.

The other is the Richard Wagner Festival in Wels, Austria. It only performs one Wagner opera a year, and in 2014 it will celebrate twenty-five years of *Werktreue* productions that follow the original directions of the composer. *Werktreue* translates roughly as "faithful to the original," and the excesses of Eurotrash are anathema to the Wels team, led by the Festival's director, Renate Doppler, daughter of the founder.

Since it was established it has performed seven of the main canonical works in the small theatre in the Hotel Greif in Wels. The technical facilities are limited, but that has not dissuaded some of the top Wagnerian singers in the world from participating. The list includes Theo Adam, Gwyneth Jones, Janis Martin, Uta Priew, Gabrielle Schnaut, Falk Struckmann, Bernd Weikl, Ekkehard Wlaschiha, Nadine Secunde, Hans Sotin, Stig Andersen, and John Treleaven.

It all started when Walter Just looked at the theatre that formed part of the newly acquired hotel. He was a lifelong Wagnerian, so when he spotted an alcove in the small theatre, he decided to place a bust of the Meister in the vacant niche. Then it seemed appropriate to celebrate the installation of the Wagner bust with a concert of Wagner's music. It was such a success that annually for the next few years, a concert version of a different Wagner opera was staged. Then the prominent stage designer Günther Schneider-Siemssen encouraged the Wels team to mount fully staged productions; they have now become an annual event, starting with *Tristan and Isolde* in 1995.

The three operas not yet staged in Wels are *Das Rheingold*, *Götterdämmerung*, and *Meistersinger*. The latter is a daunting prospect for a small company, but hopefully Wels will get round to it one day. They have an additional reason: Hans Sachs was a frequent visitor to Wels, and the local choir is named after him.

It's OK Provided You Don't Look

Although conductors are reluctant to criticize the work of another member of the production team, it was rumored that Bernard Haitink was so unhappy about a Covent Garden production that he came close to walking out. He refused to make a public statement on the row but was reported to have said that he often conducted *The Ring* while averting his eyes from the stage.

In 1940 Herbert von Karajan decided to solve the problem of inappropriate stagings by doing the job himself. For a production of *Meistersinger* he combined the role of conductor and producer. In his autobiography he wrote about the difficulty "that arises time and again in every opera house in the world, when a conductor notices during the rehearsals that the producer he's working with does not know the work that he's producing." In the following years, Karajan served as both producer and conductor of several Wagner operas, including *Rheingold*, *Walküre*, *Siegfried*, *Götterdämmerung*, *Tristan and Isolde*, *Tannhäuser*, and *Parsifal*.

I'm Not Going to Take This Any More!

Wagner seems to suffer more than most other composers from the self-indulgent, high-octane pretentiousness of opera directors. In a column in the *Times*, Stephen Pollard addressed BBC Radio 4 enthusiasts attending the Covent Garden *Ring* in October 2007. "My advice to them tomorrow—advice that, I've realized, is widely applicable—is simple: pretend you are listening to the radio. Keep your eyes closed." That may be good advice, but it is hard to take after paying a small fortune for a ticket. Maybe we should follow the example of Peter Finch in the film *Network*. Open the windows now, put your head outside and shout to your neighbors, "I'm a Wagnerian, I'm as mad as hell, and I'm not going to take this anymore!" It won't change anything or even scratch the ego of

Eurotrash directors, but it might make you feel better for a few minutes.

Stephen Wadsworth has said: "I can think of *Ring* cycles when I haven't had the foggiest idea of what's going on. When an audience sits there trying to decipher the director's concept—I don't think that's what opera is about." An exasperated participant at a Wagner Society event in England had a similar idea. He asked if it was generally accepted that after seeing the Royal Opera House *Ring*, it was necessary to attend a seminar to find out what it was all about.

More than thirty years after he conducted the first *Ring* in 1876, the conductor Hans Richter wrote to a friend in England: "In *The Ring*, the aural experience must not be disturbed by the visual." Sadly, many modern directors ignore this sage advice.

Most directors have an ego the size of Valhalla. The eminent Wagnerian Father Owen Lee has suggested that the problem is that some of them love themselves more than they love Wagner. It is therefore refreshing to quote one who is prepared to take a back seat. Sven-Eric Bechtolf, director of the Vienna State Opera *Ring* in 2008, told journalists: "But if the composer isn't at the center, there's something rotten. A director is only a manager. Our names should come last, after those of the conductor, the orchestra, the soloists."

Bechtolf is in a lonely minority. His compatriots will continue their efforts to show us what clever people they are. They will continue to foist irrelevant creativity on long-suffering audiences.

A patch of red poppies now growing where Fasolt was bludgeoned to death in an earlier scene is relevant creativity. An aircraft theme running through a *Ring* is irrelevant creativity, in my opinion. Anti-*Regie* Wagnerians can provide numerous other examples.

"When was the last 'traditional' *Ring* production staged anywhere in Europe?" I asked during a discussion on *Regie* versus "traditional" productions. "Uh, that would have been Bayreuth in 1876," said one joker.

> "But if the composer isn't at the center, there's something rotten."
> **—Sven-Eric Bechtolf, opera director**

Not true, of course; but the question may be academic, because few younger Wagnerians have seen a *Ring* in Europe that was about giants, myths, and human weakness with sets that included trees and rocks. Those of us who have been able to see beautiful, relevant *Ring* productions in Seattle, New York, or San Francisco are fortunate indeed.

Now Here's a Great Idea

Philip Kennicott is the chief art critic of the *Washington Post* and a regular contributor to *Opera News*. In an article headed "Ring of Truth" in the April 2012 issue of the magazine, he criticized productions that "strive for shock value, unnecessarily alienating large swaths of the audience and adding little more than another kind of 'cloak' over the events of the drama." Earlier he quoted from a 1966 series of essays by Susan Sontag, *Against Interpretation and Other Essays*. "'Interpretation,' she wrote, wasn't "'simply the compliment that mediocrity pays to genius.' It had become a wall that separated us from art itself." Sontag was not talking about *The Ring*, but what she said hits the nail on the head for Wagnerians tired of *Regie* productions. Or as I sometimes say, hit the nail on the thumb.

Then Kennicott offered a brilliant idea. He suggested doing away with the director who imposes his own interpretation of what a great work is all about and proposed that this task be left to the singers. Most of the top Wagnerian singers have performed in multiple *Rings* in many countries, during which they have developed a deep knowledge of the drama. They know better than most directors what it is all about and would likely eschew *Regie* stagings that leave Wagner newcomers mystified and old hands exasperated.

Three cheers for the "singers' *Ring*." While suspecting that Philip Kennicott had his tongue in his cheek, it is a great idea, and I hope some producer will have the courage to give it a try. Then, hopefully, we could say goodbye to irrelevant creativity and the nonsense imposed by lesser minds on the works of a genius. Goodbye to hypodermic "magic sleep" inducers, Rubik's-cube Tarnhelms, and cheap candles serving as "magic fire." I can't wait. ■

Act Four

Der Ring des Nibelungen (*The Ring of the Nibelung*)

The Ring took twenty-six years to write, takes fifteen hours to perform, and requires a massive orchestra of more than a hundred musicians. It includes the longest uninterrupted stretches of classical music ever composed, and some believe it includes some of the most stunningly beautiful music ever written. Wagner wrote the texts of the four operas in reverse order and worked forward through the composition. *The Ring of the Nibelung* is one of the supreme accomplishments of a single human mind.

The story of *The Ring* according to Nietzsche:

> In *The Ring of the Nibelungen*, the tragic hero is a god (Wotan), who covets power and who, by following every path to obtain it, binds himself with contracts, loses his liberty and is at last engulfed in the curse which rests upon power. He becomes conscious of his loss of liberty, because he no longer has the means to gain possession of the golden ring, the essence or symbol of all earthly power, and at the same time of greatest danger for himself as long as it remains in the hands of his enemies. The fear of the end and the "twilight" of all the gods comes over him and likewise despair, as he realizes that he cannot strive against this end, but must quietly see it approach. He stands in need of the free, fearless man, who without his advice and aid, even battling against divine order, from within himself accomplishes the deed which is denied to the gods. He does not discover him, and just as a new hope awakens he must yield to the destiny that binds him. Through his hand the dearest must be destroyed, the purest sympathy punished with his distress.
>
> Then at last he loathes the power that enslaves and brings forth evil. His will is broken, and he desires the end which threatens from afar. And now what he had but just desired occurs. The free, fearless man appears. He is created supernaturally, and they who gave birth to him pay the penalty of a union contrary to nature. They are destroyed, but Siegfried lives.
>
> In the sight of his splendid growth and development the loathing vanishes from the soul of Wotan. He follows the hero's fate with the eye of the most fatherly love and anxiety. How Siegfried forges the sword, kills the dragon, secures the ring, escapes the most crafty intrigues, and awakens Brünnhilde; how the curse that rests upon the ring does not spare even him, the innocent one, but comes nearer and nearer; how he, faithful in faithlessness wounds out of love the most beloved, and is surrounded by the shadows and mist of guilt, but at last emerges as clear as the sun and sinks, illuminating the heavens with his fiery splendor and purifying the world from the curse—all this the god, whose governing spear has been broken in the struggle with the freest and who has lost his power to him, holds full of joy at his own defeat, fully participating in the joy and sorrow of his conqueror. His eye rests with the brightness of a painful serenity upon all that has passed. "He has become free in Love, free from himself."
>
> Friedrich Nietzsche, quoted in Ludwig Nohl, *Life of Wagner*, 1884

In 1863 Wagner had the text of *The Ring of the Nibelung* printed; only a few copies were distributed. In the preface he spelled out his dream:

• **Perhaps the marketing ploy that started the interest in collecting trade cards. The Stollwerck company first issued cards with their chocolate around 1840. This one featuring Wagner and a Valkyrie is believed to have been produced around 1910.**

> He had with Semper [the architect] conceived the design of a theatre which after the Grecian style should confine the attention of the entire audience to the stage, by its amphitheatric form, thus rendering impossible the mutual staring of the public or at least making it less likely to occur. Because of the oft repeated experience of the deeper effect of music when heard unseen, the orchestra was to be placed so low that no spectator could see the movements of the performers, while at the same time it would result in the more complete harmony of sound from the many and various instruments. In such a place, consecrated to art alone and not to pleasure of the eye, the "stage festival-play" was to be produced. But would it be possible for lovers or art to provide the means, or was there perhaps a prince willing to spend for this purpose only as much as the maintenance for a short period of this imperfect Opera-house cost him?
>
> Ludwig Nohl, *Life of Wagner*, 1884

Wagner ended with a gloomy postscript: "I no longer expect to live to see the representation of my stage festival-play, and can barely hope to find sufficient leisure and desire to complete the musical composition." Few beyond his own circle of friends took any notice of the small volume bound in red and gold.

In the spring of 1864 Wagner, still on the run from his creditors, had taken refuge in the Stuttgart home of Carl Eckert. When an unexpected visitor called, Wagner, fearing that a bill collector had caught up with him, hid upstairs. Even when a card introducing the Royal Bavarian Secretary was sent up to Wagner, he suspected trickery. He was so used to dodging his creditors that he feared a creative ruse by one of them. But the visitor was King Ludwig's Cabinet Secretary Franz von Pfistermeister, who came from the new King of Bavaria, Ludwig II. The weary emissary had been seeking the equally weary Wagner for some time and had visited Munich, Vienna and Basel in an effort to deliver good news to the elusive composer. The new King intended to support Wagner

Wagner's most recent reform does not represent an enrichment, an extension, a renewal of music; it is, on the contrary, a distortion, a perversion of basic musical laws, a style contrary to the nature of human hearing and feeling . . . That it will ever become popular in the way of Mozart's or Weber's operas are popular appears improbable.
—Eduard Hanslick's review of the first performance of *The Ring* in 1876

When criticism has said the worst it can against *The Ring*, there remains nothing but to bow the knee and worship.
—Ernest Newman, in *A Study of Wagner*, 1899

Wagner's music drama is a work of a giant who in the history or art perhaps only has his equal in Michelangelo.
—Edvard Grieg, after seeing *The Ring* in Bayreuth in 1876

It is claimed to be an attack on capitalism, a sexual interpretation of history, a psychological drama of inner discovery—and some people have even thought it is a story about gods, and giants, and a race of dwarfs.
—Richard Somerset-Ward, *The Story of Opera*, 1998

Today I read out, from a Berlin paper, the news of the death, at Bayreuth, of a member of the Wagner orchestra. "The first corpse," said Brahms, dryly.
—George Henschel, in *Personal Recollections of Johannes Brahms*, 1907

Impatient Ludwig Jumps the Gun

• **King Ludwig II and Wagner on a sticker commemorating the hundredth anniversary of the composer's birth.**

Wagner wanted to stage the whole of his colossal *Ring* in a specially designed theatre, but King Ludwig II of Bavaria couldn't wait. Against Wagner's wishes, he decided that the first two operas of *The Ring*, *Das Rheingold* and *Die Walküre*, would be produced in Munich in 1869–70. This resulted in a major split between the composer and his impatient patron, and it was to be several years before the rift was healed.

The full *Ring* was first performed in Wagner's newly built Festspielhaus in Bayreuth in 1876. An English cleric, the Reverend Hugh Haweis, was there for one of the cycles and wrote about the experience in his 1884 book *My Musical Memories*.

> At the close of it the pent-up enthusiasm of the public rose to a pitch of frenzy. They stood up, and, turning to the royal box, which Wagner had left, shouted to the king, who remained seated and bowed graciously. The plaudits continuing, His Majesty motioned to the stage. The people turned, and in a moment Wagner, dressed in plain black, with his hat in one hand, stepped out from the middle of the curtain and stood motionless with his grey head uncovered until repeated cries of "Sit down!" "Sit down!" and "Hush!" had calmed the assembly. Wagner then spoke very quietly, and I regret that not hearing him quite distinctly at moments I am unable to render verbatim a speech which has doubtless been elsewhere recorded. I understood him to say he had taken many years in preparing this work; that he had presented a Saga of the Nibelung in the belief that it dealt with subjects peculiarly congenial to the Germanic races; that a new and national development of the drama was now within their reach; he believed that they had been satisfied with what they had listened to, so that it had been to the many assembled there a real Festspiel. He then thanked the king for his support and encouragement; and, the curtain being suddenly lifted, all the crowd of musicians and actors who had taken part in the Festival stood ranged, and Wagner, turning round, thanked them in the warmest terms for their devotion and assistance.
>
> Hugh Haweis,
> *My Musical Memories*, 1884

So ended the first great Bayreuth Festival in 1876.

To say the truth, I have not for years willingly attended a performance of *The Ring*; my spirit groans and protests at the thought of Fricka and Wotan and their arguments; at the thought of the riddles of the Wanderer; at the thought of the barkings and snarlings of Alberich; at the thought of the whinings of Mime. But only in advance do these fears afflict me; as soon as Wagner begins his work I am placed under an enchantment.
—Neville Cardus, *Composers Eleven*, 1958

In music there are only two brains—those of Bach and Beethoven—to compare with his [Wagner's] in breadth and span. Say what we will about the repetitions and the *longueurs* of *The Ring*, there is nothing in all music, and very little else in any other art, to compare with that wonderful work for combined scope and concentration of design. Wagner had in abundance the rarest of all gifts—the faculty, as a great critic has put it, of seeing the last line in the first, of never losing sight of the whole through all the tangle of detail. Wagner forgot nothing in his work: at any stage of it he could summon up at a moment's notice not only any figure he wanted, in all its natural warmth of life, but the very atmosphere that surrounded it, the very mood it induced in others.
—Ernest Newman, *Wagner as Man and Artist*, 1914

and encourage him in his work. The prince that Wagner had prayed for had come to his rescue and Wagner's life had changed forever. "Now all has been won, my most daring hopes surpassed. He places all his means at my disposal," Wagner told a friend. He lost no time in heading for Munich.

The premiere of *The Ring of the Nibelung* was a unique event in musical history. It was performed over four nights in August 1876 in the opera house that Wagner designed in Bayreuth in Germany. Those present included Tchaikovsky, Liszt, Saint-Saëns, Bruckner, Charles Gounod, Franz von Suppé, Kaiser Wilhelm, the viceroy of Egypt, the emperor and empress of Brazil, the grand duke of Baden, Prince George of Prussia, Sultan Abdul-Aziz, Prince Wilhelm of Hesse, the duke of Anhalt-Dessau, Grand Duke Vladimir of Russia, Nietzsche, and Theodore Steinway, who, it is said, paid for his ticket with a grand piano. In his biography of Cosima, George R. Marek said, "At the Palace, fifty-nine royal personages were quartered, not counting Kaiser Wilhelm's suite of thirty-eight courtiers."

> "Now all has been won, my most daring hopes surpassed."
>
> **—Richard Wagner, 1864, on receiving King Ludwig II's support**

Also in attendance were sixty news correspondents. Opera-house directors from all over Germany and elsewhere were present, including George Henschel of Covent Garden. The media representatives included reporters from the *Times* of London, the *New York Times*, and the *New York Tribune*. Grieg was in attendance as a representative of the newspaper *Bergensposten*.

One person who did not attend was Karl Marx. Travelling from London to Karlsbad in mid-August, he had planned to break his journey in Nuremberg, only to find that Wagnerians were occupying every hotel bed there and in all the other towns and villages of Franconia. After passing the night seated on a hard bench in a village railway station near the Czech border, he wrote to Friedrich Engels denouncing "the Bayreuth Fool's Festival of the State Musician, Wagner." Wagner was no more a state

What's in a Name?

Newcomers to *The Ring* are sometimes confused by the use of several different names for some of the characters. Wotan, the chief god, is referred to as Wälse, Wolf, or the Wanderer. Erda, the earth goddess and mother of Brünnhilde, is sometimes called Wala.

The same confusion confronts readers of Cosima Wagner's diaries, where family members are referred to by a variety of names. Son Siegfried is mostly referred to as Fidi but also as Fidichen, Fidel, or Friedel. Daniela was LouLou, Lulu, Lusch, or Luschen. Blandine was Boni or Bonichen. Isolde was Loldi or Lodchen, and Eva was just Eva or Evchen.

> musician than Marx was a state economist, but the philosopher's petulance was forgivable since he was known to suffer from carbuncles on his backside.
>
> Frederic Spotts, *Bayreuth: A History of the Wagner Festival*, 1994

King Ludwig II of Bavaria attended the final rehearsals but not the August 13 premiere. This could have been because of his aversion to crowds, or maybe he just wanted to avoid a meeting with Kaiser Wilhelm. Ludwig was so enthusiastic about *The Ring* that he returned for the third cycle ten days later.

The first year in Bayreuth was a financial disaster, and it would be twenty years before *The Ring* would be mounted again in the theatre designed to stage it. After the three performances in 1876, it was not performed in Bayreuth again before its creator died in 1883.

Three years after the premiere performance of *The Ring* in Bayreuth, a production was planned for Mannheim, home of the first of the Wagner Societies. Naturally, the Society's founder, Emil Heckel, invited Wagner to attend, but he declined. After the three cycles in Bayreuth in 1876, he never saw *The Ring* again.

> What defies ordinary people's understanding is the truth that one man could carry in him the totality of that design, could somehow construe from the first note to the last, a coherent immensity of a complexity which defies analysis.
>
> George Steiner, University of Cambridge, in BBC TV's *Great Composers: Wagner*, 2006

The *Siegfried Idyll*

Music is so omnipresent today that it is difficult to imagine the impact of something that occurred in Switzerland on Christmas Day, 1870. In today's smartphone and iPod era, we can enjoy music wherever and whenever we wish, and it is easy to forget that in 1870 the only music was live music, a rare occurrence outside the concert halls and opera houses. "People could go weeks without hearing any music at all. Even in the nineteenth century you might hear your favorite symphony four or five times in your whole lifetime," says the composer and conductor Howard Goodall.

At Tribschen on Christmas Day, 1870, Cosima Wagner was awakened by her thirty-third-birthday gift. It was a composition using two motifs from *The Ring*, and Wagner conducted a fifteen-piece orchestra on the staircase leading to Cosima's room. The secretly rehearsed group included the versatile Richter, who played second viola and then switched to play thirteen bars on a trumpet that he had learned to play especially for the

• **Christmas Day, 1870, the first performance of the *Siegfried Idyll* on a staircase in Tribschen, Wagner's Lucerne home, on a Liebig card circa 1910.**

event. (Richter was originally a horn player.)

Nietzsche was also present for the historic first performance of what was originally known as the *Tribschen Idyll*. The following day, Cosima noted in her diary: "About this day, my children, I can tell you nothing—nothing about my mood, nothing, nothing. I shall just tell you, drily and plainly, what happened." She then told how when she woke up she heard the sound of music. She thought she was dreaming as the beautiful music grew louder.

When the *Idyll* ended, Wagner and the five children entered the bedroom and presented Cosima with the manuscript of her birthday gift. Cosima wrote in her diary that everyone wept. After breakfast, the musicians returned and played the *Idyll* again. They repeated it for a third time later in the day.

Wagner promised Cosima that what came to be known as the *Siegfried Idyll* would never be published, but ten years later, in 1880, his debts were troubling him, and he sold the rights to his publisher, Schott. Both Cosima and Wagner were fond of the work. Wagner wrote several verses on the manuscript, and Cosima wrote in her diary, "The *Idyll* is going off today. My secret treasure is becoming common property. May the joy it will give mankind be commensurate with the sacrifice that I am making." Wagner conducted the first public performance in Mannheim on December 20, 1871.

In 1938 Arturo Toscanini conducted the *Sieg-*

> "The *Idyll* is going off today. My secret treasure is becoming common property."
> **—Cosima Wagner, 1880**

fried Idyll in the park outside Tribschen at the inaugural concert of what became the Lucerne International Music Festival. The Italian maestro returned the following year to conduct the *Idyll* again, this time inside the house where it was first heard. He directed a small group of musicians who played in one of the ground-floor rooms while the audience listened outside through the open windows. The only two people in the room with Toscanini and the orchestra were Cosima's daughters, Daniela and Eva.

In 1893 Henry T. Finck wrote in *Wagner and His Works*:

> It was in honor of Siegfried [the new baby son], and to celebrate his mother's birthday, that Wagner wrote his exquisite *Siegfried Idyll*. It was composed secretly, and the first performance was a surprise to Cosima. Hans Richter brought the necessary musicians from Zürich and rehearsed the piece with them at Lucerne. On the morning of the birthday the musicians placed themselves on the steps of the villa at Tribschen, Wagner conducted, and Richter took the trumpet part. It was a serenade such as no other mortal has ever been honored with. The *Siegfried Idyll* is a piece not only of ravishing musical beauty, but it breathes a spirit of refinement, of delicacy, of tenderness which alone would suffice to refute all the aspersions on Wagner's character; no one but a man whose inmost nature is love and kindness could have penned such an Idyll. And with such simple means too! Wagner, in his tragedies, asks for an orchestra of from sixty to one hundred, he has his reasons for it. In the *Siegfried Idyll* he has shown that he can write music as tender and melodious as Schubert's and as full of the most exquisite color as any part of his own music-dramas, with the diminutive orchestra consisting only of strings, woodwinds, one trumpet and two horns.

• The stairs in more recent years. The *Siegfried Idyll* was a birthday gift for Cosima. The portrait on the wall is of Eliza Wille, a novelist and supporter of Wagner's during the Swiss years. It has since been removed.

In 1941 Otto Klemperer was invited to conduct the *Idyll* with a full-sized orchestra. He refused,

• **Reggie Goodall conducting. Sketch by David Mitchell.**

arguing that the *Siegfried Idyll* is a chamber work with single woodwinds and strings and that he wanted to conduct it the way Wagner intended it. He wrote later: "They wouldn't agree so I said, 'Well, you can do it without me. Goodbye.'"

Helden Wagnerians 9
REGINALD GOODALL
A Private Line to Erda

Reginald Goodall was a British conductor whose *Ring* performances were much admired in the 1970s. Affectionately known simply as Reggie, he was on the staff of the Royal Opera House during the Solti years but switched to what is now the English National Opera at the London Coliseum, where all operas are sung in English. Goodall will be best remembered as an outstanding conductor of Wagner's works, and his *Ring* recording is still very popular with many Wagnerians. Enthusiasts point to his hallmark slow, glorious flow and superb sense of movement. His *Ring* has a magnificent majesty, but its slow pace was not popular with everyone. His recording of *Götterdämmerung* is an hour longer than that of Pierre Boulez.

Despite his reputation as one of the greatest British Wagner conductors, Goodall never recorded the three early works, *Tannhäuser*, *The Flying Dutchman*, or *Lohengrin*. He never conducted at Bayreuth. In fact, he never conducted Wagner anywhere outside Britain. He was invited to conduct in several European cities but declined. He did, however spend some time in the Bayreuth orchestra pit during performances conducted by Hans Knappertsbusch and Herbert von Karajan.

In his splendid biography *Reggie: The Life of Reginald Goodall*, John Lucas quoted the conductor: "When you conduct other things—things other than by Wagner—you find something lacking. You miss the richness and the depth and the potency of the music." The British music critic Ronald Crichton once said, "Reginald Goodall conducted Wagner as if communicating by private line with Erda."

On one occasion Goodall turned up to conduct *Das Rheingold* at the English National Opera without his dress suit. The costume department had difficulty finding something small enough for the diminutive conductor, and he entered the pit wearing a jacket with sleeves that were a few inches too long. Reggie rarely used a baton, and when he gave the subtle downbeat to start the famous E-flat, the musicians could not see the hands hidden up his sleeve and continued to wait. After a couple of seconds, Reggie leaned across to the concertmaster and whispered, "I've started." The bass singer Robert Lloyd suggested later that an appropriate response might have been, "Maybe, Sir Reginald. But how long ago?"

In his biography of David Webster, *The Quiet Showman*, Montague Haltrecht told the story of Goodall's move from the Royal Opera House to Sadler's Wells Opera, now the English National Opera. Goodall had been involved in other Wagner productions at Covent Garden, but at Sadler's Wells he would have overall responsibility for their new *Mastersingers*. Goodall took a year to prepare, during which time he coached the singers and the orchestra, section by section. The conductor's painstaking preparation paid off: the production was hailed as a triumph.

Solti conducted Covent Garden's own *Meistersinger* a year after the Sadler's Wells production, but many thought that it inferior to Goodall's, whose recording of *Meistersinger* was not issued until the middle of 2008.

In 1987, at the age of eighty-six, Goodall conducted Act III of *Parsifal* at the Proms. He died three years later while listening to his beloved *Ring* on headphones. Appropriately, *Götterdämmerung* was playing when he went into a coma, from which he never emerged. He died on May 5, 1990.

How Many Leitmotifs? Think of a Number

Opinions vary on how many leitmotifs there are in *The Ring*, and much depends on how the combination motifs are counted. J. K. Holman includes 145 motifs in his book *Wagner's Ring: A Listener's Companion and Concordance* (1996), Ernest Newman lists 198 in his book *Wagner Nights* (1949), and there are 124 examples included on the interactive disc produced by Monte Stone (see below).

In his book *An Introduction to Richard Wagner's "Der Ring des Nibelungen,"* William Cord writes:

> In 1896 a French musicologist published a study of that year's *Ring* performance in Bayreuth and included in his work an inventory of the musical motifs, each titled and catalogued according to its initial and subsequent appearances throughout the tetralogy. The list included a total of 82 leitmotifs with the following breakdown in order of their first appearance: *Das Rheingold* 34, *Die Walküre* 22, *Siegfried* 18, and *Götterdämmerung* 8. A later work cited a total of 70 motifs of which only 30 were considered to be "root" themes. Other studies that have since been published have shown numeric totals that ranged from 116 to 245, the latter including a quantity of ingenious, but nevertheless revealing interpretations. In 1891, the Mainz publisher Schott & Co. issued a libretto of *The Ring* in which each leitmotif is indicated, as well as its location in the music drama. The total number of motifs cited in this work is 367, a number that included some musical variations of earlier musical themes as independent leitmotifs.
>
> William O. Cord, *An Introduction to Richard Wagner's "Der Ring des Nibelungen,"* 1983

The relevance and appropriateness of Wagner's leitmotifs is that they say something even to people who cannot identify them. The main love motif needs no explanation or label. It is inexpressibly beautiful and perfectly matched to the stage action. The Rhine motif could be nothing but flowing water, and the thumping great giant's motif signals power and strength. Wagnerians will argue that some knowledge of the leitmotifs can add immeasurably to enjoyment of Wagner's magnificent music, and that only those who have taken the trouble to become familiar with individual motifs will spot the many combinations that make the fabric of the operas so complex and rich.

Fifty years ago, when the new Wagner enthusiasts tried to learn about the leitmotifs, they could not get a lot of help. Today numerous books and recordings are available for those wishing to increase their enjoyment by familiarizing themselves with the magic of the leitmotifs. Three of them are introduced below.

What's That Motif?

"I dream of a *Ring* recording combined with a computer program that would display the music and libretto, information on the stage action and indicators of what leitmotifs are playing at any instant," I wrote in an email message in early 1996.

"Your dream is about to come true," was the reply from Monte Stone, creator of *The Ring Disc*, issued in April 1997. Billed as *An Interactive Guide to Wagner's Ring Cycle*, it took Stone and his team of more than forty people over three years to produce. The single CD-ROM includes a complete audio recording of the Vienna Philharmonic recording of *The Ring* conducted by Georg Solti. To get the whole *Ring* on one disc is amazing enough, but *The Ring Disc* has much more. It includes a piano-vocal score and the libretto in German and English, all scrolling in synchronism with the music. When *The Ring Disc* is played, the music and librettos scroll down the screen, and at the top information is given on the stage action and details of each of the leitmotifs playing second by second. It also includes a lengthy synopsis of each of the four operas, over one hundred essays by Stone and J. K. Holman, and more than seventy photographs, most from an earlier San Francisco production of *The Ring*.

The magic of *The Ring Disc*, however, is the provision of a major aid to recognizing and understanding the leitmotifs. There are short essays on each of the motifs, and no fewer than 124 individual leitmotifs have been inserted together with examples of Wagner's many variations that reflect the stage action or a changing range of emotions.

The Ring Disc is a truly remarkable achievement. It is proving invaluable to anyone interested in a better understanding of Wagner's great work.

An Introduction to *The Ring*

The other major aid to decoding the leitmotifs is the recording by Deryck Cooke, issued at the time of the first *Ring* recording of Solti conducting the Vienna Philharmonic. Cooke was a brilliant musicologist and the first to articulate some of the nuances of the motifs of *The Ring*. He was the first to demonstrate for a mass audience the linking of the motifs into family groups and the use of inversions and combinations. He was among the first to draw attention to the evolution of some

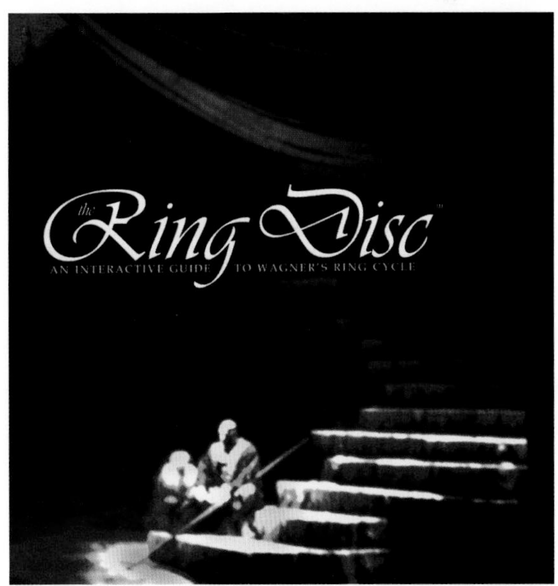

• **The entire Solti *Ring* on one disc—and a whole lot more.**

of the motifs and to offer reasons for Wagner's treatment of some of them. One classic example was the Fate leitmotif, which appears frequently throughout *The Ring*. Cooke drew attention to the way Wagner constantly changed the key of the three-note motif but then, at the end of Act III of *Die Walküre*, with Brünnhilde asleep on her rock, the motif is "locked in a single key signifying that, for the time being anyway, time has been frozen."

Cooke's *An Introduction to "Der Ring des Nibelungen"* was issued in 1968 by Decca and is still available.

Leitmotifs? There's an App for That

A useful addition to the tools available for decoding *The Ring* leitmotifs is *Wagner Ring*, a simple iPhone app with more than 150 motifs played on a piano. They are arranged by opera, and there is a search facility for finding a given motif.

The app was created by Richard Fackenthal, a piano performance and music theory graduate. He recalls that late in his years at Oberlin Conservatory, he attended a course on *The Ring* taught by Warren Darcy, whose book *Wagner's "Das Rheingold"* was published by Oxford University Press in 1993. "[The course] completely captivated me," says Fackenthal, "and I have been a *Ring* fanatic ever since. Several months ago while cleaning the house I came across my notebook of *Ring* leitmotifs that I used twenty-six years earlier in Mr. Darcy's course and the idea for this app occurred to me." Twenty years ago he changed career tracks and now designs chips and in his spare time creates apps for the iPhone and iPad. The leitmotif app is very simple but enormously useful in explaining how a given motif sounds. Just touch on the motif name on a list for each opera and it plays. The *Wagner Ring* app is available from the Apple App Store.

• ***Meine Leitmotive? Ja . . .* there's an app for that! Graphic by permission of Richard Fackenthal.**

Present for the Birth of a Ring Motif

Judith Gautier (1845–1917) was an eminent French writer, musicologist, and leading orientalist. Her father was Théophile Gautier, a prominent author, and her mother was Ernesta Grisi, a celebrated Italian contralto. According to Joanna Richardson, one of her biographers, Judith Gautier was almost certainly a mistress of Victor Hugo, and another biographer, Bettina Liebowitz Knapp, suggested that she may have been a lover of artist John Singer Sargent, for whom she posed. Prominent writers, artists, and musicians—Flaubert, Baudelaire, and Meyerbeer, among others—were regular visitors to the Gautier home.

While father and daughter were discussing music one day, Théophile mentioned a review he had written in 1857 of a performance of *Tannhäuser* in Wiesbaden that year. He told his daughter that he was the first to write in France about *Tannhäuser*. The fiasco of the aborted performances was still four years away.

Perhaps as a result of her father's enthusiastic comments about Wagner ("For some he was a sublime genius, for others, a delirious maniac—

a god—an ass—there was no middle ground"), Judith became a lifelong Wagner advocate and supporter. She was also moved by Baudelaire's reaction to the *Tannhäuser* music and while still a teenager developed an intense passion for Wagner's music. She became a friend and confidante of Cosima Wagner and stood godmother to Siegfried. Many of Wagner's passionate letters to her are available, but most of her responses were either lost or destroyed, possibly during Cosima's disinfection program following the composer's death.

In 1869 Judith Gautier visited Wagner at his home near Lucerne with her husband, Catulle Mendès, and a friend. Later during the stay, the twenty-five-year-old went out alone to Wagner's house, Tribschen. She wrote later:

> The garden door of the salon was open wide, and, as I reached the threshold, I heard very gentle chords. They were coming from the little sanctuary where the Master worked . . . I hardly dared to breathe. I sat down on the nearest chair, extremely moved, troubled, and even frightened. Was it not indiscreet, even sacrilegious, to surprise the sacred mystery like this? . . . And yet, what rare happiness! To hear Wagner compose! . . . Motionless, unblinking, I listened in devout silence.
>
> What I heard appeared to me incomparably suave . . . It was a series of chords, very slow, which seemed to escape from a harp rather than a piano: a distant, mysterious, supernatural harmony . . . I discovered later that it was the first sketch of Wotan's evocation of Erda, in the third act of *Siegfried*, when the goddess rises up with closed eyes, all covered with dew.
>
> Judith Gautier, *Wagner at Home*, 1910

The Ring for Children

The flood of books about Wagner and his works in the latter part of the nineteenth century and the early years of the twentieth catered to all interests, including those of children. In 1905 J. Walter McSpadden wrote his version of *The Ring* for children in a charming if slightly naive style. The author, who admits to taking some poetic license, describes the start of *Das Rheingold* thus:

> Hundreds of years ago in a wonderful time called the dawn of the world there lived many strange beings which do not now exist. Gods and goddesses dwelt in the clouds that hovered about the mountain peaks. Great untamed giants roamed amid the valleys. Swarthy, misshapen dwarfs, called Nibelungs, toiled in the caves of the underworld heaping up treasures of gold and silver which never did anyone any good. Ugly dragons crawled about on the earth, while beautiful water nymphs lived in the rivers and seas. Lastly there were heroes and savage men who struggled together for the mastery in that far-off day when the world was in the making.
>
> J. Walter McSpadden, *The Stories of Wagner's Operas*, 1905

In 1876 Judith attended the premiere of *The Ring* at the newly built Festspielhaus. Wagner insisted that she sit next to him at one point. It is hard to imagine what she must have felt when she heard the mysteriously beautiful chords of the Erda motif that she had heard being composed seven years earlier. She might have been one of the first to experience Wagnerian horripilation.

> "What rare happiness! To hear Wagner compose!"
> **—Judith Gautier, *Wagner at Home*, 1910**

Gautier went on to become the first woman academician in France and a Chevalier of the Legion of Honor. For the rest of her life she was a tireless promoter of Wagner and his works.

The Toughest Test in Opera

There can be no question that creating a new production of *The Ring* is the most daunting task in the whole of opera and drama. Its enormous complexity, puzzling ambiguities, casting difficulties, and seemingly impossible staging requirements make it the final examination project for any director. And that assumes that someone else is taking care of the financing.

Perhaps the most difficult task for the director is finding something new to say. After Wagner's setting, with its trees, rocks, and wooden huts, successive directors have placed *The Ring* in every imaginable setting. Some have worked very well but many have been ridiculed. At the same time, finding new interpretations and new psychological angles has become increasingly difficult. A director setting out to create a new production of *The Ring* might be forgiven for thinking that there is nothing new to say.

Some who accepted the challenge succeeded brilliantly and were acclaimed for their genius—Wieland Wagner and Patrice Chéreau in Bayreuth, Schneider-Siemssen in New York, and Stephen Wadsworth in Seattle, for example. But many fail miserably. Some even give up before reaching the

• Judith Gautier, circa 1880. One of the few people to hear Wagner compose a leitmotif.

first hurdle, let alone Becher's Brook. Lars von Trier accepted the challenge in 2002 when invited by Wolfgang Wagner to create a new *Ring* to be unveiled at Bayreuth in 2006. After two years' work he gave up, leaving his successor only two years to create a replacement from the wreckage.

The replacement *Ring*, by the director Tankred Dorst, was disliked by many of the critics and public alike—probably an unfair reaction given that when he took over the sets were already under construction and casting completed. The eighty-year-old director had only half the time normally regarded as a minimum for the job. Some of the August 2006 audiences were enthusiastic about the production, but they were in the minority.

One of the glaring failings of at least some of the so-called modern productions is the lack of cohesion between what we see and what we hear. Wagner used all of the creative arts tools available when he conceived his *Gesamtkunstwerk*, and each element supported and reinforced the others. Much of his genius lies in the way the story told by the sung words is confirmed, defined, and expanded by what we hear from the orchestra. It sometimes seems that new directors have not recognized this. Failure to understand the role of the music in the storytelling can result in disastrous contradictions if what the audience sees on the stage is out of sync with the music it hears.

A Record That Stood for 140 Years

Designing and building a new opera house is a colossal undertaking requiring the talents and skills of many people. Creating a new production of *The Ring* and staging all four operas in a week or so is comparable in terms of complexity and the need for a wide range of superior talents, some of them quite rare. Wagner achieved both tasks simultaneously in 1876 with the first production of *The Ring* in the newly completed Festspielhaus in Bayreuth.

This massive logistical and artistic achievement was not repeated for 130 years, when the British-born Richard Bradshaw inaugurated the new Four Seasons Center for the Performing Arts in Toronto with a production of *The Ring*. Born in Rugby, Bradshaw's career included spells as a chorus director at Glyndebourne and then the San Francisco Opera. The Canadian Opera Company appointed Bradshaw chief conductor in 1989, and he was made general director in 1997. His production of the first complete *Ring* to be staged in Canada was widely acclaimed. Bradshaw died in August 2007. His considerable achievement in emulating Richard Wagner was recognized with the naming of the new opera house the Richard Bradshaw Auditorium.

The first production of *The Ring* in Canada was a triumph despite numerous setbacks that could have been show enders. There were several health problems in the cast and production team, and it must have seemed like they were falling like flies. First, Pavlo Hunka (Wotan) left town before opening night, with the media speculating that the problem was laryngitis or maybe diabetes. But Adrianne Pieczonka (Sieglinde) was certainly no wimp. After she suffered an ankle injury while playing tennis, it was decided that she would sing from the side of the stage. The audience was therefore delighted when she insisted on following the original blocking that she used in the first cycle.

That was not the end of the health problems for the Canadian National Opera's *Ring*. The *Rheingold* mezzo Judit Németh (Fricka) had a dental emergency and had to be replaced. And finally Philip Boswell, the artistic administrator, hobbled around with his leg in a cast during all three cycles. He had broken his foot before opening night.

Lights, Music, Chaos

Herbert von Karajan insisted that lighting was so closely linked to the music that he had to have full control. When he worked with Rudolf Bing on the Metropolitan Opera *Ring* in the 1960s, the conductor insisted on a major investment in more powerful lighting units and additional staff to operate them. Money was tight at the Met in those days, but after some sparring by transatlantic cable and mail, Bing conceded to the maestro's wishes. However, when Karajan requested that one of his associates from Salzburg be hired to work in the lighting booth at the Met, Bing replied that this would only be possible if Karajan paid all of the expenses. The maestro declined and relied on the regular Met lighting team.

It was, perhaps, inevitable that a combination of labor union regulations and the hierarchic communications channels of the Austrian contingent would lead to some problems, and Rudolf Bing began to wish that he had agreed to pay for the Salzburg lighting man. He told the story in his memoirs:

> Lighting instructions cannot go from the designer to the men under American union procedures; they must pass through Kuntner [the Met's technical chief]. With Karajan the system was complicated, because at several rehearsals he was conducting the orchestra and studying the lighting at the same time. In his additional role of lighting director he first passed instructions to his assistant, Lehnhoff, who crouched beside him at the podium and relayed them to Kuntner, who would in turn tell the men.
>
> "More light on Wotan!" Karajan said to Lehnhoff. "More light on Wotan!" Lehnhoff said into the telephone to Kuntner. "More light on Wotan!" Kuntner said into the mike to the man in the booth, whose mike, unfortunately, was live into the house. "Who," he wanted to know, "is Wotan?"
>
> Rudolf Bing, *5000 Nights at the Opera*, 1972

Headaches for Stage Designers

The Tricky Problem of Fire

Staging technology in the second half of the nineteenth century was primitive, but this did not prevent Wagner calling for a rainbow bridge, giants, hopping frogs, flying ravens and horses, a fearsome dragon, and fire on the stage.

An intensely emotional scene at the end of *Die Walküre*, the second opera of *The Ring*, sees the chief god, Wotan, punish his daughter Brünnhilde by putting her to sleep on a mountaintop. He tells her that she will sleep there until some man comes along to claim her for his own. Brünnhilde pleads with Wotan to surround her rock with fire that only a true hero can brave. Wotan agrees and calls for Loge, the god of fire, to create the flames that will protect the sleeping Brünnhilde. And that is where the problems began for stage directors—starting with Wagner himself.

In 1876 stage smoke had not been invented, so Wagner used steam lit by colored lights. This became the norm for many years, and the idea of real fire remained an impossible dream. Cosima was therefore amused by a letter from a man in Rostock who sent her a polite complaint about the absence of real fire on the stage.

Creating a realistic illusion of fire in the opera house continued to be a problem for many years. However, outdoor productions made real flame possible, and in an early production of *Götterdämmerung* in Germany, kerosene was poured over the rocks that formed part of Valhalla. The kerosene was ignited, and the astonishing result was possibly the first time that real fire was used in *The Ring*.

The arrival of stage smoke made things easier for designers, and this, combined with the magic of modern stage lighting, made it possible to create astonishingly convincing illusions. Inevitably, once this became something of a cliché, directors sought more creative approaches to the problem of fire. Some minimalist productions involved little more than a suggestion of fire. In Bayreuth in 1995, Brünnhilde's rock was a perfectly circular Wielandesque mound that almost filled the stage. When Wotan called for Loge to surround the rock with flames, a convoy of toy railway wagons carrying flashing red lights appeared from behind the mound on previously invisible tracks. Another

Bayreuth production saw Brünnhilde lying in a huge clamshell that closed as Wotan bade his farewell. When he called for Loge's help, a thin red line traveled around the surface of the white shell to represent the fire.

But Seattle Opera has set the standard. "We have the largest fire, I believe, ever seen on a stage anywhere—230,000 BTUs of heat from propane," claims Speight Jenkins. In productions of *Die Walküre* in 1997, gas was used to create the barrier of flame around Brünnhilde's rock. In the Stephen Wadsworth productions in 2001, 2005, 2009, and 2013, the flames were even more realistic. First, a few gas-fueled flames flickered into life from gaps in the rock face and gradually spread and grew in intensity. Soon flames were leaping into the air from several points around the rock, and as the scene neared its climax, even one of the trees growing from a rock fissure burst into flame. The audience in the first few rows of the auditorium could feel the percussion waves created when the gas was ignited.

Real flame appeared again at the conclusion of *Götterdämmerung*, and the effect was truly stunning. Speight Jenkins told audience members later that the only way they could have made that scene even more impressive would have been to burn down the theatre. "And then flood it," he added.

Best not to even think about it. The Grand Theatre in Geneva is a beautiful building inspired by the Opéra Garnier in Paris. During a performance in the Geneva building on May 1, 1851, a fire broke out that caused so much damage, the theatre had to be completely restored. The inauguration of the essentially new building did not take place until December 1862. The opera that was playing when fire broke out in 1851? *Die Walküre*. It is not known whether the Swiss were experimenting with real fire on stage on that fateful night.

An inevitable consequence of the long history of fires in theatres and opera houses is extreme caution and the use of every possible safeguard when real flames are used. In Seattle the fire department is closely involved in both the planning and execution of scenes involving real flames. "We always have firefighters on the scene during all the special fire effects," said Captain Eddie L. Nelson, of the Seattle Fire Department, a few years ago. At first his men were not enthusiastic about duty in an opera house, but that changed when at least some of them were bitten by the Wagner bug. "This is one of the few jobs where they came back asking for more and apparently they are all now Wagner fans," he once told local newspapers.

If Seattle wins the top prize for the scenes involving fire, Stuttgart takes the booby prize. A 2003 Staatsoper production directed by Christof Nel must have appeared as a feeble joke to some audience members. As Wotan called for Loge to surround the rock with fire, he rummaged in a bag and retrieved five small candles that he handed to Brünnhilde, who was seated at a small table. Brünnhilde took the candles and arranged them in a semicircle on the table. She then produced a cigarette lighter from somewhere and *voilà*—instant magic fire.

This was probably the first example of do-it-yourself magic fire. I pray to Wagner's ghost that it will be the last. Unfortunately, what should have been one of the most moving scenes in the whole of opera was turned into an infantile joke. Once again, beauty in the music fought with irrelevant creativity on the stage.

In 1871 Wagner conducted three fund-raising concerts in Vienna. The Magic Fire Music was on the program, and during one performance a violent thunderstorm hit the area. At the moment when Wotan calls upon Loge to surround Brünnhilde's rock with fire, a brilliant flash of

• **Real flames surround Wotan and Brünnhilde on the rock. Photo by Gary Smith, courtesy of Seattle Opera.**

lightning lit up the concert hall. Wagner rose to thunderous applause at the end of the performance and, never one to miss an opportunity, said: "When the Greeks undertook a great work, they invoked Zeus to send them his lightning, in token of his favor. Let us too, who are united here in the desire to found a hearth for German art, interpret today's lightning in favor of our national undertaking—as a sign of blessing from above."

The Large Problem of Fafner the Dragon

Wagner's instructions for *The Ring* placed other impossible demands on directors and stage designers. In addition to fire, his stage directions call for mermaidlike creatures swimming underwater, a man who changes into a toad, a bridge made of a rainbow, a sword that shatters, and an anvil that splits in two.

One of the most difficult challenges has been Fafner the dragon in *Siegfried*, the third of the four operas in *The Ring*. The giant Fafner uses the magic Tarnhelm to turn himself into a dragon to defend the gold, including the ring, that he hoards in a cave. A bass-baritone sings the role, usually offstage, and the dragon is not required to do much more than appear onstage to be killed by Siegfried with a sword through its heart. The dragon is difficult not just because of the technical problems, but because of the risk that something intended to be fierce and frightening could so easily jeopardize the drama by appearing comical and trivial.

The dragon in the premiere performance of the full *Ring* in Bayreuth in 1876 did not go according to plan. In 1875 Wagner entrusted the creation of the first Fafner to Richard Keene of Wandsworth. After hearing about the British theatrical company Wagner told his stage technology guru, Carl Brandt, "I believe we may trust this man, as the English in this particular point are somewhat ahead of us."

The London company was commissioned to create a dragon, and it was subsequently shipped to Bayreuth in several sections. The neck, however, was shipped to Beirut by mistake. It is easy to guess what happened. Even today, it is not unusual for Bayreuth-bound Wagner enthusiasts to be asked why the Festival is being held in Lebanon. The stage crew had to improvise to cover the missing neck, but some viewers were not impressed. The ballet master, Richard Fricke, was so disgusted that he cried, "Away to the attic with such a monster!"

Hugh Haweis was not impressed either. In his 1884 book *My Musical Memories*, he wrote:

> The dragon is no doubt the weak point. I believe Mr. Dannreuther gave three hundred pounds for him in London, and brought him over with the utmost care. His tail, I am told, was worked by one man inside him and his jaws by another; but somehow he could not be got to show fight at the right time. He was a poor beast; the steam came out of his mouth too late; his tail stuck halfway on the wag, and he had evidently some difficulty in opening his jaws. He was easily slain, and rolled over conveniently enough, leaving the treasure in the hands of Siegfried.

Even Wagner himself was dissatisfied with the first dragon. In April 1878, two years after the Bayreuth premiere, Wagner sent for a representative of the Munich theatre to discuss the problem. Cosima noted in her diary, "They have in fact constructed a winged dragon, which makes R. ask why, if it could fly, it has laboriously to crawl up, and anyway it is nowhere called a dragon, but a serpent." He should have known.

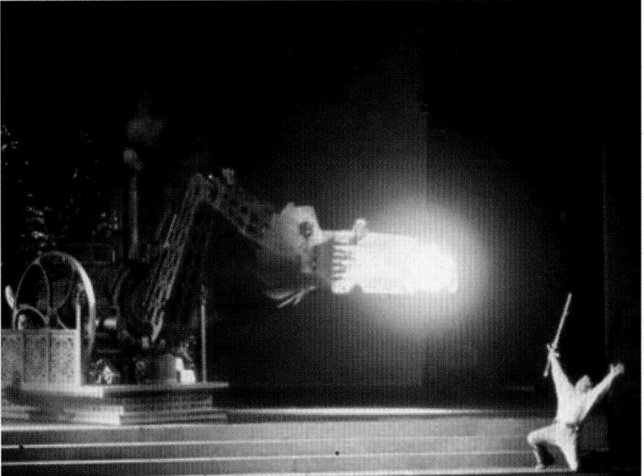

• **Robert Israel designed a dragon made from a converted backhoe in Seattle in 2001. It breathed smoke and fire and was manipulated by black-clad stagehands. Photo by Gary Smith, courtesy of Seattle Opera.**

It was his creation, yet Wagner's comment has been ignored. To this day, Fafner turns himself into a dragon, not a serpent.

Getting the dragon right continued to be a problem for stage designers for many years after that beginning in 1876. Bernard Shaw said of the dragon in a June 1892 production in London:

> The dragon, whose vocal utterances were managed jointly by Herr Wiegand and a speaking-trumpet, was a little like . . . the Temple Bar griffin, and a little like a camel about the ears, although the general foundation appeared to be an old and mangy donkey. As usual, people are complaining of the dragon as a mistake on Wagner's part, as if he were the man to have omitted a vital scene in his drama merely because our stage machinists are such duffers as to be unable, with all their resources, to make as good a dragon as I could improvise with two old umbrellas, a mackintosh, a clothes-horse, and a couple of towels. Surely it is

The dragon was shipped to Bayreuth in several sections. The neck, however, was shipped to Beirut by mistake.

> within the scope of modern engineering to make a thing that will give its tail one smart swing round, and then rear up.

In another column, Shaw wrote, "The unwieldy toy dragon, emitting its puff of steam when its mouth opened, about as impressively as a mechanical doll that says 'Mamma': did that realize the poet's vision of Fafner?"

Enthusiasts agreed that the wimpish dragon was one of the few weak points in the staging of the otherwise excellent 1997 Seattle *Ring* designed by Robert Israel. The production team was determined to come up with something more convincing, and fortunately they had four years before the dragon was to make its next appearance. They agreed to keep their plans secret and went to work behind closed doors. The new dragon was given the code name Fluffy.

The dragon thrilled the audience in August 2001: there were gasps and even a flutter of hastily suppressed applause when it came into view. Seattle's Mark 2 Fafner was based on an enormous mechanical backhoe, the bucket converted into a fire-breathing, smoke-belching head with flashing eyes. The machine was mounted on an air-cushion unit steered by six black-clad stagehands who collapsed onto the stage when the dragon was killed by Siegfried. The effect was stunning.

Four years later, in a new *Ring* production, the designer Thomas Lynch had to cap the earlier Seattle *Ring* dragon. The audience was lulled into believing that the huge coiled tail showing in the entrance to a cave would unspool to show the dragon's head. There was a rumble from the normally well-disciplined Seattle audience when the scaled coils began to move. But they realized they had been deceived when an enormous dragon's head appeared not from the cave but from behind a cliff face. The beast had huge wings and a fearsome mouth that drooled saliva. No fewer than fifteen stagehands were required to operate this dragon-to-beat-all-dragons.

• In the Seattle *Ring* designed by Thomas Lynch, the audience was fooled into believing that the coiled serpent in a cave was all there was of the dragon. It turned out to be much more, with a head that drooled slime and took fifteen stagehands to operate. Photo by Chris Bennion, courtesy of Seattle Opera.

During a visit to Thailand in 2003, Wolfgang Wagner was asked by a local English-language newspaper about his favorite Bayreuth dragon. He responded:

> For me, all attempts to create this "dragon" on stage have proved ultimately dissatisfying. What is this creature supposed to be? A winged beast as shown on fantastic images? A worm? If so, what kind of

worm? In my own *Ring* interpretation, I chose not to show this fabulous creature directly. I opted to stir the imagination by using steam effects. Clouds of steam erupted from various spots on the stage, as if coming out of the dragon's nostrils. Thus I left the image of the actual dragon to the imagination of the audience.

Another clever designer had a similar idea: create the impression of a dragon without running the risk of making it wimpish or unintentionally comical. The problem was solved by showing only an enormous scaled claw that filled most of the width of the rear of the stage, creating the thought that if that is just the foot, the whole dragon must be the size of the opera house.

In the Chicago *Ring* in 1995, Fafner took the form of a gigantic dinosaur skeleton. Designed by John Conklin and choreographed by the puppetmaster Lisa Aimee Sturz, the skeleton was manipulated by sixteen handlers dressed all in black; according to the *Chicago Sun-Times*, the result was "truly terrifying with claws that loomed over Siegfried like the prehistoric beasts in 'Jurassic Park.'"

Recording *The Ring*

Until 2006 most Wagnerians believed that the first full stereo recording of *The Ring* was the famous Vienna Philharmonic version conducted by Hungarian-born Georg Solti. Recorded between 1958 and 1965, the recordings by the Vienna Philharmonic and a stellar cast were launched in a blaze of publicity and acknowledged as a landmark in music recording technology. It was a technological triumph: the complete *Ring* on only eleven discs. The Decca producer John Culshaw estimated that the full *Ring* on the old 78-rpm shellac discs would have required 112 records.

An important part of the final complete set was a supplementary recording in which the great musicologist Deryck Cooke identified the leitmotifs and showed how they were related and how some of them evolved throughout the fifteen hours of the work. The awards and accolades flowed in, and for many years the Solti *Ring* was the only one available. Even today it is the favorite version with many Wagnerians who believe it to be the first complete recording of the great work.

Yet as many insiders knew, that was not true—the Solti *Ring* was not the first stereo recording. Ten years earlier a recording had been made during the now-legendary Wieland Wagner *Ring* at Bayreuth between 1951 and 1955. But because Decca was responsible for both, the earlier recording, by the German conductor Joseph Keilberth, was not issued.

Then, some fifty years later, Testament, a small British record producer, acquired the rights. The original tapes were remastered, and the Keilberth *Ring* was released in 2006–7. The recordings fea-

The Stagehands' *Ring*

Sing Faster: The Stagehands' Ring is a one-hour documentary film that tells the story of *The Ring* through the eyes of the union stagehands at the San Francisco opera production in 1990. With *The Ring* going on in the background, the men and women who make it happen on the stage provide a commentary on the themes of love, power, and greed. In one sequence a group of stagehands agree that *The Ring* is too long and discuss ways in which it could be shortened. "They could sing faster," was one suggestion. *The Stagehands' Ring* was produced and directed by John Else.

ture a stellar cast, including Hans Hotter as Wotan, Astrid Varnay as Brünnhilde, Gré Brouwenstijn as Sieglinde, and Ramón Vinay as Siegmund. It was produced by Peter Andry, then just beginning a distinguished career. The new first stereo *Ring* was an immediate success. It was acclaimed by the critics and soon attracted a cult following.

So Decca was both the first company to record *The Ring* (the Keilberth version) and the first to market stereo recordings (the Solti set). But not everyone was pleased with the success of the latter. When it became known that the BBC had made a television program about Culshaw's project, *The Song Writer's Guild News* protested about spending public money on such a venture. It asked, "Can the BBC find no British work of comparable stature to film? If not, surely they could have commissioned one."

Unhappily, the BBC failed to rise to the challenge, and so it may be that the world was deprived of another great masterpiece.

The Ring in a Day—a Rather Long Day

In April 2006 the British Broadcasting Corporation's classical music radio channel broadcast *The Ring in a Day*—the entire *Ring* in a unique daylong marathon. The E-flat that opens *Das Rheingold* was transmitted shortly after 8 A.M. on BBC Radio 3, and the glorious closing chords at the end of *Götterdämmerung* sounded sixteen hours later, shortly before midnight. There were short breaks between operas and only enough between acts for the presenter, Donald Macleod, to give a synopsis of the coming action.

But this was radio with a difference—supertitles. UK listeners on digital (DAB) radios were able to see live streaming supertitles in English. Those listening on the *Ring in a Day* mini–Web site were also able to see a continuous English translation of the libretto. According to a BBC spokesman, this was a unique use of digital technology and the Internet.

There is no way of knowing how many listeners tuned in from outside the United Kingdom, but comments were posted to the Web site from there as well as France, Italy, Sweden, Malta, Ireland, and the United States. Audience reactions were enthusiastic and overwhelming positive, but there were some tongue-in-cheek exceptions.

The version chosen for the broadcast was the 1988 Bayreuth recording conducted by Daniel Barenboim, which was tied into his delivery of the BBC's 2006 Reich Lectures. The Barenboim/Kupfer *Ring* featured Anne Evans as Brünnhilde, Siegfried Jerusalem as Siegfried, and John Tomlinson as Wotan. During the transmission, listeners were invited to submit *Ring* aphorisms. Two of the better entries' limericks read:

If Erda was wondrously wise,
Was she fooled by the Wanderer's disguise?
Or did he so vex
With his special effects
That she no longer cared to advise?

Deborah Rohan

The Ring is enormously long,
but it is full of music and song.
There's incest and theft,
drugs, deception and death,
and staging that's usually wrong.

Bert Coules

Shortening *The Ring*

Longborough's Abbreviated *Ring* . . .

Take a large empty barn in Gloucestershire, add a stage with lighting, scrounge 480 seats discarded by Covent Garden, and you have the beginnings of an opera company. The tiny Longborough Festival Opera (LFO) was established in 1991 in just this way, but unlike most small companies that limit themselves to Mozart and Gaetano Donizetti, the company's founder, Martin Graham, was determined to think big. In 2002, after warming up on *The Marriage of Figaro*, *The Barber of Seville*, and other "easier" productions, this little company took on the massively complex *Ring*. The four operas were presented in 2002–3.

Martin Graham proved that you do not have to be the Metropolitan Opera or the Royal Opera House to stage a Wagner opera, but he soon learned that it is an almighty struggle. He faced massive problems, such as finding singers who could handle the role yet be affordable for a small company. He needed to rearrange the score for fifty musicians, the most he could fit into the orchestra pit. And he had to handle all of *The Ring*'s difficult staging requirements in a theatre with minimal technical wizardry. Despite the difficulties, the production was a success.

Martin Graham and his small team are proud of their *Ring*, but in some ways they are even prouder of a great triumph over the British tax man in 2006. Britain's Revenue and Customs wanted to remove an exemption from payment of Value Added Tax (VAT) and took the LFO to court. If the opera company had lost, the tax authorities would have been encouraged to harass other artistic companies with charitable tax status. The LFO won a significant victory when the appeals court refused to give Revenue & Customs the right to appeal the original decision. The *Times* reported, "Mr. Graham celebrated yesterday outside court with members of the company dressed as Valkyries carrying the fake corpse of a VAT man." Two trumpeters stood outside the entrance to the court holding a placard reading *THE ROUT OF THE VATKYRIES*.

In 2013 Longborough staged a full *Ring*, an amazing achievement for a small company.

. . . And Even Shorter *Ring*s Elsewhere . . .

Would music lovers who cannot bring themselves to sit through the fifteen or sixteen hours of a full *Ring* come to an abbreviated, single-evening production? "Yes" was the answer in Iceland in 1994. Five sold-out performances of a three-act mini-*Ring* were given during the Reykjavik Arts Festival and greeted enthusiastically by audiences. *Das Rheingold* was covered in Act I, *Die Walküre* in Act II, and both *Siegfried* and *Götterdämmerung* were compressed into Act III. Great chunks of the story and music were axed, and Mime and the Norns were given the night off—they did not appear at all.

As with other abbreviated *Ring*s, the major cuts were immediately obvious to experienced Wagnerians. However, properly done, some of the cuts can appear to be seamless, and Reykjavik certainly had some top-class talent to help pull it off. The artistic consultant was none other than Wolfgang Wagner.

Berkeley Opera in California repeated that *Ring* one evening in 2004. They managed to get the epic down to three and a half hours with only eight singers and a twelve-piece orchestra. "Zip! *Rheingold*, done. *Walküre*—blink, you missed it. Act breaks? Dream on," commented Joshua Kosman in the *San Francisco Chronicle*.

. . . And the Shortest

The prize for the shortest full *Ring* on record must go to an animated version, *The Ring of the Nibelung (in 2.5 minutes)*. It can be found on the Go!Animate Web site.

My favorite line from this funny high-speed *Ring* is the Songbird singing to Siegfried, "Want to meet a pretty girl?"

Got two and a half minutes to spare? Go to http://goanimate.com/videos/0_rLZQOHoiAs.

Stray *Ring* Notes

In the completed second prose draft of *Rheingold*, there is no mention of Wotan's spear. Loge is mentioned, but there is no reference to him as the god of fire.

In *Opera Anecdotes*, Ethan Mordden tells of the tenor's wife who complains to the impresario: "Three days before he sings Siegfried, he's too tense; so he won't. Three days after, he's exhausted; so he can't. Your *Ring* cycles are ruining our marriage!"

Wotan and other characters in early productions of *The Ring* wore winged helmets that have become a symbol of both Wagner and Norse history. Yet there is no evidence that the Vikings ever wore anything like Wagner's creations. The only Viking helmet ever found was in southern Norway. The helmet has no wings or horns, nor any sign that they ever existed.

Staging *The Ring* is an enormous undertaking that will stretch the financial and physical resources of any opera company. The Seattle *Rings* of 2001, 2005, and 2009 required a total investment of around $15 million.

The Met went a million dollars better in 2011–13: Robert Lepage's production cost $16 million, a big chunk of it going for a forty-five-ton machine made up of twenty-four huge planks that served sometimes as a platform for the singers and more often as a backdrop for the video projections.

In 2006 a billionaire philanthropist offered up to $6 million to help underwrite a *Ring* in Los Angeles. In Toronto the Canadian Opera Company invested $11 million in the country's first production of *The Ring*.

The World's Slimmest Brünnhilde

It had all the ingredients for a dream production of *The Ring*. Music by world-class orchestras conducted by Furtwängler, Solti, Tennstedt, and Karajan, and a cast that included a twenty-year-old with the looks of a Greek god playing the role of Siegfried, a stunningly beautiful Brünnhilde whose age and waist measurement in inches both appeared to be about twenty-two, and not one person over thirty or an ounce overweight in the rest of the cast of fifty. I saw such a *Ring* in Germany in April 2008. I swear to Wotan!

But this was a *Ring* with a difference: it was a ballet. *Ring um den Ring* (*Ring Around the Ring*) was created by Maurice Béjart; this most recent production was restaged by the Staatsballett Berlin. The French-born Béjart was an enthusiastic Wagnerian who wanted to use his skills to create a new dimension for the masterpiece. Judging by the capacity audience's fifteen-minute ovation at Deutsche Oper in Berlin in April 2008, he succeeded.

Maurice Béjart was born in France in January 1927 and died in November 2007, aged eighty.

The Ring also stretches the stamina and dedication of singers and the management staff. Speight Jenkins estimated that in Seattle in 2009 the orchestra spent more than 130 hours on rehearsal. The three singers who played the role of the Rhinemaidens were suspended on moving trapezes thirty feet above the stage, and their acrobatic performances were the result of more than a hundred hours of rehearsal. Even management staff felt the strain. Middle and senior managers spent a minimum of ten hours a day on the project from mid-May until the first cycle commenced in early August.

Writing of the end of Act III of *Die Walküre*, Saint-Saëns wrote:

> Here nothing would have prevented the composer from writing an air and a duo in the traditional style; but no air, no duo, could have, from a theatrical point of view, the value of this monologue and this dialogue scene. Melodic flowers of the most exquisite fragrance spring up at every step, and the orchestra, like a boundless ocean, rocks the two lovers on its magic waves. Here we have the theatre of the future; neither the opera nor the simple drama will ever rouse such deep emotions in the soul. If the composer had completely succeeded in no other scene but this, it would suffice to prove that his ideal is not an impracticable dream; the cause has been heard. A thousand critics writing each a thousand lines a day for ten years would injure this work about as much as a child's breath would go towards overthrowing the pyramids of Egypt.
>
> Camille Saint-Saëns, quoted in Henry T. Finck, *Wagner and His Works*, 1893

> Wotan's tragedy is that his life is too long, Siegfried's that his is too short.
>
> Cosima Wagner in her diary, October 20, 1870

In *Conducted Tour*, Bernard Levin told about a 1976 visit to Bayreuth by Peter Diamond, one-time director of the Edinburgh Festival. He was there as a guest of Wolfgang Wagner for Patrice Chéreau's centenary *Ring*. The two men chatted in Wolfgang's office so long that they missed the start of *Das Rheingold*. Wolfgang hurried him to the door of the auditorium and thrust him inside. He stood motionless, trying to get his bearings in the darkness. He observed later that he was struck by the total darkness on the stage, with only a strip of light across the set. He had heard about Bayreuth's avant-garde lighting, so he was not surprised. It was only when his eyes adjusted to the light that he realized he was facing away from the stage and that what he had been staring at so intently was the faint light from the exit sign on the other side of the Festspielhaus.

Early in 1882 Angelo Neumann formed a troupe to take to the main cities of several countries. A few months later they reached London, and the cast included several of those who made history at the premiere in Bayreuth in 1876. The conductor was Anton Seidl, making his first appearance in London; he was praised by the critics for the clearness and refinement of his reading. Most of the audience would have been unaware of the extensive cuts made to *Siegfried* and *Götterdämmerung*.

The first city to follow Bayreuth with a full *Ring* cycle was Munich in 1878, followed by Leipzig in 1879, Vienna also in 1879, and Hamburg in 1880. In the first fifteen years after the 1876 premiere of *The Ring*, *Das Rheingold* was performed 358 times, *Walküre* 623, *Siegfried* 322, and *Götterdämmerung* 314 times in German cities alone.

The Graphic Novel *Ring*

In 1991 came the *Ring of the Nibelung* graphic novel, by Roy Thomas and Gil Kane, with Jim Woodring. It employed all of the illustrative and storytelling techniques commonly seen in modern graphic novels. The book was one of the surprise publishing success stories of the decade, and many experienced *Ring*-goers could not resist the temptation. Some said that the clarity of the book

> "Wotan's tragedy is that his life is too long, Siegfried's that his is too short."
> **—Cosima Wagner in her diary, 1870**

helped to explain some aspects of the complex plot and to make the mighty work more approachable. It seems likely that this book helped to create new Wagner enthusiasts.

The Black Cloud of Anti-Semitism

While fully understanding the views of Jewish people, and particularly those whose families and friends were subjected to the evils of the Nazi regime, the fact that so many people deny themselves access to Wagner's music saddens me. I have nothing to say in Wagner's defense about his abhorrent views. However, Daniel Barenboim, himself a Jew, has said, "Wagner's anti-Semitism, despicable, horrible, unacceptable. But you could not be a German nationalist, which he was, at the end of the nineteenth century without being an anti-Semite." For many years now, Barenboim has tried to separate Wagner the obnoxious anti-Semite from Wagner the musical genius.

Wagner's anti-Semitism became more virulent toward the end of his life, and he said some terrible things.

> You can go at that in a number of ways. My own conviction is that people like ourselves, perfectly ordinary people, cannot grasp what is going on in the mind of a titanically complex creator who can create *Parsifal* and then say absolutely barbaric inhumanities. I prefer to say that the man who has given us what he has musically lies outside of my range of understanding. That doesn't mean that it doesn't make me bitterly, bitterly disturbed, ill at ease. But to put it very vulgarly if I may, that's my problem, and not his.
>
> George Steiner, University of Cambridge

Matthew Boyden hit the nail on the head.

> For the Nazis *The Ring* was a celebration of the indomitable Teutonic spirit, though it's

Who's Got the Ring?

During the fifteen to sixteen hours of performance of *The Ring of the Nibelung*, the ring changes hands nine times, from

1. **Alberich,** who made it, to
2. **Wotan,** who steals it from the unfortunate dwarf, to
3. **Fasolt,** as part of Wotan's payment for the building of Valhalla, to
4. **Fafner,** who steals it from his brother after killing him, to
5. **Siegfried,** who kills Fafner as the dragon and takes the hoard, to
6. **Brünnhilde,** who receives it as a gift from Siegfried, to
7. **Siegfried,** who steals it back while impersonating Gunter, to
8. **Brünnhilde,** who takes it from the hand of the dead Siegfried, to
9. **The Rhinemaidens,** who retrieve it when Brünnhilde rides into Siegfried's funeral pyre, which then collapses into the Rhine.

> hard to see how a tale in which the gods are brought crashing down by their own stupidity could ever have been seen as suitable to the glorification of the Aryan race.
>
> Matthew Boyden, *Opera: The Rough Guide*, 1999

> How can you have among the highest achievements of beauty or . . . elegance and audacity in the human mind and conscience and guts and viscera on the one hand and the awfulness on the other. Wagner's music, as they'd say in a law court, is exhibit A.
>
> George Steiner, University of Cambridge

Wagner and Meyerbeer

While Wagner was enduring a miserable existence in France, Meyerbeer attempted to help with introductions. But apart from a brief period of grateful subservience, Wagner had nothing but contempt for the German-born composer.

Jacob Liebmann Beer was born in Vogelsdorf, Germany, in 1791. After several years of music study, he moved to Italy at the suggestion of Antonio Salieri. He composed several operas in the Italian style and thought it expedient to change his name to Giacomo Meyerbeer. He later moved to Paris and became one of the most popular European composers of the mid-nineteenth century.

Wagner's dislike of Meyerbeer was probably caused by a mix of jealousy about Meyerbeer's undoubted success and Wagner's failure to win recognition for his own talents. But his anti-Semitism was certainly a major cause of Wagner's disdain, and Meyerbeer was one of his prime targets in his much-criticized essay on *Judaism in Music*.

In another of his essays, *Opera and Drama*, Wagner wrote:

> In Meyerbeer's music there is shown so appalling an emptiness, shallowness and artistic nothingness that—especially compared with by far the larger number of his musical contemporaries—we are tempted to set down his specific musical capacity at zero.

Then a few lines later, Wagner contradicted himself.

> We observe, namely, that for all the renowned composer's manifest inability to give by his unaided musical powers the slightest sign of artistic life, nevertheless in certain passages of his operatic music he lifts himself to the height of the most thoroughly indisputable, the very greatest artistic power.

Later, he added:

> And now the composer who had exhausted all the resources of his musical ancestry without being able to strike one solitary spark of real invention, is at a blow empowered to find the richest, noblest, most heart-searching musical expression. I here would chiefly call to mind certain features in the well-known plaintive love-scene of the fourth act of the Huguenots, and above all the invention of that wondrous moving melody in G-flat major, by [the] side of which—sprung as it is, like a fragrant flower, from a situation which stirs each fiber of the human heart to blissful pain—there is very little else and certainly none but the most perfect of music's works, that can be set.

That might have been the last kind word Wagner ever wrote or said about Meyerbeer. When he was hired to conduct the Philharmonic Society orchestra in 1855, he suggested that the British media were antagonistic because they were in the pay of Meyerbeer. *(continued on page 206)*

Stamps of Approval

Commemorative postage stamps and cards featuring Wagner or his works have been published by many countries, including some that might seem surprising. Several examples are included in this book, but these are just a sampling of the rich variety from around the world.

• **Germany. Perhaps the only Wagner-related stamp to include some of his music. This one celebrated the 1968 centenary of the first performance of *Die Meistersinger*.**

• **Chad. The Republic of Chad issued a block of nine beautiful stamps featuring works by Brahms, Offenbach, Verdi, Strauss, Schubert, Puccini, Paganini, Mozart, and Wagner. The latter is represented by a scene with Wotan and Brünnhilde.**

• **Panama. Not the best portrait of Wagner, but at least they avoided the temptation to feature one of the over-used portraits.**

• **USSR. Wagner visited Russia in 1863, and his music was greeted with enthusiasm.**

• Austria. Lohengrin is towed in by the swan.

• Congo. Interest in Wagner has spread to many seemingly unlikely parts of the world.

• **Hungary. Tannhäuser makes a rather half-hearted effort to resist the allure of Venus.**

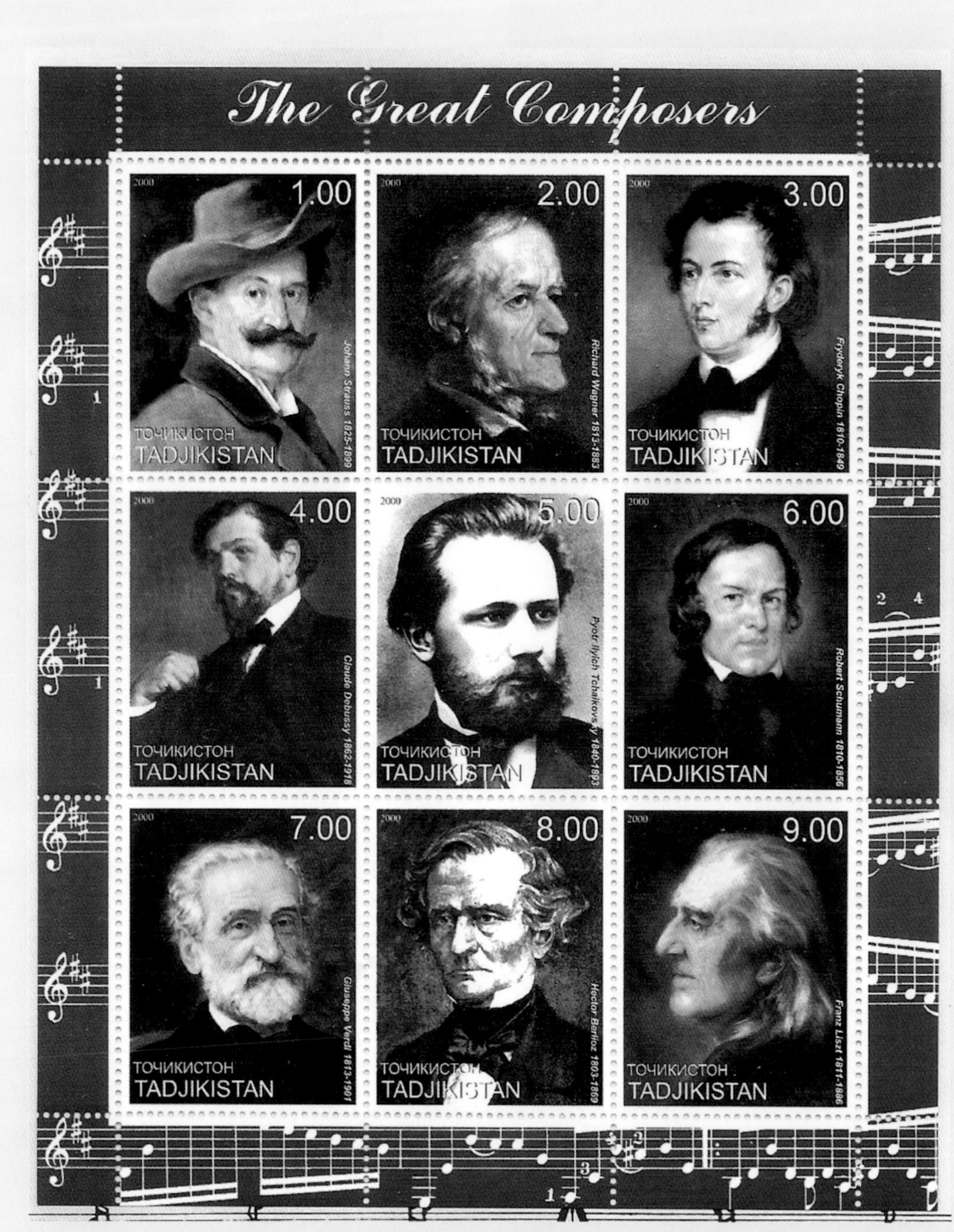

• **Tajikistan. Wagner joined by other musical greats, including his father-in-law, Franz Liszt.**

• **Giacomo Meyerbeer, who tried to help Wagner but was rewarded with contempt.**

(continued from page 199) He must have been mightily displeased to find that the management of the Society had included some of Meyerbeer's works on the program.

In November 1872 Wagner attended a performance of Meyerbeer's *Le prophète* in Frankfurt and said afterward, "The presentation of such a Meyerbeer opera in our larger and smaller theatres is the most nonsensical and undignified procedure that a tortured fantasy can imagine, and the worst of it is the stupid seriousness with which the most ridiculous things are accepted by a gaping public."

Hans Richter, that loyal lieutenant and conductor of the first performance of the full *Ring*, clearly did not share the Meister's opinion. He conducted six of Meyerbeer's works a total of 169 times. Although performances of Meyerbeer's works are rare today, he still has supporters and an online fan club.

The Golden Ages of Music

The 1880s

In the five years between 1886 and 1891 there were 128 performances of Wagner operas at the Metropolitan Opera in New York. During the same period there were 149 productions of all the French, Italian, and other German composers combined. Box-office receipts were an even better indicator of the popularity of Wagner's works: they grossed $590,021, versus $410,332 for the non-Wagner productions. It was a golden age indeed.

1935: A Very Good Year in New York

When Kirsten Flagstad sang for the first time in New York's Metropolitan Opera, *Time* magazine wrote, with more than a hint of cynicism, "Critics were so excited to hear a really great voice that everything Flagstad did was greeted with praise, some of it so indiscriminate that readers were led to believe that the greatest Wagnerian of all time had suddenly popped from the blue." Well, guess what? Commentators and critics were soon claiming that she was the voice of the century. *The New Grove Dictionary of Music* said, "No one within living memory surpassed her in sheer beauty and consistency of line and tone."

In 1934 the Met auditioned her to sing the role of Sieglinde in *Walküre* because Frida Leider had decided that the prevailing exchange rates made it more profitable for her to sing in Europe. The following year, 1935, Flagstad sang Sieglinde and four days later sang Isolde for the first time in New York. "All hats were in the air," commented *Time*.

Flagstad had sung other Wagner roles in her native Norway, but only in Norwegian or Swedish. Over the next three months or so she learned the roles of Elsa in *Lohengrin* and Elisabeth in *Tannhäuser*, both in German. *Time* magazine went into raptures.

Her most amazing accomplishments were the Brünnhildes in *Die Walküre* and *Götterdämmerung* and Kundry in *Parsifal*, roles she had never sung before. Only for these last two did she have the benefit of stage and orchestra rehearsals. But no one could have guessed it. To her colleagues she scarcely seemed human—until the final *Parsifal*, when she fell asleep on the stage and nearly missed her cue.

Kirsten Flagstad died in Oslo in 1962 at the age of sixty-seven. The Web site of the Kirsten Flagstad Museum is appropriately headed, "Voice of the Century."

Oh, and there were a few other crowd-pleasers that made that 1935 Met season rather special. The season's singers included Lauritz Melchior, Ezio Pinza, Lotte Lehmann, and Lily Pons.

1937: A Very Good Year in London

Wagner's operas are frequently performed in London, New York, San Francisco, and some of the world's other leading opera houses, However, Wagner enthusiasts in smaller cities consider themselves lucky when even one Wagner opera is included in the annual program, and they are truly delighted when the annual offerings include two Wagner operas or maybe a complete *Ring*. Patrons of London's Royal Opera House must have been overjoyed when the brochure for the 1937 Coronation Year program dropped onto their doormat. The plans for the year included two full *Ring* cycles conducted by Furtwängler, and each cycle featured a dream team. The first had Frida Leider and Max Lorenz; the second, Kirsten Flagstad and Lauritz Melchior. As if that was not enough, the rest of that year's program included *Parsifal*, *The Flying Dutchman*, and *Tristan and Isolde*.

Recordings were made of Furtwängler conducting excerpts from *Die Walküre* and *Götterdämmerung*. They were remastered in October 2008 and reissued on the Pristine Classical label.

The Golden Age of Composition

Wagner lived during the golden age of classical music. Other composers alive at some point during Wagner's life included Auber, Bartók, Berlioz, Beethoven, Bellini, Bizet, Borodin, Brahms, Bruckner, Cherubini, Chopin, Delius, Donizetti, Dukas, Dvořák, Elgar, Falla, Franck, Glazunov, Glinka, Gounod, Grieg, Holst, Victor Hugo, Humperdinck, Janaček, Kodály, Liszt, Mahler, Mendelssohn, Meyerbeer, Mussorgsky, Offenbach, Puccini, Rachmaninoff, Ravel, Rimsky-Korsakov, Rossini, Saint-Saëns, Schoenberg, Schubert, Schumann, Sibelius, Smetana, Strauss (Richard), Stravinsky, Sullivan, Tchaikovsky, Vaughan Williams, and Weber.

Other prominent people who lived during some part of Wagner's life were the painters Constable and Rossetti; the writers Balzac, Browning, Dickens, Ibsen, Keats, Scott, Shelley, Swinburne, Thackeray, and Tennyson; the philosophers Hegel, Nietzsche, and Schopenhauer; and Darwin, who introduced to the world a new view of life.

Warning! Wagner Can Be Bad for Your Health

"Wagner's music can cause horripilation," warned a lecturer on classical music in California. One

• **The program for the 1937 season at the Royal Opera House, London.**

or two Wagner enthusiasts in the audience exchanged puzzled looks. "In fact, recent research has shown that a very high percentage of audiences for *The Ring* and *Tristan and Isolde* suffer from horripilation during the operas," he went on. "But don't worry about it," he said. "Horripilation won't kill you. It is the medical term for goose bumps!" Cutis anserine is another name for goose bumps or goose pimples.

"Don't listen to Wagner in your car," warned a British traffic-accident researcher. The announcement was about the dangers of loud music that can distract drivers and cause accidents; Wagner's music was singled out as particularly dangerous in this regard.

Even animals are not immune from the health threats posed by Wagner's music. The Copenhagen Zoo blamed Wagner for the death of an okapi, a rare African animal related to the giraffe. It was claimed that six-year-old Katanda, a female, died from stress after hearing a group of singers from the Royal Theatre rehearsing *Tannhäuser*. A zoo official said that the singers were rehearsing for an outdoor performance in a park three hundred yards from the animal's enclosure. The okapi "started hyperventilating, went into shock, and collapsed." The official added that okapis are sensitive to unusual sounds and that an autopsy revealed that the animal died from a severe stress attack. Fortunately, neither the male okapi nor the eight-month-old calf was affected by the music. As a precaution, however, opera officials said that they were considering transferring the performance to another location.

Several prominent conductors and singers have died while performing Wagner's works, and there is plenty of anecdotal evidence of fatal heart attacks among audience members. But it is the conductors who appear to be affected most. In his 2005 book *The Virtuoso Conductors*, Raymond Holden told of the deaths of three eminent conductors during or shortly after conducting works by Wagner.

Felix Mottl, who had been the lead conductor at Bayreuth in 1886, collapsed while he was conducting a performance of *Tristan* in Munich in 1911. As his mistress, who was singing Isolde, delivered the words, "His heart is destined for death," the unfortunate Mottl in the orchestra pit felt the first stabs of the heart attack that was to kill him a few days later. He was only fifty-five.

Joseph Keilberth's premature death has also been linked to *Tristan and Isolde*. The stage director Rudolf Hartmann recalled that Keilberth often said that he would like "to die, if possible, on the podium, best of all like Felix Mottl, during a performance of *Tristan*." He should have been more careful what he wished for: his end came on June 20, 1968, during the second-act love scene. He was only sixty. According to his son, Thomas Keilberth, sometime before that fateful end his father had marked the date in his diary with a cross.

Wilhelm Furtwängler felt unwell during his journey home after recording *Die Walküre* in Vienna in 1954. When his condition deteriorated, he was moved to a clinic in Baden-Baden. He died there less than a month after completing his final recording.

Stefan Minde felt faint while conducting *Das Rheingold* in Phoenix, Arizona, in 1998. His assistant, Byron Dean, stood by his side following the score, ready to step in if necessary. Somehow the maestro managed to get through the two-and-a-half-hour opera, and over the following days he completed all four. During the second cycle, he conducted *Die Walküre* and then suffered a heart attack. He was rushed to a hospital, where he underwent quadruple bypass surgery. He survived, and in 2011, when the seventy-five-year-old was asked about his health, he replied, "I'm above ground."

> **"**
> His heart is destined for death."
> **—words sung by conductor Felix Mottl's mistress, as Isolde, when Mottl felt the heart attack that would kill him**

Fortunately, not all of the health problems suffered by conductors are fatal. In 2012 Antonio Pappano, music director of the Royal Opera House in London, was ordered by his doctors to rest because of acute tendinitis in his right arm. Not surprising, perhaps, as most conductors give most of the work to their right arm.

Love and Money from Three Crucial Supporters

It is unlikely that any of Wagner's mature works—*The Ring*, *Die Meistersinger*, *Tristan and Isolde*, and *Parsifal*—would have been written and composed without the support of three people. King Ludwig II of Bavaria usually gets the lion's share of the credit for supporting the struggling composer, and it is unquestionably true that without him, not only would *The Ring* not have been completed, but there would have been no Festspielhaus in which to perform it. However, another supporter who is perhaps not sufficiently credited with Wagner's success: Liszt, Wagner's close friend over more than forty years, his father-in-law, and a tireless promoter of Wagner and his works. The Hungarian keyboard virtuoso was perhaps the first to recognize Wagner's genius and supported Wagner's ideas against seemingly overwhelming opposition and obstacles.

In his 1962 book, *Man and His Music*, Wilfred Mellers wrote: "Liszt reverenced Wagner with something approaching idolatry; he was prepared to abandon his own creative work if only he could raise adequate funds to finance a production of *The Ring*." If this had not been true, the friendship could not have survived Wagner's relentless importuning of his friend, who was not a wealthy man. Wagner pleaded for money for transportation, food, clothing, or help for his first wife, Minna. And effusive acknowledgment letters were quickly followed by further demands for support and help in acquiring princely sponsors.

Wagner was convinced that the world owed him a living and was mystified when requests for help were declined or ignored. Liszt never turned a deaf ear, even when his own finances were stretched. Although Wagner was aware of the difficulties that he caused, most of the time he seemed to be oblivious to behavior that makes even card-carrying Wagnerians cringe. Just occasionally a hint of awareness showed through. In 1849 he wrote to Liszt asking yet again for financial support. Liszt replied, "My purse is completely dry at this moment." In a December 1849 response Wagner expressed appreciation for the great friendship Liszt had shown him "in spite of many sides of my nature which cannot possibly be agreeable to you."

The third critically important supporter was Cosima. Her role has been devalued in recent years because of her overzealous protection of "the Meister's way" when she ran the Bayreuth Festival after Wagner's death. It was commonly agreed that her refusal to change even the staging minutiae, let alone consider alternative approaches to the ten works, had a stultifying effect that could have ended in disaster. In the years immediately following Wagner's death, there was also great resentment of her bullying demands for the return of her dead husband's letters and other documents, some of which she is believed to have destroyed.

• King Ludwig II stands guard at Wagner's house, Wahnfried.

• **Cosima Liszt, Wagner's second wife, who supported and inspired him and ran the Festival after his death. Caricature in *Der Floh*, Vienna, 1891.**

However, during her long marriage to the composer, Cosima provided complete, unquestioning support and encouragement. She was a strong-willed woman, and Wagner benefited from her support and total commitment to his ambitions. Scholars believe that Cosima was involved in several of the most important letters that Wagner wrote and may have been the sole author of some of them. At least one letter begging for support was written to King Ludwig without Wagner's knowledge. In early 1878 the deficit from the Festival of August 1876 was still almost 100,000 marks. Friedrich Feustel, who had played a leading part in getting the theatre built and staging the first Festival, did not know what to do about it. He did not want to interrupt Wagner's work on *Parsifal*, so he gave Cosima the bad news. But he included a possible solution: he suggested that advance royalties, payable over a ten-year period, be sought from the Munich Royal Theatre. The idea was anathema to Cosima, who had never forgiven Munich for staging *Rheingold* and *Walküre* against her husband's wishes. Without consulting Wagner, she wrote to King Ludwig asking him to cover the deficit, concluding her appeal: "I hope that my step will not be disapproved by my most gracious lord, whom I have ventured to approach with the most respectful and grateful feelings, and for whom I remain unto death, His Majesty's most obedient servant, Cosima Wagner-Liszt." The ever-generous Ludwig paid up yet again, and Cosima's intervention permitted the ailing Wagner to continue uninterrupted with the composition of his final work.

• Liszt consoles Wagner after the fiascos in France. Caricature by J. Blass.

Greater Love Hath No Man

Despite losing his wife to Wagner, Hans von Bülow continued to support the composer and conducted the first performance of *Tristan and Isolde* in 1865 and of *Die Meistersinger* in 1868. To the great surprise of many, von Bülow never showed any sign of bitterness or resentment. After Cosima left him to live with Wagner in Lucerne in 1866, von Bülow wrote to her: "You have preferred to devote your life and the treasures of your mind and affection to one who is my superior and, far from blaming you, I approve your action from every point of view and admit you are perfectly right. I swear that the only consoling thought has been this: Cosima is happy over there."

During a visit to New York, von Bülow visited William Mason, a violinist and composer whom he had befriended in Leipzig. Mason later told of the meeting in his memoirs.

I know from what von Bülow himself told me that he accepted philosophically the trouble between himself and his wife Cosima Liszt. Soon after he arrived in New York, in 1876, I called on him and during the conversation I broached the subject in a tentative way. I was not sure that his feelings toward Wagner were not so hostile that mention of the Bayreuth master would have to be avoided and I thought it just as well to arrive immediately at a clear understanding of the matter.

"Bülow," I said, "you will excuse me if I touch on a rather delicate subject. Of course your friends abroad know just what your present attitude is toward Wagner; but over here we know little or nothing about it. Perhaps you would like to enlighten me. I hope, however, I have not touched on a painful subject."

"Not at all," he exclaimed. "What happened was the most natural thing in the world. You know what a wonderful woman Cosima is—such intellect, such energy, such ambition, which she naturally inherits from her father. I was entirely too small a personality for her. She required a colossal genius like Wagner's, and he needed the sympathy and inspiration of an intellectual and artistic woman like Cosima. That they should have come together eventually was inevitable."

William Mason, *Memories of a Musical Life*, 1901

The Symphonic *Ring*

The overtures and preludes to the operas of many composers have been recorded as orchestral highlights. However, very few recordings are made of orchestral excerpts from the main body of an opera. Wagner is an exception, and many such extracts are frequently heard in concert halls or on recordings by all of the world's leading orchestras and conductors. Popular favorites include the Entry of the Gods into Valhalla from *Das Rheingold*, Wotan's Farewell and the Magic Fire Music from *Die Walküre*, Forest Murmurs from *Siegfried*, and Siegfried's Funeral March from *Götterdämmerung*.

Wagner called such concert-hall favorites "bleeding chunks" because he believed that performance in the context of the complete opera would communicate much more than musical extracts. The composer conceded, however, and was persuaded to produce new arrangements to cover the bleeding edges.

Many Wagnerians regret that Wagner did not live long enough to fulfill his ambition to devote his mature talents to symphonic works. This aim might have been on his mind in Venice in his final weeks, when he conducted his youthful Symphony in C as a Christmas surprise for Cosima.

In 1997 Henk de Vlieger, a percussionist with the Netherlands Radio Philharmonic, decided to reweave some of the motifs from *The Ring* into a symphonic treatment. He selected the most important orchestral excerpts from the work and linked them to create a unified sixty-seven-minute symphonic work. The notes accompanying the CD explained: "The choice of the various components and the manner in which they follow one another is mainly determined by the principle of 'exposition, development and recapitulation' of the most important themes and motifs. The excerpts have been taken over without alteration, where possible, and only sporadically has an essential line for voice been replaced by wind instruments. The transitions between the excerpts were 'composed' again, with strict adherence to Wagner's idiom."

Der Ring: An Orchestral Adventure was recorded in Amsterdam in 1992, conducted by Edo de Waart. The orchestra has also played this symphonic *Ring* on tours in Germany and elsewhere.

An Operatic Hit Parade

In a survey of 252 professional opera companies and festivals whose schedules are reported in *Opera* magazine (included in his 1992 book *The Ultimate Art: Essays Around and About Opera*), David Littlejohn listed the top one hundred operas by number of performances in the calendar years 1988 and 1989. The top three were *The Marriage of Figaro* (Mozart, 1786), *Tosca* (Puccini, 1900), and *Don Giovanni* (Mozart, 1787). The positions of Wagner's works were:

16. *The Flying Dutchman*
32. *Die Walküre*
33. *Parsifal*
39. *Lohengrin*
40. *Das Rheingold*
48. *Die Meistersinger*
51. *Götterdämmerung*
54. *Tannhäuser*
62. *Siegfried*
75. *Tristan and Isolde*

Littlejohn noted that the sheer cost of staging operas such as *Die Walküre* (or *Aida*, for that matter) is a major factor. He also suggests that "singers, conductors, producers, and designers equal to the task of an adequate *Aida* or *Die Walküre* may be among a hundred or fewer people available in the world. Some observers put the number of 'great' sopranos or tenors performing at any time at no more than twenty, as if some sort of global gene pool limited the available talent. In a market economy, such people, like star athletes and other popular entertainers, can ask for, and expect, very high rewards indeed."

Das Rheingold (The Rhine Gold)

Text completed: Around December 1853.
Music completed: September 26, 1854.
Premiere performance: September 22, 1869, National Theatre, Munich.
First performance in the full *Ring*: August 13, 1876, Festspielhaus, Bayreuth.
UK premiere: May 5, 1882, Her Majesty's Theatre, London.
US premiere: January 4, 1889, Metropolitan Opera, New York.

The Bare-Bones Plot

Alberich is able to steal the gold from the Rhinemaidens because he has renounced love. He creates the Ring and the magic Tarnhelm, which give special powers to their owner. The giants complete Valhalla, but Wotan tries to renege on the deal he made with the giants Fasolt and Fafner, which required him to hand over his sister-in-law Freia as payment. Loge searches the world for an alternative way to pay the giants and tells Wotan about the Nibelung's gold. The pair leave to steal the gold, but the giants insist on holding Freia until the deal is completed. While Freia is absent, the gods are weakened, since they do not have access to the golden apples that Freia supplies to keep them strong.

Wotan and Loge steal the gold, the ring, and the Tarnhelm from the Nibelung Alberich, who then places a curse on the ring. Wotan is forced to hand over all the gold, the ring, and the magic Tarnhelm to the giants, and Fasolt becomes the first victim of the curse when he is slain by his brother in a fight over the loot. Fafner leaves with the gold, the ring, and the Tarnhelm. Freia is freed, and the gods get their supply of golden apples and enter their new home, Valhalla.

The opening trio of the Rhinemaidens was the first music heard in the Festspielhaus in 1875.

The Beginning of Time

Das Rheingold and *The Ring* start with something unique in all of classical music, a single E-flat that continues unchanged for anywhere up to fifteen seconds. It is one of the most magical moments in musical history and it signifies the beginning of time. It might be compared to the background noise in the universe, the residual drone from the Big Bang. The effect is stunning in any opera house, but coming from the sunken pit at the Bayreuth Festspielhaus it is truly electrifying: the mystical sound comes from everywhere and nowhere. It is hard to imagine any more appropriate way to start this colossal cycle.

Wagner claimed that he first thought about the opening when he was staying in an inn in La Spezia, but some commentators believe that this is another example of Wagner's postcreation creativity. His original idea was for an E-flat chord, but the use of a single note played on double basses is even more dramatic.

The opening trio of the Rhinemaidens was the first musical sound heard in the Festspielhaus on June 24, 1875. The whole creative team had been assembled in the almost completed building to inspect the scenery for *Rheingold* and *Walküre*. Then Wagner clapped his hands and said, "Now, children, go on the stage and let us hear something."

The Rhinemaidens, Lilli and Marie Lehmann and Minna Lammert, who would be the first voices to be heard in *The Ring*, were also the first to sing from the huge new stage.

The Magic Tarnhelm

The Tarnhelm is the magic helmet created by Mime in *Das Rheingold*. It gives its wearer the power to assume any appearance or to transport himself instantly between locations. It is used by Fafner to appear as a fearsome dragon to protect his hoard of gold and by Siegfried to assume the appearance of Gunther and to transport himself instantly from Brünnhilde's rock back to Gibichung Hall. In most *Ring* productions the Tarnhelm is a metallic mesh or fabric. In the 2007 Royal Opera House production audience members were puzzled when the Tarnhelm appeared as a large Rubik's cube that Alberich wore on his head like a colorful tin box.

The leitmotif for the Tarnhelm is a perfect example of Wagner's genius in creating musical themes that fit the person, object, or emotion. The Tarnhelm motif, played on six muted horns, paints an eloquent picture of something magical, mystical, or just plain spooky. Some critics of the Royal Opera House production have suggested that the jokey Rubik's cube conflicted with the magical sound of the Tarnhelm motif.

Richard Has Left the House!

Wagner left the theatre before the end of *Das Rheingold* because he was annoyed about staging problems. The thunderous applause at the end went on for ten minutes, with calls for Wagner to take a bow. The calls went unanswered despite the presence of two emperors and three grand dukes.

Wagner did not approve of applause during the performance and had got the agreement of the singers that no curtain calls would be taken at the end. At the conclusion of *Götterdämmerung*, the applause was so tumultuous that Wagner was forced to come onto the stage. He made a short speech which ended with, "You have seen what we can do; it is now for you to will. And if *you* will, we

• A *Ring* conductor surrounded by his anvil-playing percussionists for Wotan and Loge's descent into Nibelheim. Cartoon by Emil Wagner, date unknown.

When you step on to the rostrum for *Das Rheingold*, you look at your hand, knowing that it will not stop for two and a half hours. You wonder: Can I sustain it? What shape will I be in? Will I want to go to the toilet?
—Georg Solti

The first time you hear it [the Rheingold motif] it's brilliantly placed as a very memorable, sonorous image. You just hear the girls sing "Rheingold" to those two chords. It's beautifully orchestrated. Once you've heard that you cannot forget it. So whenever that recurs throughout the next fourteen or fifteen hours, it will have that connotation. The whole adventure of the gold is carried by those two chords which in turn decay and become blackened and besmirched. The sound of *Rheingold* in *Götterdämmerung* is one of the blackest sounds ever made.
—Robin Holloway, composer, in BBC TV's *Great Composers: Wagner*, 2006

What other man could have written two Rhinemaidens' trios like those in *Das Rheingold* and *Götterdämmerung*, each so liquid, so mobile, so sweet with the primal innocence of the world, and therefore so alike in some respects, yet so absolutely different?
—Ernest Newman, *Wagner as Man and Artist*, 1914

At the end of *Rheingold*, or the other three *Ring* operas for that matter, we sit in a state of emotional shock. We are in the grip of a theatre experience as intense as we are ever likely to have, exposed to everything that is beautiful and difficult and hateful in life. We have been connected with all we have longed for and with the presentiment of inevitable disappointment.
—J. K. Holman, *Wagner's "Ring": A Listener's Companion and Concordance*, 1996

I think I've been rung!
—A dazed John Diedenhofen at the end of the Seattle's Opera's *Ring* in 2005

In one of his productions of *Das Rheingold*, he cast his Rhine maidens without a stitch of clothing. Reproached by a critic for allowing the girls to appear naked, Wagner, who ran the festival for 57 years, retorted: "You are quite wrong. I let them keep their contact lenses in."
—Richard Kay, in a *Daily Mail* report on the retirement of Wolfgang Wagner

You use a mirror to see your face: you use works of art to see your soul.
—Bernard Shaw, in *Back to Methuselah*, 1920

shall have an art!" Wagner was possibly referring to his combination of poetry and music to create what had already been dubbed "the artwork of the future." However, the German press did not see it this way. They accused Wagner of massive conceit for daring to suggest that art did not exist before him. What about Homer, Goethe, Bach, Mozart, or Beethoven, they asked.

The attendance of the future King Edward VII at a London performance of *Lohengrin* in 1875 may have played a role in imposing Wagner's wish that applause be withheld until the end of an act. There was contingent of Germans living in London led by Edward Dannreuther, a German writer, lecturer, pianist, and music teacher who founded the London Wagner Society in 1873. In an article in the *Monthly Musical Record*, Dannreuther wrote of "the utter absurdity of the dramatic grimace known as grand opera." He was talking about the perception that the main purpose of an opera was to provide a showcase for singers to display their vocal skills.

After the performances of *Lohengrin* at Covent Garden and Her Majesty's Theatre, the *Musical Times* reported: "The Teutonic element in the house had a marvelous effect in teaching the audience that *Lohengrin* was not to be judged by the ordinary standard; so when the usual round of applause was given for the favorite singers on their entrance and the boisterous marks of approbation burst forth after an effective *morceau*, a very decided 'hush' convinced the astonished opera habitués that the vocalists must be considered secondary to the work they were interpreting, and that any congratulations to individual performers must be reserved for the fall of the curtain."

Enter the Wagner Societies

Despite generous assistance from King Ludwig for the planned festival theatre, still more financial support was needed. Emil Heckel, a Mannheim piano maker, came up with the idea of encouraging the formation of Wagner Societies to raise funds, and Wagner, delighted with the idea of ensuring a steady flow of funds, urged him to go ahead. The original plan was to allocate tickets to Society members only, excluding the public (and unwanted critics, an idea Wagner liked very much) from performances of *The Ring*. Heckel was instrumental in establishing the first Wagner Society in Mannheim in June 1871. Then Vienna, Munich, and Leipzig climbed onto the bandwagon, and by 1874 there were Societies in Brussels, London, St. Petersburg, and New York. The drawing room at Wagner's house, Wahnfried, was decorated with the coats of arms of all the German cities that had signed up to support the cause. In 1877 an umbrella association, the Richard Wagner Verband, was formed, with headquarters in Bayreuth.

Other countries soon followed, and within a few years Wagner Societies were established from Munich to Melbourne, London to San Francisco, and Finland to South Africa. Today around 135 Wagner Societies in forty-four countries provide opportunities for members to share their knowledge of the composer and their experiences of his works. The total membership in 2010 was more than 23,000 in 135 countries that now include member associations in Abu Dhabi, Armenia, China, India, Taiwan, and Thailand.

The London Wagner Society was influential in popularizing Wagner's music, and its founder, Dannreuther, assisted with arrangements for Wagner's 1877 visit to London to conduct at the Albert Hall. Harry Edmonds reformed the Wagner Society in 1953, and today its objective is to promote knowledge, understanding, and appreciation of the life and works of Wagner.

In 1884 the UK group was refounded as the London Branch of the Universal Wagner Society with fifty-four members. By 1890 it had grown to 309 and was led by William John Manners, the

The Floral *Ring*

Bob Bauer breeds Japanese irises at Ensata Gardens in Michigan. He is also a Wagner fan. So when he and his partner were searching for a name for their new white iris, they called it "Tarnhelm." The catalogue says, "*Rheingold* purity in this Nibelung magic helmet."

"We would have many more Wagner character names on our flowers if they hadn't already been used over the past sixty years," says Bob. The Ensata Gardens iris is a multipetal white iris and sells for $15.

Plant breeders of the Botanic Park in Adelaide, Australia, introduced a new bush rose to mark the International Wagner Symposium, held in the Botanic Garden Restaurant in 1998. The rose was given another appropriately Wagnerian name, "Magic Fire."

A Test for Opera-House Administrators

David Webster, the eminent general administrator of the Royal Opera House for a quarter of a century after World War II, was once asked what qualifications he had to do the job. He thought about it and then listed three qualities.

1. I don't want to conduct.
2. I don't want to produce.
3. I don't have a mistress who wants to sing.

ninth earl of Dysart. There are more than twenty Societies in English-speaking countries, including those based in Adelaide, Auckland, Boston, Cambridge University, Cape Town, Chicago, Christchurch, Dallas, Dublin, Dunedin, Edinburgh, Florida, Honolulu, London, Los Angeles, Manchester, Melbourne, Minneapolis, New York, Ohio, Perth, Queensland, San Francisco, Sydney, Toronto, Vancouver, Washington, D.C., and Wellington.

Contact details for most of the Societies may be found on the Web site of the Richard Wagner Verband International at http://www.richard-wagner-verband.de/index.html. In addition to the Verband Societies, there are unaffiliated groups in several countries.

From 1888 to 1995 the original UK Wagner Society published a quarterly journal titled simply *The Meister*. It was edited by William Ashton Ellis, a physician remembered today as the author of several books and translator of Wagner's prose works. Excerpts of many of Ellis' translations were published in *The Meister*. Ellis did his best to present the subject of the journal in the best possible light. He included extracts from Glasenapp's sycophantic biography, and in the very last issue of the publication he recommended Chamberlain's biography. If these were misjudgments, Ellis was proven right when he exposed Ferdinand Praeger's 1992 book, *Wagner as I Knew Him*, as a fraud.

> *The Meister*'s cover design illustrated its preoccupations. The theme was the pre-Socratic division of the universe into the four elements—water, earth, air and fire—in the same order as they occurred in *The Ring*. A female figure resembling a mermaid and carrying a shield typified the dual nature of man—animal and material in the lower part of the body, human and spiritual in the upper. Her shield presented on its left the sword of power, Nothung, and the Nibelung's ring, the symbol of "self-devouring Time"; on the right of the shield was the swan of Lohengrin, representing the soul, and the chalice, or vessel of divine reason. Other aspects of the picture included a laurel wreath of victory, a lance—Parsifal's spear—denoting the power of spiritual truth, and the masks of comedy and tragedy. Crossing the entire composition and uniting it was a flamboyant scroll bearing the name of the journal; the flames of the scroll symbolized the purifying fire of love.
>
> Anne Dzamba Sessa, *Richard Wagner and the English*, 1979

Bernard Shaw complained that the cover was "excessively exuberant."

One interesting piece by Ellis was an analysis of Wagner's letters to Liszt that some believed to have been dominated by requests for financial help. Anne Dzamba Sessa summed it up: "Of 314

• **The cover of the first London Wagner Society magazine included more symbols than many modern productions of the operas.**

letters of Wagner to Liszt, only 12 were direct appeals to Liszt's own purse."

After the eighth year of publication, *The Meister* ceased publication without warning or explanation.

Bernard Shaw and the UK Wagner Society

Shaw was a massive Wagner enthusiast, but he had a love-hate relationship with the Wagner Society.

> I have to announce an important move on the part of the London branch of the Wagner Society, which has almost led to reconciliation between me and that body. The misunderstanding came about in this way. I once gave them a guinea for the good of the cause and they spent thirteen shillings of it on a horrible evening party. To appease me, they bought a ticket for a Richter concert, and made me a present of it—a pretty treat for a man who was almost dead of concerts, and was throwing half a dozen tickets per day into the waste-paper basket. Naturally I received an application for a second guinea with speechless indignation. It may be asked what they did with the other eight shillings. Well, they sent me four numbers of their quarterly, *The Meister*, for half of it—and I admit that *The Meister* was good value for the money—but they sent the remaining four shillings to the Bayreuth people, who had just cleared a profit out of a series of performances to which I had contributed four pounds. This was enough to make any man mad; and as there was nothing to prevent me from getting *The Meister* from Messrs. Kegan Paul for four shillings paid across the counter (not to mention that I always get review copies), I forswore the Wagner Society, as I thought, forever. Now, however, the Society makes a fresh bid.
>
> The translations of Wagner's writings in *The Meister* have deservedly proved a success; for they are good Wagner and good English, being made by men who understand the language of the philosophy of art in both languages.

Then after a diatribe against the enforced contribution to the Bayreuth coffers, Shaw continued:

> We are immeasurably worse off than the Germans in musical matters, I have to sit in our vulgar diamond-show at Covent Garden, listening to scratch performances of *Faust* and *Les Huguenots*, whilst Mottl is producing *Les Troyens* in Carlsruhe, Levi conducting *Siegfried* at Munich, and Richter using his left hand at Vienna to conduct *Carmen*, because his right is fatigued with perpetual Wagner. Next autumn I shall have to pay £20 to hear *Tannhäuser* properly done at Bayreuth because I have not the remotest chance of hearing it even decently done at home . . .
>
> And since there must be many others of the like mind, why in the name of common sense does not this London branch of the Wagner Society declare itself an autonomous English Wagner Society, and save up the fifty pounds a year which it now spends in sending coals to Newcastle, to form a fund for placing a Wagner Theatre on Richmond Hill? The only objection to it is that it is impossible. What of that? The Bayreuth theatre was ten times as impossible when it was first conceived; yet it has been an accomplished fact these fifteen years. Besides, it does not become gentle-

men who propose that the English should keep their Wagner theatre in Bavaria to talk about impossibility. The arrangement to which they are contributing 4s [shillings] per head per year is not only impossible, but impracticable, which is a real objection.

On the whole, I am inclined to conclude that I can do no good by holding one opinion and backing the other to the extent of 12s a year. I had rather give the money to Mr. Grein's Theatre Libre, which is likely to help Wagnerism more than all the £20 pilgrimages in the world. When the Bayreuth reserve fund is replaced by the Richmond Hill reserve fund, then it will be time enough to open my hand.

Bernard Shaw, in the *World*,
February 25, 1891

Die Walküre (The Valkyrie)

Completed: March 1856.
Premiere performance: June 26, 1870, National Theatre, Munich.
First performance in the full *Ring*: August 14, 1876, Festspielhaus, Bayreuth.
UK premiere: May 6, 1882, Her Majesty's Theatre, London.
US premiere: April 2, 1877, Academy of Music, New York.

The Bare-Bones Plot

Exhausted, Siegmund enters a hut in the forest to seek shelter from a storm. Sieglinde gives him refreshments, and there is an immediate attraction between the couple. They soon realize that they are the twin children of Wälse (Wotan) and that Sieglinde's husband, Hunding, is Siegmund's enemy. She points out the sword buried in a tree by Wotan. Siegmund removes it, and the pair flee to the forest to begin an incestuous relationship.

Fricka, the goddess of marriage, insists that Wotan end the liaison by allowing Siegmund to be killed in a fight with Hunding. Wotan's daughter Brünnhilde defies her father and tries to protect Siegmund. But Wotan intervenes and shatters the sword, and both Siegmund and Hunding are killed. Brünnhilde helps Sieglinde to hide with the remains of the sword and tells her that she is pregnant with Siegmund's child. The orchestra confirms that the child is Siegfried.

Wotan is furious with Brünnhilde for disobeying him. He removes her godhood and banishes her to sleep on a rock surrounded by magic fire that only a hero will be able to penetrate.

In the first fifteen years after the premiere of the full *Ring* in 1876, *Die Walküre* was the most frequently performed of the cycle's four operas. Much to Wagner's annoyance, it was given 823 performances in German cities alone; *Das Rheingold*, with 358 performances, was a distant second. Wagner wanted only complete productions of the tetralogy, but what annoyed him even more was the common practice of starting *The Ring* with *Die Walküre* instead of *Das Rheingold*.

Die Walküre is still the most popular opera in *The Ring*. It is frequently performed by companies who have never mounted a full cycle, and many of those who do often tack a few extra *Walküres* on to the program.

Walküre is popular because of the strength of the story and the extraordinary quality of the music. Yet the end of *Walküre* is a paradox. The emotions we feel at the close of Act III are not the emotions that we should feel after a rational consideration of the plot. Most people in the audience feel an over-

• **Who struggles most, Siegmund trying to remove the sword or the stagehand holding up the flimsy stage set? Cartoon by Emil Wagner, circa 1927.**

whelming sense of sadness and sympathy for both Brünnhilde and her father, Wotan. Many consider Brünnhilde's treatment unjustified because she did what she believed her father wanted, so we feel sorry for her. We also feel for Wotan, who is about to banish his favorite daughter from his court. Some in the audience empathize with the god because he is only doing the duty required by his position as leader of the gods and keeper of the rules.

But wait a minute. The god who is keeper of the runes engraved on his spear is the same guy who broke them by using trickery and force to steal the ring from Alberich in the first opera of the cycle. And just hours before singing a fond farewell to Brünnhilde, did he not cause the death of his beloved son Siegmund? And did not this upholder of ethics and principles cause his daughter Sieglinde to flee into the forest, where she died giving birth to Siegfried?

Why do we feel such sympathy for Wotan? Why is Brünnhilde not the sole object of our pity?

Perhaps it is because we have been taken in by Wagner's consummate ability as a dramatist. He has led us to a point where we forget Wotan's sins and feel only sympathy for his remorse about what he is getting ready to do.

Or could it be the beauty of the music? The final scene of *Die Walküre* includes some of the most beautiful music Wagner wrote, and the leitmotifs have been admired because they are so appropriate to the stage action. The magic sleep motif, with its dreamlike, lulling quality; the beauty of Brünnhilde's slumber motif; the flickering fire motif; the inspiring motif of Wotan's love for Brünnhilde; and, all the way through, the oh-so-appropriate three-note fate motif are overwhelming. This is the reason why Wotan's Farewell and the Magic Fire Music are such popular choices for the concert hall.

The final element in the mix that is such a drain on our emotions is the drama of the staging. In most productions stage smoke and lighting are used to surround Brünnhilde's rock. As the flames rise, the music reaches a climax and then fades to

I find *Walküre* the most exhausting opera in *The Ring*, the conflict between father and daughter is draining and heart-wrenching. I love the characters, though, and they don't haunt me afterwards. Quite the opposite—I enjoy reaching into myself and getting into them. At the end of the night, I turn off the emotions, but I don't turn off the energy, I go home and I'm still wound up. I'm usually up 'til at least three in the morning.

—Linda Watson, soprano, quoted in an *Opera Magazine* article by Richard Speer, October 2007

I once found myself tearing up during Wotan's monologue. I had to remind myself [he said while pointing backward over his shoulder]: they cry, I conduct.

—Robert Spano, conductor of the Seattle *Ring*

When the actors are silent, the orchestra speaks, and what a language! Wagner, the man of noise, the tamer of ferocious instruments, employs here nothing but string instruments. By the manner in which a composer makes the string quartet speak, the master is shown. The goddess reveals herself as such by her bearing.

—Camille Saint-Saëns, on Wagner's orchestration in the first act of *Die Walküre*

From the technical standpoint, they're marathon roles. You know why you're tired the next day. It's not your voice that's tired, it's your body that's tired, it's your feet, it's your knees, it's your back. It's maybe the muscles you need to make your support system work properly. It's physically exhausting. That's what a lot of people don't realize.

—Deborah Polaski, soprano, on singing Wagnerian roles, in BBC TV's *Great Composers: Wagner*, 2006

Herr Vater ist loaded."

—Heidi Krall, as a Valkyrie, noting a replacement Wotan's inebriation

the dominant fate motif. We feel only sadness as Wotan takes one last look at the sleeping Brünnhilde and walks off through the smoke. Wagner, the wizard of Bayreuth, has wrought his magic again.

Ethan Mordden's delightful book includes this hilarious story under the heading "Unusual Commotion at the Valkyries' Rock."

> Mignon Dunn recalls the night she doubled as Fricka and Waltraute in a Met *Walküre* that was riddled with substitutions . . . at the second intermission, Otto Edelmann, the Wotan, was asked to surrender Act 3 to his cover. Edelmann insisted that he felt fine, but management feared he might have been overworked in a heavy season and wanted to save his voice for an imminent Saturday broadcast.
>
> Unfortunately, Edelmann's cover, not expecting to be called upon at such a late hour, had been hoisting one or two with the boys and was in no shape to go on. On he went, however, staggering onstage to the cry of "Wo ish Brünnhild?"
>
> Valkyrie Heidi Krall leaned over to Dunn. "Herr Vater," she whispered, "ist loaded."
>
> He was indeed. Erich Leinsdorf, in the pit, spurred the players on to ever greater waves of sound to effect a *cordon sanitaire* between the helpless Wotan and his audience, the Valkyries created a distraction by violently overacting, the prompter was screaming, the bass's wife praying. Finally, Wotan dropped his spear, leaned over to the prompter and roared, "*What?*"
>
> The curtain came down and the public was promised a resumption of the opera if it would kindly wait while the makeup man prepared a third Wotan.
>
> Otto Edelmann.
>
> Ethan Mordden, *Opera Anecdotes*, 1985

It had been calculated that the full score of *Die Walküre* alone contains at least a million notes.
—May Byron, *A Day with Richard Wagner*, 1911

The motifs at work in *Das Rheingold* are exclusively deceit, prevarication, violence, and animal sensuality. Even the gods are characterized by covetousness, cunning and breach of contract. Not a single ray of noble moral feeling penetrates this suffocating mist. *The Valkyries* stands out among the four episodes by virtue of its great dramatic and musical beauties; but we will never overcome the moral repulsion of so ecstatic a revelation of incest.
—Eduard Hanslick, 1876

Mme. Flagstad is that rara avis in the Wagnerian woods—a singer with a voice, with looks, with youth. She is not merely another of those autumnal sopranos who passed their prime when the Kaiser was a boy, and whose waistlines have gone to that bourne from which no slenderness returneth.
—Lawrence Gilman, in a *New York Herald Tribune* review of Flagstad's first appearance at the Metropolitan Opera in February 1935, when she sang Sieglinde

Brünnhilde a Hit at Glastonbury Pop Festival

In one of the most unlikely pop-concert billing decisions, one act from *The Ring* was included at the Glastonbury Festival in England in the summer of 2004. The Festival is normally devoted to performances by top pop bands playing for an audience of up to 150,000. That year, the program included Paul McCartney, Oasis, and Muse. The surprise addition was Act III from the English National Opera's 2004 production of *Die Walküre*. The second surprise was that Wotan and Brünnhilde were a hit with the predominantly young audience. Wotan was cheered at the beginning but noisily booed when he banished Brünnhilde to her mountain rock. Some of the huge audience was in tears at the end of Wotan's Farewell and the Magic Fire Music. The ovation was long and enthusiastic.

Paul Daniel conducted the ENO orchestra, with Robert Hayward singing Wotan and Kathleen Broderick as Brünnhilde.

Tristan und Isolde (*Tristan and Isolde*)

Completed: August 1859.
Premiere performance: June 10, 1865, National Theatre, Munich.
UK premiere: June 20, 1882, Theatre Royal, Drury Lane, London, in Italian.
US premiere: December 1, 1886, Metropolitan Opera, New York.

The Bare-Bones Plot

Tristan is sailing back from Ireland to bring Isolde, who is betrothed to Marke, king of Cornwall. Isolde, who had once saved Tristan's life, is angry that he ignores her during the voyage. She plans to poison him and herself, but her loyal maid, Brangäne, substitutes a love potion for poison. They fall in love and are discovered by an emissary of the king during a nocturnal tryst. Tristan is wounded and is taken to his home in France. Isolde follows, believing she can cure him, but before she arrives, Tristan dies. The distraught Isolde collapses over his body, and the lovers are united in death.

Tristan Commemorated in Cornwall

At the side of the B3269 road approaching Fowey in Cornwall stands a seven-foot high weather-worn stone that is believed to have been erected in 550 AD. The stone was moved from its original location some two hundred yards to the north. In 2013 local authorities planned to move it again as a result of road improvements. A plaque on the base reads:

> The Tristan Stone
> This Stone, Erected Nearby About 550 A.D.
> Has On Its North Side A Raised T,
> An Early Form Of The Christian Cross.
> On Its South Side, In 6th Century Letters,
> Is Inscribed—
>
> Drvstans Hic Iacit
> Cvnowori Filivs
>
> Translated This Reads "Trystan Here Lies
> Of Cunomorus The Son."
> Cunomorus Was Marcus Cunomorus Of The
> Medieval Life Of St. Sampson And King Mark
> Of Cornwall In The Love Story Of
> Tristan And Iseult.

In at the End

In 1859 the twenty-three-year-old composer Felix Draeseke visited Wagner for a month in the Hotel Schweizerhof, Lucerne. He left some valuable notes on his experiences with the composer.

> At six in the evening I came to him and was received with the words: "Wait a moment, the *Tristan* is just being completed." [The young composer told Wagner that he would like to be present for that important milestone.] . . . I experienced how the beautiful introductory motif flowed into the

• **Temperatures rise as Materna seeks another hug from Wagner. Caricature in *Der junge Kikeriki*, Vienna.**

The First Cast Party

Wagner hosted a celebration party at Wahnfried after the close of the first Bayreuth Festival in 1876. The guests included Hugh Haweis, who wrote afterward:

> [Amalie] Materna, the unique Brünnhilde, was there. Wagner had taken endless trouble in forming her for the *Nibelungen Ring* and the great part she was to play; and master and pupil always entertained the liveliest admiration and affection for each other, which sometimes took an amusing and demonstrative form. That night, when Brünnhilde, an immense woman, arrived *en grande toilette*, and wearing some of her best jewels, she bore directly down upon Wagner—a spare, short, fragile little man. Her enormous bulk seemed to extinguish him for a moment. On reaching him with difficulty in the midst of the glittering crowd she embraced him rapturously—German fashion—with; "Ach, Herr Wagner!"
>
> Wagner stood it like a man; but toward the close of the evening I beheld the Materna bearing down upon him again, and as she neared him he held up both his hands energetically repelling a second attack, "Nein, nein, Frau Materna, das will ich gar nicht" [I don't want to do that], and poor Brünnhilde had to put up with a handshake instead.
>
> Hugh Haweis, *My Musical Memories*, 1884

The Curse of the Mobile Phone

It was embarrassing enough when the mobile phone of someone in the audience at Lincoln Center rang during a live broadcast from the Met in 2012. But it was made worse by the ring tone on the offending mobile phone. It was the Ride of the Valkyries making a surprise return during the first act of *Götterdämmerung*. "Wrong opera," muttered one of the more tolerant audience members.

When the conductor Daniel Barenboim spoke at a press conference about his decision to ignore the taboo on public performance of Wagner's music in Israel, he was interrupted by the sound of a mobile phone. Once again, it was the Ride of the Valkyries.

> glorious B major chord and the tones of the full orchestra were painted in an astonishingly brief space of time. When I noticed that in this last chord the tuba employed earlier was missing and I enquired after the reason, he said to me: "What use are the old villain's grunts now?" Artistically he was absolutely right. For without this uncouth instrument the end sounded much nobler.

Later the same year, the Wesendoncks visited Wagner at the Schweizerhof. Of course, he was quick to grasp the opportunity to give them a sample of his newly completed work. Draeseke noted:

> Wagner played the second act of Tristan for them, in that characteristic manner of his, that is he raced up and down the piano keys, added vocal accompaniment, unfortunately all too often out of tune, sweated, worked himself into a passion, in short, gave a performance that no way resembled what one could expect from a thoroughly well-trained practical musician. Yet he had a gift, shining through a veil as it were, of explaining his intentions and making the dramatic situations and the various characters recognizable.

• **The Tristan Stone supposedly marked the historical Tristan's burial place.**

Following the success of a performance of *Lohengrin* in Vienna in 1861, Wagner was keen to have *Tristan and Isolde* performed in the same city. It took two years to agree on contracts, and finally rehearsals began. But it all went horribly wrong.

• **Isolde with Brangäne on a postcard circa 1902.**

The opening phrase of *Tristan and Isolde* ends on a chord which leaves us all up in the air, waiting for a resolution which doesn't come. Wagner gives a kind of prominence to a feeling of non-resolution which was unique in the history of harmonic language up to that time. And in that way alone, it stands out in his work as one of the two or three major musical events of the whole nineteenth century.
—Rowland Cotterill, biographer, in BBC TV's *Great Composers: Wagner*, 2006

Do Isolde and Tristan confess their love? They don't need to; the music does it for them. Up wells music of such torrential passion, such ineffable tenderness, that its poor human protagonists seem dwarfed and foolish.
—Deems Taylor, *Of Men and Music*, 1937

What a lot of harm this *Tristan* style has wrought in music! . . . The only person who did not succumb to it was its creator. Immediately after *Tristan* he started work on *Die Meistersinger*, which represents the greatest imaginable contrast with *Tristan*, not only in its message, but especially in its idiom.

In writing *Tristan*, Wagner had no intention at all of creating something "new," of "expanding" the laws of harmony, of "forcing" progress, but was solely and exclusively concerned with finding the most . . . impressive language for his poetic vision, for his *Tristan* world. This is proved not only by every bar of *Tristan*, but also in another sense by the works that he wrote after *Tristan* and that represent without exception more or less serious "falls from grace" in the eyes of the believers in progress. [Yet] in finding adequate expression for the spiritual world he wanted to portray . . . he discovered the chromatic system that was of such significance for the future. [This] was far from essential as far as he was concerned; it was a mere accident.
—Wilhelm Furtwängler, quoted in John Ardoin, *The Furtwängler Record*, 1994

In 1863, after no fewer than seventy-seven rehearsals, including one led by Wagner himself, the musicians rebelled and declared that the music of *Tristan and Isolde* was unperformable. The production was abandoned. It was to be another two years before *Tristan* was premiered in Munich.

Years later, in 1882, Hans Richter conducted a triumphant *Tristan* in Vienna, although he did cut the work by about 20 percent. Even then, Eduard Hanslick was not satisfied. "A blue pencil is not enough," he said. "What is needed here is a sword." Another critic, Daniel Spitzer, wrote: "Anyone who can survive the ordeal of Act Three without closing his eyes is amply qualified to apply for the job as a night-watchman." But Marcel Prawy, author of *The Vienna Opera*, thought that yet another critic, Ludwig Spiedel, won the battle of put-downs with: "In order to concentrate on what the singers were doing I shut my eyes during a passage in the second act. The first thing I heard was a cavalry charge riding down 100 defenseless women. There was a terrible mêlée of groans and screams and cries for help, and behind it all the roar of artillery. What had happened? I cautiously opened my eyes. Isolde had heaved a sigh."

Tristan was the first opera conducted by Gustav Mahler when he started a series of three-month seasons with the New York Metropolitan Opera on January 1, 1908. During that first season he also conducted Met productions of *Walküre* and *Siegfried*. The following year, Mahler arrived for his second three-month stint to discover that the Met's new management had also signed up Arturo Toscanini, who was reportedly enthusiastic about conducting *Tristan*. The New York press had a field day speculating on a shoot-out between the two star conductors. Mahler dug in his heels and conducted *Tristan* again. Toscanini had to settle for *Götterdämmerung*.

Child! This *Tristan* is turning into something frightful! That last act!!! I fear the opera will be forbidden—unless the whole thing is turned into a parody by bad production—nothing but mediocre performances can save me! . . . good ones are bound to drive people crazy,—I can't imagine what else would happen! To such a state have things come!!! Alas!
—Wagner, in a letter to Mathilde Wesendonck in 1859

The music of *Tristan and Isolde* would kill a cat or turn rocks into scrambled eggs because the harshness of the chords would just dissolve them.
—Richard Strauss

To the student, no work of the Master's gives such unbounded delight, such intense pleasure. *Tristan* is positively terrible in its greatness.
—Landon Ronald, writing in *The Lady's Realm* in 1898

And beyond Faust here is *Tristan und Isolde*, which is at last music for grown men.
—Bernard Shaw, writing in 1890

On my return from one of my walks I jotted down the incidents of the three acts in a concise form, with the intention of working them out more elaborately later on. In the last act I introduced an episode, which, however, I did not develop eventually, namely, the visit to Tristan's deathbed by Parsifal during his search for the Holy Grail. The picture of Tristan languishing, yet unable to die of his wound, identified itself in my mind with Amfortas in the Romance of the Grail.
—Wagner, *Mein Leben*, 1911

Before the first act was over, a knowing audience . . . was aware that a great star was flashing in the operatic heavens. At the end of the act . . . they roared like the stadium fans when [Charlie] Conerly [a New York Giants football player] throws a winning touchdown pass . . . At the final curtain the audience began a thunderous demonstration . . . People seemed disinclined to go home. The lights in the theatre were dimmed, but men and women throughout the house remained near their seats, applauding for Miss Nilsson's return. After more than fifteen minutes of plaudits, the enthusiasts let Miss Nilsson return to her dressing room.
—Howard Taubman, in a *New York Times* review of Birgit Nilsson's first Isolde at the Metropolitan Opera in December 1959

> Less than forty years after the composition of the Ninth Symphony of Beethoven, Wagner composed *Tristan*. A new texture of sound, a new significance, a new instrumentation, a new vocal melody; a new musical psychology—and a music that not only was potent in itself, as music, but one which changed ways of life, ways of conceiving love and death.
>
> Neville Cardus, *Ten Composers*, 1945

When Herbert von Karajan conducted *Tristan and Isolde* in Vienna in 1937, he was duped by the management and again by the musicians. He was originally promised three rehearsals, but just two weeks before the performance date a management representative got in touch to advise that only two rehearsals would be possible. There is no record of how Karajan reacted to this, but he seems to have accepted quietly because closer to the performance date, Karajan received a second letter from the management advising that he would have to manage with only one rehearsal. Who knows whether there was a legitimate reason for this or whether it was a ruse to keep expensive rehearsal time to a minimum?

Three Influential Women

In September 1857 Wagner read the newly completed text of *Tristan and Isolde* to a group of friends. It was probably the only time that the three most influential women in Wagner's life sat with him in the same room. They were Minna Planer, his first wife; Mathilde Wesendonck, who was a powerful influence while he was composing *Tristan*; and Cosima von Bülow, who would later become his second wife. Her first husband, Hans von Bülow, would conduct the first performance of *Tristan and Isolde* in Munich some eight years later.

• **Minna Planer, Wagner's first wife. Painting by Alexander von Otterstedt, 1835.**

• **Mathilde Wesendonck, who inspired the passionate music in *Tristan and Isolde*. Painting by Karl Ferdinand Sohn, 1850.**

• **Cosima in the Festspielhaus gardens, Bayreuth. Bust by Arno Breker, 1982.**

When Karajan arrived in Vienna, he met with the leader of the orchestra, who expressed the opinion that one rehearsal was useless. He promised the young conductor that if he would forego this single, worthless rehearsal, he was in a position to promise that his colleagues in the orchestra would play their hearts out. Karajan agreed and probably thought that he had made a good decision, because the production was a success and the twenty-nine-year-old conductor was applauded enthusiastically.

Karajan only discovered later that he had been conned by a group of lazy musicians who pulled this same trick with every unsuspecting young conductor.

Wieland's *Tristan* Goes Up in Flames

In 1962 Wieland Wagner's Bayreuth production of *Tristan and Isolde* featured a dream cast of megastars, including Birgit Nilsson, Wolfgang Windgassen, Grace Hoffman, and Hans Hotter and Gustav Neidlinger alternating in the role of Kurwenal, with a young Wolfgang Sawallisch conducting. But it was the staging that had such a profound effect, not only on productions of Wagner's works but on all of opera. Wieland stripped away all of the detail, leaving the stage empty but for a prominent phallic symbol. The rest was achieved by the team that I have always thought of as the Bayreuth Lighting Magicians. Despite Wieland's untimely death in 1966, productions of his groundbreaking *Tristan* continued until 1970.

The final production of Wieland's *Tristan* was memorable for several reasons. Wolfgang Windgassen had announced that it was to be his farewell appearance in Bayreuth; and although she had not told anyone, it was to be Birgit Nilsson's swan song too. Then, at the first intermission, a new, unique, never-to-be-repeated piece of theatricality was added. Immediately after the end of the first act, the minimal stage sets from Act I were carried outside to the front of the Festspielhaus and set aflame. At the second intermission, more of the iconic elements of Wieland's *Tristan* were burned.

Nilsson later recalled the end of the opera in her 2007 autobiography, *La Nilsson*: "As the last chord died away, there was a great stillness that seemed to last forever until the audience could bring itself to applaud. It was one of the most deeply felt moments for me in all the years at Bayreuth."

As the audience left, the final sets were burned in front of the Festspielhaus. Within an hour, all of the sets of what some believe to have been Wieland's greatest triumph were reduced to a pile of ashes.

In *The Literary Clef*, Edward Lockspeiser recounted the reactions of Emmanuel Chabrier after a Bayreuth performance of *Tristan and Isolde*. The Frenchman turned to his neighbor: "Ten years," he exclaimed, literally sobbing, "ten years I've been waiting for that A on the cellos!"

In 1936 Arturo Toscanini sat in the auditorium during one of Bruno Walter's rehearsals for a performance of *Tristan and Isolde*. Margaret Wallman recalled in her memoirs that at the end of the long second-act love scene, Toscanini turned to her and said, "If they were Italians, they would already have seven children; but they are Germans, so they're still talking."

The German conductor Hans Richter had a similar thought. He once stopped a rehearsal of the introduction to *Tristan*, turned to the cellists, and said, "Bravo celli! Quite correct, but you play like married people; a little more like the young lovers, please."

And Victor Borge, the Danish comedy musician, put it this way.

To enjoy *Parsifal*, either as a listener or an executant, one must be either a fanatic or a philosopher. To enjoy *Tristan* it is only necessary to have had one serious love affair.

—Bernard Shaw, writing in the *Star*, August 1889

The prelude to *Tristan and Isolde* sounded as if a bomb had fallen into a large music factory and had thrown all the notes into confusion.

—*Berlin Tribune*, 1871

***Tristan* . . . was a favorite opera of Tsar Nicholas II. Who knows why? I had heard of this unexpected taste of the Tsar from the brother of the Tsarina at a dinner in Mainz in 1931 or 1932.**

—Igor Stravinsky, quoted in Robert Craft, *Memories and Commentaries*, 1981

So there I sat in the topmost gallery of the Berlin Opera House, and from the first sound of the cellos my heart contracted spasmodically . . . Never before had my soul been so deluged with floods of sound and passion, never had my heart been consumed by such yearning and sublime bliss, never had I been transported from reality by such heavenly glory. I was no longer in this world . . . My ecstasy kept singing within me through half the night, and when I awoke on the following morning, I knew that my life was changed. A new epoch had begun; Wagner was my god, and I wanted to become his prophet.

—Bruno Walter, quoted in Phil G. Goulding, *Classical Music*, 1993

To enjoy *Tristan* it is only necessary to have had one serious love affair, and though the number of persons possessing this qualification is popularly exaggerated, yet there are enough to keep the work alive.

—Bernard Shaw, *The Perfect Wagnerite*, 1898

Wagner completed the libretto for *Tristan and Isolde* in four weeks, which isn't half bad, considering the interruptions. The music took him two years, though, and by that time he and Mathilde [Wesendonck] were just good friends. Fortunately, Wagner had an excellent memory, so the love scenes were as torrid as ever. In fact, he may have overdone them a little.

Victor Borge with Robert Sherman, *My Favorite Intervals*, 1974

“Ten years I've been waiting for that A on the cellos!”

—Emmanuel Chabrier, after a performance of *Tristan* at Bayreuth

---

Not until the turn of the century did the outlines of the new world discovered in *Tristan* begin to take shape. Music reacted to it as a human body to an injected serum, which it at first strives to exclude as a poison, and only afterwards learns to accept as necessary and even wholesome.

Paul Hindemith, *The Craft of Musical Composition*, 1937

Even now when I hear the opening bars of the prelude to *Tristan*, or the merest growl from Fafner as a snatch of *Siegfried* passes by, or the shimmering wonder of the Good Friday Spell from *Parsifal*, the passion flares up, and in a few seconds, I am once again drunk beyond breathalyzers.

Bernard Levin, *Conducted Tour*, 1982

When asked about her favorite roles, Birgit Nilsson responded without hesitating, “Isolde and Turandot.” She thought for a couple of seconds and went on: “Isolde made me famous. Turandot made me rich.”

Lord Beaverbrook, the newspaper publisher, was not a regular operagoer, but someone persuaded him to attend a performance of *Tristan*. After five hours of passion from the stage and the orchestra pit, Beaverbrook asked a companion, “This Wagner, was he a clean-living man?”

Apropos of contretemps, in one performance of *Tristan*—not in the “grand” season, I am happy to say—the prima donna was so completely sung out in the first two acts that the Liebestod had to be sung by the conductor.

J. A. Fuller-Maitland,
A Door-Keeper of Music, 1929

An official of La Fenice was dispatched from Venice to Milan to sign up Maria [Callas] for the production of *Tristan and Isolde* that the Maestro [Tullio Serafin] would be conducting in Venice. In fact it was a package deal: Isolde in December, Turandot in January, and 50,000 lire per performance. Maria signed the contract without reading it, and only after she had signed, did she turn her attention to the fact that she had agreed to sing a part she did not know. She revealed this to Serafin when he arrived in Milan the next day, and fully expected Serafin to be appalled. Instead he was amused. "One month of study and hard work is all you need," he assured her.

Arianna Stassinopoulos,
Maria: Beyond the Callas Legend, 1980

The following might have been said about *Tristan and Isolde*:

But who could paint in words the infinitely manifold but inexpressible sentiments which pass from pain to the highest exultation and from exultation to the softest grief, until they come to rest in a bottomless pondering? The tone poem alone could do this in this wonderful composition. But only in the master's tone-speech could that unspeakable meaning be uttered which my confined words have attempted to describe with the greatest modesty.

It could have been said about *Tristan and Isolde*. But it was not. It was written about Beethoven's *Eroica* Symphony. The writer was Richard Wagner.

He laid aside *The Ring* in 1857, and calmly proceeded to compose *Tristan*. Then he turned to the world of *Meistersinger*, two works as different as night from day; the one glorifies, in fact, night and death, the other glorifies life and day. The miracle of it!—to interrupt *Siegfried* and to think himself into the shot-silk tragedy of *Tristan and Isolde*; then to think himself into the radiant sunshine of the greatest of comedies in music; not only the genius but the effrontery of it . . . He interrupted his work on *Siegfried* in the second act, where Siegfried rests under the trees; not for a dozen years did Wagner again pick up the score of *Siegfried*, but when at last he did pick it up he wrote and imagined from the place, the very bar, exactly where he had left off, took up the identical strands in the orchestral tissue and began again to weave the great fabric of *The Ring* . . . and nobody today can place his finger on the score of Act II of *Siegfried* and show the point of interruption; there is no "joint" or hiatus, no caesura of style, for Wagner transformed his whole being as artist and technician back to the old legendary universe of gods and dragons and wood-birds.

Neville Cardus, *Ten Composers*, 1945

I have just conducted my first *Tristan*. It was the most wonderful day of my life.

Richard Strauss, in a letter to
Cosima Wagner in 1892

Sounds Different

The Earliest Recordings?

In October 2003 the Munich City Museum mounted an exhibition titled "Wagner's Worlds." While they were working on plans for the exhibit, a group of the curators came up with the idea of scouring the museum's large stock of mechanical musical instruments for recordings of Wagner's music. They assembled an assortment of self-playing musical instruments from the puppet theatre museum as well as from the musical instrument section. There were pneumatic instruments such as fairground organs, portable hand-cranked barrel organs, and player pianos, as well as many smaller domestic devices with such euphonic names as Ariosa, Ariston, Chordophone, Euphonium, Calliope, Piano Melodico, and Polyphone. Many of these instruments originate from the late nineteenth century, and it is said that some were regularly used at Wahnfried during Wagner's life at birthday parties and other celebrations.

Some of the most interesting sounds were later issued on a CD titled *Wagner Mécanique* that includes selections of music from *The Flying Dutchman*, *Tannhäuser*, *Lohengrin*, *Walküre*, *Siegfried*, *Meistersinger*, and *Parsifal*. One of the oldest machines used was the Concert Orchestrion, made by Josef Stern around 1880 near Baden, in the Black Forest. An original model of this pinned cylinder-driven device was restored in 1983. It includes 334 pipes and seven registers and a percussion register consisting of large and small drums, triangle, and cymbals. Selections from *Lohengrin* and *Tannhäuser* are included on the CD, and the huge instrument has a familiar fairground-organ sound, with punctuation in the form of loud thumps on a bass drum.

Around 1890 the company Paul Ehrlich AG was established in Leipzig to manufacture the Ariston Organette, a hand-cranked system using air suction and a punched disc. The discs rotated only once, so the repertoire was limited. An example on the Munich Museum CD is the march from *Tannhäuser* in forty-four seconds and *Lohengrin*'s Wedding March at thirty-nine seconds. According to its own records, by the middle of 1896 the firm had sold approximately 350,000 instruments and four million discs. Could it be that someone owed Wolfgang Wagner one of the world's first platinum discs for his grandfather's work?

Of special interest are works played by several musicians on the Steinway player piano, first manufactured in 1904. By use of a carefully guarded secret method, the Welte-Mignon system captured the individual playing and personal interpretation of a musician and then reproduced them faithfully through the Steinway, making it possible to "record" interpretations played by musicians who had worked closely with Wagner and some of his closest associates. The CD includes two "recordings" by Felix Mottl (1856–1911), who

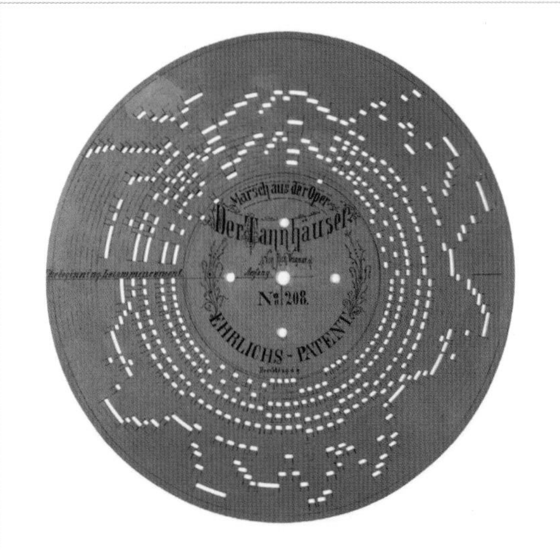

• The *Tannhäuser* march reduced to forty-four seconds on a large mechanical music disc, circa 1890.

assisted at the first Bayreuth Festival in 1876 and was chief conductor at Bayreuth in 1886: "Am stillen Herd zur Winterzeit" (By the quiet hearth in wintertime), from *Meistersinger*, and the Transformation Music and Entrance of the Knights of the Holy Grail from the first act of *Parsifal*.

Wagner Mécanique was issued on the Oehms Classic Label, catalogue number OC 330.

The Tuned-Up Organ

Martin Fischer and Hansjörg Albrecht were looking for an organ on which to record a transcription of *The Ring*—not any old organ, but something rather special. The two Germans, an organist and a sound engineer, visited monasteries, churches, and cathedrals from Berlin to Waldsassen and from Bochum to Leipzig. They eventually found what they were looking for—excellent acoustics and Germany's largest organ, built by the French company Cavaillé-Coll-Mutin—in the Cathedral of St. Nikolai at Kiel, erected in the fourteenth and fifteenth centuries: in fact, this cathedral has two organs, which can be played either separately or together from one keyboard.

A special feature of the recordings made by Fischer and Albrecht in April and May 2006 is that they made several different recordings of the organ, with its various voicings and registrations, which are then superimposed on one another—in other words, overdubbing. This technique is quite common in the realm of pop music but probably unique in recordings of organ music. The result is more of an orchestral arrangement than a straight transcription for two hands and two feet.

The CD, issued in 2006, includes extracts from all four *Ring* operas. It begins with the Vorspiel to *Rheingold*, where the famous E-flat goes on for close to thirty seconds and rattles the windows when played on large enough speakers. The Forest Murmurs from *Siegfried* has a wonderfully light, open feel, and the acoustics of the cathedral pay off. Brünnhilde's Immolation Scene has such tremendous power, depth, and richness that it is easy to forget that it was all played by a single organist but with a lot of help from technical wizardry. The CD is on the Oehms Classics label, catalogue number OC 612. The arrangement and organ playing are by Albrecht, and the sound concept and recording are by Fischer.

Wagner with a Latin Beat

In 1890 the German consul in Cuba gave a garden party at which his guests were entertained with selections from *Tannhäuser*. One of the guests, Sindo Garay, a famous Cuban folk singer, was deeply moved by the music and returned to his host's house a few days after the party with a gift: a Wagner-inspired composition that he titled *Germania*. It was probably the first crossover music that linked Wagner's themes with a Cuban beat.

A hundred and fifteen years later Ben Lierhouse, a German-born record producer, followed in Garay's footsteps with a recording created by combining a group of twenty-six Latin American musicians and singers with a thirty-eight-piece classical orchestra. The result was a series of CDs released in 2005 with titles like *Parsifal Goes La Habana*, *Siegfried's Olé in Spain*, *Tristan Meets Isolde in Harlem*, and *Parsifal's Trip to Brazil*.

Lierhouse's affection for Wagner shows through in several of the titles given to his tracks. A *fado* theme transitions into Sieglinde's motif on a track labeled "Mother, Where Are You?" "La Andalusia" becomes the march from *Rienzi*. No prizes for guessing which operas some of the tracks come from—for example, "Just Married," "Flying over the Sea," and "Wintertime."

Some of it is quite subtle. A soft Latin American beat is ambling along, and suddenly in comes "Winterstürme." Or the opening bars of *Tristan* give way to a bossa nova beat.

I own the four-disc set, and I enjoy picking out the Wagner themes that suddenly emerge from a totally different genre. The discs are great for a barbecue or dinner-party music, and Wagnerian guests enjoy the surprise appearance of familiar themes. I feel a certain satisfaction from conning my anti-Wagner philistine friends. They appreciate the lively beat and the pleasant melodies but most of them are totally unaware that Wagner wrote some of the themes that weave in and out.

Strict Wagnerians who believe that none should mess with the works of the master might disapprove, but in a Bayreuth record store the discs sold like hotcakes when they were first issued. It is hard to say what Wagner would have made of a bossa nova or tango beat, but he enjoyed parodies of his own music.

Coincidentally, one of the musicians Lierhouse found for his project was the aptly named Wagner Tiso. It seems that his parents had been Wagnerians and hoped that their newborn son would grow up to become a musician like their idol. Perhaps it was not the direct route that his parents hoped for, but with his involvement in this recording, Wagner Jr. got there in the end.

The Ukulele Band

Wagner's music has been played at the Proms on many occasions, but the performance of the Ride of the Valkyries in August 2009 was different: it was performed by the eight members of the Ukulele Orchestra of Great Britain. Their version of the ride was a gentle trot rather than a gallop. It took a few seconds for the audience to recognize the music they were hearing, but once they did, they were enthusiastic.

Founded in 1985, the group is made up of seven ukuleles in high and low registers. The eighth is really a bass guitar. Most of the Prom performance was devoted to pop music, but in addition to Wagner, Beethoven made an appearance with the "Ode to Joy" from the Ninth Symphony.

Missed Opportunities

Because of Too Much Verbose Prose

Wagner completed the composition of *Lohengrin* on August 28, 1847, and for the next six years he did not compose a bar of music. He did write a series of theoretical works including *Art and Revolution* (1849), *Artwork of the Future* (1850), *Opera and Drama* (1851), *A Communication to My Friends* (1851), and *Judaism in Music* (1852).

Henry T. Finck said in *Wagner and His Works* in 1893:

> With the exception of the last part of *Opera and Drama*, these writings are not among Wagner's best literary productions and some of them are so dry, abstruse and uninteresting that only an enthusiast for his operas could ever be expected to work his way through them from beginning to end . . . [This] means that the world lost two or three immortal operas, which he might have, and probably would have, written in those six years had not an unsympathetic world forced him into the role of an aggressive reformer and revolutionary.

He Never Visited the United States—but Almost . . .

Wagner never visited the United States, but in letters written in 1848 and 1849 he mentioned the possible benefits of such a journey. And in 1854, he wrote to Liszt: "While I live here like a beggar, I hear from America that in Boston they are already giving Wagner Nights. Someone implores me to come; he says that interest in me is rapidly growing there; that I could make much money with concert performances, etc."

In 1855, shortly after he conducted the London Philharmonic in London, he was invited to go to New York for six months. He had been told that he would be well paid, but it was not enough to tempt him. Then Boston tried again with an invitation to conduct a Beethoven festival. He wrote to Liszt saying that it was fortunate that no large sums of money had been offered; otherwise, he might have been tempted to accept and neglect his work. Liszt replied with a question. Would $10,000 to $12,000 for six months be enough to persuade him? Wagner replied by imploring Liszt not to offer further temptation. He said that ten years earlier he might have accepted, but that to do so now might mean that his *Nibelungen* would never be completed. The discussions ended, but when he became despondent about the prospects for his *Ring*, he hinted that he might put the project on a shelf and go to America to earn a small fortune.

New offers for transatlantic projects came later. In 1857 an approach was made on behalf of the emperor of Brazil. Later Chicago went one better: the city offered to build Wagner a new theatre to celebrate its renaissance after the Great Fire of 1871. Again Wagner declined. But he never completely rejected the idea of a visit to the United States. In March 1880 he wrote to Feustel that he was once again seriously considering a trip to America. A few weeks later the composer told his banker friend, "I must look elsewhere for personal support; five months in America shall secure me an independent income."

He never made it.

Quote—End Quote

Tell your friend Wagner that I thank him for the book, but he should give up music; he has more genius for poetry.

Arthur Schopenhauer, after reading the newly printed *Nibelung* poem

I am reading a book on Wagner . . . What an artist—one like that in painting would be something. It will come.

Vincent van Gogh, in a June 1888 letter to his brother Theo

Wagner is Wagner whether writing of Cornwall or Nuremberg, Elgar is Elgar whether writing of Poland or of the Severn Valley, Gounod showed his nationality most clearly in a German subject, Bizet in a Spanish one.

Gustav Holst, in a letter to the *Musical Herald* in 1915

There is no law against composing music when one has no ideas whatsoever. The music of Wagner, therefore, is perfectly legal.

The National, Paris, 1850

It was necessary that he should suffer, for he was a man of genius.

Heinrich Heine

I don't like Wagner. Whatever I do, I cannot like the unpleasant creature that he was.

Dietrich Fischer-Dieskau, during an interview in Israel

"9W."

Answer to the question: "Do you spell your name with a V, Mr. Vagner?"

Steve Allen

Wagner is the Puccini of Music.

J. B. Morton

The longest duration of any opera should be two hours.

Arthur Schopenhauer

Wagner wrote operas that were colossal and bombastic yet also moving and almost unbearably beautiful.

Michael Portillo, *Music That Shook the World: The Ring Cycle*, BBC TV, 2002

Wagner was one of those dynamically charged personalities after whose passing the world can never be the same again . . . Wagner is probably the only figure in the whole history of music of whom this can be said. Bach created no such upheaval . . . We were not fit for Bach until Beethoven and Wagner—and Wagner, perhaps, even more than Beethoven—made us so.

Ernest Newman

The Germans are a cruel race. Their operas last seven hours and they have no word for fluffy!

Rowan Atkinson, in *Blackadder*

A musicologist is a man who can read music but can't hear it.

Thomas Beecham

I can't listen to too much Wagner, you know? I start to get the urge to conquer Poland.

Woody Allen, *Manhattan Murder Mystery*, 1993

The American composer Silas Gamaliel Pratt deserves immortality, if only for the alleged conversation with Wagner. When Wagner said: "You are the Richard Wagner of the United States," the polite rejoinder was made, "And you, Sir, are the Silas G. Pratt of Germany."

Percy A. Scholes, *The Oxford Companion to Music*, 1938

Is it possible that he has musical talent?

Ludwig Geyer on hearing the eight-year-old Richard playing the piano while the stepfather lay dying in an adjoining room ■

Act Five

Die Meistersinger von Nürnberg (The Mastersingers of Nuremberg)

Completed: October 1867.
Premiere performance: June 21, 1868, National Theatre, Munich.
UK premiere: May 30, 1882, Theatre Royal, Drury Lane.
US premiere: January 4, 1886, Metropolitan Opera, New York.

The Bare-Bones Plot

At the close of a church service a young knight, Walther von Stolzing, meets and falls in love with Eva, the daughter of a rich goldsmith. But her father, Pogner, had already offered his daughter as the prize in a song contest, so Walther decides to compete. First he has to join the Mastersingers, in whose pedantic rules he is instructed by David, apprentice to the shoemaker and poet Hans Sachs. Beckmesser, the town clerk and a rival for Eva's hand, is the Marker, and as a result of his assessment Walther's application for membership is rejected.

Walther and Eva decide to elope. But before they can do so, Beckmesser arrives to serenade Eva. Hans Sachs, who has decided to champion Walther's cause, interrupts Beckmesser by singing humorous songs and hammering at a shoe. David arrives and mistakes Beckmesser's serenade as intended for his own sweetheart, Magdalena; he attacks the town clerk, starting an uproar among the townspeople.

Walther spends the night talking with Hans Sachs and tells of the wonderful melody that came to him in a dream. Sachs writes it down, but Beckmesser steals it, believing that it was written by the shoemaker.

• **Medal commemorating the four-hundredth anniversary of Hans Sachs' death.**

The next day Beckmesser tries to sing the song in the competition but makes a hash of it. Hans Sachs then proposes that anyone who can sing the song should be declared the winner, even if he is not a member of the Meistersingers. Walther steps onto the podium and wins the competition and the hand of Eva.

Wagner's Debt to Wagenseil

Wagner told in his autobiography *Mein Leben* about how he set out to obtain the information he would need to work on the plot for *Die Meistersinger*.

> My first idea was to make a thorough study of Grimm's controversy on the Song of the Meistersinger; and the next question was how to get hold of old Wagenseil's Nuremberg Chronicle. Cornelius accompanied me to the Imperial Library [where the book was found]. I remained at my hotel, eagerly making extracts of portions of the Chronicle,

• **The Nuremberg sculpture of Hans Sachs. Appropriately, he is sitting on a pile of books. Statue by Johann Konrad Krausser.**

> which to the astonishment of the ignorant I appropriated for my libretto.

The book that Wagner referred to was a chronicle produced by Johann Christoph Wagenseil (1633–1708), a professor at the university in Altdorf, near Nuremberg. The chronicle, written mostly in Latin with a scattering of Greek and Hebrew, is an amazingly detailed record of the affairs of Nuremberg's institutions. An appendix was headed:

> Johann Christoph Wagenseil's Book of the Master-singers' Gracious Art; its origin, practice, utility, and Rules.

The early part of the book rambles on about a woman novelist, printing errors, the delicate skin of French ladies, and traveling entertainers. In his 1927 book *Wagner and Wagenseil*, Herbert Thompson wrote: "The first three chapters of the Professor's message may be dismissed very briefly. They contain some interesting particulars, it is true, but for irrelevant discursiveness the author deserves to rank with Mrs. Nickleby."

After a detailed account of the origins of the Mastersingers, which Thompson dismisses as "mythical," Wagenseil reached the fourth chapter of his work—the section that Wagner found so valuable in developing his version of the Mastersingers story. Wagenseil spelled out in great detail the rules relating to prosody, measures, rhymes, syllables, stanzas, and much more. He then lists the thirty-two faults that the markers must watch for and even spells out the punishment to be meted out.

Wagner used much of this detail in developing the plot for *Die Meistersinger von Nürnberg*. He even used descriptions of the Nuremberg trial song setting for his staging instructions. Wagenseil wrote:

> Markers are known as those who, as the most prominent and most eminent members of the Guild, sit at the table and before the great desk in the curtained platform, and are generally four in number. The senior has lying before him the Holy Scriptures according to the translation of Herr Luther; opens them at the place indicated by the singer as that from which his song is taken, and gives careful attention whether the song agrees not only with the tenor of Scripture, but also with Luther's very words. The second Marker, who sits opposite the first, notices whether in the wording of the song all is in accordance with the rules of the Tablature, and if any should be broken, makes a note of the mistake with a piece of chalk upon the desk, and of the corresponding forfeit, that is to say, how many marks (Sylben) he is to lose in respect thereof. The third Marker writes down the last syllable of each verse or rhyme, and sees that all are correctly rhymed, at the same time noting down the mistakes. And the fourth Marker pays attention to the Tone (melody), so that the right one be adhered to, and not falsified; also that all the Stanzas and After-songs conform together.

In the interests of dramatic effect, Wagner reduced the work of four men in medieval Nuremberg to one, Sixtus Beckmesser.

Meistersinger Stray Notes

Herbert von Karajan frequently impressed audiences by conducting without a score, but on at least one occasion he probably regretted it. Karajan lost his place while conducting a performance of *Die Meistersinger* at a June 1939 gala performance for the king and queen of Yugoslavia, with Adolf Hitler also present. He did not just stumble; he completely lost his way, forcing the management to ring down the curtain while Karajan found his bearings. Hitler was furious and told Winifred Wagner, "Herr von Karajan will never conduct at Bayreuth in my lifetime." Winifred made sure that he never did.

> After working all day at copying, [Hans] Richter would often row out to a small island on the Lake [Lucerne]). It would not be unusual for him to take his horn with him and, in the solitude of his surroundings, play phrases from *Meistersinger* amongst his repertoire. Many years later in 1885, after the degree ceremony at Oxford at which he received an honorary doctorate in music, he was approached by an academic. During the course of the conversation it emerged that this professor was holidaying in Lucerne at the time of Richter's apprenticeship with Wagner. He asked Richter if he knew the identity of a mysterious horn player whose music used to waft across the lake at dusk. Richter confessed that it was he, adding that the professor could consider himself the first member of the public to hear music from what was then the unperformed opera *Meistersinger* by Richard Wagner.
>
> Christopher Fifield, *True Artist and True Friend: A Biography of Hans Richter*, 1993

The original Hans Sachs was a contemporary of Martin Luther and lived in the medieval town of Nuremberg in Bavaria until his death in 1576. According to his own reckoning, at one point Sachs had already written 4,275 master-songs, 208 dramas, 1,558 comic stories, fables, histories, figures, comparisons, allegories, dreams, visions, lamentations, controversial dialogues, psalms and religious songs, street and tavern songs, and a few prose dialogues—all in all, 6,048 pieces, large and small.

Of all the affected, sapless, soulless, beginningless, endless, topless, bottomless, topsiturviest, scrannel-pipiest, tongs and boniest doggerel of sounds I have ever endured, that eternity of nothing was the deadliest.
—John Ruskin, in a letter to a friend after attending *Die Meistersinger* in 1882

To this day Richard Wagner, though undoubtedly in the great line of German classics, has his detractors, and it is easy to see what it is in the vast romantic canvases of *The Ring* and *Tristan* that can repel the more severe kind of modern taste. But the man who cannot enjoy *The Mastersingers*, surely one of the wisest and most humane works of art ever created, must have a cold heart: let no such man be trusted!
—Desmond Shawe-Taylor and Iain Lang, *A Basic Record Library*, 1959

He became a shoemaker but continued to compose poems and songs that covered every aspect of life in medieval Germany. There are poems still in existence signed by Sixtus Beckmesser and Veit Pogner, but Hans Sachs' works fill whole volumes, and his memory is so revered that he is looked upon almost as the patron saint of his city.

> That Wagner was able to return from the orgiastic world of Tristan to life as it is lived by men in this world, from the murky shadows of a distended chromaticism to the clear and

brave light of diatonicism, from the shrieks of "highest rapture" to well-turned melody; that he was able to overcome the irresistible attraction of "consuming fire-death" in favor of the living humanism of the medieval artisan-poets—this remains one of the incomparable feats in the history of the arts.

Paul Henry Lang,
The Experience of Opera, 1973

It was popularly believed at one time that Hitler's off-duty troops flocked enthusiastically to the opera houses to relax at a performance of *The Ring*, *Tristan*, or *Meistersinger*. Not so, says Jonathan Carr, author of *The Wagner Clan* (2007). According to Albert Speer, Hitler's architect and later minister of armaments, most Nazis were bored by Wagner's long music dramas and preferred lighter fare. At the 1933 gala performance of *Die Meistersinger*, for instance, so few turned up that a furious Hitler sent patrols to drag party members out of beer gardens and brothels, recalled Speer in his memoirs. He added that many of those who did show up slept through most of the performance—this despite the fact that the meadow scene must have been quite stunning. There were more than seven hundred people crowded onto the stage of the Festspielhaus.

Jonathan Carr researched operatic performances in Germany in the 1930s and confirmed Speer's comment. In the 1932–33 season, *Carmen* was the most frequently performed opera in the country, followed by Weber's *Der Freischütz* and then four Wagner operas. Five years later, Wagner's most-performed opera was *Lohengrin*, but it occupied twelfth place—behind works by Leoncavallo, Mascagni, and Puccini. During the war years Verdi's works were the most often performed. "The Master's market share dropped to under 10 percent. Wagner was already considered by the younger generation to be rather old-hat," said Carr.

The villain in *Die Meistersinger von Nürnberg* is the town clerk, Sixtus Beckmesser, who schemes and cheats to win the contest and the hand of Eva in marriage. Beckmesser is a pompous buffoon without any redeeming features. At one stage in the early development of *Die Meistersinger*, Wagner planned to call the town clerk Veit Hanslich, a thinly veiled insult directed at Eduard Hanslick, the Viennese music critic who had been a detractor of many of Wagner's works. E. W. Engel's *Richard Wagners Leben und Werke im Bilde*, published in Vienna in 1913, includes a facsimile of a list of dramatis personae for *Die Meistersinger*. There in Wagner's hand the town clerk is shown as "Hanslich." Wagner later changed his mind and reverted to the name in his source material.

In May 1931 John Barbirolli made a historic recording of the *Meistersinger* with a dream team: Elisabeth Schumann, Gladys Parr, Lauritz Melchior, Ben Williams, and Friedrich Schorr. For years afterwards Barbirolli enjoyed telling the story of the obstacles that he had to overcome to complete the recording. Barbirolli's friend and biographer recounted it:

> Take after take was ruined by wrong entries by Melchior while Elisabeth Schumann became hoarser with each new beginning. Eventually, after a day and a half, Barbirolli told Melchior to watch him implicitly. He conducted the final take with his eyes riveted on no one but Melchior and with one hand over his mouth. When he moved it away was the signal for Melchior to sing: when he didn't, Melchior was under orders to keep his mouth firmly shut. Yet the result was one of the classics of the gramophone.
>
> Charles Reid, *John Barbirolli: A Biography*, 1971

• **Wagner's nemesis, Eduard Hanslick. Caricature by Peter Cornelius.**

Die Meistersinger was one of the favorite Wagner operas of the journalist Bernard Levin. In one of his *Times* essays, reprinted in *Enthusiasms*, an anthology of his works published in 1983, Levin wrote:

> If the pages of a book could sing, my task would be considerably easier, for I could then lay down my pen and let them sing to you, starting their programme with the Quintet from Act Three of *The Mastersingers*. How many times have I seen that work? Thirty, perhaps; yet every time, as the five voices blend, part, exchange themes, blend again, soar, swoop, exult, dream, rise, fall, and finally come to a climax and die away, I find tears filling my eyes. Four of the five voices are singing of love, the fifth of wisdom; and the orchestra, which knows everything they know and more, makes the sixth voice. Imagine being so locked against feeling as to be unable to respond to such beauty in sound, conveying feelings so deep! It is not even necessary to have loved to respond to the *Mastersingers* Quintet; it explains—with its sound, not with its words—what love is, in terms that enable even the most inexperienced to comprehend.

Levin was therefore thoroughly delighted when he was given a surprise performance and the manuscript of a work dedicated to him by his friend, the composer Richard Blackford. It was a fantasia for wind quintet (flute, oboe, clarinet, horn, and bassoon) and, appropriately, it featured themes from *Die Meistersinger*. Levin wrote about it in the *Times* in February 1990: "It was presented to me first in a surprise performance; the circumstances were festive, and reminiscent of Wagner's birthday present to Cosima, the surprise of the *Siegfried Idyll*."

"It explains—with its sound, not with its words—what love is."

—Bernard Levin, on the Act III quintet from *Die Meistersinger*

Blackford called his composition *Portrait of Hans Sachs*, and Levin said that he would not part with it for any amount. "It is no use," he wrote, "your waiting until I die and going to the auction of my effects, for I shall have bequeathed it to one who loves music and Richard as much as I do."

Bernard Levin died in August 2004. The fantasia was played at his memorial service later that year in St.-Martin-in-the-Fields.

A few years after Wagner's death in 1883, Puccini traveled to Bayreuth to determine whether *Die Meistersinger* could be cut for performance in Italy. A shortened version was subsequently staged at Milan's La Scala in December 1889.

Preparing for the premiere performance of *Meistersinger* in Munich in 1868, the conductor Hans Richter insisted on no fewer than sixty-six chorus rehearsals. The performance was a sell-out, and King Ludwig was present in the audience.

It was to be another twenty years before *Meistersinger* would be performed in Bayreuth. Cosima Wagner was in charge of production in 1888 and must have been delighted with the response. It was her first sold-out performance in the Festspielhaus.

Early in 1868 Bruckner wrote to Wagner inviting him to become an honorary member of the Frohsinn (Happy Spirit) Choral Society and send a suitable work for the male choir to sing in Linz. Wagner quickly accepted the honorary membership and added: "However, as you must realize, a work of such a nature is hard to find among my compositions. Yet after thinking the matter over, since you mention a festival concert in which an orchestra and a female chorus will take part, I think I can offer you something appropriate. It is the closing section of my latest dramatic work, *Die Meistersinger*."

This is how Bruckner, who at that point had never met Wagner, came to conduct the first excerpt from *Meistersinger* outside Germany.

> The overture is hardly calculated to win the listener. All the leitmotifs of the opera are dumped consecutively into a chromatic flood and finally tossed about in a kind of tonal typhoon . . . The only thing which prevents one from declaring it to be the world's most unpleasant overture is the even more horrible Prelude to *Tristan and Isolde*. The latter reminds me of the old Italian painting of that martyr whose intestines were slowly unwound from his body onto a reel.
>
> Eduard Hanslick, 1868

Wolfgang Wagner and his wife, Gudrun, visited London during the 1993–94 season for the Graham Vick production of *Meistersinger*, conducted by Bernard Haitink, with John Tomlinson singing the role of Hans Sachs. Jeremy Isaacs, then the general director, later recalled the visit in his memoirs, *Never Mind the Moon: My Time at the Royal Opera House*. He said that the Wagner couple enjoyed everything about the production and the performance. Gudrun wrote to Isaacs: "We thought we saw not a *Meistersinger* but THE *Meistersinger*."

Three years later the couple was in London again for the Richard Jones production of *The Ring*. Many Wagnerians remember it as the one where Brünnhilde is dragged onstage with a brown paper bag over her head. This time Gudrun's thank-you letter was sent to Isaacs' assistant and mentioned only the "excellent arrangements."

The first performance of *Meistersinger* in Vienna in February 1870 was a fiasco that approached the *Tannhäuser* shambles in Paris. The performance was conducted by the very popular Johann Herbeck, a true-blue Wagnerian. There were many Wagner supporters in the audience, and they reacted with enthusiasm to the first act. The anti-Wagner forces took over in Act II when they greeted Beckmesser's serenade with a storm of booing and catcalls. Johann Beck, who was singing Hans Sachs, went to pieces when he heard the audience booing and gave up. Fortunately, Herbeck was a trained singer, and while continuing to conduct, he picked up where Beck left off and sang the Hans Sachs role.

However, the Viennese Wagnerians won out in the end, and the performance was greeted with loud cheering. Despite this, Wagner was furious when he received reports of the Viennese premiere. He learned that some ninety minutes of *Die Meistersinger* had been cut, and he bore a grudge for years. The rift was not healed until 1875, when Hans Richter made his Viennese debut by conducting *Meistersinger*. All of it.

Siegfried

Completed: February 1871.
Premiere performance: August 16, 1876, Festspielhaus, Bayreuth.
UK premiere: May 8, 1882, Her Majesty's Theatre, London.
US premiere: November 9, 1887, Metropolitan Opera, New York.

The Bare-Bones Plot

Siegfried wants to weld the broken sword that his mother left when she died in childbirth. The Nibelung dwarf Mime, son of Alberich, fails to repair the sword that he knows will help to regain the ring and the gold from the dragon Fafner. After the Wanderer (Wotan) visits Mime's cave, Siegfried forges the sword himself.

Mime leads Siegfried to the cave where Fafner sleeps. Siegfried kills Fafner and retrieves the ring and the magic Tarnhelm. He accidentally tastes the dragon's blood, which gives him the ability to understand the birds. The Woodbird warns him that Mime wants to poison him and describes the beautiful Brünnhilde, who lies sleeping on a rock surrounded by a protective wall of fire.

The Wanderer consults the earth goddess, Erda, but fails to halt the movement toward catastrophe. On his way to Brünnhilde's rock, Siegfried encounters the Wanderer and removes his power by shattering his spear. Siegfried awakens Brünnhilde and they fall wildly in love.

One of the Problems in *Siegfried*: You!

Arturo Toscanini could be brutally rude to anyone, frequently for no reason. An Italian composer reported the following exchange between the maestro and a member of the orchestra when Toscanini conducted *Siegfried* in Bologna in 1905:

> At the first Bolognese performance of *Siegfried*, one of the singers (an excellent one), who was treading the boards of the Comunale for the first time, showed signs of great fear and worry. A few minutes before the curtain was to go up, Maestro Toscanini passed next to him, serious and morose as usual.
>
> "Good evening, Maestro," said the singer, greeting him. "How will the opera go?" "Eh!" answered Toscanini, "I really don't know. There are too many beasts in this opera. There are birds, there's the dragon, there's the bear, and there's you." And he went quickly down to the orchestra.
>
> Francesco Vatielli, quoted in Harvey Sachs, *Toscanini*, 1978

The music triples the intensity of the feelings with which the characters are animated—that is all one can say to those who have not heard it . . . It is impossible to give the faintest idea of such music; it resembles no other.

—Camille Saint-Saëns on *Siegfried* after a performance at Bayreuth

Nap Time for Brünnhilde

The soprano Jane Eaglen once admitted that she fell asleep as she was lying on Brünnhilde's rock, waiting to be awakened by Siegfried while the magic fire blazed around her. "It was only the dress rehearsal, so I was more relaxed than usual," she explained.

One of the problems with the libretto of *Siegfried* is the unintended laugh when Siegfried first sees the uncovered breast of Brünnhilde and declares, "That is no man!" It is unfortunate that the laughter in the audience comes at a moment of great tenderness and drama. In recent years, clever translations have sometimes avoided the problem, but in most productions a collective snigger is considered inevitable.

The soprano did not make it any easier for the tenor in a Manchester production of *Siegfried* in the mid-1970s. Siegfried prepared himself for

• **Siegfried slays the dragon. Artist unknown.**

the audience reaction as he started to remove the breastplate from the sleeping Brünnhilde, but on this occasion, it was the tenor who had to suppress a belly laugh. Under the armor of the sleeping maiden was a note reading: "Do Not Disturb. Early Morning Tea 7:30 A.M."

Because of illness and other problems, three different singers appeared as Siegfried in the 1957 *Ring* at Covent Garden. One critic, Philip Hope-Wallace, wrote in the *Manchester Guardian* that each of the tenors had a different way of dying: Wolfgang Windgassen "collapses slowly like a chloroformed dog and one is never quite sure if he is dead yet"; Set Svanholm "goes over on his back with such a bang that one is rather alarmed"; and Bernd Aldenhoff simply "takes it with resignation."

During the first years of his exile after the 1849 uprising, Wagner corresponded with Theodor Uhlig, his friend from the Dresden orchestra. In one letter Wagner said: "In the first act of *Valkyrie* he [Siegfried] is conceived almost before the eyes of the public." Then in an apparent reference to his own son, he added: "How Siegfried will enjoy seeing how he was made: I should like to see his expression!"

Tchaikovsky was an enthusiastic Wagnerian and attended the premiere of *The Ring* at Bayreuth in 1876. He later complained that there were so many visitors that it became difficult to find food. Around the same time, Tchaikovsky wrote a fairy story about a young man named Siegfried who was bewitched on his wedding night.

In Lucerne one day, Wagner was visited by Judith Gautier. She recalled looking out from

> two windows of the little room that we were in [that] faced the lake [Lucerne], [and] a third, a side window, [that] was open and overlooked the court, where a blacksmith was at work. Wagner listened to the ringing stroke of the hammer on the anvil. Suddenly he opened the piano and began to play the motif of Siegfried forging the sword. At the measure where the blade is struck, he stopped, and it was the blacksmith who, striking the iron with an astonishing precision, unconsciously completed the theme.
>
> "You see," said the Master, "how well I have calculated the time, and how exactly the blow falls."
>
> Judith Gautier, *Wagner at Home*, 1910

"Do Not Disturb. Early Morning Tea 7:30 A.M."

—note to a tenor playing Siegfried, revealed after he removed the sleeping Brünnhilde's breastplate

In the summer of 1875 singers, musicians, scenic artists, and technicians assembled in Bayreuth for rehearsals, coaching, stage work, conducting tests, and experimentation. Singers had been tried and roles established, but at this eleventh hour, before work was to begin on building *The Ring*, Wagner had still not found a singer for the key role of Siegfried. His ideal was Ludwig Schnorr von Carolsfeld, the first Tristan, but unfortunately, he had died ten years earlier.

Then he found Georg Unger. He had reservations, though, and set some apparently harsh conditions.

> This choice was due not so much to Unger's unusual vocal gifts as to his personal appearance and great stature, which fitted him admirably for the joyous youthful hero, Siegfried.
>
> The conditions upon which he was accepted at Bayreuth were that he should leave the stage for a year and devote himself

exclusively to the preparation of the rôle, and in addition devote himself to serious voice work with Professor Julius Hey in Munich.

Wagner himself studied the rôle with him word by word, note by note, and wrought a marvelous transformation in Unger both as an actor and an artist. Hey, in his *Reminiscences*, writes that "The sixty-two-year-old Wagner not only made clear to Unger every passage of the *Siegfried* score, in regard to meaning, mood, vocal technique, and plasticity in the treatment of the text, but also endeavored to influence his entire character, so as to bring Unger into closer harmony with that of the 'hero without fear.'"

Wagner, according to the testimony of his artists, had a marvelous gift of vitalizing the music, and as a singer without a voice he made the dramatic situation so vivid as to create an indelible impression upon all present.

Hey relates a little anecdote from the *Siegfried* rehearsal, where at the point where Mime utters his second distressed cry of "Fafner!" Wagner's voice broke on the high A, producing an irresistibly comical effect. He laughed immoderately, as did everyone else, and cried: "Where shall I hide myself! There is no anvil here!"

To quote Hey further: "How did this voice, which in reality was no voice at all, succeed in producing such moving tone nuances, so as to present in the clearest manner every varying phase of emotion! In addition a dramatic declamation which penetrated to the very bottom of the listener's soul!"

Caroline V. Kerr, *The Bayreuth Letters of Richard Wagner*, circa 1912

A Cuckoo in *The Ring*? Thankfully Not

Since the earliest days of music, composers have tried to translate the music of birds into the music of the orchestra with varying degrees of success. Many used the call of the cuckoo, because it is simple and unmistakable. Everyone can point immediately to Beethoven's cuckoo in the *Pastoral* Symphony, but how many can single out the nightingale also present in the Scene by the Brook? Other composers have tried to signify thrushes, linnets, larks, doves, and even roosters in their compositions but the keenest birdwatcher would be hard-pressed to find all the hidden birds.

When Wagner conceived the idea for the Woodbird that would guide Siegfried to Brünnhilde's rock, he needed a musical theme. If he even considered the easy solution of using the two-note call of the cuckoo, he quickly rejected the idea. He chose instead to feature an anonymous bird that Richard Aldrich called "the most eloquent and the most beautiful singer of them all, unmatched by any other bird in music."

How much less pleasing Siegfried's dialogue with the bird would have been if Wagner had taken the easy way out.

Helden Wagnerians 10

KING LUDWIG II OF BAVARIA

The First Helden Supporter

For the first two days of his life, Ludwig was Otto. He was born on August 26, 1845, and the next day he was christened Otto Friedrich Wilhelm. A few days later, at the request of his grandfather, the baby's name was changed to Ludwig. In March 1864, upon the death of his father, Maximilian II, the young man became King Ludwig II of Bavaria. He had just turned eighteen.

• Lohengrin enthusiast King Ludwig II of Bavaria rides a swan and plays the music. Caricature in *Der Floh*, Vienna, 1885.

Ludwig had been entranced by Wagner's music from an early age and owned the librettos of both *Tannhäuser* and *Lohengrin*. His father prevented him attending performances of the operas until he was fifteen, when he was at last allowed to see *Lohengrin* performed in Munich. That event changed his life, and an interest became a passion for Wagner's music that would last the rest of his life and that even, it may be argued, led to his death.

Ludwig is known to many as the "Mad King," but some believe that his diagnosis as insane is questionable. There can be no doubt, however, that Ludwig was extremely eccentric, a dreamer, and a fantasist. In his biography of Ludwig, Greg King paints a picture of the difficult life that led to Ludwig's eccentricity:

> Ludwig II stood apart from the world around him. Raised without warmth or affection, he grew into an aloof, emotionally starved young man, curiously detached from everyday life. In his loneliness, he found comfort in glowing accounts of life at the court of Louis XIV at Versailles, in the tales of ancient gods and dark Teutonic history, and in a world of dreams. He so hated his own century, his own surroundings, that he actively sought refuge in another, less hostile environment, one filled with granite and marble castles and palaces where he could relive the glories of past ages and peopled not with the unfriendly faces of the Munich court but with the ghosts of Parsifal and Lohengrin, Louis XIV and Marie Antoinette. Through the musical dramas of Richard Wagner, he managed to escape, however briefly, into a place and time where he felt himself truly accepted, an era of chivalry and fair maidens, of heroic knights and divinely inspire rule. All around him, the realities of his position—the political pressures and wars with Prussia, the intrigues of Bavarian politics, the impotence of the democratic monarch in Bavaria—drove him further and further into this world of illusion, and with the passing years, he severed all but the last links with the world beyond his own rarefied existence. His struggles, against Otto von Bismarck, against the court officials who blocked his friendship with Wagner, against his own desires for solitude, and against his homosexuality, crushed Ludwig's spirit.
>
> Greg King, *The Mad King: A Biography of Ludwig II of Bavaria*, 1996

Within days of acceding to the throne, Ludwig sent his cabinet secretary Pfistermeister on a journey to find Wagner. When he eventually tracked him down in Stuttgart, he gave a servant his card, which read, "Franz von Pfistermeister, Secretary to the King of Bavaria." On seeing it Wagner panicked, assuming that this must be one of his creditors. The next morning, however, Wagner agreed to meet the stranger. Thus did the fifty-year-old composer learn that an eighteen-year-old king was to be his patron.

Ludwig spent the rest of his life worshipping Wagner and providing him with everything he needed to complete *The Ring*. He largely financed the building of the Festspielhaus and Wahnfried, Wagner's home in Bayreuth.

Ludwig's eccentricity and extravagance made enemies of powerful courtiers, for whom his being diagnosed as insane was an easy solution. None of the four psychiatrists who declared Ludwig insane examined him, and three of them had never even met him. Following the declaration of insanity, Ludwig was deposed, and days later the bodies of the king and his psychiatrist were found drowned in Lake Starnberg. He was only forty. Most scholars are uncertain about what happened. In 1978 the Elmcrest Psychiatric Institute of Portland, Connecticut, published an article in the *American Journal of Psychiatry* titled "The Commitment and Suicide of King Ludwig II of Bavaria."

Their conclusion is in the title, but most scholars still classify Ludwig's death as simply mysterious.

Götterdämmerung (*Twilight of the Gods*)

Completed: May 1874.
Premiere performance: August 17, 1876, Festspielhaus, Bayreuth.
UK premiere: May 9, 1882, Her Majesty's Theatre, London.
US premiere: January 25, 1888, Metropolitan Opera, New York. However, it was decided that New York audiences were not ready for the whole nine yards. The Norns' prologue and the long Waltraute scene were cut.

The Bare-Bones Plot

The three Norns recap the saga, and when the rope of destiny breaks, they return to Erda because they know that the end of the gods is inevitable. Siegfried gives Brünnhilde the ring as a pledge of his love. Brünnhilde gives him her horse, and he leaves on a journey. He arrives at Gibichung Hall, the residence of Gunther, his sister, Gutrune, and their half-brother, Hagen, the evil son of Alberich. They give Siegfried a magic potion that causes him to forget Brünnhilde and fall in love with Gutrune. He agrees to brave the fire and bring Brünnhilde to Gibichung as a bride for Gunther.

Waltraute visits Brünnhilde on the rock and tries to persuade her sister to return the ring to the Rhinemaidens to save the gods. Brünnhilde refuses, and Waltraute leaves in despair. Then Siegfried arrives, but because of the magic Tarnhelm, he has taken on the appearance of Gunther. He forces the ring from her finger.

Alberich visits his son, Hagen, and encourages him to plot Siegfried's murder to win back the ring. Gunther takes Brünnhilde back to Gibichung Hall by force, and a double wedding is arranged for Siegfried to Gutrune and for Gunther to Brünnhilde. When Brünnhilde sees the ring on Siegfried's finger, she screams that she has been betrayed. After mutual swearing of oaths, Hagen persuades Brünnhilde to agree to a plan that will result in the death of Siegfried.

On a hunting expedition Siegfried encounters the Rhinemaidens, who try unsuccessfully to coax the ring from him. Hagen kills Siegfried with a spear in the back, and his body is carried back to Gibichung Hall. Gunther tries to claim the ring and is killed by Hagen. Brünnhilde takes the ring from the finger of the dead Siegfried and orders a funeral pyre for the dead hero. She follows him into the flames. Valhalla and the gods are destroyed in the fire, the river rises, and the Rhinemaidens reclaim the ring.

On November 21, 1874, twenty-six years after he first outlined *Götterdämmerung*, Wagner composed the final notes. He was exhausted; the normally garrulous composer could manage only six words on the last page of the score: "Completed at Wahnfried—no further comment."

Before a performance of *Götterdämmerung* at Covent Garden, a friend suggested to Thomas Beecham that he should not attempt to con-

• **Hagen kills Siegfried. Liebig card circa 1910.**

duct without the score because of the difficulty of handling the changes in rhythm. Beecham replied, "There are no rhythmical changes in *Götterdämmerung*; it goes straight on from half past five till midnight like a damned old cart horse!"

Beecham was excluded from the Covent Garden organization in 1945. Although polite in public, he took frequent private potshots at David Webster, the general administrator. Beecham once remarked, "You know, I was walking past Covent Garden the other day and saw, to my great surprise, that they were actually announcing *The Twilight of the Sods*. It's about time." ("Sod" is a British general term of contempt for an unpleasant person.)

"It ain't over till the fat lady sings" is an expression popular with sports commentators. It is a somewhat cryptic answer to any question about when something will be over.

So who was the fat lady, and why will her singing mean that we have reached the end? While there are other explanations, most experts believe that the fat lady is Brünnhilde, who sings at the end of *Götterdämmerung*, the final opera of *The Ring*. Most, though not all, of the sopranos who sing this difficult role are large ladies. It seems likely that the colloquialism was popularized by baseball commentators when a long game was reaching its conclusion.

In *Götterdämmerung* the hero, Siegfried, sings his heart out during much of the five-hour opera, while the singer playing Brünnhilde enjoys long breaks in her dressing room. (Jane Eaglen, one of the top Brünnhildes of recent years, is known to have watched baseball on television while awaiting her call to the stage.) When she gets back to the stage late in the third act, she launches into a ten-minute performance that

I find the last opera of the *Ring* cycle, *Götterdämmerung*, almost unbearable in its clash between Siegfried's short-sighted masculine prowess and Brünnhilde's dawning enlightenment. It culminates in his murder and her suicide, but there is no resolution in *The Ring*, although some critics—and Wagner himself—have tried to find redemption in Brünnhilde's death. What there is, however, is the strong message that she is the only one who has understood what has happened, not just intellectually, but also emotionally. As Wagner said: "It all happens so that a woman can become wise."

And extraordinarily, given the massive number of phrases that Wagner has to draw upon by the end of *Götterdämmerung*, the last music we hear is the return, saved up for so long, of that hopeful phrase that drifted up from Sieglinde's trust in Brünnhilde. We have not heard it in all the intervening eight hours of music, and as it spirals out across the exhausted audience, we are staggered that everything comes to rest in these achingly plangent tones. After all these male heroes have battled themselves to a standstill, this melody that grew out of a sense of sisterhood has returned.

Is it true, we ask, wrapping ourselves in our coats, that this hopefulness that arises between women should be what remains at the end of all wars, at the end of all empires? Have we travelled through these great mazes of myth and music to have this suggestion about the power of a woman's empathy laid at the end of it all? If we allow him to, Wagner truly has the power to surprise us.

—Natasha Walter, "Wagner's Women," the *Guardian*, © Guardian News & Media Ltd., 2006

The Norns as Suffragettes

• "Vote, sister, I pass it to you." The Norns as suffragettes give new meaning to the rope of destiny in a 1929 *Punch* cartoon. Reproduced with permission of Punch Ltd., www.punch.co.uk.

This cartoon appeared in a May 1929 issue of *Punch* shortly after the Representation of the People Act of 1928 gave women equal voting rights to men. Coincidentally, the cartoon appeared just weeks before the death of Emmeline Pankhurst, aged sixty-nine, one of the founders of the British woman suffrage movement. The cartoon is signed simply "BP," for Bernard Partridge.

few thin ladies have the strength or stamina to deliver. Eventually she throws herself onto Siegfried's funeral pyre, and it's over. The fat lady has sung.

When Arturo Toscanini was preparing to conduct *Götterdämmerung* in Turin in December 1895, he was afraid that the audience would not be able to cope with the massive work. Wagner's works were not well-known there at the time, so he tried to ease his audience into the opera by making several major cuts, including the whole of Waltraute's impassioned plea to Brünnhilde. The performance was a major success, and the audience did the very thing that Wagner did not want at the end of Siegfried's Funeral March: they applauded enthusiastically. They called loudly for a *bis*, but this time the wishes of the composer prevailed, and there was no encore.

It is impossible to tell whether Toscanini's cuts of about 25 percent of the opera had anything to do with the audience's reaction. However, *Götterdämmerung* was a major success in Turin, where it was performed twenty-one times that year.

What do the singers do when they are not onstage? While singing Brünnhilde in the August 2005 Seattle *Ring*, the Lincolnshire-born soprano Jane Eaglen watched baseball on television. She now lives in Ohio, where she is professor of voice at Baldwin-Wallace University. She leads a "Wagner Intensive" workshop there.

Kirsten Flagstad preferred to knit during intermissions or when awaiting her cue. What she created during the hours of knitting at the Met during her first appearances there in 1935 is not known. Perhaps some lucky tenor was given a new scarf to protect his instrument from the chill of a New York wind.

"

As Wagner said: 'It all happens so that a woman can become wise.'"

—Natasha Walter, in the *Guardian*, 2006

The World Wide Wagner Web

I sit in my study surrounded by bookshelves holding more than five hundred books on opera, the majority of them with a Wagner connection. I have been working on *Richard Wagner: The Lighter Side* for many years and regularly need to get additional information or check a fact. What was the date of the first performance of *Parsifal* in the United States? Who was the Flower Maiden singer rumored to be one of Wagner's conquests? When did Reginald Goodall die? There have been many such questions every day, and in the early years I got up to find the relevant books with the information I needed, decided which might be best, and then thumbed through to find the answer.

Today, I Google the information I need, and within seconds I have the answer.

A Google search for "richard wagner" produces more than 20 million hits in under a second. Because some of those have nothing to do with the magician of Bayreuth, I try again. A search for "richard wagner opera" results in almost 17 million hits. When I try a more specific search, "richard wagner's parsifal" scores 1.4 million. Information on the Web is growing at such a rate that all of these numbers will probably have increased significantly by the time this is read.

Not many years ago I wrote for another project that "it is unfortunate that only a few of the top opera houses have their own Web site." Now even the smallest offers comprehensive information on programs, casts, librettos, and much more.

The Bayreuth Festival

The site has a section in English, but some of the detailed pages are in German only. As might be expected, the site includes details of the each season's program with cast names and a performance database back to 1951.

An interesting feature of the site is headed "Backstage." The opening illustration of the entire Festspielhaus complex shows that the auditorium is dwarfed by other facilities, including workshops, rehearsal rooms, restaurants, and the huge stage. Click on any of the fourteen headings and you get a short video sequence on key features, including the famous hidden orchestra pit, costumes, makeup, chorus, stage machinery, and lighting. The stage at Bayreuth is unique because there are no wings, and the area behind is massive, with huge rear doors to permit the movement of set elements from the workshops directly onto the stage. The lighting video reveals that what I have called elsewhere the Bayreuth lighting magicians have at their disposal more than eight hundred light sources employing the very latest technology.

Online ticketing is now included on the Bayreuth Web site (www.bayreuther-festspiele.de/english/english_156.html), but don't expect tickets until you have tried every year for about ten years.

The Wagneropera.net site (www.wagneropera.net/Bayreuth) includes another Bayreuth section with much information, including something not included on the official site: *Stukas*, a 1941 Nazi propaganda film. A distressed member of a bomber crew is miraculously cured after a performance in the Festspielhaus. Anyone who can stand the Nazi element will be interested in snips of a 1941 *Siegfried* performance.

Monsalvat, a Mecca for Parsifal Enthusiasts

Possibly the most comprehensive Web site devoted to a single Wagner opera, Monsalvat was created by Derrick Everett in Norway. After an introduction, there are sections on sources and contexts, creation, interpretation, references, performance, the music, and reactions. The site includes numerous essays on every aspect of the work by eminent Wagnerians, including Adolphe Appia, Bernard Shaw, Charles Dudley Warner, Thomas Mann, and Bernard Levin. The leitmotif guide is particularly valuable. It includes audio files of some forty motifs, musical notation, and extensive notes. This brilliant Web site is must reading for *Parsifal* enthusiasts or newcomers who would like to know more about Wagner's final work. Interested readers can check it out at www.monsalvat.no/index.htm.

The Wagnerian

With a title like that, this Web site (www.thewagnerian.com) has to be of interest to readers of this book. The site provides information on broadcasts, new productions, recordings, and books on Wagner and his works. Future performances of Wagner's operas are given with cast lists and video clips. A valuable search feature enables users to seek information from the site's archive, and there are links to other Wagner-related Web sites, including many of the Wagner Societies.

Membership in The Wagnerian is free, and members receive email roundups of news and information.

Wagneropera.Net

This is a beautifully designed and presented general Wagner site that has been voted one of the top seventy-five music and arts Web sites. It includes lists of books, recordings, articles, a calendar of performances, details of opera houses, and lists of Wagner Societies around the world. The section on how to get tickets for the Wagner Festival in Bayreuth even includes a seating plan.

This Web site (www.wagneropera.net) was developed by Per-Erik Skramstad in Norway. He is a professional Web designer, which explains why the site is so attractively presented.

YouTube

The already massive selection of Wagnerian material on YouTube grows every day. Search for "leitmotifs" and select "Let there be leitmotifs" to hear a demonstration by members of the Metropolitan Opera brass section. Search for "nibelungen" and select "Anna Russell" to hear her live presentation at New York Town Hall in 1953.

Another brilliant clip combines footage from *Wagner and Me*, by Stephen Fry, with footage from TV's *X Factor* featuring a pop singer called Wagner. In the original, Fry climbs the stairs to the Festspielhaus auditorium, puts a hand on the door handle, and says in a hushed tone that he has waited all his life to enter. But when he opens the door we see the third-rate pop singer and band performing on the hallowed stage. Irreverent but hilarious.

Search for any of the characters in *The Ring* and select from dozens of clips. One of my favorites is a doctored version of a segment from Disney's *Fantasia*. The final music in *Fantasia* is Schubert's "Ave Maria." The animation shows a procession of shadowy monklike figures carrying torches through an abstract landscape. Someone looked at that sequence and thought that it could be improved, presumably without permission from Disney. The doctored version shows the same animated scene, but with the music from the end of Act III to *Parsifal* replacing the Schubert composition. It is quite beautiful and as one viewer observed, it transcends the original.

The original plans for Walt Disney's *Fantasia* included a segment featuring the Ride of the Valkyries. The animation was created by a Danish artist, Kay Nielsen, who was responsible for other segments in the 1940 film. Unfortunately, Disney was concerned about anti-German sentiment and Hitler's hijacking of Wagner, so the Ride was dumped. If it had remained in the award-winning animated movie, Francis Ford Coppola might not have felt free to use the popular music in his movie *Apocalypse Now*.

Parsifal

Text completed: April 1877.
Music completed: April 1879; the full orchestral score was completed in January 1882, just months before rehearsals started for the first performance.
Premiere performance: July 26, 1882, Festspielhaus, Bayreuth.
UK premiere (concert version): November 10, 1884, Royal Albert Hall, London.
First full UK performance: February 2, 1914, Royal Opera House, London.
US premiere (concert version): March 4, 1886, Metropolitan Opera, New York.
First full US performance: December 24, 1903, Metropolitan Opera, New York.

Parsifal was Wagner's thirteenth and final complete opera. It took him four years to write. In 1878, while he was composing the work, Wagner told Cosima at lunch one day that he had spent the entire morning working on a modulation for just two words—"nach ihm," from Amfortas' lament. He told her later that he had crossed out everything he had composed the day before.

(Oscar Wilde went Wagner one better. He is

• A postcard showing Gurnemanz, Amfortas, and Kundry in a scene from the English-language production of *Parsifal* in the US by the Henry W. Savage touring company in the early 1900s.

quoted as saying, "I was working on the proof of one of my poems all the morning, and took out a comma. In the afternoon I put it back.")

The Bare-Bones Plot

Kundry is condemned to an eternity of tempting the virtuous. She tempts Amfortas, a knight from the Grail, and while in her embrace he is wounded by the evil magician Klingsor. Amfortas suffers agonies because his wound will not heal: it can be healed only by a "wise fool." Parsifal arrives on the scene, but Kundry's wiles fail to tempt him. The wise fool defeats Klingsor and takes possession of the holy spear that the magician had used to wound Amfortas. Parsifal is hailed by the knights of the Grail when he cures Amfortas' wound. Kundry is released from her wanderings and falls dead.

Engelbert Humperdinck worked with Wagner in Bayreuth in 1881–82. He was employed to copy the score of *Parsifal*, a boring, painstaking task that offered little glamour or excitement. It is said that toward the end of the orchestration stage, the composer was working at such a pace that his copyist could barely keep up. The young Humperdinck got his big chance after rehearsals started when one scene change took longer than expected and the stage managers needed more time. Humperdinck was asked to compose an extra six bars of music and add them to the score. He did so and looked forward to a brief moment of fame. Unfortunately, his contribution was deleted when improved stage procedures removed the need for the extra time. His six bars were unceremoniously scrapped.

That was not the worst indignity Humperdinck suffered. The producer of a performance of *Hansel and Gretel* in the United States made a speech in which he referred to "the wonderful work of this great composer Pumpernickel."

Footsies

The slippers worn by the Flower Maidens in the first production of *Parsifal* were open-toed. This shocked one Berlin critic, who confessed that he had never before seen a female foot. He added that he was disappointed by the experience.

Perhaps he was simply continuing a tradition started by Wagner himself, who regularly took liberties with his assistants' names. He once wrote an instruction to Hermann Levi about performance of *Parsifal*: "The six solo Magic Maidens are to be coached by Humperting! . . . Have you a score? If not, you can get one from Hump!"

When *Parsifal* was first performed at Bayreuth in 1882, the conductor was Hermann Levi. Henry T. Finck claimed that Wagner wanted to assign the honor to his longtime assistant Anton Seidl. However, as King Ludwig had lent him his royal orchestra from Munich, Wagner felt obliged to use the king's conductor. Years later Seidl was given the privilege of taking the podium for the one-hundredth performance of *Parsifal* at Bayreuth, and it turned out to be the last full opera he ever conducted.

Wagner did not describe *Parsifal* as an opera or even a music drama. He called it a *Bühnenweihfestspiel*—a "festival play for the consecration of the stage." At the last of the sixteen performances in August 1882, Wagner took the baton from Levi and conducted the final scene. It was the first and only time he conducted at a public performance in the Festspielhaus.

Maria Callas sang the role of Kundry but did not consider it an important part of her repertoire. She sang the part in a 1950 radio broadcast from Rome, and fortunately it was recorded. The Italian

At the last performance of *Parsifal* in 1882, Wagner took the baton and conducted the final scene. It was the first and only time he conducted publicly in the Festspielhaus.

director Franco Zeffirelli said later, "Like thousands of other people, I was immediately taken by the extraordinary quality of this warm personality and the sound of that voice. I remember my ears were absolutely buzzing—the power of this woman and the presence . . . There was something unique happening."

Years later, while London was abuzz with enthusiastic reaction to her famous *Tosca* performances, Neville Cardus, the critic for the *Guardian*, wrote an open letter to Callas. "Really, Madame Callas . . . your admirers are your worst enemies. They actually protest overmuch that your voice is 'better than ever.' For my own part, I could almost wish that it had worsened. Then there would be some hope of your liberation from more or less brainless parts in Italian opera. A high shriek is fatal to a singer appearing as Norma, Elvira, Lucia, or any of that kind. A high shriek could be a histrionic asset if you are acting with body, eyes, temperament, as well as voice, Kundry in *Parsifal* or Electra or Salome in Strauss's operas . . . Opera for you now is the ranging world of Wagner, Strauss, Berg, and other composers who could give your intelligence something to get its teeth into and kindle the Callas imagination, flammable now surely from hot kindling of personal experience . . . There is still time left to you to fulfill this destiny."

Callas ignored the plea, but who can deny that she succeeded in adding intelligence and depth to the "brainless parts"?

Henry T. Finck told a story about Anton Seidl hearing Wagner at the piano while he was working on the composition of *Parsifal*. What became the Flower Maiden score made an indelible impression on him: "Some years later, when he was putting the sketches into rough shape for practical use, Wagner played various parts for him. When he came to the *Flower Maiden* music, Seidl remarked, 'Ah, I know that.' Whereupon Wagner jumped up excitedly, almost angrily, and wanted to know where he had heard it. He was pacified on being told where, but for a long time the shock affected him, for he often said to Seidl: 'Well, have you found any more familiar things in my music?'"

Bruckner dedicated his Third Symphony to Wagner, but some commentators have suggested that his Seventh Symphony would have been more appropriate. The slow movement has been described as a lament upon Wagner's death just a few weeks earlier. The use of Wagner tubas strengthens the connection.

Puccini was so enthusiastic about *Parsifal* that he obtained tickets for three separate performances in 1923. He intended to stay for only one act on each occasion so that he could absorb the work bit by bit. However, he could not bring himself to leave and stayed for the entire performance each time.

Wagner audiences listen to overtures and preludes without chattering and allow the final notes at the end of a work to fade away before applauding. They also respect the composer's request that applause be withheld until the end of the act. But before the first performance of *Parsifal*, Wagner's wishes were misinterpreted as meaning "no applause at all." For years after Wagner's death, first Cosima and then Winifred imposed the "no applause" rule, but by then it had become more of a requiem to the master. Even today it is traditional in some opera houses to withhold applause after the first act.

Bernard Levin believed that directing opera, as opposed to drama, requires a long apprenticeship, and that the works of Wagner required significant postgraduate qualifications and experience. Therefore it was with some trepidation that he entered the Royal Opera House in 1979 for a production directed by Terry Hands. It was only the second opera that the Englishman had ever directed. What made Levin even more nervous was that the production onstage that night was *Parsifal*.

The performance was to be conducted by Bernard Haitink, whom Levin much admired. In his critique in the *Times*, Levin wrote: "Musically, it was without exception the finest *Parsifal* of my life; I have never before been so entirely overwhelmed by its force and meaning."

But the staging lived up to his worst fears:

> Let's get it over quickly: the idea of the production is that Parsifal is the end-of-term play at a minor public school in the 1930s, put on in the ruined church next door, with the doting parents of the performers scattered round the stage—handbags, hats, three-piece suits and all (Gurnemanz is the headmaster incidentally); from time to time the parents are called upon to do things, such as light candles and hold them in their laps. I truly believe that it was only by the direct intervention of Almighty God—who, after all, has a substantial interest in the matter—that the grail was not inscribed, The Mrs. Featheringay-Fawcett Cup for Outstanding Prowess in the Gymnasium. (Perhaps it was; my sight is not of the keenest.)

Terry Hands went on to become artistic director and later chief executive of the Royal Shakespeare Company and winner of a string of awards and honors. His biographical entry on Wikipedia lists an impressive sixty-six stage productions between 1968 and 2005, but no operas are mentioned—not even the 1979 *Parsifal*.

> For the life of me I cannot see why the recent suggestion that the score of *Parsifal* may find a place on Signor Mancinelli's desk at Covent Garden should be scouted as "profane." I leave out of the question the old-fashioned objection, founded on the theory that all playhouses and singing-halls are abodes of sin. But when a gentleman writes to the papers to declare that "a performance of *Parsifal*, apart from the really religious surroundings of the Bayreuth Theatre, would almost amount to profanity," and, again, that "in the artificial glare of an English opera-house it would be a blasphemous mockery," I must take the liberty of describing to him the "really religious surroundings," since he admits that he has never seen them for himself. In front of the Bayreuth theatre, then, on the right, there is a restaurant. On the left there is a still larger restaurant and a sweetstuff stall. At the back, a little way up the hill, there is a café. Between the café and the theatre there is a shed in which "artificial glare" is manufactured for the inside of the theatre; and the sound of that great steam-engine throbs all over the Fichtelgebirge on still nights.
>
> Between the acts the three restaurants are always full, not of devout Wagnerites (the Meister advocated vegetarianism), but of Spiers & Pondites, who do just what they

will do at the Star and Garter when my Festspielhaus on Richmond Hill is finished. The little promenade in front of the theatre is crowded with globe-trotters, chiefly American and vagabond English, quite able to hold their own in point of vulgarity, frivolity, idle curiosity, and other perfectly harmless characteristics, with the crowd in the foyer at Covent Garden or the Paris Opéra. When they have seen every celebrity present pass and repass some twenty times, they become heavily bored, and are quite excited at seeing a small contingent from the orchestra, with the familiar German-band equipment of seedy overcoat and brass instrument, assemble under the portico and blare out a fragment of some motif from whatever music-drama is "on" that evening. This is the signal for entering the theatre, but nobody moves, as everyone knows that it is only the third blast that means business, when you do not happen to be at a distance—in which case, however, you hear nothing, unless you are dead to windward, with a strong gale blowing. Inside, the "honorable ladies" are requested by placard to remove their towering headgear; and not one of them is sufficiently impressed with the really religious surroundings to do so. Then the famous "Bayreuth hush" is secured by a volley of angry sh-sh-sh-es, started by the turning down of the lights; and the act begins. What sanctity there is in all this that is not equally attainable at Boulogne or Bayswater remains to be explained.

Mr. Charles Dowdeswell's position on the subject is safer than that of his fellow-correspondent. He claims special sanctity, not for Bayreuth, but for *Parsifal*, and says (what is perfectly true) that the Bayreuth Festspielhaus is the only existing theatre in which justice can be done to the work. But as to his practical conclusion—that for the immense majority here who cannot afford to go to Bayreuth it is better that they should never see any performance of *Parsifal* at all than see one even as good as the Covent Garden Meistersinger—no practical Wagnerite critic can endorse it. Let us build a Wagner Theatre, by all means, as soon as possible; but if, in the meantime, Mr. Harris will produce even the second act of *Parsifal*—and he could quite easily do it—I, for one, will forgive him for *La Favor-*

**I am still under the spell of *Parsifal* . . .
I found many innovations in the music . . .
It is amazing that a man of seventy could write anything as fresh as the Flower Maiden's love song.**
—Béla Bartók after his 1904 visit to Bayreuth

The Good Friday music from *Parsifal*, the enchantments of which pass all sane word-painting.
—Bernard Shaw, writing in 1890

***Parsifal* is the kind of opera that starts at 6 o'clock. After it has been going on for three hours you look at your watch and it says 6:20.**
—David Randolph

"*Parsifal* is daft" was the refreshingly straightforward verdict of Winifred Wagner's children on their grandfather's complex and significant work.
—Guido Knopp, *Hitler's Women*, 2001

Yesterday, I heard *Parsifal* for the first time. I have never in all my life had an artistic experience at all comparable to this; it is overwhelming; one comes out after each act (I do, at least) absolutely overcome with admiration, bewildered, distraught, with tears running down one's cheeks.
—Emmanuel Chabrier

About this lady a story was current at one time that she had entreated Wagner to write her a part and let her "create" it. It was perhaps rather cruel of the master to tell her, when *Parsifal* was preparing, that he had written a part with special regard to her vocal powers, and to extract from her a promise that she would fill it at every performance. The promise was given, and it is to the lady's great credit that it was faithfully kept. The older visitors to Bayreuth will not have failed to be impressed with the reverent walk of the Bearer of the Grail, who, of course, has not a note to sing!
—J. A. Fuller-Maitland, *A Door-Keeper of Music*, 1929

Bloomer instead of Blume also panicked the New York Chorus of Bridesmaids in *Lohengrin* when German conductor Karl Muck reprimanded them in rehearsal for raising their bouquets to their noses at the wrong time. He announced, "Ze ladies are sniffing zer bloomers too zoon."
—Stephen B. Tanner, *Opera Antics and Anecdotes*, 1999

> *ita*, and applaud his artistic enterprise to the skies the whole season through.

Bernard Shaw, in the *World*, March 25, 1891

Not Everything Was Masterly

Bell's Miniature Series of Musicians, published in the early part of the twentieth century, included books on Henry Purcell and Richard Wagner by John F. Runciman (1866–1916). The music critic and author had strong views that resulted in several libel suits.

Although Runciman found *Rheingold* to be tedious and boring, his book on Wagner's works was enthusiastic about all of the other works, with one exception. He said of *Tannhäuser*: "There are enough beautiful and passionate tunes there to make the fortune of half a dozen Italian operas." Of *Lohengrin*: "sheer sustained loveliness." *Meistersinger* "is full of sweet sunlight and cool morning winds." *Walküre* includes "some of Wagner's finest and freshest love-music," and "the continuous sweep of the music, with its ever-changing colors and emotions, is almost supermasterly." But when it came to *Parsifal*, Runciman had only a few lines of angry denunciation.

> This disastrous and evil opera was written in Wagner's old age, under the influence of such a set of disagreeable immoral persons as has seldom if ever been gathered together in so small a town as Bayreuth. The whole drama consists in this: At Monsalvat there was a monastery, and the head became seriously ill because he had been seen with a lady. In the long-run he is saved by a young man—rightly called a "fool"—who cannot tolerate the sight of a woman. What it all means—the grotesque parody of the Last Supper, the death of the last woman in the world, the spear which has caused the Abbot's wound and then cures it—these are not matters to be entered into here. Some of the music is fine.

John F. Runciman, *Wagner*, 1905

According to the *London Musical Times* in 1883, *Parsifal* was the second-shortest of Wagner's operas in terms of number of bars of music. It has 4,347, compared to the 3,905 of *Das Rheingold* and the 4,432 of *The Flying Dutchman*. Yet *Parsifal* is a much longer opera: "Most of this beautiful music is so solemn and slow that more time is consumed than usual. The first act alone lasts an hour and three-quarters; but I have never yet met anyone at Bayreuth who found it too long."

In *Parsifal* Wagner adapted a rising four-note melody that Liszt had used in his cantata *The Bells of Strasbourg Cathedral*. Two months before Wagner died in Venice in February 1883, Liszt had a dream in which he saw his son-in-law's black-draped funeral gondola. The next day he sat down in Wagner's Palazzo Vendramin home and took the four notes back. As a tribute to his friend, he incorporated the theme from *Parsifal* in an elegy that he called *At the Grave of Richard Wagner*.

Régine Crespin once claimed that Wieland Wagner persuaded her to sing Kundry at Bayreuth by demeaning the other Wagnerian heroines. She had expected that Wieland would invite her to sing one of the roles that the French call *les Wagnériennes blondes*—Elsa, Eva, Sieglinde, and Elisabeth. "Oh, those dummies," he is reported to have said. "I don't like them. Look, you are not born for that, you have a better job to do." He then astonished the soprano when he told her that the role he wanted her to sing was Kundry. She agreed and sang Kundry for the next three years. Many believe that it was this role that propelled her to international stardom.

Years later Herbert von Karajan persuaded Crespin to sing the notoriously difficult *Walküre*

The whole drama is calculated for hysterical women and blasé men of the world.
A complete absence of melodic charm.
Wagner—The Doctor of Cacophony.
The *Parsifal* motifs: piano-tuning with impediments.

—Extracts from media reports on the premiere of *Parsifal*

***Parsifal* deals with momentous matters but with a richness of symbolism that has often obscured as much as it has enlightened . . . Christian imagery is . . . a key element in the work but that does not necessarily mean that it is an essentially Christian drama.**

—Barry Millington, in the Metropolitan Opera Guild's *Talking About Opera*, 1991

***Parsifal* is Christianity arranged for Wagnerians.**

—Friedrich Nietzsche in 1874

Was *Parsifal* meant to represent Christ, someone once asked Wagner. He replied, "Christ, a tenor! God forbid!"

—Milton Brener, *Opera Offstage*, 1997

***Parsifal* is scored in a surprisingly discreet manner. In the art of orchestration Wagner has not grown old; in *Parsifal* this art has developed into pure magic, and for every change of mood conjures the most wonderful sounds in infinite shades and variety.**

—Wagner's arch critic Eduard Hanslick, after the premiere of *Parsifal*

An ideal Kundry is difficult to find, i.e. one who combines the beauty called for in the second act with the histrionic talent required in the first and second acts. In case of doubt, it is better to sacrifice the beauty; at least Wagner seemed to think so. When he invited Frl. Brandt to be one of the Kundrys, she was delighted, but expressed doubts of her fitness, on account of the directions, "Kundry, a young woman of the greatest beauty." "Never mind the beauty," interrupted the Meister: "I need a clever actress, and that you are; cosmetic will make up the rest."
—Henry T. Finck, *Wagner and His Works*, 1893

The first act of the three occupied two hours, and I enjoyed that in spite of the singing.
—Mark Twain, *At the Shrine of Wagner*, 1891

And, oh, those voices of children singing under the dome!
—Paul Verlaine

Like it or not, most 20th-century music could not have been written without *Parsifal*.
—Robert Thicknesse, in the *Times Opera Notes*, 2001

Then I went out front for the next rehearsal and had my first "Nicht dagewesen," meaning it was a truly " out of this world" experience. I was exalted. I was pole-axed. I had never been so affected, so spiritually lifted out of this world in my thirteen years of theatre. I walked out of the [Festspielhaus] theatre into the misty rain to go home and walked a half mile in the wrong direction. I was a different person. I had experienced an epiphany beyond my understanding or reach. It was like the consideration of afterlife.
—Glynn Ross, after witnessing a rehearsal of *Parsifal* in Bayreuth in 1953; quoted by Trish Benedict in *Leitmotive*, a publication of the Wagner Society of Northern California

Brünnhilde at Salzburg by employing a similar line of flattery. "I want a woman's voice, not a trumpet. I want a human being," he told her.

> Nothing in the world has ever made so overwhelming an impression on me. All my innermost heart-strings throbbed. I was beginning to think of myself as a dry old stick but it is not the case . . . I cannot begin to tell you how *Parsifal* transported me. Everything I do seems so cold and feeble by its side. That is really something.
>
> Jean Sibelius, in a letter to a friend after his 1894 visit to the Bayreuth Festival

Wagner wrote to his London friend Edward Dannreuther in 1878 on two important matters. The first was probably a consequence of a new taste acquired in London the previous year. "Please send me some Yorkshire hams," he asked. Then there was news of *Parsifal*. "The Vorspiel is finished," he told Dannreuther. "It sounds very nice!"

A few weeks later, the *Parsifal* Vorspiel had its first public performance when it was played in the hall at Wahnfried.

The sets for the original 1882 production of *Parsifal* were used for over fifty years: designed by Wagner's friend Paul von Joukowsky, they continued in use at Bayreuth until 1934.

Parsifal in New York

With the support of King Ludwig, Wagner decreed that *Parsifal*, the "stage festival play," would never be performed anywhere but Bayreuth, and his wishes were observed for twenty years after his death. The score could be bought, but the enforcers in Bayreuth prevented foreign performances with threats of legal action. That was not enough to discourage Heinrich Conried, director of the New York Metropolitan Opera, who was determined to stage *Parsifal* in his city. He had no musical training and his only prior experience of musical production was the first American staging of Humperdinck's *Hansel and Gretel*.

Conried went ahead with his plans, triggering a sensational court case in which Cosima's lawyers tried to protect the exclusive right of Bayreuth to Wagner's final work. Cosima lost, and *Parsifal* took New York by storm. The first performance was given on Christmas Eve, 1903, and the 3,700 seats were sold at $10, double the usual price. As the performance date approached, the scalpers did very well, with $10 tickets selling for $75.

The first performance was a major event in the cultural history of New York City, and media coverage was splashed over the front pages the next day. The *New York Times* filled two columns on its front page, followed by further extensive coverage on the inside pages. As was the norm at the time, the front-page lead headline was followed by subheads and sub-subheads. The newspaper said:

"PARSIFAL" A TRIUMPH
Production Unrivaled in History of Opera in New York—
Immense Audience, Deeply Impressed with Wagner's Festival-Play,
Listens Breathlessly Throughout the Performance

The coverage even extended to the editorial page, where the editor suggested that opera had been elevated to a new high and that *Parsifal* had raised serious and deep questions.

Parsifal was performed eleven times in New York that season, and every house was a sell-out, due in part to a special *Parsifal* train from Chicago. The embargo had been broken, but most opera companies waited until the copyright expired before mounting their own productions.

The first "legal" performance was staged in Barcelona. The copyright expired at midnight on December 31, 1913, and the Spanish performance began one minute later.

Otto Klemperer was better prepared than most. When he conducted *Parsifal* in the small opera house in Barmen on January 4, 1914, he did it from memory.

The first performance of *Parsifal* in English in the United States was given by the touring company of Henry W. Savage. Amazingly, it was given no fewer than 320 times during the forty-week tour of 1904–5. Taking such a production around the United States must have been a logistical challenge. Eight performances were given every week, requiring three separate casts. Finding even one singer to handle each of the main roles would have been tricky; three complete sets must have been a nightmare.

But Savage's problems did not end there: most of the singers he recruited did not speak a word of English. The impresario therefore asked the British music writer and critic Herman Klein to coach the singers on clear enunciation. Klein took all of the singers to Germany in the summer of 1904, and with the help of the two conductors, he coached the singers on clear and understandable pronunciation. He drilled them parrot fashion until they could recite the unfamiliar language. It seems to have worked: the New York critics later wrote that the text was "exceptionally audible."

Stray Notes

In Heidelberg in the summer of 1877, Wagner met Ulysses S. Grant, but there was no great meeting of minds because communication was difficult. Grant spoke only English and Wagner only German and some French. If a dialogue had been possible, it would probably have been about something other than music. Grant once said, "I know only two tunes: one of them is 'Yankee Doodle,' the other isn't."

Wahnfried was the first house in Bayreuth to have a working telephone.

The first Wagner opera to be performed in Italy was *Lohengrin*, in Bologna on November 21, 1871. It was sung in Italian.

In 1931 Wilhelm Furtwängler was the first conductor to have a concert broadcast over two hundred radio stations worldwide. The broadcast was a performance of *Tristan and Isolde* from the Bayreuth Festspielhaus.

Winifred Wagner was the first woman in Bayreuth to get a driving license.

The first full recording of *Tristan and Isolde* was made at the Metropolitan Opera in March 1935; it featured Kirsten Flagstad and Lauritz Melchior. The Met orchestra was conducted by Artur Bodanzky.

Winifred Wagner was the first woman in Bayreuth to get a driving license.

> The vocal life of a soprano has four stages: 1. Bel canto, 2. Can belto, 3. Can't belto, 4. Can't canto.
>
> Madame Vera Galupe-Borszkh

Shavian Wit and Wisdom

Bernard Shaw was a master of the cutting phrase, and there were some wonderful examples in his columns in the *World* in 1890–94.

> At Covent Garden there is nothing new before the curtain except a lining of mirrors to the walls of the corridors; so that on diamond nights box holders who are tired of being admired by the audience can go outside and admire themselves.
>
> April 15, 1891

> The *Tannhäuser* on Saturday was a rather desperate business. To begin with, [Enrico] Bevignani made his first bow amid a gust of fiddle-rapping from the band, and proceeded at once to give us a more than sufficing taste of his quality. He treated the unfortunate opera exactly as the Chigwell donkey-boys treat their steeds, literally *walloping* it from one end of the course to the other.
>
> I purposely refrain from saying anything about the praiseworthy points in the past (Covent Garden) season. The

critic who is grateful is lost. Sir Augustus [Harris, administrator of Covent Garden] has given us *Otello* and revived *Fidelio*. Instead of thanking him, I ask why he has not given us *Siegfried*. When he gives us *Siegfried* (which he can do by engaging [Ernest] Van Dyck for it), I shall complain of the neglect of *Die Walküre*. Let him add that also to his obsolete repertory, and I shall speak contemptuously of an opera-house where *Tristan* is unknown. After that, I can fall back on *Das Rheingold*, *Götterdämmerung*, and *Parsifal*; but by that time, at the present rate of progress, I shall be celebrating my hundred and fiftieth birthday. If even then I say that I am satisfied, let there be an end of me at once; for I shall be of no further use as a critic.

August 5, 1891

The modern lyric drama owes to the German nation three leading features. First, the works of Wagner. Second, tenors who never sing in tune. Third, prima donnas who dress badly. I plead earnestly with Sir Augustus for a strenuous resistance to the two last, combined with a hearty welcome to the first . . . The performance of *Die Walküre* improved as it went on. The first act was bad—very bad. Sieglinde was a cipher. [The tenor Max] Alvary began by singing out of the key. Later on he found the key, and merely sang out of tune. He posed with remarkable grace and dramatic eloquence: I can imagine no finer Siegmund from the point of view of a deaf man.

June 3, 1891

It is all very well to represent Bayreuth as a quiet spot where Nature invites the contemplative peace in which Wagner's message comes to you with the full force of its deepest meaning (or words to that effect); but in solemn truth the place is such a dull country town that the most unmusical holiday-maker is driven into the theatre to avoid being bored out of his senses.

February 3, 1892

Wagner: The Nine-Hour Epic

Tony Palmer's film of Wagner's life is appropriately epic in every way. The nine-hour film was originally shown as a ten-part TV series and was made to commemorate the one-hundredth anniversary of Wagner's death. The cast looks like a *Who's Who* of the stage, screen, and opera house and includes Richard Burton as Wagner, Vanessa Redgrave as Cosima, and Gemma Craven as Minna. Other roles are played by John Gielgud, Laurence Olivier, Gwyneth Jones, Peter Hofmann, Joan Greenwood, William Walton, Liza Goddard, Bill Fraser, Arthur Lowe, Prunella Scales, Corin Redgrave, Joan Plowright, Andrew Cruickshank, Cyril Cusack, Manfred Jung, and Jess Thomas. In total, the huge cast wore more than two thousand costumes.

The film took seven months to shoot in more than two hundred locations in eight countries, including King Ludwig's castles and Wagner's apartment in Venice. Richard Burton was in pain during the filming of this, his penultimate screen role, but he has been praised for his portrayal of the composer's mix of arrogance and tenderness.

The music was conducted by Georg Solti and played by the London Philharmonic, the Vienna Philharmonic, and the Budapest Symphony Orchestra.

• Richard Burton on the cover of a brochure for a lavish charity premiere of the movie *Wagner* in London, 1983.

Wagner's latest reform is . . . a perversion and violation of the fundamental laws of music, a style opposed to the nature of human hearing and sentiment . . . What torture it is to follow this musical goose-march four evenings, he only knows who has experienced it.

—Eduard Hanslick's review in the *Neue freie Presse*

From the point of view of opera mythology offers one advantage in the use of the miraculous. But the rest of the mythical element offers, rather, difficulties. Characters who never existed and in whom no one believes cannot be made interesting in themselves. They do not sustain, as is sometimes supposed, the music and poetry. On the contrary, the music and poetry give them such reality as they possess. We could not endure the interminable utterances of the mournful Wotan, if it were not for the wonderful music that accompanies them. Orpheus weeping over Eurydice would not move us greatly, if Gluck had not known how to captivate us by his first notes. If it were not for Mozart's music, the puppets of *The Magic Flute* would amount to nothing.

—Camille Saint-Saëns, *Musical Memories*, 1919

The movie included in the cast the three British theatrical knights: Laurence Olivier (Pfeufer), John Gielgud (Pfistermeister), and Ralph Richardson (Pfordten). It was the first and perhaps the only film in which they acted together. It was also the only film in which Burton and Olivier appeared together.

. . . And the 1913 Bioflick

Probably the first biographical film on Wagner's life, *The Life and Works of Richard Wagner*, was made in 1913 by Carl Froelich. At seventy minutes, the black-and-white film is one of the longest surviving movies from that time. Paul Fryer, of Rose Bruford College in Kent, has upgraded the film with English subtitles and commissioned a new soundtrack. The film, made only thirty years after Wagner's death, is of special interest and has been shown to Wagner Societies and *Ring* Festivals in Europe and the United States over the past several years.

Wagner loved to read his poems to friends and was intolerant of interruptions. During a get-together in Switzerland around Christmas 1852, Wagner read his Nibelung tetralogy to friends at Mariafeld. He expected their complete attention for three full evenings. At one point his friend Eliza Wille had to leave the room while Wagner was still reading. Her young son had a fever and was calling for his mother.

The next morning Wagner remonstrated with the unfortunate Frau Wille. He commented that the boy was not dangerously ill and that leaving the room was a disagreeable criticism of an author. Eliza Wille knew that he was serious when he called her Fricka!

The Essential Wagner Library

A new convert to Wagner wanting to know more about the composer has an amazing selection of books from which to choose. Every aspect of his life has been examined in detail. There are several dozen biographies and numerous books on the staging of his works, family squabbles, singers, producers, conductors, things that went well, and things that went wrong. There are books on the stories and the meanings behind the stories, and biographies of—and sometimes by—several members of the family.

Most Wagner enthusiasts have several books on the composer, and more are added each year. So with so many books to choose from, where should the new convert begin? The following is a personal recommendation. These are the ten books that I find the most interesting, useful, or inspiring. The list ranges from the slim *Aspects of Wagner* to the gigantic two-volume edition of Cosima Wagner's diaries. This is not one to be attempted in a few days but savored and sampled over weeks, maybe months.

My personal top ten are:

William O. Cord, *An Introduction to Richard Wagner's "Der Ring des Nibelungen"* (Ohio University Press, 1983)

Christopher Fifield, *True Artist and True Friend: A Biography of Hans Richter* (Clarendon, 1993)

M. Owen Lee, *Wagner: The Terrible Man and His Truthful Art* (University of Toronto Press, 1999)

Bryan Magee, *Aspects of Wagner* (Oxford University Press, 1968)

Barry Millington, ed., *The Wagner Compendium: A Guide to Wagner's Life and Music* (Thames and Hudson, 1992)

Ernest Newman, *Life of Richard Wagner*, 4 vols. (Alfred A. Knopf, 1933).

Ernest Newman, *Wagner Nights* (Bodley Head, 1949)

Frederic Spotts, *Bayreuth: A History of the Wagner Festival* (Yale University Press, 1994)

Cosima Wagner, *Cosima Wagner's Diaries, Vol. 2: 1878–1883*, edited and annotated by Martin Gregor-Dellin and Dietrich Mack; translated and with additional notes by Geoffrey Skelton (Harcourt Brace Jovanovich, 1980)

Derek Watson, *Richard Wagner: A Biography* (Schirmer Books, 1979)

Regrettably, none of Wagner's extended family inherited his immense genius for composition. It was not for want of trying.

Wagner and Family Publishing Ltd.

For many years it was part of Wagnerian folklore that more books had been written about Wagner than anyone else in history except Jesus Christ and Napoleon Bonaparte. This is now discounted as Wagnerian hyperbole, but the idea had been around for a long time. In the preface to his book *The Music Dramas of Richard Wagner*, Albert Lavignac, professor of harmony at the Paris Conservatoire, apologized for writing what he called the "thousand and first book on Richard Wagner." Yet Lavignac's book was published in 1898, just fifteen years after Wagner's death. Nikolaus Oesterlein's *Katalog*, which lists items published only during Wagner's lifetime, includes no fewer than ten thousand titles.

With so many books published about the composer and his works, trade in used books on Wagner and his world became a new industry. Many antiquarian book dealers established sections in their catalogues devoted to the magician of

Bayreuth, and some of the earlier publications became sought-after collector's items. It is no surprise to find several such dealers in Bayreuth; they are essential stops on the itinerary of Festival attendees each August.

The Wagnerian, an online book retailer, lists several thousand titles about Wagner, every one of them currently available. A mid-sized German bookstore currently has 773 German-language Wagner books and another 200 in English. About half of these titles were first published or reissued in 2012–13.

In the United States one dealer specialized in Wagnerian literature and became a respected expert. George Herget operated his business from New Orleans but traveled extensively around the country seeking out Wagner enthusiasts. Whenever *The Ring* was staged by one of the major houses, Herget would arrive and set up his table, which was filled with old and not-so-old books on almost any aspect of Wagner and his world. He usually offered some discounts at the end of each cycle. On *Götterdämmerung* night a new sign would appear above George's table reading: "IMMOLATION SALE." Herget died in 1994.

Regrettably, none of Wagner's extended family inherited his immense genius for composition. It was not for want of trying, and in fact his only son, Siegfried, tried to follow in the famous footsteps. He made up for a lack of quality with quantity and composed more operas than his father. Although they enjoyed a degree of success in their day, they are rarely performed today, and since then none of the extended family has shown much interest in composing.

But Wagner did seem to pass on a few genes: his prolific writings started a Wagner family publishing industry. His descendants and families have written several works on the man and his music. In chronological order, they include:

Richard Wagner (Houston Stewart Chamberlain [husband of Wagner's daughter Eva], 1895)

Heritage of Fire (Friedelind Wagner, 1945)

The Wagner Family Albums (Wolf Siegfried Wagner, 1976)

Acts: The Autobiography of Wolfgang Wagner (Wolfgang Wagner, 1994)

Twilight of the Wagners (Gottfried Wagner, 1997)

He Who Does Not Howl with the Wolf: The Wagner Legacy (Gottfried Wagner, 1997)

The Wagners: The Dramas of a Musical Dynasty (Nike Wagner, 1998)

Wagner Theater (Nike Wagner, 1999)

The Wagner Journal

Almost all of the 135 Wagner Societies that exist in more than forty countries distribute publications to their members. Some of them are modest newsletters covering the activities of the societies and reports on performances in their areas. Some of the larger societies, such as those in New York, San Francisco, and London, publish more elaborate magazines that include scholarly features on virtually every aspect of the composer's life and works.

Only one independent publication is published in English. *The Wagner Journal* is published in London and edited by Barry Millington, the well-known British Wagner scholar. The publication's stated objective is "to examine Wagner and his works from a variety of perspectives—musicological, historical, literary, philosophical and political—and to illuminate the unique appeal of this endlessly fascinating composer."

Some five hundred to six hundred copies of the journal are distributed three times a year (March, July, and November) to twenty-four countries. It

The Critic's Fate

Max Reger (1873–1916) was a Bavarian composer, conductor, pianist, and organist. Despite a prodigious output, his compositions are rarely performed today. Perhaps his best-known work was a letter to a critic who had written an unfavorable review. "I am sitting in the smallest room in my house. Your review is in front of me. Soon, it will be behind me."

is available in both print and online forms. Although independent, the *Journal* is supported by the Wagner Societies in Washington, D.C., and London. The distinguished editorial board includes Wagner specialists in the United Kingdom, the United States, Canada, and Germany. Some of them, including Mike Ashman, John Deathridge, and Millington himself, are quoted elsewhere in this book.

Millington is uniquely qualified to edit *The Wagner Journal*. He is the chief music critic for the *London Evening Standard*, and his name is on the cover of eight books on Wagner, including *The Wagner Compendium*. His most recent book, published in 2012, is titled *Richard Wagner: The Sorcerer of Bayreuth* and sets out to reassess received notions about the composer and his work.

Further information on *The Wagner Journal* may be obtained from the Web site (www.thewagnerjournal.co.uk).

Death in Venice

Wagner's health deteriorated in his final years, and there were several warnings of the heart condition that would end his life in Venice. It is believed that he suffered several heart attacks, and he collapsed during the fifth performance of *Parsifal*. When he recovered he said, "Another narrow escape."

In September 1882 Wagner, Cosima, their children, Count Gravina and his wife, Blandine (née Bülow), Liszt, the painter Paul Joukowsky, the children's teachers, and four servants arrived in Venice. Wagner wanted rest, peace, and quiet after the exhaustions of the Bayreuth Festival. After a week in the Hotel Europa, the party moved into a suite of twenty-eight rooms in the Palazzo Vendramin.

He relaxed, walked, and visited local watering holes. One of his favorite strolls took him to Lavenna's pastry shop to buy treats for the children. While walking in Venice one day wearing his overcoat and slouched hat, Wagner went up to the bandmaster and asked him to play something from Rossini's *La gazza ladra*. Hugh Haweis wrote in *My Musical Memories*:

> The conductor, not recognizing Wagner, answered civilly that he had none of the music there, and otherwise could not well arrange the programme. On Wagner retiring, a musician told the bandmaster who the stranger was. Filled with confusion and regret, the worthy man instantly sent for copies of the *Gazza Ladra* selection and played it for two consecutive days. Wagner was much pleased and, again going up to the band, expressed his thanks, and praised especially the solo cornet, who had much distinguished himself.

It seems that Wagner chose to ignore frequent chest pains and spells of dizziness. On at least two occasions he suffered from faintness and was taken home in a gondola. He begged his companions

• **The Palazzo Vendramin in Venice, where Wagner died on February 13, 1883. Etching from the *Graphic*, March 3, 1883.**

not to tell his family about these events, but they already knew that he was a sick man. At home he had been found one day groaning in pain, his hand pressed to his heart.

On January 12 Paul Joukowsky sketched the composer as he was reading, and later Wagner played the piano. After playing the Rhinemaidens' final song from *Das Rheingold* he said, "I like them, those creatures of the deep."

During those last days of his life, Wagner also worked on an essay titled "The Feminine Element in Humanity" in his room at the Palazzo Vendramin. The first page of the manuscript was dated February 11, 1883.

The next day Wagner had a major row with Cosima—probably over the pending visit of Carrie Pringle, the English singer believed to have been one of Wagner's conquests and one of the Flower Maidens in the first *Parsifal*. Wagner went to his room to work, and Cosima did something she had never done before: she interrupted Siegfried's piano lesson, sat down, and played Schubert's "In Praise of Tears." It was the first time that twelve-year-old Siegfried had ever heard his mother play the piano. She wept as she played.

Wagner worked in his room all morning and broke off after writing the words "The process of women's emancipation is under way, but only amid ecstatic convulsions." In the margin, he wrote "Love-Tragedy." They were to be the last words he ever wrote.

At one o'clock Betty Bürckel, the maid who

• **The funeral cortege in Bayreuth on its way from the railway station to Villa Wahnfried. From an etching in *Illustrirte Zeitung*, March 1883.**

had been instructed by Cosima to stay in an adjacent anteroom, heard her master's bell. Wagner told her that as he felt unwell he would take lunch, just a bowl of soup, alone in his room. A little later she heard him calling her name faintly; when she went in, he was lying on his sofa, his face distorted in pain. He told her, "Call my wife and the doctor." According to some reports, these were his last words.

There are several alternative stories. When Wagner was moved, his watch slipped out of his pocket. "My watch!" said Wagner, and according to Ernest Newman, one of his first reliable biographers, these were his last words. Newman's opinion on Wagner's last words had been included in *Wagner: History of an Artist*, a 1932 biography by Guy de Pourtales, and Derek Watson's *Richard Wagner: A Biography*, published in 1979.

Adolphe Jullien included another alternative in his 1892 book *Richard Wagner: His Life and Works*: "In drawing his last breath he indistinctly murmured a few words, which some have thought to be a last call to his servant, Betty Bürckel; others, a supreme command to his son: Siegfried soll . . . ('Siegfried must . . .')."

Yet another biographer claims that Wagner's

last words were spoken about the Rhinemaidens: "I wish them well, these creatures of the deep." Most believe that these words were uttered earlier when he sat at the piano and played the lament of the Rhinemaidens.

Ludwig Nohl wrote in 1884, "At 3 o'clock he went to dinner with the family, but just as they were assembled at table and the soup was being served he suddenly sprang up, cried out 'Mir ist sehr schlecht' (I feel very badly) and fell back dead from an attack of heart disease."

Wagner was dying when Cosima arrived, but, thinking that he had merely fainted, she tried to revive him. When the doctor arrived and confirmed that it was all over, Cosima let out a piercing cry, clasped her husband's body, and fainted.

For the rest of the day and all through the night after Wagner's death, Cosima refused to leave the body. She went without nourishment until, after twenty-six hours, she fainted again and could be moved.

Details of Wagner's illness were included in a book by M. H. Perl, *Richard Wagner at Venice*, published in Augsburg in 1883. He wrote about Wagner's final days, including information he had received from the composer's physician in Venice, a Dr. Keppler, as noted by Adolphe Jullien:

> "Richard Wagner was afflicted with hypertrophy of the heart already far advanced, affecting especially the right ventricle, and with fatty degeneration: he suffered besides from dilatation of the stomach and from a rupture which the prolonged use of a badly made truss had greatly aggravated." . . . Add to this, says he, Wagner's agitated life, his passion to discuss upon matters of art, science or politics, and one may see that the master was daily at the mercy of an accident; as to the precise occasion which determined this sudden death, no one can even conjecture in regard to it.
>
> Adolphe Jullien, *Richard Wagner: His Life and Works*, 1892

The news of Wagner's death was all over Venice within an hour. The mayor offered a funeral pageant, but Cosima declined. A wreath arrived from King Humbert of Italy and another from King Ludwig of Bavaria with the message, "To the Master, Richard Wagner, from his devoted admirer and King, Ludwig." The king's messenger, one Herr Gross, of Bayreuth, arrived to supervise arrangements for the return of the body to Wahnfried. Some of those present wanted to have a death mask made by the sculptor Augusto Benvenuti. Cosima refused permission, but her daughter Daniela gave her approval, and the mask was made. Cosima arranged for the settee on which Wagner died to be shipped back to Wahnfried, where it remains to this day.

Before the coffin was closed, Cosima cut off some of her long hair and placed it on a red cushion under his head. At her request, there was no music as the coffin was transported by gondola to the station, where it was placed in a special mourning car that had been sent from Vienna. By the time the train left Venice, thousands of telegrams had been addressed to Cosima and the family from all parts of the world. Two train carriages were required to hold the fourteen hundred floral wreaths.

The train arrived in Bayreuth on Saturday, and on Sunday public tributes were paid by the city's mayor and others before the cortege left the Bayreuth station for Wahnfried. A regimental band played Siegfried's Funeral March, and King Ludwig's wreath was laid on the coffin by his aide-de-camp. The coffin, carried on an open hearse drawn by four black horses, was followed by a long

• Cosima mourning at Wagner's grave. Etching from *Illustrirte Zeitung*, March 10, 1883.

procession. Silent crowds lined the streets and black flags were flown on almost every house. Snow was falling when the composer's remains were lowered into the tomb that Wagner himself had arranged years before. He had also specified the heavy granite slab that covered the vault.

Two months after Wagner's death, a memorial concert was given in front of the Palazzo Vendramin. Anton Seidl conducted a program that included the overture to *Tannhäuser* and Siegfried's Funeral March, and the audience filled more than four hundred gondolas.

Years earlier Cosima had written in her diary, "My only prayer is this: to die with Richard in the very same hour." Her prayer went unanswered. She was ninety-three when she died in 1930. She had outlived her husband by "47 years of mourning," said an obituary in the *Daily Express*.

Breaking News Worldwide

By the end of the day on February 13, 1883, some five thousand telegrams had been sent from Venice, and the tributes started immediately. The next morning daily newspapers in every corner of the globe carried the news of Wagner's death in virtually every language.

Although effusive and fulsome language was not unusual in the late nineteenth century, Britain's *Daily Telegraph* must have been a strong contender for the most over-the-top tribute to the dead composer.

> We learn by telegraph from Venice that the greatest of contemporary composers, Richard Wagner, died there at four o'clock yesterday afternoon. Within two months of attaining the scripturally-appointed age-limit of three-score-and-ten, the potent magician who, during the latter twenty-five years of his life, revolutionized musical style throughout the civilized world, trampled underfoot all the most cherished operatic traditions, and peopled the stage with romantic and heroic figures of inimitable grace, stateliness, and beauty, has been taken suddenly from a world in which—to the apprehension, at least, of many thousands of its inhabitants—he occupied a loftier station and fulfilled more important functions than King or Kaiser, Pope or President. No monarch, indeed, was ever more enthusiastically served or loyally reverenced than had been Richard Wagner. Infallibility, embodied in a Roman Pontiff, has never been more implicitly believed in by the most orthodox Catholic than it has been in the person of the Bayreuth Prophet by his innumerable followers. If to wield power, to be adored as a demi-god, and to attain unprecedented and unequalled conspicuity amongst one's fellow-men is to be happy, the dead composer's felicity, during fully one-third of his allotted span, should have been complete.
>
> *Daily Telegraph*, February 14, 1883

When Giuseppe Verdi first heard Wagner's music, he said, "He's mad." But when he received news of Wagner's death, he wrote to a friend: "Sad, sad, sad! Frankly when I heard the news yesterday I was crushed. Let us say no more about it. A great individuality has gone, a name that will leave a powerful imprint on the history of art." Then on reading his letter again before it was posted, he crossed out the word *potente*, or "powerful," and wrote above it *potentissima*—"most powerful."

Verdi's wife, Giuseppina, commented in a letter to a friend:

Verdi, who is in the country at the moment, never knew or even saw Wagner. This great individuality, now departed, was never afflicted with the little itch of vanity, but devoured by an incandescent, measureless pride, like Satan or Lucifer, the most beautiful of fallen angels!

Alas! For great and small a few feet of earth suffice, to shut him up forever and give him that peace which, I think, he never enjoyed, even when he was glorified by kings, by his country, and overwhelmed with riches.

Mahler ran around sobbing and howling after hearing the news from Venice. He ran through the streets shouting, "The Master has died," and was distraught for several days.

Tchaikovsky was in Paris when he heard of Wagner's death. In their 1965 biography of the Russian composer, *Tchaikovsky: A New Study of the Man and His Music*, Lawrence and Elisabeth Hanson wrote:

> Drinking punch at a café—the winter and spring were bitterly cold—Tchaikovsky read the newspapers and listened to the flood of talk caustically. All of a sudden Wagner had become the rage, every orchestra competing with its Wagner programme. Men could talk of nothing but his greatness. Pyotr Ilyich could remember, if the French could not, the time when Wagner's operas were howled down and the critics excelled themselves in vituperation. Though he was no great admirer of the composer—he had recently seen and described *Tristan and Isolde* as "an endless voice, without life or movement"—he could see in him the fate of all artists. He could with particular clarity see the French and art: "Curious people, the French. One has to die to catch their attention."

Wagner's Short Pinky

Casts of Wagner's hand have been on display for several years at Wahnfried in Bayreuth and at the Wagner museum at Tribschen in Lucerne. The version shown here is believed to be privately owned. Note the unusually short little finger. Could this be one of the reasons that Wagner never became an accomplished pianist?

• Cast of Wagner's right hand.

An obituary in the February 26, 1883, *Harper's Weekly* observed that "history deals lightly with the weaknesses of great men, and so compensates them for their courage and devotion to the cause in which they have become great. It is impossible now to estimate the vastness of Wagner's genius."

> Oh, how I wept!
>
> Anton Bruckner

In a postscript to his 1884 translation of Ludwig Nohl's *Life of Wagner*, George P. Upton wrote:

> After a life of strife such as few men have to encounter; of hatred more intense and love

> "Sad, sad, sad! . . . A great individuality has gone."
> **—Giuseppe Verdi, after hearing of Wagner's death**

more devoted than usually falls to the fate of humanity; of restless energy, indomitable courage, passionate devotion to the loftiest standards of art and unquestioning allegiance to the God that dwelt within his breast, he rests quietly under the trees of Villa Wahnfried. He lived to see his work accomplished, his mission fulfilled, his victory won and his fame blown about the world despite the malice of enemies and cabals of critics. As the outcome of his stormy life we have music clothed in a new body, animated with a new spirit. He has lifted art out of its vulgarity and grossness. The future will prize him as we today prize his great predecessor—Beethoven.

In the United States Gustav Kobbé, the music critic and author of the well-known opera guide, wrote:

> If a man's greatness may be measured by the number of his enemies, then Wagner was very great. Hardly had his tendency made itself felt when opposition began to develop itself on all sides. No advance has ever been made in art without a struggle. But Wagner's enemies were unusually virulent. Not content with vilifying his character, they even questioned the sincerity of his artistic purpose. On the other hand, there arose a band of young musicians and critics burning to join the master in the new crusade.
>
> Wagner found the opera a succession of levels of dull recitative, relieved here and there by arias which, as a rule, bore no special relation to the text, and simply furnished singers with an opportunity to display their skill. Interpretive talent was overpowering creative genius. He saw at once that the true opera would be that in which the music would give the exact dramatic meaning of the text and situations. For such an opera a fine drama was as necessary as fine music. Voltaire's remark, "What is too stupid to be spoken is sung," was no longer to hold true.
>
> Wagner accomplished this by a simple process. He originated the Leitmotif, or leading motive. In his music drama each character and the prevailing moral ideas were denoted by motives. His musical genius enabled him to develop these themes, and so combine them that the music reflects all the varied life and action of the stage.

Gustav Kobbé, *Harper's Weekly*, February 24, 1883, eleven days after Wagner's death

The Wagner Story: Dramatis Personae

The star of the Wagner story had left the stage. As for the other players in his extraordinary drama:

- **Minna Wagner,** Wagner's first wife, died of heart disease in Dresden in 1866, four years after separating from the composer. She had suffered heart problems for several years. Wagner did not attend her funeral; he was in France and could not make it back to Dresden in time.
- **Cosima Wagner,** Wagner's second wife, died at Wahnfried in April 1930. She was

In Memoriam: The Story of a Statue

In the years following Wagner's death, numerous statues, busts, plaques, and other commemorations were erected all over Europe, and in many German towns and cities, streets were named after the dead composer.

One of the largest statues included Wagner on a massive plinth surrounded by characters from his operas. The statue was commissioned by a wealthy cosmetics manufacturer and former singer, Ludwig Leichner, and carved by the Berlin-born Gustav Eberlein (1847–1926).

The characters around the base of the large plinth are Tristan and Isolde, Tannhäuser, Alberich, the Rhinemaidens, and Walther von Stolzing.

The huge statue was unveiled in Berlin's Tiergarten on October 1, 1903, in the presence of Prince Eitel Friedrich, the second son of Wilhelm II, together with the great and good of Berlin dressed in their finery. Five years later the scene was recreated in a painting by Anton von Werner, who had been present for the unveiling and had been one of the speechmakers.

The gleaming white statue has suffered greatly during the century since its unveiling. The statue was covered by a large metal and glass canopy several years ago to protect it from the combined effects of weather and bird droppings. Sadly, this did nothing to deter the attention of human vandals, who damaged the carving or painted graffiti on several occasions. Several of the figures have lost a nose or parts of fingers or arms.

• TOP: The unveiling of the Wagner memorial in Berlin's Tiergarten in 1903 was a major social occasion attended by the great and good. Painting by Anton von Werner, 1908. BOTTOM: A detail of the Berlin memorial shows Tristan and Isolde.

ninety-three. During her final years she was barely aware of events around her, yet she had clear memories of the past. She lived on the upper floor of Wahnfried and spent most of her days in a darkened room. Her vision was poor and her eyes were sensitive to light, so she dictated her letters and had to have correspondence and books read to her. This led to a belief that she was virtually blind, but Winifred Wagner said that this was untrue. Her mind did wander toward the end, and in one conversation with her daughter Eva, she thought she was still married to Hans von Bülow. Cosima was buried alongside her second husband in the tomb at Wahnfried.

- **Siegfried Wagner** died in Bayreuth in August 1930 during the Festival and just a few months after his mother. He is buried in the Bayreuth cemetery in the same grave as his sons, Wieland and Wolfgang, and their wives.
- **Wieland Wagner** died of lung cancer on October 17, 1966. He was only forty-nine. Wieland's first name came from *Wieland the Smith*, his grandfather's planned but unwritten opera. After a difficult birth, Wieland suffered from lung problems all his life. Even his death did not end the feud with his mother, Winifred, over her support for Hitler: she was not allowed into Wahnfried, where her son was laid out.
- **Wolfgang Wagner** (full name: Wolfgang Manfred Martin Wagner) was named after Goethe, his cousin Manfredi Gravina, and Martin Luther. Wolfgang ran the Bayreuth empire single-handedly for almost forty-three years following the death of his brother. His closest associate was his second wife, Gudrun. Shortly after she died in 2007, Wolfgang decided to hand over to his daughters, Katharina and Eva, who now carry the torch. Wolfgang died in March 2010 and is buried in the family grave in Bayreuth Cemetery.
- **Hans Richter,** conductor of the first full performance of *The Ring*, died in 1916. He ended his career in England, where he was conductor of the Hallé Orchestra from 1899 to 1911. He became a friend of Edward Elgar and conducted the premiere performances of the *Enigma Variations*, *The Dream of Gerontius*, and the First Symphony. He died in Bayreuth and is buried in the Bayreuth cemetery.
- **Hans von Bülow** died in Cairo, Egypt, in February 1894. Despite losing Cosima to his idol, he maintained a sense of humor and demonstrated great magnanimity. When a woman asked him, "Oh, Monsieur von Bülow, you know Mr. Wagner, don't you?" Bülow made a low bow and said in French, "But of course, Madame, he's my wife's husband."
- **Blandine von Bülow** was one of the two daughters of Bülow and Cosima and was unofficially adopted by Wagner. She maintained a distance from the rest of the family and raised four children. In her later years she lived in Italy and rarely came to Bayreuth. She died in 1941.
- **Daniela von Bülow,** the other daughter of Bülow and Cosima, spent much of her life supporting her mother at Wahnfried. She died in July 1940, and as a staunch Party member and holder of the Party's Gold Badge, she was buried in Bayreuth cemetery with full Nazi honors.
- **Isolde Wagner** (Mrs. Franz Beidler) died in 1919. Had DNA testing been possible

then, it would almost certainly have confirmed that she was a daughter of Wagner, but Cosima denied this. Isolde was banished and never met Winifred Wagner, who managed the Festival after Siegfried's death.

- **Eva Wagner** born in Switzerland, at Tribschen, and married Houston Stewart Chamberlain in Bayreuth in 1908. She died in 1942 and is buried in Bayreuth cemetery. She, too, was given full Nazi Party honors at her funeral.
- **Houston Stewart Chamberlain** was born in Southsea, England, in 1855 but lived most of his adult life in Germany. He married Eva Wagner in 1908 and became a German citizen in 1916. He was one of the early biographers of Wagner. He died in 1927.
- **Mathilde Wesendonck** died in 1902. Her husband, Otto, a wealthy partner in a New York silk company, had died seven years earlier. It is not known for sure whether her passionate relationship with Wagner was consummated, but we can be confident that Mathilde Wesendonck was the inspiration behind *Tristan and Isolde*.
- **King Ludwig II of Bavaria** drowned in mysterious circumstances in 1886. Just days before his death, he had been deposed after being certified insane by four psychiatrists. One scholar has said that none of the psychiatrists had even met the king, let alone examined him. Ludwig's remains are buried in St. Michael's Church in Munich.
- **Franz Liszt** died in Bayreuth in 1886 shortly after leaving a performance of *Tristan and Isolde* at the Festspielhaus. He is buried in the Bayreuth cemetery in a mausoleum designed by Siegfried Wagner. The conductor Felix Weingartner observed in 1937 in *Buffets and Rewards*, "The Wagner family gave no outward sign of mourning. The daughters wore black dresses and that was all. We had confidently expected that at least one of the festival performances would be cancelled."
- **Hermann Levi** died on May 13, 1900. He was the son of a rabbi and one of Wagner's closest Jewish associates, and it was he who was selected to conduct the first performance of *Parsifal* at Bayreuth in 1882. Five years after Wagner's death, Levi conducted the first performance of *Die Feen*, Wagner's first completed opera. Levi was buried in a private mausoleum in his garden, which was destroyed by the Nazis in the late 1930s.
- **Friedrich Nietzsche** died in Turin in 1900. He was almost blind and suffered mental health problems over the final years of his life. It was commonly believed that he died of tertiary cerebral syphilis, but a 2006 study suggested that the cause of death was a form of dementia.
- **Winifred Wagner** died on March 5, 1980, in Switzerland. The previous Christmas she had traveled to Lake Constance to stay with her daughter Verena. She was weak after earlier cancer treatment. Her body was returned for burial with her husband in Bayreuth. ■

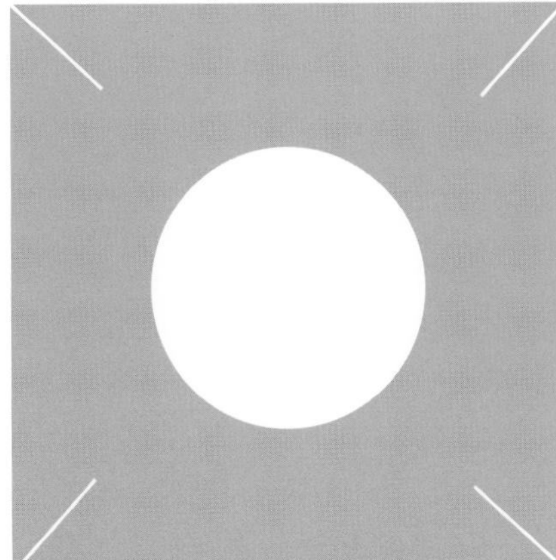

Coda

How to end a collection of information, memorabilia, and trivia on this extraordinary man? I can do no better than to reprint "The Monster," by Deems Taylor (1885–1966).

The New York–born Taylor was a composer, music critic, and promoter of classical music. He was a frequent intermission commentator for the New York Philharmonic and was closely involved in the selection of the music featured in Walt Disney's *Fantasia*. His voice is heard in the film as the master of ceremonies, and he is seen in a live-action sequence with the Philadelphia Orchestra and Leopold Stokowski. As a Wagner enthusiast, Taylor was probably the man most responsible for proposing the use of the Ride of the Valkyries in *Fantasia*. This segment was storyboarded but did not make it to the animation stage.

"The Monster" was originally featured in an intermission broadcast from New York's Metropolitan Opera House; it was later included in a collection of Taylor's works published in 1937.

"The joke was on us . . . The world did owe him a living."
—**Deems Taylor**

"The Monster"

by Deems Taylor

He was an undersized little man, with a head too big for his body—a sickly little man. His nerves were bad. He had skin trouble. It was agony for him to wear anything next to his skin coarser than silk. And he had delusions of grandeur.

He was a monster of conceit. Never for one minute did he look at the world or at people, except in relation to himself. He was not only the most important person in the world, to himself; in his own eyes he was the only person who existed. He believed himself to be one of the greatest dramatists in the world, one of the greatest thinkers, and one of the greatest composers. To hear him talk, he was Shakespeare, and Beethoven, and Plato, rolled into one. And you would have no difficulty in hearing him talk. He was one of the most exhausting conversationalists that ever lived. An evening with him was an evening spent in listening to a monologue. Sometimes he was brilliant; sometimes he was maddeningly tiresome. But whether he was being brilliant or dull, he had one sole topic of conversation: himself. What *he* thought and what *he* did.

He had a mania for being in the right. The slightest hint of disagreement, from anyone, on the most trivial point, was enough to set him off on a harangue that might last for hours, in which he proved himself right in so many ways, and with such exhausting volubility, that in the end his hearer, stunned and deafened, would agree with him, for the sake of peace.

It never occurred to him that he and his doings were not of the most intense and fascinating interest to anyone with whom he came in contact. He had theories about almost any subject under the sun, including vegetarianism, the drama, politics, and music; and in support of these theories he wrote pamphlets, letters, books—thousands upon thousands of words, hundreds and hundreds of pages. He not only wrote these things, and published them—usually at somebody else's expense—but he would sit and read them aloud, for hours, to his friends and his family.

He wrote operas; and no sooner did he have the

synopsis of a story, but he would invite—or rather summon—a crowd of his friends to his house and read it aloud to them. Not for criticism. For applause. When the complete poem was written, the friends had to come again, and hear *that* read aloud. Then he would publish the poem, sometimes years before the music that went with it was written. He played the piano like a composer, in the worst sense of what that implies, and he would sit down at the piano before parties that included some of the finest pianists of his time, and play for them, by the hour—his own music, needless to say. He had a composer's voice. And he would invite eminent vocalists to his house, and sing them his operas, taking all the parts.

He had the emotional stability of a six-year-old child. When he felt out of sorts, he would rave and stamp, or sink into suicidal gloom and talk darkly of going to the East to end his days as a Buddhist monk. Ten minutes later, when something pleased him, he would rush out of doors and run around the garden, or jump up and down on the sofa, or stand on his head. He could be grief-stricken over the death of a pet dog, and he could be callous and heartless to a degree that would have made a Roman emperor shudder.

He was almost innocent of any sense of responsibility. Not only did he seem incapable of supporting himself, but it never occurred to him that he was under any obligation to do so. He was convinced that the world owed him a living. In support of this belief, he borrowed money from everybody who was good for a loan—men, women, friends, or strangers. He wrote begging letters by the score, sometimes groveling without shame, at others loftily offering his intended benefactor the privilege of contributing to his support, and being mortally offended if the recipient declined the honor. I have found no record of his ever paying or repaying money to anyone who did not have a legal claim upon it.

What money he could lay his hands on he spent like an Indian rajah. The mere prospect of a performance of one of his operas was enough to set him to running up bills amounting to ten times the amount of his prospective royalties. On an income that would reduce a more scrupulous man to doing his own laundry, he would keep two servants. Without enough money in his pocket to pay his rent, he would have the walls and ceiling of his study lined with pink silk. No one will ever know—certainly he never knew—how much money he owed. We do know that his greatest benefactor gave him $6,000 to pay the most pressing of his debts in one city, and a year later had to give him $16,000 to enable him to live in another city without being thrown into jail for debt.

He was equally unscrupulous in other ways. An endless procession of women marches through his life. His first wife spent twenty years enduring and forgiving his infidelities. His second wife had been the wife of his most devoted friend and admirer, from whom he stole her. And even while he was trying to persuade her to leave her first husband he was writing to a friend to inquire whether he could suggest some wealthy woman—any wealthy woman—whom he could marry for her money.

He was completely selfish in his other personal relationships. His liking for his friends was measured solely by the completeness of their devotion to him, or by their usefulness to him, whether financial or artistic. The minute they failed him—even by so much as refusing a dinner invitation—or began to lessen in usefulness, he cast them off without a second thought. At the end of his life he had exactly one friend left whom he had known even in middle age.

He had a genius for making enemies. He would insult a man who disagreed with him about the weather. He would pull endless wires in order to meet some man who admired his work, and was able and anxious to be of use to him—and would proceed to make a mortal enemy of him with some idiotic and wholly uncalled-for exhibition of arrogance and bad manners. A character in one of his operas was a caricature of one of the most powerful music critics of his day. Not content with burlesquing him, he invited the critic to his house and read him the libretto aloud in front of his friends.

The name of this monster was Richard Wagner. Everything that I have said about him you can find on record—in newspapers, in police reports, in the testimony of people who knew him, in his own letters, between the lines of his autobiography. And the curious thing about this record is that it doesn't matter in the least.

Because this undersized, sickly, disagreeable, fascinating little man was right all the time. The joke was on us. He *was* one of the world's greatest dramatists; he *was* a great thinker; he *was* one of the most stupendous musical geniuses that, up to now, the world has ever seen. The world did owe him a living. People couldn't know those things at the time, I suppose; and yet to us, who know his music, it does seem as they should have known. What if he did talk about himself all the time? If he had talked about himself for twenty-four hours every day for the span of his life, he would not have uttered half the number of words that other men have spoken and written about him since his death.

When you consider what he wrote—thirteen operas and music dramas, eleven of them still holding the stage, eight of them unquestionably worth ranking among the world's great musico-dramatic masterpieces—when you listen to what he wrote, the debts and heartaches that people had to endure from him don't seem much of a price. Eduard Hanslick, the critic whom he caricatured in *Die Meistersinger* and who hated him ever after, now lives only because he was caricatured in *Die Meistersinger*. The women whose hearts he broke are long since dead; and the man who could never love anyone but himself has made them deathless atonement, I think, with *Tristan und Isolde*. Think of the luxury with which for a time, at least, fate rewarded Napoleon, the man who ruined France and looted Europe; and then perhaps you will agree that a few thousand dollars' worth of debts were not too heavy a price to pay for the *Ring* trilogy.

What if he was faithless to his friends and to his wives? He had one mistress to whom he was faithful to the day of his death: Music. Not for a single moment did he ever compromise with what he believed, with what he dreamed. There is not a line of his music that could have been conceived by a little mind. Even when he is dull, or downright bad, he is dull in the grand manner. There is greatness about his worst mistakes. Listening to his music, one does not forgive him for what he may or may not have been. It is not a matter of forgiveness. It is a matter of being dumb with wonder that his poor brain and body didn't burst under the torment of the demon of creative energy that lived inside him, struggling, clawing, scratching to be released; tearing, shrieking at him to write the music that was in him. The miracle is that what he did in the little space of seventy years could have been done at all, even by a great genius. Is it any wonder that he had no time to be a man? ■

All truth passes through three stages.
First, it is ridiculed. Second, it is violently opposed.
Third, it is accepted as being self-evident.
—Arthur Schopenhauer

Acknowledgments

I have been collecting the information in this book for more than twenty years, so it is inevitable, regretfully, that I will have omitted some who have helped in some way. To those who were missed, my sincere apologies.

My sincere thanks to Lee Acaster, Liese Bauer, Chris Bennion, Elizabeth Clarke, John Constable, the late Professor Bill Cord, Robert Court, John Diedenhofen, Corrine Diedenhofen, Peter Ede, Lee MacCormick Edwards, Rich Fackenthal, Robert Fisher, Cameron Gant, Dale Gant, Sara Gant, Alec Gustafson, Sophie Gustafson, Barry Higgs, Jane Horton, Monte Jacobsen, Speight Jenkins, Jenny Labbett, Dr. Lisa Lagadec, Dr. Marc Lagadec, Father Owen Lee, the late Perry Lorenzo, Bryan Magee, Barry Millington, David Mitchell, Verna Parino, Prof. Dr. Peter Pachl, Sandra Rhodes, Dr. Andrew Rombakis, Melanie G. Ross, Paul Schofield, Robert D. Schaub, Thea Seese, Mike Shaw, the late Steve Sokolow, John Staedke, Roy Troth, Dr. Nicholas Vick, John Wagner, Linda Watson, Peter West, Luke Woodhead, and Peter Young.

Many books on Wagner, including this one, are dependent on the work of scholars who have shed light on the life and works of the composer. The list is long and grows each year. The following are those that I have found most useful and inspirational: Henry T. Finck, for an early biography and other works; Ernest Newman, for *The Life of Richard Wagner*, the first comprehensive and reliable biography; Martin Gregor-Dellin, Dietrich Mack and Geoffrey Skelton, for the invaluable English volumes of Cosima Wagner's diaries; and finally, Barry Millington, who has written eight books on Wagner and edits *The Wagner Journal*. I gratefully acknowledge their valuable contributions and those of the many other fine scholars cited throughout this book.

Best efforts have been made to identify the copyright owners of all materials in this book. Still, some may have been missed, and I apologize in advance if this is the case. I acknowledge the following authors, publishers, and copyright holders for granting permission to use excerpts from various writings.

John Ardoin: Excerpts from *The Furtwängler Record* (Amadeus Press, 1994).

Cook & Taylor Publishers: "The Monster" by Deems Taylor from *Of Men and Music* (1937). Copyright © 2013 Michael Cook. Reprinted with the permission of Cook & Taylor Publishers (www.worthyshorts.com/cooktaylor).

Guardian News & Media Ltd.: Excerpts from "W Is for Wagner, X Is for Xenakis," by Joe Queenan, the *Guardian*, January 29, 2007; and from "Wagner's Women," by Natasha Walter, the *Guardian*, April 2006.

Jeanne Henny: Excerpts from the works of Neville Cardus, including *Ten Composers* and *Composers Eleven* (Jonathan Cape, 1958).

Guido Knopp: Excerpts from *Hitler's Women* (Sutton, 2001).

Bryan Magee: Excerpts from *Aspects of Wagner* (Oxford University Press, 1968).

Mike Shaw: Excerpts from the works of Bernard Levin.

The Society of Authors on behalf of the Bernard Shaw Estate: Excerpts from the works of Bernard Shaw.

Illustrations

Images not included in the list below, including reproductions of vintage prints, engravings, newspaper clippings, and ephemera—such as postcards, ticket stubs, promotional trading cards, and program covers—are from the author's personal collection.

Page 3: Portrait photographed by permission of the Jean Paul Museum, Bayreuth.

Pages 5, 12, 27, 41, 46, 47, 53, 117 (right), 150, 212, 213, 228, 250, 254, 257: Caricatures from John Grand-Carteret, *Wagner en caricatures* (Librairie Larousse, 1891), and Ernst Kreowski and Eduard Fuchs, *Richard Wagner in der Karikatur* (B. Behr's Verlag, 1907).

Pages 6, 13, 43, 44, 74, 108, 146, 147, 154 (left and right), 156 (top), 158, 180, 211, 229, 233 (right), 245, 246, 289 (bottom): Photos by the author.

Page 21: Photo courtesy of Luke Woodhead, Woodhead Horn Repair, Bedfordshire, UK.

Page 42: Photo of Luxembourg stamp © Olga Popova/Shutterstock.

Page 72: Photo by Iain Scott.

Page 81: Photo by Chris Bennion, courtesy of Seattle Opera.

Page 82: Photo by Ron Scherl, courtesy of Seattle Opera.

Page 92: Photo provided by Bryan Magee.

Page 97: Photo by C. Yuen Lui, courtesy of the Seattle Opera.

Pages 103, 145, 181: Sketches by David Mitchell.

Page 117 (left): Photo courtesy of Peter West.

Page 184: Graphic courtesy of Richard Fackenthal.

Page 190: Photo by Gary Smith, courtesy of Seattle Opera.

Page 191: Photo by Gary Smith, courtesy of Seattle Opera.

Page 192: Photo by Chris Bennion, courtesy of Seattle opera.

Page 200: Photo of German stamp © Lefteris Papaulakis/Shutterstock.

Page 201: Photo of Chad stamp © Sergey Goryachev/Shutterstock.

Page 202 (top): Photo of Panama stamp © Bocman1973/Shutterstock.

Page 202 (bottom): Photo of USSR stamp © Olga Popova/Shutterstock.

Page 203 (top): Photo of Austrian stamp © Neftali/Shutterstock.

Page 203 (bottom): Photo of Congo stamp © IgorGolovniov/Shutterstock.

Page 204: Photo of Hungarian stamp © rook76/Shutterstock.

Page 221: Cover of *The Meister*, Wagner Society, London Branch, 1888.

Page 233 (center): Portrait photographed at Tribschen by permission of Lucerne Museums.

Page 237: Photo of *Tannhäuser* disc courtesy of Munich Museum.

Page 262: Cartoon by Bernard Partridge from *Punch* magazine, May 1929. Reproduced with permission of Punch Ltd., www.punch.co.uk.

Page 287: Photo courtesy of Peter West.